The **ABORTION RIGHTS** Controversy in America

The **ABORTION RIGHTS** Controversy in America

Controversy in America

A LEGAL READER

. . .

Edited by **N. E. H. HULL, WILLIAMJAMES HOFFER,**

and **PETER CHARLES HOFFER**

The University of North Carolina Press

Chapel Hill and London

Set in Charter and Meta types by Keystone Typesetting, Inc.

The paper in this book meets the guidelines for
permanence and durability of the Committee on
Production Guidelines for Book Longevity of the Council
on Library Resources.

Permission is required for the use of material from this edited collection
in classroom coursepacks or in electronic reserve that exceeds fair-use limits.
Please contact either the Copyright Clearance Center at <www.copyright.com>
or the publisher at uncpress@unc.edu.

Excerpts from the following works have been reprinted with permission: *The
Supreme Court in Conference, 1940–1985*, edited by Del Dickson, © 2001 by Oxford
University Press, Inc., used by permission of Oxford University Press, Inc.; John Hart
Ely, "The Wages of Crying Wolf: A Comment on *Roe v. Wade*," reprinted by
permission of The Yale Law Journal Company and William S. Hein Company from
The Yale Law Journal 82 (1973): 920–49; and Tom Wicker, "Abortion and the
G.O.P.," © 1989 by the New York Times Co., reprinted by permission.

Library of Congress Cataloging-in-Publication Data
The abortion rights controversy in America : a legal reader / edited by N. E. H. Hull,
Williamjames Hoffer, and Peter Charles Hoffer.
p. cm.
ISBN 0-8078-2873-4 (cloth: alk. paper)
ISBN 0-8078-5535-9 (pbk.: alk. paper)
1. Abortion—Law and legislation—United States. I. Hull, N. E. H., 1949–
II. Hoffer, Williamjames. III. Hoffer, Peter Charles, 1944–
KF3771.A937   2004
342.7308′4—dc22
2003027750

cloth   08 07 06 05 04   5 4 3 2 1
paper   08 07 06 05 04   5 4 3 2 1

CONTENTS

. . .

Introduction 1

3. The "Right" to an Abortion 85

4. *Roe v. Wade* before the High Court 124

5. Regulating and Funding Abortions 165

6. Nineteen Eighty-Nine: A Year of Decision 206

7. Regulation and Controversy in the Post-*Webster* Era 247

INTRODUCTION

. . .

It is the summer of 2002. We are driving along a suburban four-lane road, past a local hospital and spa, ballfields, and a small outdoor shopping center. A bright Saturday morning in South Jersey. We come upon a series of demonstrators along the berm, holding aloft larger-than-life banners with actual (we supposed) but color-enhanced pictures of dismembered fetuses. Placards remind the drivers, who have slowed to view the display, that Jesus would not have approved laws that sanctioned the murder of the unborn. The demonstrators are young and clean-cut white men and women, wearing white shirts and shorts. They are the picture of health and make a startling contrast with their sanguinary billboard-size photographs. The demonstrators jump up and down and call to the drivers like high school boosters soliciting car washes. But no one can take their eyes off the visual display. After all we have seen of terror and war, these gruesome pictures still have the power to shock us.

We did not stop to ask who was demonstrating. Perhaps the youth group of a local church. The South Jersey churches are divided on the issue of abortion, and the state has a liberal law—there is no waiting period, parental consent is not required for a minor seeking the procedure, and medical insurance is not barred from paying. As a result, New Jersey has one of the highest abortion rates (36.3 abortions per 1,000 women aged 15 to 44) in the country. Only New York (39.1) and the District of Columbia (68.1) are higher.[1] The whole point of the demonstration was to gain support for an amendment to the state constitution requiring parental consent for all abortions sought by minors.

Perhaps the demonstrators belonged to the loose national confederation of "rescue" groups. The most violent of these, the Army of God, destroyed abortion clinics and threatened doctors until its leaders were indicted and convicted for criminal assault. Operation Rescue, once a powerful national coalition, is now largely defunct and nearly bankrupt; even its name has changed, to Operation Save America. A decade ago, the organization could summon thousands of protesters to shut down urban clinics, and demonstrators used bullhorns so loud that patients in the clinics could hear the chanting through the walls of the building. There were no bullhorns in sight this morning, and the demonstrators did not try to prevent anyone from entering the hospital. But the placement of the pictures at the entrance to the medical facility was not accidental.

In one of the many ironies of the controversy, rescues, state-imposed waiting periods, refusal to use public Medicaid funding and hospital facilities, and other pro-life measures have combined with improved chemical contraceptives, some of which are actually abortifacients, to reduce the national rate of abortion from a high of 30 per 1,000 women aged 15–44 in 1979 and 1980 to a low of 22 per 1,000 at the end of the 1990s. Still, there are over 1.3 million abortions in America every year. Even if some abortion clinic entrances are quieter than they were in past years, fewer exist now than a decade ago. Over 87 percent of counties in the United States have no abortion provider. As we write, the pro-life movement is as strong as it ever was, with support from President George W. Bush, Attorney General John Ashcroft, and a majority of both houses of Congress. Pro-life forces have won many victories in the last few years and look forward to the day when the U.S. Supreme Court reverses its decision in *Roe v. Wade* (1973) affording constitutional protection to women seeking abortions.[2]

Unlike many other demonstrations against abortion, there were no counterdemonstrators that morning. Few today defend abortion as a positive good, even when done in the most medically safe manner. As the poet, essayist, and feminist Adrienne Rich has written, "No free woman, with 100 percent effective, nonharmful birth control available, would 'choose' abortion."[3] The pro-choice argument is that women should have the right to decide whether to remain pregnant. It is their body and their future that is at stake. To underline the point, the National Association for the Repeal of Abortion Laws (NARAL) has changed its name to NARAL Pro-Choice America.

The day after the demonstration we had witnessed, August 11, 2002, the *Philadelphia Inquirer Sunday Review* carried a feature by Jane Eisner. In an eastern Pennsylvania court, a judge first barred and then allowed a young unmarried woman to have the abortion she sought. He had stopped her at the request of her estranged boyfriend, then decided that her rights outweighed his. Eisner expressed her sympathy for fathers but concluded, "Ultimately, reproductive rights are women's rights, unless and until a man is biologically able to endure the joy and hell of pregnancy and childbirth."[4] Eisner's report was moderate in tone—hardly as confrontational as the demonstration by the side of the road the day before. But the implication of her reports, that the decision was one for the conscience of individual women, is the essence of the pro-choice campaign.

The results of that campaign vary from state to state. Some, such as New

Jersey, New York, New Hampshire, New Mexico, Florida, Hawaii, Oklahoma, Oregon, and Vermont, as well as the District of Columbia, have almost no restrictions on abortion sought in the first trimester of pregnancy. Other states, including Idaho, Kentucky, Mississippi, North Dakota, Ohio, Pennsylvania, Rhode Island, and Virginia, have many restrictions on who can perform the abortion, where it may be performed, and various kinds of permissions, waiting periods, and "consent forms" (warnings about the dangers of abortion and the availability of alternatives). Some states allow a judge to permit the abortion when a minor cannot get or will not ask permission from a legal parent or guardian. On one reported occasion, in Montgomery, Alabama, a state judge named Walter Mark Anderson III faced a number of requests for "judicial bypasses" to parental consent. Under the state's law, if he deems the young woman mature enough to understand the implications of her decision, he is required to grant her request. A conservative Republican, he is personally opposed to abortion, "but I have an oath to uphold," he recently told a journalist, "and as much as I hate it, if I find, by the facts, that the girl is in compliance with [the state] law, I have to grant it."[5]

Our experience this weekend was a microcosm of an ongoing national agony. During the eight years of President Bill Clinton's term in office, many of the restrictions on abortion information—for example, on military base hospitals, in birth control funds for foreign countries, and in federal family assistance plans—were lifted. In 2001, with the inauguration of President George W. Bush, federal policy returned to its pre-Clinton course. Restriction on information and funding returned. Pro-life organizations celebrated; pro-choice organizations warned that all of the gains of the past quarter century were in jeopardy. John Ashcroft, who as state legislator, attorney general, governor, and senator from Missouri had opposed all abortion measures except to save the mother's life, was confirmed as U.S. attorney general. Why should the innocent unborn suffer for the misconduct of the father and the plight of the mother, he worried. He promised to uphold the law as it stands when it is "settled" but did not indicate whether he regards *Roe* as falling in this category. Norma McCorvey, who in the early 1990s proudly revealed her service in an abortion clinic, now ran the Roe No More Ministry in Dallas, a referral service for speakers against the decision.

It is often said, and with much truth, that our country defines itself by its laws. We take justifiable pride in our constitutions and codes because they express our ideals as well as the realities of political life. Controversy over law performs a parallel cultural function by highlighting important divisions among us. As we will see in this reader, abortion and abortion rights are among the legal issues in American history that both define our character and delineate the fissures in our thinking. Over a decade ago, litigator and law scholar Catharine A. MacKinnon put the "abortion right" at the center of her case for "Feminism unmodified."[6] In the same year as MacKinnon argued for abortion rights, another leading law scholar, Mary Ann Glendon, warned against regarding such court-defined rights as absolutes. "A people that lacks a common religion, history, or customs is apt to regard law, especially criminal law and constitutional law, as an expression and source of common values. But at the same time that law is increasingly treated as a value-carrier, there is an almost total lack of agreement about how and where the values it carries are to be discovered."[7]

As both MacKinnon and Glendon go on to argue, abortion and abortion rights disputes are central to our conception of ourselves because they reach out beyond the realm of courts and legislatures to everyday life. They touch the most intimate areas of women's lives and family styles and the most dearly held notions of religion and personal autonomy. At the same time, they fuel the most hotly contested public debates. Finally, they bring together doctors, lawyers, elected officials, judges, and scholars as few other legal issues do.

Roe v. Wade has given the focus to the recent debate, but controversy roiled long before the U.S. Supreme Court attempted to define a right to abortion and gained even more intensity after its ruling was handed down. As the documents in the following chapters demonstrate, the course of the debate follows the larger outlines of increasing state interest in ordinary people's everyday lives. The ancient and early modern state took little interest in abortion. The premature end of a pregnancy was regarded as the concern of the family. In societies where the father had absolute control of the rest of the family, abortion and infanticide were widely practiced and not illegal. In ancient Egypt, Greece, and Rome, abortion was a common form of birth control. Christian teachings prohibited abortion after God implanted the soul in the infant. "Ensoulment" was tied to "quickening," when the woman could feel the child moving of its own volition in the womb. In the Bible, a fine was levied on anyone performing an abortion after quickening, and an abortionist faced death if the woman died as a result of the abortion or the attempted abortion. The Koran does not mention abortion specifically, but Islamic thinkers in early times did not regard abortion before 120 days (or, for some theologians, 40 days) as a crime in itself. Talmudic scholars decided that the harm had to befall the woman, not the fetus, for an attempted abortion to be a crime. The rabbis also concluded that there was no crime unless the fetus had quickened, but abortion was still permitted if the pregnancy endangered the mother's life. Some Jewish jurists went so far as to allow abortion if the pregnancy hurt the mother's reputation. Medieval European medical writings referred to the early fetus as a toad or a parasite, not as an unborn child, but the same writers saw abortion after quickening as a mortal sin, for the fetus then had a soul. Although the Roman Catholic Church frowned on contraception of all kinds, it was not until 1869 that the papacy denounced all abortions, even those that were undertaken before quickening, under the theory that the soul was implanted at conception. Many modern Islamic theologians restrict abortion to situations where the health of the mother or a nursing child is at stake.

In the nineteenth century, the state became far more concerned about day-to-day life, particularly for young people. Compulsory public education plans fundamentally restructured the lives of school children, the taxing responsibilities of governments, and family values. Education became the focal point of domestic life. Public commissions to investigate and regulate hospitals, asylums, and medical care also changed the way parents cared for their children. State legislatures began to pass laws limiting or forbidding the dissemination of birth control information. The federal government came to regard materials describing contraception as a form of pornography and banned them from the mails. Under new laws, states began to prosecute individuals for performing abortions and women for seeking them.

This thoroughgoing anti-abortion regime lasted well into the twentieth century, but the drive for birth control that began in the 1920s eroded the antipathy to abortion in certain kinds of cases, and the number of abortions skyrocketed during the Great Depression. A movement for "reform" of abortion law came from the ranks of doctors who treated victims of botched abortions. The doctors called for a broadening of the so-called therapeutic exceptions to abortion law for women whose pregnancies came about through incest or rape, as well as for women whose pregnancies for them posed physical or mental problems. The "reform" movement gained the support of lawyers and law professors concerned about the rights of women to choose to end pregnancies. A different approach to abortion law, based on the concept of women's rights, became a centerpiece of the women's liberation movement in the 1960s and 1970s. A number of states had passed reform legislation by the end of the 1960s, but many advocates of choice were also working through the courts for an end to all laws criminalizing abortion. By the beginning of the 1970s, a few federal courts had ruled that women had a constitutional right to end their own pregnancies. In 1973, the U.S. Supreme Court adopted this stance in *Roe v. Wade*.

That decision was supposed to end the controversy. Instead, it made the dispute even more vituperative. The abortion question became what many journalists called a "litmus test" in politics, as both major political parties took sides on the issue. State legislatures passed a bewildering variety of regulations governing doctors, hospitals, and counseling centers regarding abortion, and the U.S. Congress chimed in by denying public funds for abortion procedures and birth control centers that provided information on abortion to their clients. Instead of ending lawsuits over abortion rights, the decision in *Roe* seemed to spawn them. Soon the Supreme Court was hearing cases about abortion regulations and funding, and even cases about anti-abortion picketing of clinics. Plainly, the study of abortion and abortion rights remains, as it was for MacKinnon and Glendon over fifteen years ago, a way to understand American law and American life.

On a subject so varied, vast, and controversial as abortion and abortion rights, no single work can be comprehensive. There are dozens of collections of firsthand accounts and dozens more scholarly studies, not to mention the thousands of articles, opinion pieces, and news reports and a number of encyclopedias and multivolume resource books—and this in the past decade alone. Many of them are mentioned in the recommended reading at the end of this book. Navigating through this archipelago of writings is a daunting task, even for the expert. One must assess not only the validity of arguments but also the biases of the authors. In this book we focus on the legal and historical story, attempting to offer a balanced, reflective review of the many voices raised in the course of the controversy. Two of the editors have already published a narrative of the abortion rights controversy in American history.[8] That book was designed as a kind of primer for college students and lay readers. The format of the series in which the book appeared forbade us from wandering far from the case itself into the many other public forums where *Roe*'s emanations reached. Neither were we able to present more than squibs from the rich documentation of the public debate over the case and subsequent holdings of courts on regulation of abortion.

Whether abortion is a matter of choice or an abomination; whether the right to it can or cannot be found in our fundamental law; whether it should be left to the courts or to the legislatures; whether the fetus has rights that the state must protect or the state should respect the woman's right to determine her reproductive fate; and whether and when the fetus should be considered a person under the law—all are questions considered in the following readings. We take no position on any of them, save to explain a little bit about them in the headnotes that precede each selection. The focus questions in some headnotes are intended to help the reader spot key issues, think about alternatives to the argument the author of the selection has made, and master content. Our questions are not intended to be definitive in any way, nor is anything in them to be taken as showing a preference or displaying either disrespect or disagreement with the authors of the selections.

Throughout the book we have tried as well to put the case into the long context of abortion controversy in our history. If there is no clear answer to the problems that abortion and abortion rights raise in law, perhaps a historical view of these subjects will allow us to see them in their largest context. It is a rule of thumb in law that apparently intractable issues can sometimes be resolved when one puts them in a longer time frame. Then we can examine a much larger piece of the social and political situation. Thus it is not surprising that legislators and judges facing the abortion question have routinely taken history into account.

A Note on Editorial Method

In this collection we have tried to include a portion from every crucial legal text on the abortion/abortion rights controversy over the years. We aimed at a documentary history of ideas, events, and opinions. Unfortunately, often the documents themselves were long, repetitive, and sometimes bad tempered. The opinions of Supreme Court justices in abortion cases sometimes ran on for dozens of pages and addressed very obscure points of law or highly technical matters of pleading and procedure not actually related to abortion or abortion rights. In the interests of clarity and utility for the reader, we concluded that we had to omit portions of these documents. Indeed, in some instances the selections in the following chapters represent only a small fraction of the original. At the same time, we did not want to prepare a collection of snippets unrepresentative of the texture or the coherence of arguments in the original. As a rule, we excised all text not unique to its author or to the ongoing debate. In addition, we routinely excluded "citations" (references) to other cases and footnotes in the judicial opinions and scholarly pieces except when these were necessary for clarity. We indicate missing text with ellipses.[9]

With a few noteworthy and in our judgment necessary exceptions, we have reproduced only what historians call primary sources. These reflect the ideas of participants in the story and were uttered or written at the time or shortly after their involvement. The recommended reading section lists many fine secondary sources on the controversy that readers may use to gain the insights of scholars, jurists, and journalists. "Briefs," arguments that parties and "friends of the Court" made to the U.S. Supreme Court, are taken from the Supreme Court's own files. Sources of ready access to these are indicated where the document appears in this book.

Finally, we have occasionally added material in square brackets to identify a person, place, or thing or to clarify a technical term. In similar fashion, we have identified the majority and dissenting opinions of judges by the names of their authors. Although the courts sometimes speak as oracles of the law, wherein the specific identity, interests, prior experience, and personal views of the justices do not matter, the historian knows otherwise. To be understood as historical documents, the opinions must be put in their chronological context and their authors must be recognized as real men and women with political, social, and economic perspectives of their own.

Some of the accounts in these primary sources, particularly those describing the act of abortion, are quite explicit. However one comes down on the issue of abortion rights, the act itself is not pretty. Reader discretion is therefore advised.

The authors gratefully acknowledge the assistance of James Mohr, Karen O'Connor, James W. Reed, and Mark Tushnet as well as reprint permissions from Neal Devins, Cynthia Karmarck, Cass Sunstein, and Sarah Weddington, the *North Carolina Law Review*, the *Yale Law Journal*, the *New York Times*, the *Boston Globe*, and Oxford University Press. The support of University of North Carolina Press assistant director Chuck Grench and his associate, Amanda McMillan, copyeditor Nancy J. Raynor, and assistant managing editor Paula Wald is gratefully acknowledged as well. A special thanks to the students in the legal history classes at Rutgers University–Camden School of Law, Seton Hall University, and the University of Georgia who helped us prepare and evaluate these documents and the secretarial staff at Rutgers who scanned, downloaded, and typed them.

NOTES

1. Alan Guttmacher Institute figures, reported in *New York Times*, January 20, 2003, A16.

2. 410 U.S. 113. A note on citation form: U.S. is the abbreviation for the official reporter of opinions for the Supreme Court of the United States, *United States Supreme Court Reports*, in which all opinions of the justices are printed. By convention, the volume number of the report precedes "U.S.," and the first page of the case follows.

3. Adrienne Rich, *Of Woman Born: Motherhood as Experience and Institution* (New York, 1986), 269.

4. Jane Eisner, "Fathers Count, but Pregnancy Choices Belong to Mothers," *Philadelphia Inquirer Sunday Review*, August 11, 2002, C2.

5. *New York Times*, January 20, 2003, A16.

6. Catharine A. MacKinnon, *Feminism Unmodified: Discourses on Life and Law* (Cambridge, Mass., 1987), 1.

7. Mary Ann Glendon, *Abortion and Divorce in Western Law* (Cambridge, Mass., 1987), 139.

8. N. E. H. Hull and Peter Charles Hoffer, *Roe v. Wade: The Abortion Rights Controversy in American History* (Lawrence, Kans., 2001).

9. All of the materials we edited out of the judicial opinions can be found in the printed versions of the full opinions in the *United States Supreme Court Reports*, for which we have given citations at the start of each selection, as well as online at <www.lexis.com> and <www.oyez.com>.

CHAPTER 1

. . .

Abortion Becomes a Crime

Although the controversy over *Roe v. Wade* has made it seem that the last quarter of the twentieth century is the most important historical era for understanding abortion and abortion rights in America, the law of abortion changed just as dramatically in the first half of the nineteenth century in our country as in the last fifty years. In the formative era of our nation's history, both women's roles in reproduction and the regulation of reproduction became the object of intense public scrutiny. For complex reasons, many states and then the federal government began passing laws that made abortion a crime. By the end of the century, performing or attempting to perform an abortion was punishable in almost all states by fines and imprisonment. Sending abortifacients or abortion information through the mails was also punishable under federal and state law.

Until the nineteenth century, bearing and birthing children primarily involved women, and within the community of women, it was a private affair. Women helped other women through the rigors of pregnancy, and midwives delivered the infant. This is not to say that fathers and husbands were uninterested in children. In Anglo-American law, children were the possession of the fathers, and last names, inheritance, and status passed through the male line. But fathers and husbands ordinarily did not invade the private world of pregnant women. By the same token, although the state took an active interest in general matters of population size and growth, as well as the ethnic composition of the citizenry, governments did not intrude into the reproductive decisions of families.

In the nineteenth century, two new and powerful currents of thinking about domestic life and women's roles in society came to compete with each other, and abortion law became one focal point of the struggle. On the one hand, it was a century of individualistic and liberal ideas about family life which stressed the importance of privacy and self-expression. Among these liberal reform ideas about the family was the notion that women ought to control their reproductive fate. They should be able to decide whether to marry, whether to have children, and whether to continue a pregnancy. Leading nineteenth-century feminists such as Elizabeth Cady Stanton toured the lecture circuit to advance "enlightened motherhood" and "a gospel of few children and a healthy happy maternity."[1] These notions ran against the strong, older, and more conservative current of paternalism, under which women's roles were to remain those of dutiful wife and fecund mother. Some advocates of this stance argued that women who elected not to have children were guilty of the offense of "race suicide." A few proponents of the "race suicide" thesis added to it their fear that if middle-class northern European women did not have large families, the "blood" of the "ruling races" would be tainted by inferior peoples. As sociologist Edward Ross summarized this view in the *American Journal of Sociology* in 1907, "exaggerated individualism that avoids marriage or else dodges its natural consequences [i.e., procreation] forebodes the extinction of the class, the people, or the race that adopts it. . . . The one-child or two-child ideal growingly in favor with the middle class would, if popularized, hurry us to extinction."[2]

On the other hand, the debate over reform of domestic life had a public side—that is, many reforms were imposed on families by government. Reformers who believed that moral standards should be dictated by the state often had the best intentions. Their reforms included the ending of slavery by a constitutional amendment, the restriction of alcohol and drug use by statute, and the introduction of child welfare programs funded by states. Reform "from above," as some historians have termed these efforts, also included the most sweeping of all governmental intrusions into domestic life in our history—the introduction of compulsory public schooling. Similar intellectual and political impulses among legislators led to state intervention into the most private aspects of family life: consensual sexual activity. Some states, such as Georgia, even prescribed the allowable manner of sexual congress in the marital bed. By the end of the century, state and federal law also included a ban on sending birth control information through the mails, which was regarded as a form of pornography.

Government interest in what married people did or did not do with regard to reproduction followed a high tide of abortion in the middle of the nineteenth century. Abortionists advertised openly in newspapers. The most well known of these, Ann Lohman, an English immigrant to New York City who called herself Madame Restell, pioneered abortion referral agencies in a number of cities and an abortion clinic in New York City. Arrested repeatedly, she defied the prosecutors until the 1870s. Her rivals included a Dr. Carswell, who guaranteed in his advertisements to "remove the difficulty in a few days" and swore that "strict secrecy is observed." Sarah

Blakeslee Chase, a homeopathic physician, sold douche syringes used to prevent conception. Arrested five times for performing abortions, she was routinely acquitted by juries until one patient in her care died. Private female clinics opened in a number of cities and treated "all diseases peculiar to women." There rose a brisk trade in over-the-counter and mail-order abortifacients, including pills, powders, and solutions. Many of these were potentially harmful, and some were poisons.[3]

· As the rate of abortion rose to the range of one per every five or six live births in some areas, and perhaps even higher among slaves, doctors and state governments began to focus their attention on abortion. At first the aim of governments was to protect pregnant women, and the first laws they passed regarded women as the victim of a crime. Attempted or successful abortions that killed the mother were capital offenses. If an abortion killed a viable fetus, it was a serious misdemeanor. Pregnant women were not prosecuted even when they solicited and cooperated in the abortion.

Connecticut was the first state to make abortion a crime, in 1821, and New York followed in 1828. The 1828 New York anti-abortion act introduced a clause explicitly legalizing abortion when "the same shall be necessary to preserve the life of such woman, or shall have been advised by two physicians to be necessary for such purpose." This "therapeutic exception" to the anti-abortion law was an elastic one, for doctors might (and in later years did) argue that mental health and future physical health could be considered acceptable reasons for abortions under the therapeutic exception.[4]

◯ In 1845, Massachusetts's law on abortion for the first time made attempted abortion, at any time in the pregnancy, punishable by jail and fines. Under Massachusetts State Laws 1845, chapter 27, "whoever maliciously or without lawful justification, with intent to cause or procure the miscarriage of a woman then pregnant with child, shall administer to her, prescribe for her, or advise or direct her to take or swallow, any poison, drug, medicine or noxious thing, or shall cause or procure her, with like intent, to take or swallow any poison, drug, medicine or noxious thing, and whoever maliciously and without lawful justification shall use any instrument or means whatever with the like intent, and every person with the like intent knowingly aiding and assisting such offender or offenders, shall be deemed guilty of felony, if the woman die in consequence thereof . . . and if the woman doth not die in consequence thereof, such offender shall be guilty of a misdemeanor." But juries still resisted the idea that one could indict for a crime when the victim—under the law the mother, not the fetus—wanted the procedure. Over the next decade there were thirty-two trials in Massachusetts for attempted abortion under the new law and no convictions.

New York revised its anti-abortion laws in 1845, making the death of the fetus (as opposed to the death of the mother) a criminal offense. Attempted abortion at any time in the pregnancy, as in Massachusetts, was a crime. New York added a second novelty to its laws: women who sought an abortion or attempted to perform one on themselves were subject to a fine of up to one thousand dollars. This portion of the act, almost unenforceable (for the best evidence was still the testimony of the mother), was never imposed, but it indicated a shift in official attitudes.

In the following years, the example of Massachusetts and New York (the two states were regarded as leaders in many areas of law) influenced other states to add statutes against abortion to their codes or to revise their earlier laws. For example, in a series of anti-abortion laws passed in the 1850s, Texas made any attempted abortion a felony. If the woman died as a result, the charge was changed to murder, even if the woman had consented to the procedure.

State and federal governments did not stop with the imposition of criminal penalties for abortion. They also turned their attention to birth control itself. In 1873 the federal government passed a law colloquially known as the Comstock Act, in its way as fundamentally intrusive to family life as the introduction of public schools. The government made it illegal to sell, prescribe, buy, publish information about, and send through the mails birth control information.

The interpretation of all of these new statutes (legislative acts) was not easy for courts. In our legal system, courts of appeals are charged with the task of deciding whether lower (trial) courts have correctly applied statutes in particular cases. Appellate courts also determine if the statutes themselves violate provisions of constitutions (the highest law in our state and federal legal systems). Many abortion cases raised legal issues that trial court judges misunderstood. Often, attorneys for the defendant asked the judge to instruct the jury on a particular matter of law at the end of the trial, and he refused. Sometimes the grounds for appeal lay in the judge's decision to admit or refuse to admit evidence of some kind. When defendants appealed their convictions to appellate (or supreme) courts, the judges there had to decide if the lower court had applied the law correctly. Thus the statute law on abortion led to "case law" or a set of "precedents" in the rulings of appeals courts.

. . .

The nineteenth-century debate between those who favored "liberal" reform and those who preferred reform ordered by government had a direct influence on the abortion/abortion rights issue. Although they were not allowed to vote, hold office, or serve in professions such as the law, women took part in these debates. Women's rights movements did not fulfill their major aims of full legal and civil rights for women until the next century, but advocates like Stanton insisted that reform of women's lives required the end of unfair state-imposed restrictions on women. She explained her position to the delegates at the women's rights convention in Seneca Falls, New York, in the summer of 1848.

Elizabeth Cady Stanton, "Address to the Seneca Falls Convention," July 19, 1848, in *Elizabeth Cady Stanton, Susan B. Anthony: Correspondence, Writings, Speeches*, ed. Ellen Carol Dubois (New York, 1981)

We have met here today to discuss our rights and wrongs, civil and political, and not, as some have supposed, to go into the detail of social life alone. We do not propose to petition the legislature [of New York] to make our husbands just, generous, and courteous, to seat every man at the head of a cradle, and to clothe every woman in male attire. . . .

We are assembled to protest against a form of government existing without the consent of the governed—to declare our right to be free as man is free, to be represented in the government which we are taxed to support, to have such disgraceful laws as give man the power to chastise and imprison his wife, to take the wages which she earns, the children of her love; laws which make her the mere dependent on his bounty. It is to protest against such unjust laws as these that we are assembled today, and to have them, if possible, forever erased from our statute books, deeming them a shame and a disgrace to a Christian republic in the nineteenth century. . . .

There seems now to be a kind of moral stagnation in our midst. Philanthropists have done their utmost to rouse the nation to a sense of its sins. War, slavery, drunkenness, licentiousness, gluttony, have been dragged naked before the people, and all their abominations and deformities fully brought to light, yet with idiotic laugh we hug those monsters to our breasts and rush on to destruction. Our churches are multiplying on all sides, our missionary societies, Sunday schools, and prayer meetings and innumerable charitable and reform organizations are all in operation, but still the tide of vice is swelling. . . . Verily, the world waits the coming of some new element, some purifying power, some spirit of mercy and love. The voice of woman has been silenced in the state, the church, and the home, but man cannot fulfill his destiny alone, he cannot redeem his race unaided. There are deep and tender chords of sympathy and love in the hearts of the downfallen and oppressed that woman can touch more skillfully than man. . . . So long as your women are slaves you may throw your colleges and churches to the winds. You can't have scholars and saints so long as your mothers are ground to powder . . . as in women all have fallen, so in her elevation shall the race be recreated.

. . .

Stanton's call for women's equality under the law did not require the intervention of the state in behalf of women. She envisioned instead a negative state that would free women from the oppression of unequal laws. At the same time as she was speaking to the Seneca Falls Convention, Massachusetts was adopting a revolutionary state-sponsored and supervised program of compulsory public education. The best-known and most effective advocate of state-funded public education was Massachusetts's Horace Mann, and he connected compulsory public reform with the rights of the very young.

Horace Mann, *Tenth Annual Report of the Board of Education Together with the Tenth Annual Report of the Secretary of the Board* (Boston, 1847), in *Lectures and Annual Reports in Education* (Cambridge, Mass., 1867)

The expediency of [free public] schools is sometimes advocated on grounds of political economy. An educated people is always a more industrious and productive people. Intelligence is a primary ingredient in the wealth of nations . . . the moralist, too, takes up the argument of the economist. . . . And yet, notwithstanding these views have been presented a thousand times with irrefutable logic . . . there is not at the present time, with the exception of the States of New England . . . a country or a state in Christendom which maintains a system of free schools for the education of its children.

I believe that this amazing dereliction from duty, especially in our own country, originates more in the false notions which men entertain respectiving the nature of their right to property than in any thing else. . . . The rich man who has no children declares that the exaction of a contribution from him to educate the children of his neighbor is an invasion of his rights of property. The man who has reared and educated a family of children denounces it as a double tax when he is called upon to assist in educating the children of others . . . or if he has reared his own children without educating them, he thinks it peculiarly oppressive to be obliged to do for others what he refrained from doing even for himself. Another, having children, but disdaining to educate them with the common mass, withdraws them from the public school, puts them under what he calls "selecter influences," and then thinks it a grievance to be obliged to support a school which he contemns. . . .

The rich farmer, the opulent manufacturer, or the capitalist, when sorely pressed upon his natural and moral obligation to contribute a portion of his means for the education of the young, replies—either in form or in spirit— "My lands, my machinery, my gold, and my silver are mine: may I not do what I will with my own?" There is one supposable case, and only one, where this argument would have plausibility. If it were made by an isolated, solitary being—a being having no relations to a community around him, having no ancestors to whom he had been indebted for ninety-nine parts in every hundred of all he possesses, and expecting to leave no posterity after him. . . . But is this the relation which any man amongst us sustains to his fellows? In the midst of a populous community to which he is bound by innumerable ties . . . the objector can no longer shrink into his individuality. . . . ọ The case of a child, then, to a portion of pre-existent property, begins with the first breath he draws. The new-born infant must have sustenance . . . and care. If the natural parents are removed or parental ability fails, in a word, if parents either cannot or will not supply the infant's wants, then society at large—the government having assumed to itself the ultimate control of all property—is bound to step in and fill the parent's place. To deny this to any child would be the equivalent of a sentence of death, a capital execution of the innocent—at which every soul shudders. . . . If a child has any claim to bread to keep him from perishing, he has a far higher claim to knowledge to preserve him from error and its fearful retinue of calamities. Any community, whether national or state, that ventures to organize a government, or to administer a government already organized, without making provision for the free education of all its children, dares the certain vengeance of Heaven.

• • •

The two styles of nineteenth-century reform—the liberal demand for women's reproductive autonomy within the family and the conservative insistence on state-imposed standards of morality for the family—collided when abortion advertising became popular in the first half of the nineteenth century. The following is a selection of one of the many newspaper advertisements for abortifacients that appeared in newspapers in the middle of the century, although the word "abortion" is not in the advertisement.

"French Lunar Pills" advertisement,
Boston Daily Times, January 8, 1845

MADAME DRUNETTE. Female Physician, is happy in complying with the urgent solicitations other friends and patrons who have tested the efficacy of her invaluable medicines, that she still remains at the old stand 9 EN-DICOTT ST. where ladies may consult her personally with confidence upon all cases incident to their nature arising from irregularities . . . and a cure warranted in all cases where her directions are strictly followed, and furthermore feels warranted in saying from her long personal experience and attention to patients that the FRENCH LUNAR PILLS are the only preparation ever discovered that has proved invariably certain in its operations, acting as they do to eradicate all impurities, thereby assisting nature in performing its office. Madame D. particularly cautions females against advertisements of medicines purporting to be in such eminence for the cure of all female complaints, for they originate from the love of money and not from a sufficient knowledge of medicines to be of use to the patient, but on the contrary of different nature. Married ladies had best consult personally. . . .

FRENCH PREVENTATIVE POWDERS for ladies in delicate health; these powders was long used in Europe before their introduction into this country, and have been extensively used in this city with unprecedented success. They can be had only at Madame Drunette's Office, No. 9 Endicott street. P.S. All letters directed to Madame Drunette; No, 9 Endicott street [postpaid], will meet with immediate action.

. . .

Connecticut was the first state to pass a statute regarding abortion, in 1821. The primary purpose of the law was to spell out the conditions under which the state could prosecute. The victim was not the unborn child, however.

Connecticut General Statutes, Title 22 (1821)

SECT. 14. Every person who shall, wilfully and maliciously, administer to, or cause to be administered to, or taken by, any person or persons, any deadly poison, or other noxious and destructive substance, with an intention him, her or them, thereby to murder, or thereby to cause or procure the miscarriage of any woman, then being quick with child [i.e., the fetus was moving in the womb], and shall be thereof duly convicted, shall suffer imprisonment, in new-gate prison, during this natural life, or for such other term as the court having cognizance of the offence shall determine.

SECT. 15. If any woman shall conceal her pregnancy, and shall willingly be delivered in secret, by herself, of any issue of her body, male or female, which shall by law be a bastard; every such woman, so offending, being thereof duly convicted, before the superior or county court, shall pay a fine not exceeding the sum of one hundred and fifty dollars, or be imprisoned not exceeding three months, at the discretion of the court having cognizance of the offence.

. . .

In the first cases of criminal abortion to arise, the problem was one of evidence: how can there be an abortion if the fetus was already dead in the womb? How can an accusation of attempted abortion be proved if there is no evidence that the woman was pregnant at the time of the attempt? The Massachusetts courts faced this question in the Parker *case below.*

Commonwealth v. Luceba Parker, 50 Mass. 263 (Massachusetts Superior Judicial Court, 1845)[5]

The indictment against the defendant contained three counts. The first alleged that the defendant . . . unlawfully, knowingly and inhumanly, did force and thrust a sharp metallic instrument into the womb and body of a married woman . . . "being then and there pregnant with child, with a wicked and unlawful intent . . . to cause and procure the said" married woman "to miscarry, and prematurely bring forth the said child, with which she was then and there pregnant . . . and that she by means of the said forcing and thrusting of said instrument into the womb and body of the said" married woman, "in manner aforesaid, did bring forth the said child, of which she was so pregnant, dead." . . .

At the trial in the municipal court, it appeared in evidence that the acts alleged in the indictment were done, by the defendant, with the consent of the [woman]. . . . The jury found the defendant guilty. . . . Her counsel thereupon moved in arrest of judgment on the first count, "because no indictable offence is set forth in said count, inasmuch as there is no allegation that the woman therein mentioned was quick with child [that the fetus was alive], at the time the operation was performed." . . . The judge overruled these motions; but . . . he deemed the questions arising thereon to be so important as to require the decision of the supreme judicial court. . . .

Shaw, C. J. [chief justice, the author of the opinion] Without stating particularly the formal grounds of the motions in arrest [to prevent execution] of judgment and for a new trial, it is sufficient to say that they resolve themselves into one question, namely, whether it is an indictable offence, at common law [i.e., the English common law on the subject], to administer a drug, or perform an operation upon a pregnant woman, with her consent, with the intention and for the purpose of causing an abortion and premature birth of the foetus of which she is pregnant, by means of which an abortion is in fact caused, without averring and proving that, at the time of the administration of such drug, or the performance of such operation, such woman was quick with child. The instruction of the judge, at the trial, was, that it was not necessary to aver, or, if averred, to prove, this fact; and if this instruction was incorrect, a new trial ought to be awarded.

We must take care not to confound this case with some others, which resemble it in fact, but fall within another principle. The use of violence upon a woman, with an intent to procure her miscarriage, without her consent, is an assault highly aggravated by such wicked purpose, and would be indictable at common law. So where, upon a similar attempt by drugs or instruments, the death of the mother ensues, the party making such an attempt, with or without the consent of the woman, is guilty of the murder of the mother, on the ground that it is an act done without lawful purpose, dangerous to life, and that the consent of the woman cannot take away the imputation of malice, any more than in case of a duel, where, in like manner, there is the consent of the parties. . . .

The court are of opinion that, at common law, no indictment will lie [i.e., the case should not have even come to trial], for attempts to procure abortion with the consent of the mother, until she is quick with child. It was only considered by the ancient common law that the child had a separate and independent existence, when the embryo had advanced to that degree of maturity designated by the terms "quick with child." . . . "Life," says [the English legal authority William] Blackstone, "begins, in contemplation of law, as soon as an infant is able to stir in the mother's womb." . . . The words "quick with child" must be taken to be according to the common understanding, which was proved to be this; that a woman is not considered to be quick with child, till she has herself felt the child alive and quick within her. It is not necessary, however, to decide, in the present case, what degree of advancement in a state of gestation would justify the application of this description to a pregnant woman; because, in this case, it was not alleged, and the court ruled that it was not necessary to prove, that she was quick with child. . . .

There being no averment, in the first count in this indictment, that the woman was quick with child, or any equivalent averment . . . the court are all of opinion that, although the acts set forth are, in a high degree, offensive to good morals and injurious to society, yet they are not punishable at common law, and that this indictment cannot be sustained.

· · ·

Cases such as Parker *caused an outcry among a group of doctors who already had little regard for homeopaths, herbalists, midwives, and folk healers who performed abortions. Foremost among these reformer-doctors was Horatio Storer, a Boston physician who campaigned vigorously against all abortions. His 1865 essay against abortion, which won a prize from the American Medical Association, contained very pointed advice for doctors.*

Horatio Storer, *Why Not?: A Book for Every Woman* (Boston, 1868), 2–5

What has been done by Physicians to foster, and what to prevent, this Evil.

In our appeal we shall endeavor to go straight towards the mark, nothing concealing, undervaluing, or selfishly excusing. And, first of all, what part have physicians had in this great tragedy, wherein so many women have been chief players? For it is to the medical attendant that the community have a right to look for counsel, for assistance, and for protection, and the present is an evil more especially and directly coming within these bounds.

From time immemorial such have been the deplorable tendencies of unbridled desire, of selfishness and extravagance, of an absence of true conjugal affection, there has existed in countless human breasts a wanton disregard for foetal life, a practical approval of infanticide. This has, however, in the main been confined either to savage tribes, or to nations, like the Chinese, with a redundant population, with each of whom the slaughter of children after their birth is common, or to the lowest classes of more civilized communities, impelled either by shame, or, as in the burial clubs of the London poor, the revelations of which a year or two since so startled the world, by the stimulus of comparatively excessive pecuniary gain.

That infanticide is of occasional occurrence in our own country, the effect of vice or of insanity, has long been known; instances being occasionally brought to the surface of society, and to notice by the police, and through courts of law.

The closely allied crime of abortion also dates back through all history, like every other form or fruit of wickedness, originating in those deeply lying passions coeval with the existence of mankind. Till of late, however, even physicians, who from time to time have accidentally become cognizant of an isolated instance, have supposed or hoped (and here the wish was father to the thought), that the evil was of slight and trivial extent, and therefore, and undoubtedly with the feeling that a thing so frightful and so repugnant to every instinct should be ignored, the profession have, until within a few years, preserved an almost unbroken silence upon the subject.

Some ten years since, this matter was thoroughly taken in hand by a physician much interested in the diseases of women, the younger Dr. Storer, of Boston, with the frank acknowledgment that it was to his father, the Professor of Midwifery in Harvard University, that the credit of initiating the anti-abortion movement in New England was justly due. Prof. Hodge, of Philadelphia, like the elder Dr. Storer, had previously commented, in a public lecture to his class, afterwards printed, upon the immorality and frequency of induced miscarriage; and in Europe one or two physicians of eminence, as Dr. Radford, had endeavored to arouse the profession to the real value of foetal life. The subject had also received some slight attention in works upon medical jurisprudence, but in special treatises upon abortion and sterility, their causes and treatment, of which the most celebrated has been that of Dr. Whitehead, of England, the chance of this occurrence and condition being dependent upon a criminal origin had been almost entirely lost sight of. In investigating the cases of disease in the better classes that came under observation, it was now ascertained that a very large proportion of them were directly owing to a previous abortion, and that in many of them this occurrence had been intentional; the physician's consultation room proving in reality a confessional, wherein, under the implied pledge of secrecy and inviolate confidence, the most weighty and at times astounding revelations are daily made. In such instances as those to which we are now referring, the disclosures are in answer to no idle curiosity, but to the necessity which always exists of knowing and understanding every point relating to the causation, the treatment, the cure of obscure disease.

The profession were soon aroused to an appreciation of facts, whose existence it was shown could so easily be proved by every physician, and in 1857 a Committee, consisting of some of the more prominent and most reliable practitioners in various parts of the country, with the younger Storer as Chairman, was appointed by the American Medical Association, at its meeting in Nashville, to investigate the crime with a view to its possible suppression. The report of this Committee was rendered at Louisville, in 1859, and, supported as it was by a mass of evidence of almost boundless scope, the measures proposed, chiefly of a legislative character, were unanimously indorsed by the Association. The evidence upon which the report was based was subsequently published at Philadelphia, as a separate volume, "the first of a series of contributions to Obstetric Jurisprudence" by its writer, under the title of "Criminal Abortion in America," and was feelingly dedicated "to those whom it may concern—Physician, Attorney, Juror, Judge, and Parent."

This detail, otherwise out of place in an appeal to the community, is rendered perhaps necessary, that an exact and true impression may be given of the steps that have been taken by medical men to redeem themselves from the imputation of having been sluggish guardians of the public weal. Since the time of the Louisville report, the profession have been fully alive to the claims of the subject, and it is not with unnatural satisfaction that its author, in a subsequent publication, has taken occasion to observe that the importance and legitimacy of the investigation has now been acknowledged in the current files of every medical journal, in the published transactions of the national and minor medical associations, in many medical addresses, as that by Dr. Miller, of Louisville, at the meeting of the Association at New Haven, in 1860, over which he presided, and in nearly every general obstetric work of any importance issued in this country since that date, Bedford's Principles and Practice of Obstetrics, for instance, and in many works of criminal law and medical jurisprudence, as Elwell, Wharton and Stillé, and Hartshorne's edition of Taylor, to a much greater extent than the subject in these works had ever been treated before.

I am constrained to acknowledge my indebtedness to the various publications of the writer from whom I have quoted, for much of the evidence I shall now present upon the subject of forced abortions. I trust that thus offered it may lose none of its freshness, point, and force. My frequent extracts from one who has given more thought to the subject than probably any other person in the country, will, I am sure, need no excuse.

An opinion has obtained credence to a certain extent, and it has been fostered by the miserable wretches, for pecuniary gain, at once pandering to the lust and fattening upon the blood of their victims, that induced abortions are not unfrequently effected by the better class of physicians. Such representations are grossly untrue, for wherever and whenever a practitioner of any standing in the profession has been known, or believed to be guilty of producing abortion, except absolutely to save a woman's life, he has immediately and universally been cast from fellowship, in all cases losing the respect of his associates, and frequently, by formal action, being expelled from all professional associations he may have held or enjoyed.

The old Hippocratic oath, to which each of his pupils was sworn by the father of medicine, pledged the physician never to be guilty of unnecessarily inducing miscarriage. That the standard, in this respect, of the profession of the present day has not deteriorated, is proved by the first of the resolutions adopted by the Convention at Louisville, in 1859: "That while physicians have long been united in condemning the procuring of abortion, at every period of gestation, except as necessary for preserving the life of either mother or child, it has become the duty of this Association, in view of the prevalence and increasing frequency of the crime, publicly to enter an earnest and solemn protest against such unwarrantable destruction of human life."

It is true, however, that while physicians are unanimous as to the sanctity of foetal life, they have yet to a certain extent innocently and unintentionally given grounds for the prevalent ignorance upon this subject, to which I shall soon allude. The fact that in some cases of difficult labor it becomes imperatively necessary to remove the child piecemeal, if dead, or, if living, to destroy it for the sake of saving the mother's life, ought not to imply that the physician has attached a trifling value to the child itself. Compared with the mother, who is already mature and playing so important a part in the world, he justly allows the balance to fall, but he fully recognizes that he is assuming a tremendous responsibility, that his action is only justified by the excuse of dire necessity, and he suffers, if he is a man of any sensibility and feeling, an amount of mental anguish not easily to be described, and that none of us, who have been compelled to so terrible a duty, need feel ashamed to confess.

There are cases again, where, during pregnancy, the patient may be reduced by the shock of severe and long-continued pain or excessive vomiting, and its consequent inanition, to the verge of the grave. In such instances, it has been supposed that abortion was necessary to preserve the woman's life. The advance of science, however, has now shown that this procedure is not only often unnecessary, but in reality unscientific; the disturbances referred to occurring, as they generally do, in the earlier months of gestation, being owing not to the direct pressure of the womb upon the stomach or other organs, but to a so-called reflex and sympathetic disturbance of those organs, through the agency of the nervous system; and that a cure can in general be readily effected without in any way endangering the vitality of the child.

There are other instances that might be cited, cases of dangerous organic disease, as cancer of the womb, in which, however improbable it might seem, pregnancy does occasionally occur; cases of insanity, of epilepsy, or of other mental lesion, where there is fear of transmitting the malady to a line of offspring; cases of general ill-health, where there is perhaps a chance of the patient becoming an invalid for life; but for all these, and similar emergencies, there is a single answer, and but this one— that abortion, however it may seem indicated, should never be induced by a physician upon his own uncorroborated opinion, and, in a matter so grave, affecting, with his own reputation, the life of at least one, if not of a second human being, every man worthy of so weighty and responsible a trust will seek in consultation a second opinion. This is a matter of such importance to the welfare of the community, that long ago the law should have provided for its various dangers, and should wisely have left it to no man's discretion or purity of character to withstand the tremendous temptations which must be allowed to here exist. The law now provides, in one or more at least of our States, that the certificate of a single physician, no matter what his skill or standing, cannot commit a patient to the often necessary and beneficial seclusion of a lunatic asylum; two are required. How much more requisite is it that in the question we are now considering, to one mode of deciding which the physician may be prompted by pity, by personal sympathy, the entreaties of a favorite patient, and not seldom by the direct offer of comparatively enormous pecuniary compensation, the law should offer him its protecting shield, saving him even from himself, and helping him to see that the fee for an unnecessarily induced or allowed abortion is in reality the price of blood. As a class, it cannot be gainsaid that physicians of standing will spurn with indignation the direct bribe; let them look to it that they never carelessly permit what they condemn, by endeavoring to bring on the woman's periodical discharge when it is possible that she may have conceived, or by carelessly passing an instrument into her womb without ascertaining whether or no it contain the fruit of impregnation, or by allowing the completion of a miscarriage that may threaten or even have commenced, without resorting to every measure, of whatever character, that can possibly result in its arrest, and the consequent completion of the full period.

. . .

The New York statute was the first to drop proof of quickening as a requirement for culpability, but New York courts still had the burden of determining the intent of the suspected abortionist. Most criminal law (and all serious crimes) requires that intent be established. Intent means that the defendant wanted the outcome of his or her actions and framed them to arrive at the consequence (the crime) that the law defined. But proof of intent in abortion cases was very hard to find, as the court admitted in the following case.

ABORTION BECOMES A CRIME

People v. Van Zile, 143 N.Y. 368
(Court of Appeals of New York, 1894)

ANDREWS, C. J.

The defendant was indicted for the crime of abortion, as defined by section 294 of the Penal Code [i.e., the criminal laws of the state]. The indictment contains two counts [parts]. The first charges the use of the instruments by the defendant upon the body of one Lille M. Cook, with intent to produce a miscarriage; and he is charged in the second count with prescribing and causing to be administered to her a certain medicine, drug, or substance, with the same intent. The case was submitted to the jury under both counts, who rendered a general verdict of guilty. The court, in its charge [instructions to the jury on the law and what both sides had to prove], instructed the jury, in substance, that if they should find that the defendant either used an instrument for the purpose and with the intent charged, or prescribed for or gave drugs to the person named, with the same intent, he could be convicted. The counsel for the defendant, on the conclusion of the charge, asked the judge to charge certain propositions . . . among others, that "there was no evidence before the jury of what transpired in Dr. Van Zile's house on the 8th day of November, 1889, except what is furnished by the testimony of Dr. Van Zile himself, and that, so far as that testimony is concerned, he utterly disproved that any criminal operation was performed or attempted at that time." . . .

We think the requests to charge [the jury], so made, were improperly refused [by the judge of the trial court], for the reason that there was no evidence which justified a submission to the jury of the guilt of the defendant under the first count in the indictment, charging the use of instruments to produce a miscarriage. For the proper understanding of this point, a brief reference to the circumstances shown is necessary. So far as appears, the first connection of Dr. Van Zile with the case was an application made to him on or about the 8th day of November, 1889, by a young man named Terrell, who stated to the defendant, in substance, that it was thought he had a young woman in trouble, but he did not believe it; and he then asked the defendant if he would make an examination to ascertain the fact, and how much the defendant would charge for making it. The defendant said he would make the examination, and this his charge would be $25. The young man, Terrell, in company with a young woman, who was a saleswoman in a store, went to the defendant's office on the evening of November 8, 1889. The only evidence of what there occurred is contained in the testimony of the defendant. Terrell was in prison, and was not examined on the trial; and the girl was dead, she having died at her mother's house on the 25th of December thereafter.

Van Zile testified, in substance, that on that occasion he examined the girl for the purpose of ascertaining whether she was pregnant; that he used a speculum, and sponged the parts with a soft sponge, to aid him in making his observations, but not disturbing the cervix of the womb, or doing anything tending to produce an abortion; that a few minutes only were occupied in the examination; that he ascertained that the girl had advanced a month or two in her pregnancy, and so told Terrell, and advised him to marry her.

This was all the evidence in the case of what occurred on the occasion. It appeared from the examination of medical witnesses that an instrument called a "tent sponge" is sometimes used to produce a miscarriage, which, being introduced into the opening or neck of the womb, will gradually absorb the substance which collects there in case of pregnancy, operating as a barrier against premature delivery. But there is not evidence that the defendant had or used a tent sponge, and he positively testified that he did not use one on that occasion, but only a soft sponge, for the purpose of washing the parts. The evidence of this transaction, as given by the defendant, the only witness who spoke upon the subject, did not tend to sustain a charge of using instruments to produce an abortion.

The judge correctly stated that the jury could believe or disbelieve the defendant's narration, or believe part and reject the rest. But if the whole had been rejected there would have been no evidence whatever of what was done on the evening in question, or even that any examination was made. If the entire evidence is credited, it shows no criminal act; and if part only was believed the same result follows, because the statements, neither separately nor together, show or tend to show a violation of the statute. The jury had no right, upon mere conjecture, to assume or find that the defendant had withheld something, or that he used instruments not shown to have been used, or that he falsely denied such use. Nor was there any proof of injury to the person of the girl disclosed on the autopsy, which would justify an inference that force had been used on this occasion. On the contrary, the great preponderance of evidence is that, in case of the use of instruments, miscarriage results within a short time thereafter. . . .

Evidence was given tending to support the second count in the indictment, charging the prescription by the defendant of drugs for the purpose and with the intent charged. This was denied by the defendant on oath. The claim on the part of the prosecution was that on or about the 11th of November the defendant, at the request of Terrell, prescribed and had put up an abortive compound to be used by the girl. The coupling of the latter evidence with the former may give rise to grave suspicion that the defendant did not state the whole truth as to the transaction on the evening of November 8th. But suspicion cannot give probative force to testimony which in itself is insufficient to establish, or to justify an inference of, a particular fact; and proof of one offense cannot aid in establishing another. . . . The judgement should be reversed, and a new trial ordered.

All concur. Judgement reversed.

. . .

In 1856, Texas adopted a New York–style law, amending it in 1907 to include within the definition of abortion not only the killing of a fetus within the womb but also the premature expulsion of the fetus causing its death. The revised statute gave rise to confusion in the lower courts, and the court of criminal appeals had to decide if lower courts properly applied the new law, as in the next case.

Sam Tonnahill v. The State, 84 Tex. Crim. 517 (1919)

DAVIDSON, Presiding Judge.—The conviction was for abortion charged to have been committed by administration of a drug.

The theory of the State and testimony of the prosecutrix [the pregnant woman, Lena Ward] were that appellant gave to the prosecutrix a certain medicine which was subsequently used by her in producing the abortion. She said that when he handed her the medicine he told her to keep it and he would tell her when it was time to take it, or to keep it until she heard from him; and that she afterwards heard from him and that some time after hearing from him she took the medicine. She claimed to have received a letter from him, saying: "I suppose it was from him, as he was the only one that knew I had this medicine." The letter was lost and its existence and appellant's connection with it developed a sharp issue of fact.

In submission of the case to the jury, the appellant [Tonnahill, who is appealing his conviction] requested the following charge: "The prosecutrix, Lena Ward, testified that when the defendant gave her certain drugs which she claimed to have subsequently administered to herself and caused her to abort, he told her not to use such drugs until she heard from him. If such was the fact the defendant would not be guilty of the crime charged unless he did subsequently give her instructions with reference to the use of said drugs. Now the burden of proof is upon the State to prove beyond a reasonable doubt the defendant's guilt before you would be authorized to convict him.

You are instructed, therefore, that even though you may believe the defendant gave Lena Ward the medicine, still, unless you believe from the evidence beyond a reasonable doubt that the defendant subsequently directed the said Lena Ward to use the medicine which she claims to have been theretofore delivered to her by him, you will return a verdict of not guilty and so say."

It is conceded by the Assistant Attorney General that this charge should have been given, and that its refusal is error. In this conclusion we agree with him. Appellant was not present at the time the medicine was taken by the prosecutrix. Exception was also reserved to the charge because it submitted a state of facts for the consideration of the jury, as a basis of conviction, which were not charged in the indictment. The indictment charged the abortion was procured by administering and causing to be administered to prosecutrix, a pregnant woman, with her consent, a drug and medicine calculated to produce an abortion, and did then and there destroy the life of the fetus in the womb of the said woman, and did then and there by the use of the means aforesaid procure an abortion as aforesaid. The court, after submitting the above charge to the jury, further instructed them that if the defendant by the use, if any, of the means, if any, aforesaid, procured a premature birth, if any, of said fetus, if any, then and in that event they will find the defendant guilty. This phase of the statute was not charged in the indictment. We think the exception [the appellant's objection to the charge] was well taken, and the charge should have been corrected, and that clause of it omitted and not given to the jury.

. . . There is another question involved, and upon it special instructions were asked and refused, that is, unless the jury should find from the facts that the child in the womb of prosecutrix was a live fetus and its life destroyed by the means set out as a prerequisite to the abortion, the jury should find in favor of the defendant. This is presented in two or three ways by special charges [framed by the appellant at the time of the trial for submission to the jury], and all refused [by the trial judge to be included in his charge]. It was necessary for the State to prove the fact that the child was alive, and that the medicine administered was done for the purpose of destroying its life, and in this manner produce the abortion. If the child was not alive, then the case was not proved. The testimony upon this is very meager and quite uncertain. It left room for doubt as to whether the facts sustained this allegation. The court, therefore, was in error in not giving these instructions to the jury. They could not find appellant guilty under the indictment unless the facts would show beyond a reasonable doubt that the child was alive at the time of the administration of the drugs, and that the medicine was administered for the purpose of destroying that life as a means of producing the abortion.

For the reasons indicated the judgment is reversed and the cause remanded.[6]

. . .

Abortion law was a state preserve until 1873, when a remarkable man and his persistent campaign for state-imposed reform of morality in a wide variety of causes brought the federal government into the field. The man behind the novel federal law was Anthony Comstock, not himself a member of Congress but one of the many middle-class-morals reformers of the age, who believed, like Mann, in a positive role for the state in enforcing morality. Born in 1844 in Connecticut, a devout Protestant, he opposed all kinds of pornography, including birth control and abortion depictions. Comstock parlayed the battle against vice and pornography into national prominence for himself, and this helped him influence the passage of the first obscenity law. As explicit as the law seemed to be, it did not make clear how the federal government gained jurisdiction on this subject, what exactly the law prohibited, and who was to enforce it.

An Act for the Suppression of Trade in, and Circulation of, Obscene Literature and Articles of Immoral Use, 42d Congress, 3d session, chapter 258 (1873)

Sec. 1 *Be it enacted by the Senate and House of Representatives of the United States of America in Congress assembled*, That whoever, within the District of Columbia or any of the Territories of the United States, or other place within the exclusive jurisdiction of the United States, shall sell, or lend, or give away, or in any manner exhibit, or shall offer to sell, or to lend, or to give away, or in any manner to exhibit, or shall otherwise publish or offer to publish in any manner, or shall have in his possession, for any such purpose or purposes, any obscene book, pamphlet, paper, writing, advertisement, circular, print, picture, drawing or other representation, figure, or image on or of paper or other material, or any cast, instrument, or other article of an immoral nature, or any drug or medicine, or any article whatever, for the prevention of conception, or for causing unlawful abortion, or shall advertize the same for sale, or shall write or print, or cause to be written or printed, any card, circular, book, pamphlet, advertisement, or notice of any kind, stating when, where, how, or of whom, or by what means, any of the articles in this section hereinbefore mentioned, can be purchased or obtained, or shall manufacture, draw, or print, or in any wise make any of such articles, shall be deemed guilty of a misdemeanor, and on conviction thereof in any court of the United States having criminal jurisdiction in the District of Columbia, or in any Territory or place within the exclusive jurisdiction of the United States, where such misdemeanor shall have been committed; and on conviction thereof, he shall be imprisoned at hard labor in the penitentiary for not less than six months nor more than five years for each offense, or fined not less than one hundred dollars nor more than two thousand dollars, with costs of court.

Sec. 2 That section one hundred and forty-eight of the act to revise, consolidate, and amend the statutes relating to the Post-office Department, approved June eighth, eighteen hundred and seventy-two, be amended to read as follows:

. . . That no obscene, lewd, or lascivious book, pamphlet, picture, paper, print, or other publication of an indecent character, or any article or thing designed or intended for the prevention of conception or procuring of abortion, nor any article or thing intended or adapted for any indecent or immoral use or nature, nor any written or printed card, circular, book, pamphlet, advertisement or notice of any kind giving information, directly or indirectly, where, or how, or of whom, or by what means either of the things before mentioned may be obtained or made, nor any letter upon the envelope of which, or postal-card upon which indecent or scurrilous epithets may be written or printed, shall be carried in the mail, and any person who shall knowingly deposit, or cause to be deposited, for mailing or delivery, any of the hereinbefore-mentioned articles or things, or any notice, or paper containing any advertisement relating to the aforesaid articles or things, and any person who, in pursuance of any plan or scheme for disposing of any of the hereinbefore-mentioned articles or things, shall be deemed guilty of a misdemeanor, and, on conviction thereof, shall, for every offense, be fined not less than one hundred dollars nor more than five thousand dollars, or imprisoned at hard labor not less than one year nor more than ten years, or both, in the discretion of the judge.

Sec. 3. That all persons are prohibited from importing into the United States, from any foreign country, any of the hereinbefore-mentioned articles or things, except the drugs hereinbefore-mentioned when imported in bulk, and not put up for any of the purposes before mentioned; and all such prohibited articles in the course of importation shall be detained by the officer of customs, and proceedings taken against the same under section five of this act.

Sec. 4. That whoever, being an officer, agent, or employee of the government of the United States, shall knowingly aid or abet any person engaged in any violation of this act, shall be deemed guilty of a misdemeanor, and, on conviction thereof, shall, for every offense, be punished as provided in section two of this act.

Sec. 5. That any judge of any district or circuit court of the United States, within the proper district, before whom complaint in writing of any violation of this act shall be made, to the satisfaction of such judge, and founded on knowledge or belief, and, if upon belief, setting forth the grounds of such belief, and supported by oath or affirmation of the complainant, may issue, conformably to the Constitution, a warrant directed to the marshal, or any deputy marshal, in the proper district, directing him to search for, seize, and take possession of any such article or thing hereinbefore-mentioned, and to make due and immediate return thereof, to the end that the same may be condemned and destroyed by proceedings, which shall be conducted in the same manner as other proceedings in case of municipal seizure, and with the same right of appeal or writ of error: *Provided*, That nothing in this section shall be construed as repealing the one hundred and forty-eighth section of the act of which this act is amendatory, or to affect any indictments heretofore found for offenses against the same, but the said indictments may be prosecuted to judgement as if this section had not been enacted.

APPROVED, March 3, 1873.

. . .

Under the Comstock Act (as it came to be known) the federal courts found themselves in the business of deciding the motives of people who sent mail about birth control and abortion or received it. Although most prosecutions ended in convictions, in the case below the prosecution did not fare so well.

Bates v. United States, 10 F. 92 (Circuit Court, N.D. Illinois, 1881)

DRUMMOND, C. J. This was an indictment against the plaintiff in error [an old-fashioned way of saying "appellant"], charging him with violating different [a variety of] provisions of section 3893 of the Revised Statutes [i.e., the Comstock Act]. He was found guilty by the jury and sentenced to fine and imprisonment. A motion in arrest [to prevent execution] of the sentence on account of the insufficiency of the indictment was made in the district court, and the refusal of the court to grant the motion is one of the principal errors [grounds for appeal] relied on in this court. The section of the statutes referred to, as amended by the act of July 12, 1876, declares the following shall be non-mailable matter; Any book, pamphlet, picture, paper, writing, print, or other publication which is obscene, lewd, lascivious, or indecent, or any article or thing designed or intended or adapted for any indecent or immoral use, or any written or printed card, circular, book, pamphlet, advertisement, or notice of any kind giving information directly or indirectly where, or how, or of whom, or by what means any of these matters, articles, or things before mentioned may be obtained or made, or any letter upon the envelope of which, or postal card, upon which, indecent, lewd, obscene, or lascivious delineations, epithets, terms, or language may be written or printed; and any person who shall knowingly deposit, or cause to be deposited, for mailing or delivery, anything declared to be non-mailable matter, is deemed guilty of a misdemeanor, and liable for every offence to a fine or imprisonment at hard labor, or both.

One of the counts of the indictment charges the defendant with sending by mail a book, the title of which is given, and it is alleged that it was of so indecent and obscene a character that it was improper to state its contents. Various other counts of the indictment allege that a letter addressed to a particular person, naming him, contained indecent matter. Other counts state that circulars were sent by mail from and to a place named and to a particular person, naming him, giving information where the article referred to [about preventing conception] could be obtained.

The main ground of objection to the various counts of the indictment is that they do not set forth in language what was contained in the book, in the letters, or in the circulars. It is said that whether a book, or letter, or circular is within the terms of the law is a conclusion, and the court must be permitted to judge by the use of the special language, or if the case be a picture, or representation, or article, by a copy, or description of the same. I think this objection is not well taken. The object of the law is to exclude certain articles from the mail. If a book, pamphlet, picture, representation, or article, it is sufficient as to that to describe it so as to identify it, or by stating to whom it was addressed, and then to allege that is within the terms of the statute, as that it is an obscene book, pamphlet, paper, print, picture, or otherwise, or an indecent thing . . . so that I think it is sufficient, in an indictment under section 3893, to describe the particular book, paper, pamphlet, etc., so as to identify the same, and then allege, in the language of the statute, that it was of the character there described. Consequently, a count which declares that the plaintiff in error caused to be deposited in a post-office of the United States, (naming it,) for mailing and delivery to the address of a certain person, (naming it and him,) an envelope then and there containing a printed advertisement and a written letter, which together were then and there a notice giving information where, how, and of whom might be obtained an article (naming it) designed and intended for the prevention of conception, was sufficient.

An objection was also taken because these various communications were sent through the mail in consequence of what are called "decoy letters," addressed to the plaintiff in error. The fact was that a detective of the post-office department did send letters to the plaintiff in error under fictitious names, but he was requested to send the communications under fictitious names, and they were received by the detective under these various names. It was the case, therefore, where a person used another name to cause a communication to be sent by the mail to him under that name, and such communications sent to a real person under a fictitious name, and of course it was as much an offence against this statute for the plaintiff in error to cause non-mailable matter to be deposited for mailing as though there had been no fiction in the case. . . .

It was also objected that the district court refused to allow the defendant to prove that certain pills which were sent by mail would not, of themselves, prevent conception or procure abortion. I think the ruling of the district court was correct upon that point. The language of the statute is not that the article must necessarily procure abortion or prevent conception, but that it is designed or intended to procure the one or to prevent the other; and these pills were sent in answer to the letter asking for something which might have that effect, and they were sent with the statement that they were just what the writer wanted.

It is further objected that the deposit of the book, letters, circulars, etc., in the mail was not done by the plaintiff in error himself, but by another person. The language of the statute shows clearly that is was intended to prevent any one from violating the law by another as well as by himself, and the jury were specially instructed by the district court that they must be satisfied that the act done was authorized by the plaintiff in error; in other words, that he caused it to be done through another. . . .

This being so, it is insisted by the district attorney that this [appellate] court cannot change in any way the punishment which was imposed upon the plaintiff in error by the district court; but in proceeding to pronounce final sentence and to award execution, this court must follow the precise terms of the conviction in the district court. I am not of that opinion. . . . I think one object of the statute was to give to the circuit court authority, not only over the rulings of the district court during the trial, but also over the degree of punishment imposed upon the party, if, upon the whole record before the circuit court, it should appear in the judgment of the court that the penalty was not in conformity with law. . . . In all these cases I think the opinion of the district court is subject to review by the circuit court, and may be changed.

. . .

Federal courts still had the difficult task of divining the meaning of private correspondence that might violate the act. In the case below, the limits of the First Amendment freedoms of the defendant were at stake, as was his personal freedom.

Bours v. United States, 229 F. 960
(Circuit Court of Appeals, Seventh Circuit, 1915)

MACK, Circuit Judge. The defendant was convicted under an indictment based on section 211 of the Penal Code . . . and was sentenced to two years in the penitentiary. The indictment, after alleging a newspaper advertisement by defendant reading: "Women's Diseases a Specialty. Consult Dr. T. Robinson Bours"—and giving his address and telephone number, charged the receipt by him on September 16, 1912, of the following letter:

> Sparta, Wis., Sept. 16, 1912.
> Dr. T. Robinson Bours, 403–404 Merrill Bldg., Milwaukee, Wis.—My Dear Doctor: I am at a loss as to begin to tell you my troubles. I am about worried to death of the recent discovery of the condition of my only daughter. The dear girl has had the misfortune to repose to implicated confidence of a man who took advantage of her innocence and tried to ruin her, and now that she is in a family way the hound has deserted her. We are willing to make any sacrifice to preserve her good name and reputation. Will you take the girl and relieve her of her disgrace so she can once more face the world. How long would she have to remain there before it would be safe to move her? And what would the cost of the operation be, as well as all other charges? Please answer soon.
> Very respectfully, Mrs. Chas C. Wilson, Box 352.

It then proceeded:

And the grand jurors aforesaid, upon their oaths aforesaid, do further say and present: That on the 25th day of September, 1912, the said T. Robinson Bours, then and there designing and intending to give information directly and indirectly to one Mrs. Charles C. Wilson, of Sparta, Wisconsin, where how, and from whom, and by what means conception might be prevented and an abortion produced, unlawfully, feloniously and knowingly did at, etc., place and cause to be placed in the post office at Milwaukee, Wisconsin, *** [asterisks in original] a certain letter of the tenor following, to wit:

"Milwaukee, Wis. Sept. 25th/12.

Mrs. Chas. C. Wilson, Sparta, Wis.—Dear Madam: Your letter of the 24th I just received and believe me I feel very sorry for you. The operation you speak of would cost from $50.00 to $100. Would have to first see the patient before determining whether I would take the case or not. She could stop at a hotel near by; she would be here about three days. Hotel bill about $10.00 no other expense. (Should come right away.)

Sincerely yours, T. Robinson Bours, M.D."

—which said letter *** [asterisks in original] was then and there non-mailable matter *** and was intended by the said T. Robinson Bours, with full knowledge of its contents and import, to be delivered by the said United States post office establishment, at Milwaukee, Wisconsin, to the said Mrs. Chas. Wilson, at Sparta, Wisconsin. *** That on the said 25th day of September, 1912, the named letter in said post office, did so with full knowledge upon his part of its said contents and import, and unlawfully, feloniously and knowingly meant and intended thereby to give, and did thereby give, and convey information directly and indirectly to the said Mrs. Chas. Wilson, where, how and from, and by what means conception might be prevented, and an abortion produced.

While errors have been assigned on the admission and rejection of testimony and on portions of the charge to the jury, we shall confine ourselves to the error based on the [trial court] overruling of a demurrer [objection] to the indictment. On the adoption of the Penal Code, March 4, 1909, the clauses "where or by whom any act or operation of any kind for the procuring or producing of abortion will be done or performed or how or by what means conception may be prevented or abortion produced" were introduced into the act. Before that, the statutes forbade the use of the mails for obscene literature or writings, for articles and things adapted to prevent conception or produce abortion, and for printed or written matter giving information as to where, how, from whom, or by what means such articles or things might be obtained or made. It aimed to keep out of the mails (1) obscene matter; (2) articles or things designed or intended for use denounced by the act as immoral; and (3) written or printed matter in respect to such articles. Until the amendment, however, a letter or other written or printed information in respect, not to the articles excluded from the mails, but to the act of abortion itself, did not fall within the statute. . . .

While the indictment charges that the letter of September 25th gave information both as to conception and abortion, it is properly conceded in the supplementary brief that, if it be unmailable, it must be because it comes within the clause prohibiting the mailing of a letter giving information "where or by whom any act or operation of any kind, for the procuring or producing of abortion will be done or performed" [in other words, the intention to perform an abortion], and not "how or by what means conception may be prevented or abortion produced," or within any other clause of the act. . . .

The amendment [of the Comstock Act in 1909], closing the mails to written or printed information "where or by whom any operation for producing abortion will be performed," was adopted by Congress under the same power that was exercised in passing the original section, the national power of controlling the mails. Congress has no power to penalize or to legalize the act of producing an abortion. That is a matter for the states. In applying the national statute to an alleged offensive use of the mails at a named place, it is immaterial what the local statutory definition of abortion is, what acts of abortion are included, or what excluded. So the word "abortion" in the national statute must be taken in its general medical sense. Its inclusion in the statute governing the use of the mails indicates a national policy of discountenancing abortion as inimical to the national life. Though the letter of the statute would cover all acts of abortion, the rule of giving a reasonable construction in view of the disclosed national purpose would exclude those acts that are in the interest of national life [i.e., saving the life of the woman]. Therefore a physician may lawfully use the mails to say that if an examination shows the necessity of an operation to save life he will operate, if such in truth is his real position. If he use the mails to give information that he elects, intends, is willing to perform abortions for destroying life, he is guilty, irrespective of whether he has expressly or impliedly bound himself to operate. . . .

But while an obligation, promise, or assurance is not essential, the language of the act, in our judgment, requires that there must be the indication of a positive intent that the act [of an illegal abortion] will be done, not merely that it might perhaps be performed. This intent need not be apparent from the document itself; a letter, however innocent on its face, may, by proper allegations, be shown to convey, and to have been intended to convey, the prohibited information. The single word "Yes," if charged and proven to have been written and mailed in answer to an inquiry whether the writer would perform an illegal operation would be sufficient. No disguise or subterfuge will be of any avail. The word "rupture" may be shown to have been used to indicate abortion to the knowledge of both parties . . . the general statement that X. performs abortions, or an advertisement by X. "Women's Diseases a specialty," may be proven to have been used and understood as meaning that X. will perform a certain definite abortion, or an abortion for any woman in trouble.

The indictment, however, must charge that the apparently innocuous words were used and intended to be understood in the wrongful sense, and must allege such matters as justify the charge. . . .

The letter of the 25th, construed as written by one who had received the letter of the 16th, but as intended to be in reply to some letter of the 24th, the contents of which are not set out, conveys information that an abortion might possibly be produced, not that the act would be done. If in fact the defendant intended to operate, and to have Mrs. Wilson understand that he would operate only under such circumstances as would make it the duty of any reputable physician to perform the act, as, for example, only if an examination disclosed the conditions stated in the letter which defendant testified was dated the 24th, concededly he could not be found guilty. The indictment is fatally defective in charging that the defendant by his letter intended to give information only as to where and by whom an abortion might be produced, not as to where or by whom it would be produced and in failing to allege facts that would support a construction of the letter of September 25th as conveying and intending to convey information that the act would be performed.

Judgement reversed, and cause remanded.

. . .

The arguments of anti-abortion advocates and the efforts of state and federal officials to punish abortion providers did not end the practice of abortion, particularly among the masses of immigrants who had arrived during the previous three decades, poor people living in rural areas, and young, unmarried women. At the end of the nineteenth century, as at its inception, the motivations that the poor, the unwed, and the overburdened pregnant woman had for terminating a pregnancy were still there. Among working-class people in New York City early in the twentieth century, health care professionals found that one of every twenty pregnancies was terminated by an abortion or by the death of the mother from an attempted abortion. In Chicago alone, one doctor, whose practice included women who were the victims of their own attempted abortions, estimated that there were six to ten thousand abortions in 1904.[7] The laws against abortion simply drove it underground and made it even less safe for women than it had been in the years before the laws were passed.

But the same overcrowding, infant mortality, and poverty that led to hidden abortions was spurring another debate, this one open and engaging the talents of leading figures in politics, religion, and the sciences. This was the debate over birth control, and by the middle of the twentieth century it would reopen the question of abortion and abortion rights.

NOTES

1. Quoted in N. E. H. Hull and Peter Charles Hoffer, *Roe v. Wade: The Abortion Rights Controversy in American History* (Lawrence, Kans., 2001), 26.

2. Quoted in ibid., 61–62.

3. Ibid., 26–27.

4. Quotations from <www.lexis.com>.

5. This is the formula in which the state "reporter" (the publisher of the court record) indicated where the opinion of the court was recorded. The first number is the volume of the report; then comes the abbreviation for the state; then the first page of the opinion; then, in parentheses, the date that the opinion was rendered (not the date that the case was heard).

6. To be remanded means the cause was sent back to the lower court to be reheard or decided along the lines laid out in the appellate opinion.

7. The figures appear in Leslie J. Reagan, *When Abortion Was a Crime: Women, Medicine, and Law in the United States, 1867–1973* (Berkeley, Calif., 1997), 19–45.

. . .

CHAPTER 2

Birth Control and the Abortion Law Reform Movement

Attitudes toward women's roles in the family and society, as well as toward sexuality, birth control, and abortion, that had seemed set at the end of the nineteenth century began to shift in the first three decades of the twentieth. Although traditional condemnation of birth control and abortion continued, the horrors of World War I profoundly shook the moral self-confidence that underlay such condemnation. The generation that came of age in these years began to rethink the views of sexuality and childrearing it had inherited from the previous century. By the middle of the 1920s, the "true womanhood" of the ankle-skirted Victorian matron had given way to the "new womanhood" of the scantily clad "flapper." For a marriage to work, many writers and thinkers agreed, women and men had to find sexual pleasure in each other. This included the regular employment of birth control methods.

Despite the ban on dissemination of birth control information, many couples practiced it. Women's networks, older family members, supportive nurses, doctors, pharmacists, midwives, and pamphlets privately printed and passed from hand to hand spread information on methods of contraception. In this period of time there was a steady decline in the number of conceptions among all social and economic classes of married women, a phenomenon that became striking in the Great Depression years of 1929–41. A brief, sharp upturn in the number of births and average family size immediately after World War II was followed by an equally sharp decline in the birth rate in the 1960s. Reliable chemical forms of birth control, including "the pill," were developed and widely sold to supplement older mechanical means. Polls suggested that most women availed themselves of some sort of artificial birth control method.

At the beginning of the century, a small group of eugenicists proposed that certain people should either be encouraged or be forced to practice birth control. These advocates of selective birth control ran the gamut from those who saw birth control as a way of lifting the economic burden from the poor to those who wanted to improve the human species by selective breeding. Although many eugenics advocates did not argue for forced sterilization of any group, the movement appealed as well to those who feared the spread of supposedly inferior races and the reproduction of "dysgenic" traits among individuals.

Although the eugenics movement became popular in the first half of the twentieth century, most birth control advocates, such as Margaret Sanger of New York, founder of what would become the Planned Parenthood Foundation, wanted birth control clinics to help the poor. Sanger enlisted a legion of highly regarded medical specialists, and soon they were pressing for changes to state and federal law. The battle for the legalization of birth control continued as state after state changed its laws to allow birth control clinics and the sale of birth control devices. The federal courts would eventually join in the reform, first allowing birth control information to circulate, then, in 1965, striking down the last of the state laws prohibiting the dissemination of birth control information.

Abortion remained a crime under almost all states' laws through the end of the 1960s. In 1962, forty-two states allowed abortion only when necessary to save the life of the mother, although rarely did the law define exactly what saving the life of the mother entailed. Eight other states and the District of Columbia allowed additional therapeutic exceptions, for health or to prevent serious bodily injury or for the safety of the mother. Many doctors who supported the legalization of birth control also argued that states ought to leave to doctors and their female patients the determination of therapeutic exceptions. Doctors who wanted to reform the laws to expand the therapeutic exception understandably worried whether they would be prosecuted for helping a woman in dire need of the procedure. In 1962, the American Law Institute (ALI), an elite body of lawyers, judges, and law professors, came to agree with these doctors that some reform of abortion law was necessary. The members of the institute feared that a law so vague and varied, and so often disregarded, brought all law into disrespect. At the end of the 1960s, a few states, notably California and Georgia, followed the lead of the ALI and changed their criminal codes to allow more scope for doctors' discretion in performing abortions, but the number of abortions did not rise very much because the procedures were cumbersome and the doctors' decisions had to be approved by hospital committees. Abortion law might have been reformed, but in practice little had changed.

The argument over the role of women in bearing and rearing children begun early in the 1800s continued into the new century. Indeed, with more and more middle- and upper-class women beginning to attend college, marry later in life, and have smaller families, the controversy grew hotter. President Theodore Roosevelt was a fervid supporter of the traditional ideal of the American family and the special role in it assigned to women.

Theodore Roosevelt, "On American Motherhood," address delivered to the National Congress of Mothers, Washington, D.C., March 13, 1905, Theodore Roosevelt Papers, Library of Congress

In our modern industrial civilization there are many and grave dangers to counterbalance the splendors and the triumphs. . . . No piled up wealth, no splendor of material growth, no brilliance of artistic development, will permanently avail any people unless its home life is healthy . . . unless the average woman is a good wife, a good mother, able and willing to perform the first and greatest duty of womanhood, able and willing to bear, and to bring up as they should be brought up, healthy children, sound in body, mind and character, and numerous enough so that the race shall increase and not decrease.

There are certain old truths which will be true as long as this world endures, and which no amount of progress can alter. One of these is the truth that the primary duty of the husband is to be the . . . breadwinner for his wife and children, and that the primary duty of the woman is to be the helpmate, the housewife, and mother . . . and, therefore, after a certain point, the training of the two must normally be different because the duties of the two are normally different. This does not mean inequality of function, but it does mean that normally there must be dissimilarities of function. . . .

No ordinary work done by a man is either as hard or as responsible as the work of a woman who is bringing up a family of small children; for upon her time and strength demands are made not only every hour of the day but often every hour of the night. . . . The woman who is a good wife, and good mother, is entitled to our respect as is not one else; but she is entitled to it only because, and so long as, she is worthy of it. . . . Into the woman's keeping is committed the destiny of the generations that come after us. In bringing up your children you mothers must remember that while it is essential to be loving and tender it is not less essential to be wise and firm. . . .

There are many good people who are denied the supreme blessing of children, and for these we have the respect and sympathy always due to those who, from no fault of their own, are denied any of the other great blessings of life. But the man or woman who deliberately foregoes these blessings, whether from viciousness, coldness, shallow-heartedness, self-indulgence, or mere failure to appreciate aright the difference between the all-important and the unimportant,—why such a creature merits contempt as hearty as any visited upon the soldier who runs away in battle, or upon the man who refuses to work for the support of those dependent upon him. . . . The most rudimentary mental process would have shown . . . that if the average family in which there are children continued by having two children the nation as a whole would decrease in population so rapidly that in two or three generations it would very deservedly be on the point of extinction, so that the people who had acted on this base and selfish doctrine would be giving place to others with braver and more robust ideals. Nor would such a result be in any way regrettable, for a race that practiced such doctrine—that is, a race that practiced race suicide—would thereby conclusively show that it was unfit to exist. . . .

. . .

Although white middle-class families led the way in limiting family size (the very phenomenon that Roosevelt deplored), the same kind of drop was visible throughout all classes and ethnic groups. In the following piece, Lydia Commander suggested that the decrease in family size was voluntary and may not have had the dire consequences Roosevelt foresaw.

Lydia Kingsmill Commander, "Has the Small Family Become an American Ideal?," *Independent*, April 14, 1904, 836–40

. . . The decline in the American birth-rate has for some years been of considerable interest to those who are quick to discern national tendencies. Conventions of ministers of different denominations have repeatedly discussed the subject, and physicians have called it to the attention of the public.

But it was only when President Roosevelt sent out his trumpet-blast protest against what he termed "race suicide" that the nation, as a whole, became aware of the importance of the population question.

That the large family of the early days of this country has disappeared every one is aware. . . . In fact, about the time of the President's famous utterance my attention was especially called to this question by the exclusion from a number of New York flat houses of two families, the one containing seven and the other five children, on no other charge than that the families were too numerous to be desirable as tenants.

Apropos of these incidents, I made some investigations and found that New York landlords had decided prejudices against children and that there was a striking absence of them in the better neighborhoods of the city. Six real estate agents, controlling flats renting at from $50 to $100 a month, in locations from about 80th Street to 140th Street, on the West Side of the city, practically refused to take more than two children, and plainly indicated that even they were not desired. . . .

To discover the causes lying at the basis of these conditions I visited forty-six New York physicians, men and women, practicing in different parts of the city, and gathered their opinions upon the question. Physicians are in a position to understand this matter because they get the confidence of their patients as no other class can. These doctors based their opinions on experience covering, in many instances, thousands of cases. Of the forty-six whom I visited several declined to discuss the question at all, and others were extremely guarded in their remarks. But thirty-eight had facts and opinions which they gave me frankly, with the understanding that their names were not to be quoted.

Of the thirty-eight physicians who were willing to discuss the matter, I asked: "What do you consider the ideal American family?" Thirty said, "Two children, a boy and a girl." Six said, "one-child." One said, "Having a family is not an American ideal," and one said, "Five or six." The last, whose report varied so entirely from every other, said she had not discovered any objection to family on the part of Americans. But she qualified her statement by the explanation that her position was possibly exceptional, her practice being in the upper part of the Bronx among people who have moved to that locality because their families are too large to live comfortably in the more crowded parts of the city. She said, too: "Probably my desires color the expression of the wishes of my patients. As I always strongly advocate five or six children, it may lead women to agree with me, at least during conversation. Besides, my views being well known, I probably attract women of similar opinions. I am inclined to think this is true because when I commenced to practice I was frequently consulted in regard to the family, whereas now I seldom am." . . .

Altogether twelve physicians, practicing among people in comfortable circumstances, and generalizing in all from many thousands of cases, expressed practically these opinions—viz., that the large family does not exist and is not desired.

Nor do those doctors whose patients are less fortunately situated, financially, give a different report. Of nineteen physicians, the majority of whose patients follow the better paid trades and clerical work, such as bookkeeping, etc., with from $20 to $35 a week, all agreed that no desire for large families is to be found.

Dr. J. has practiced for eight years mainly among women. He said: "Most of my patients are people in the middle class financially. They have $1,000 to $1,800 a year. They are just the class always declared to be the bulwark of a nation. They have the vices of neither the rich nor the poor. They are steady, industrious, respectable and live comfortably. They do not want big families, tho, and they will not have them. They generally want one or two, but never more." Dr. R., who has been practicing for eighteen years among all classes, said; "I think most of my patients want children. I am often consulted by childless women who wish for family. But they never want more than one or two. I cannot recall in all my experience a woman who wished for and sought to have a family of five or six."

Dr. I., practicing twelve years among intelligent but not very prosperous people on the upper East Side, said: "I find few who wish to be childless. Most people want one or two children. A very few are willing to have three, and fewer still, four. More than that is considered too many. During my entire experience I have been looking for women willing to have all the children nature would send and have, in twelve years, found only one woman."

The reports were all practically repetitions of this, variously worded. Nor was I able to discover that the poor were more eager to add to the population. It appears that they do so more inadvertently than through intention. . . .

The opposition to large families is not only individual but social. Not only do people object to large families for themselves, they do not want others to have them. Americans disapprove of the large family as a social institution. They dislike to see it and condemn its existence. The producers of large families are considered rather in the light of social enemies than social benefactors.

A physician who has practiced in New York for over twenty years among well-off Americans, as well as having done a great deal of clinic work, said: "The large family is never anything but an unintentional misfortune at the present. Nowadays the mother of a large family feels humiliated. She is really an object of ridicule. People laugh at her at best, and blame her if she is poor. Society does not approve of many children. Unless people have plenty of money we do not excuse them for having a large family. We know that only ample means will enable parents to do justice to many children." Another doctor, who has practiced for six years among different classes of people, said: "I often have women say, 'Doctor, I can't have another. I'm getting such a family I'm ashamed. I don't like to be laughed at.'"

In a woman's club in New York, President Roosevelt's opinions on "race suicide" were discussed and his attitude generally condemned. Of thirty-four present only two agreed with Mr. Roosevelt. The remaining thirty-two indorsed the statement of one of the members: "There are thousands born that have no business to be born." . . .

. . .

The coming of World War I intensified the debate over birth control. In the selection below, the author, Professor Roswell H. Johnson of the University of Pittsburgh, inveighs against the "better sort" of people—here, women who attend college—neglecting their reproductive duties. Professor Johnson's argument, coming as the United States was mobilizing thousands of men for service in the First World War, sounded a sober note. He assumed all of the best and brightest young men would serve, and many would not return. Note how race figured into his arguments.

Roswell H. Johnson, "The Birth Rate of College Women," *School and Society*, June 9, 1917, 678

To the editor of *School and Society*: Professor Laura E. Lockwood, of Wellesley College, has contributed to your issue of March 4, 1916, a criticism of my article dealing with the Wellesley birth-rate [in *The Journal of Heredity*, June 1915]. May I be permitted this belated reply?

Miss Lockwood contends that, except in comparison with the birth-rate of women of the same social class, that of college women has no significance. This is to miss entirely the point of my article. It is precisely because college women are a superior group that I am interested in determining their birth-rate. It is disheartening to find a person in the position Miss Lockwood holds approving the present low birth-rate because superior women as a class bear "only as many children as they can safely and sanely rear and educate." Bad as it is that college women do not replace themselves, it is still more disappointing that this course is deliberately approved. If there were a recognition of the great evil of the "sub-fertility of the superior," the prospect would not be so clouded.

But let us make the comparison that Miss Lockwood considers the only fair one—that between college women and other women of the same social group. We are referred to a study by Miss Smith. But this fails to give the data we need in order to ascertain the comparative racial contributions of the groups, viz., the percentage of married women in each group. Since Miss Lockwood finds the principal findings of this paper against her, she makes the most of the irrelevant fact that more children per year of married life are born to college woman than to others of the same class—a fact of no biological effect. The onus of the situation is that college women are making a small racial contribution both because they marry late and because they have few children. Was not the questionnaire of the Association of Collegiate Alumnae sent to the unmarried as well as the married? Let the comparative marriage-rates of these two groups, as well as the birth-rates be published.

The women's college is of course not the only offending institution; this has never been asserted. Ecumenists have exposed many dysgenic agencies of the most diverse kinds. If the woman's college plays a considerable role among these agencies, however, it demands distinct attention, especially in view of the fact that college conditions are easily amenable to control. If the college deprives the young woman unduly of the society of young men, gives her an ill-balanced education, and apparently approves her limitation of offspring to "as many children as she can rear and educate in the best possible way," reform is needed.

My argument is seriously misunderstood when it is described as seeing only numbers. Its whole weight is placed on the difference in quality among children and the serious racial consequences of a low birth-rate in the superior class. This is the case with all eugenic investigations. Miss Lockwood comments on the excellent quality of the few marriages made by college women, I have (in my article on "Marriage Selection" in the *Journal of Heredity*, for March, 1914) noted the same fact. But this makes their low birth-rate all the more regrettable. How can baby-saving adequately increase the number of children, if, even were all children reared to maturity, their total number does not equal that of their parents?

Miss Lockwood seems to think that small percentages have no biological significance. But the processes of evolution, as a whole, have depended on variations far slighter than those revealed in comparative studies of marriage and birth-rates. The fact that about five per cent more women from coeducational colleges marry than do those from separate colleges, after correcting for geographical differences, to use Miss Shinnu's figures, is significant to the scientific student.

Fortunately the percentage of women attending coeducational colleges is growing very rapidly. . . .

Because men prefer that women be efficient wives and mothers, Miss Lockwood finds that "it is clear" that we want such wives "rather than comrades for ourselves." This assumes that inefficiency is the hall-mark of comradeship.

In very many cases marriage depends on the ability of girls to become efficient home makers and possible mothers. Most young men at the proper time for marriage have incomes too small to afford skilled servants. The high efficiency of these girls renders marriage possible in such cases, or prevents the man from marrying an inferior woman who is within the possibilities of his income. To relegate domestic science to the graduate year would be wholly inadvisable, for the low marriage-rate of the graduate is largely the result of her increased age when she is ready for marriage. . . .

The most discouraging aspect of Miss Lockwood's article is its shocking biology. In discussing the birth-rate of girls who do now nearly reproduce themselves, can she really mean that "we do not know whether we should be deeply concerned that college women, and women of leisure in general, are bearing fewer children, or be grateful that they are producing only the number they can wisely bring to maturity, and are thus setting an example to the poor and ignorant which they may eventually learn to follow"? If the faculties of the women's college were seriously setting out to correct the sub-fertility of their graduates, it would be comforting, even though some of their efforts were erroneous, but her smug defiance of the biological foundation of progress is appalling. Does Miss Lockwood realize the irrevocable injury to the human species she may be causing by such an assertion as this!

. . .

In response to Johnson, Dorothy Dunbar Bromley offered an array of arguments that suggested uncontrolled population increase could destroy a nation —or the world. What was more, it seemed to her that by making birth control difficult, governments were acting in an immoral fashion, a thesis that owed more than a little to some of the ideas of eugenics.

Dorothy Dunbar Bromley, "This Question of Birth Control," *Harper's Monthly*, December 1929, 34–45

. . . The problem of birth control, linked as it is with the population problem, is one of the most interesting of the modern age. Academically, at least, it has been a moot point ever since an obscure English clergyman, the Reverend T. R. Malthus, published his essay on "The Principles of Population" in the year 1798. It was his theory that "the chief cause of human strife and misery lies in the constant tendency of mankind to increase beyond the means of subsistence." And after a systematic survey of the various races of the world, he endeavored to show that this natural excess of population was invariably checked either by some such restraint on procreation as infanticide and abortion or by such destructive forces as disease, war, famine, and poverty. He offered no remedy for this dilemma short of celibacy or late marriage, and it was left for the Utilitarians, with their doctrine of "the greatest good for the greatest number," to urge birth control as the logical solution. The Reverend Mr. Malthus' theory of the ratio of human increase as compared with the ratio of the increase of the means of subsistence was destined to be upset by the industrial developments of the nineteenth century. But his general conclusions as to the dangers inherent in excess population have not yet been broken down.

It is a fact that Nature has provided in man, as in animals, for the maintenance of the species by a capacity for reproduction far in excess of its needs. It is also a fact that civilized man is not less fertile, but if anything a little more fertile than was primitive man. Darwin was convinced that the fecundity of the human race as a whole had increased during past times, inasmuch as civilized man is better able to adapt himself to such changing conditions of environment as tend to depress the fertility of savage races. As a corollary to this idea, Havelock Ellis suggests that the sex impulse has gained in strength during the ages, since civilized man is less preoccupied with the physical struggle for survival than was primitive man; and he points to the corresponding difference in the sex habits of wild and domestic animals of the same species. In any event it is true that with the emergence of the great historical races and a more steeled type of life, large families have averaged three and not more than four children. At the same time, with the rise of towns and cities, plagues and epidemics, together with wars and famines, exerted a constant check on the increase of people, so that up until the nineteenth century the population of the entire world is supposed not to have exceeded 850 millions. During the course of that century the industrial revolution and the opening up of vast continents greatly enhanced the earth's resources, while the development of medicine and the new humanitarianism saved and prolonged thousands of human lives. As a result the population of the world was approximately doubled in one short century, amazing as the fact may seem.

It can hardly be denied that this rapid multiplication of human beings in the nineteenth century set the stage for the World War. In 1901 a German writer, Herr Arthur Dix, declared that "because the German people nowadays increase at the rate of 800,000 inhabitants a year, they need both room and nourishment for the surplus." A decade later Bernhardi baldly announced, "Strong, healthy, and flourishing nations require new territory for the accommodation of their surplus population. Since almost every part of the globe is inhabited, new territory must, as a rule, be obtained at the cost of its possessors, that is to say, by conquest, which thus becomes a law of necessity." . . . A phrase with a similar intent—"necessity knows no law"—was to be used by Bethmann Hollweg when he felt called upon to justify Germany's invasion of Belgium. . . .

What the future holds for Europe—whether populations will continue to grow to the point where teeming nations must burst their bounds, or whether the female contingent will eventually become so emancipated as to cease to reproduce itself, as Dr. Robert R. Kuczynski has recently predicted in his study of "The Balance of Births and Deaths in Western and Northern Europe"—is a matter for wide speculation. It is certain, however, that at the present time most of Europe, as well as large parts of Asia, are overcrowded and underfed, and that birth control is the only practical solution thus far offered. . . .

Whether the margin between our birth and our death rates will continue to grow narrower in the years to come is a matter for blind prophecy, because no one knows how much farther science may go in conquering disease and postponing death. In any event a population must be appraised, in the opinion of Professor Henry P. Fairchild of New York University, "not according to its size, but according to whether it is too large or too small to promote the maximum human happiness."

We talk largely of American prosperity and yet we forget that thousands of families have not yet felt its golden influence. Child labor is a case in point. This barbaric practice goes on, not because parents are inherently cruel, but because they are driven to it by harsh economic necessity. An investigation of tenement home work carried on in New York in 1922 revealed that in the small families of four or less the children were allowed their freedom after school, but that in the large families, averaging seven children, the latter were obliged to come home and sew on coats or make artificial flowers. Summing up the child labor situation, Owen B. Lovejoy, formerly General Secretary of the National Child Labor Committee, has estimated that with family limitation in the poor classes, perhaps one-third of all the working children in this country could be saved from a life of exploitation.

A recent plea for funds from the New York Child Welfare Committee stated that in some families "as many as thirteen, fourteen, and even seventeen human beings sleep in three or four rooms." These are the children that often become delinquents, we are told by Miriam Van Waters, who has seen thousands of them pass through the Juvenile Courts in California and a number of other states. Agreeing with her, the eminent criminologist, Dr. George W. Kirchwey, believes that "the practice of birth control would go far towards a solution of the crime problem to-day."

Millions of dollars are spent annually by the several States of the Union for the care of the insane, mental defectives, and epileptics. To meet this problem twenty-three States have active eugenic laws providing for the sterilization of individuals so degenerate mentally or physically that their progeny would become a burden to the community. In the remaining States, however, defectives continue to spawn, and their offspring frequently become a menace to the community. Only the other day I read in the newspaper of the brutal murder in Connecticut of a three-year-old child perpetrated by two boys seven and eight, the sons of a man who had formerly been an inmate of an insane asylum. Obviously this man should have been sterilized before he was released, but in these cases they asylum doctor cannot take such a step unless the state law instructs him to do so. . . .

. . .

A renewed effort to legalize birth control was under way before the First World War had ended. Although it had a number of advocates coming from a wide variety of intellectual and political interest groups, at its center was Margaret Sanger. Sanger, a romantic reformer in some ways, was in others hard headed and practical. In her autobiography she narrated her initial experiences with problems raised by the illegality of birth control and later her refusal to obey the law.

Margaret Sanger, *Autobiography* (New York, 1938), 86–92

During these years in New York trained nurses were in great demand. Few people wanted to enter hospitals; they were afraid they might be "practiced" upon, and consented to go only in desperate emergencies. Sentiment was especially vehement in the matter of having babies. A woman's own bedroom, no matter how inconveniently arranged, was the usual place for her lying-in. I was not sufficiently free from domestic duties to be a general nurse, but I could ordinarily manage obstetrical cases because I was notified far enough ahead to plan my schedule. And after serving my two weeks I could get home again.

Sometimes I was summoned to small apartments occupied by young clerks, insurance salesmen, or lawyers, just starting out, most of them under thirty and whose wives were having their first or second baby. They were always eager to know the best and latest method in infant care and feeding. In particular, Jewish patients, whose lives centered around the family, welcomed advice and followed it implicitly.

But more and more my calls began to come from the Lower East Side, as though I were being magnetically drawn there by some force outside my control. I hated the wretchedness and hopelessness of the poor, and never experienced that satisfaction in working among them that so many noble women have found. My concern for my patients was now quite different from my earlier hospital attitude. I could see that much was wrong with them which did not appear in the physiological or medical diagnosis. A woman in childbirth was not merely a woman in childbirth. My expanded outlook included a view of her background, her potentialities as a human being, the kind of children she was bearing, and what was going to happen to them. . . .

Below this stratum of society was one in truly desperate circumstances. The men were sullen and unskilled, picking up odd jobs now and then, but more often unemployed, lounging in and out of the house at all hours of the day and night. The women seemed to slink on their way to market and were without neighborliness.

These submerged, untouched classes were beyond the scope of organized charity or religion. No labor union, no church, not even the Salvation Army reached them. They were apprehensive of everyone and rejected help of any kind, ordering all intruders to keep out; both birth and death they considered their own business. Social agents, who were just beginning to appear, were profoundly mistrusted because they pried into homes and lives, asking questions about wages, how many were in the family, had any of them ever been in jail. Often two or three had been there or were now under suspicion of prostitution, shoplifting, purse snatching, petty thievery, and, in consequence, passed furtively by the big blue uniforms on the corner.

The utmost depression came over me as I approached this surreptitious region. Below Fourteenth Street I seemed to be breathing a different air, to be in another world and country where the people had habits and customs alien to anything I had ever heard about. . . .

I remember one confinement [late pregnancy] case to which I was called by the doctor of an insurance company. I climbed up the five flights and entered the airless rooms, but the baby had come with too great speed. A boy of ten had been the only assistant. Five flights was a long way; he had wrapped the placenta in a piece of newspaper and dropped it out the window into the court. . . .

Pregnancy was a chronic condition among the women of this class. Suggestions as to what to do for a girl who was "in trouble" or a married woman who was "caught" passed from mouth to mouth—herb teas, turpentine, steaming, rolling downstairs, inserting slippery elm, knitting needles, shoe-hooks. When they had word of a new remedy they hurried to the drugstore, and if the clerk were inclined to be friendly he might say, "Oh, that won't help you, but here's something that may." The younger druggist usually refused to give advice because, if it were to be known, they would come under the law; midwives were even more fearful. The doomed women implored me to reveal the "secret" rich people had, offering to pay me extra to tell them; many really believed I was holding back information for money. They asked everybody and tried anything, but nothing did them any good. On Saturday nights I have seen groups of from fifty to one hundred with their shawls over their heads waiting outside the office of a five-dollar abortionist.

Each time I returned to this district, which was becoming a recurrent nightmare, I used to hear that Mrs. Cohen "had been carried to a hospital, but had never come back," or that Mrs. Kelly "had sent the children to a neighbor and had put her head into the gas oven." Day after day such tales were poured into my ears—a baby born dead, great relief—the death of an older child, sorrow but again relief of a sort—the story told a thousand times of death from abortion and children going into institutions. I shuddered with horror as I listened to the details and studied the reasons back of them—destitution linked with excessive childbearing. The waste of life seemed utterly senseless. One by one worried, sad, pensive, and aging faces marshaled themselves before me in my dreams, sometimes appealingly, sometimes accusingly. . . .

Then one stifling mid-July day of 1912 I was summoned to a Grand Street tenement. My patient was a small, slight Russian Jewess, about twenty-eight years old, of the special cast of feature to which suffering lends a madonna-like expression. The cramped three-room apartment was in a sorry state of turmoil. Jake Sachs, a truck driver scarcely older than his wife, had come home to find the three children crying and her unconscious from the effects of a self-induced abortion. He had called the nearest doctor, who in turn had sent for me. Jake's earnings were trifling, and most of them had gone to keep the none-too-strong children clean and properly fed. But his wife's ingenuity had helped them to save a little, and this he was glad to spend on a nurse rather than have her go to a hospital.

The doctor and I settled ourselves to the task of fighting the septicemia. Never had I worked so fast, never so concentratedly. The sultry days and nights were melted into a torpid inferno. It did not seem possible there could be such heat, and every bit of food, ice, and drugs had to be carried up three flights of stairs.

Jake was more kind and thoughtful than many of the husbands I had encountered. He loved his children, and had always helped his wife wash and dress them. He had brought water up and carried garbage down before he left in the morning, and did as much as he could for me while he anxiously watched her progress.

After a fortnight Mrs. Sachs' recovery was in sight. Neighbors, ordinarily fatalistic as to the results of abortion, were genuinely pleased that she had survived. She smiled wanly at all who came to see her and thanked them gently, but she could not respond to their hearty congratulations. She appeared to be more despondent and anxious than she should have been, and spent too much time in meditation.

At the end of three weeks, as I was preparing to leave the fragile patient to take up her difficult life once more, she finally voiced her fears, "Another baby will finish me, I suppose?"

"It's too early to talk about that," I temporized.

But when the doctor came to make his last call, I drew him aside. "Mrs. Sachs is terribly worried about having another baby."

"She well may be," replied the doctor, and then he stood before her and said, "Any more such capers, young woman, and there'll be no need to send for me."

"I know, doctor," she replied timidly, "but," and she hesitated as though it took all her courage to say it, "what can I do to prevent it?"

The doctor was a kindly man, and he had worked hard to save her, but such incidents had become so familiar to him that he had long since lost whatever delicacy he might once have had. He laughed good-naturedly. "You want to have your cake and eat it too, do you? Well, it can't be done."

Then picking up his hat and bag to depart he said, "Tell Jake to sleep on the roof."

I glanced quickly at Mrs. Sachs. Even through my sudden tears I could see stamped on her face an expression of absolute despair. We simply looked at each other, saying no word until the door had closed behind the doctor. The she lifted her thin, blue-veined hands and clasped them beseechingly. "He can't understand. He's only a man. But you do, don't you? Please tell me the secret, and I'll never breathe it to a soul. *Please!*"

What was I to do? I could not speak the conventionally comforting phrases which would be of no comfort. Instead, I made her as physically easy as I could and promised to come back in a few days to talk with her again. A little later, when she slept, I tiptoed away.

Night after night the wistful image of Mrs. Sachs appeared before me. I made all sorts of excuses to myself for not going back. I was busy on other cases; I really did not know what to say to her or how to convince her of my own ignorance; I was helpless to avert such monstrous atrocities. Time rolled by and I did nothing.

The telephone rang one evening three months later, and Jake Sachs' agitated voice begged me to come at once; his wife was sick again and from the same cause. For a wild moment I thought of sending someone else, but actually, of course, I hurried into my uniform, caught up my bag, and started out. All the way I longed for a subway wreck, an explosion, anything to keep me from having to enter that home again. But nothing happened, even to delay me. I turned into the dingy doorway and climbed the familiar stairs once more. The children were there, young little things.

Mrs. Sachs was in a coma and died within ten minutes. I folded her still hands across her breast, remembering how they had pleaded with me, begging so humbly for the knowledge which was her right. I drew a sheet over her pallid face. Jake was sobbing, running his hands through his hair and pulling it out like an insane person. Over and over again he wailed, "My God! My God! My God!"

I left him pacing desperately back and forth, and for hours I myself walked and walked and walked through the hushed streets.

When I finally arrived home and let myself quietly in, all the household was sleeping. I looked out my window and down upon the dimly lighted city. Its pains and griefs crowded in upon me, a moving picture rolled before my eyes with photographic clearness: women writhing in travail to bring forth little babies; the babies themselves naked and hungry, wrapped in newspapers to keep them from the cold; six-year-old children with pinched, pale, wrinkled faces, old in concentrated wretchedness, pushed into gray and fetid cellars, crouching on stone floors, their small scrawny hands scuttling through rags, making lamp shades, artificial flowers; white coffins, black coffins, coffins, coffins interminably passing in never-ending succession. The scenes piled one upon another on another. I could bear it no longer. . . .

I went to bed, knowing that no matter what it might cost, I was finished with palliatives and superficial cures; I was resolved to seek out the root of evil, to do something to change the destiny of mothers whose miseries were vast as the sky.

. . .

Despite the dramatic appeal of her story, Sanger was already engaged in a campaign to make the dissemination of birth control information and apparatus legal. In 1914, Sanger and her allies opened a birth control clinic in Brooklyn, New York. A police raid closed it down, and she, along with her sister Ethel and another woman, was tried for violating the state's obscenity laws, an experience she reported in her Autobiography. *Note especially how she characterized the formal processes of law and how she felt that the trial was an inadequate forum for her to reveal the realities of the problem.*

Sanger, *Autobiography*, 224–37

. . . Out of the raid four separate cases resulted: [my sister] Ethel was charged with violating Section 1142 of the Penal Code, designed to prevent dissemination of contraceptive information; Fania with having sold an allegedly indecent book entitled *What Every Girl Should Know*; I, first, with having conducted a clinic in violation of the same Section 1142, second, with violating Section 1530 by maintaining a public nuisance.

I claimed that Section 1142 which forbade contraceptive information to, for, and by anyone was unconstitutional, because no state was permitted to interfere with a citizen's right to life or liberty, and such denial was certainly interference. Experience had shown it did the case no good merely to defend such a stand in a lower court; it must be carried to a higher tribunal, and only a lawyer versed in whereases and whatsoevers and inasmuchases could accomplish this. But I was still hopeful of finding one who was able to see that the importance of birth control could not be properly emphasized if we bowed too deeply before the slow and ponderous majesty of the law.

The attorney who offered himself, J. J. Goldstein, had a background which made him more sympathetic than other lawyers, even the most liberal. He was one of those young Jewish men of promise who had been guided through adolescence by Mary Simkhovitch, founder of Greenwich House, and Lillian Wald, founder of the Henry Street Settlement. The seeds of social service had been planted in him; his legal training only temporarily slowed down their growth.

J. J. had placed himself in a difficult position for a youthful Tammany [Hall] Democrat [the regular Democratic Party in the city, a political machine], some day to be a magistrate; he might have been forgiven more easily had he received a larger fee. Though he had to be convinced that we declined to have anything to do with political wire-pulling, he fought for us valiantly.

November 20th we pleaded not guilty and trial was set for November 27th. J. J. endeavored to have the three of us tried simultaneously, but the Court of Special Sessions would have none of it. Then he asked for a jury trial, which could be granted at the discretion of the Supreme Court; application was denied. An appeal to the Appellate Division was dismissed; writs of habeas corpus were dismissed; another appeal to the Appellate Division was dismissed; adjournments pending appeal were urged but not granted. Indeed I was being swiftly educated in the technicalities of criminal law.

I felt like a victim who passed into the courtroom, was made to bow before the judge, and did not know what it was all about. Every gesture had its special significance, which must not be left out if appeals were to be possible. We had to make many more appearances than would otherwise have been necessary; everything had to be correctly on the record. . . .

Evening after evening J. J. rehearsed the arguments he was going to present and directed me to respond to questioning. I did not understand the technicalities and begged to be allowed to tell the story in my own way, fearful lest the heartaches of the mothers be lost in the labyrinthine maze of judicial verbiage. But he maintained if the case were to be appealed to a higher court, it had to be conducted according to certain formalities.

"Why should it have to be in legal language?" I demanded. "I'm a simple citizen, born in a democratic country. A court should also listen to my plea expressed in plain language for the common people. I'm sure I can make them understand and arouse their compassion."

He reiterated that I could not address a court as though I were trying to instil my views in an individual. "You can't talk to them that way. You'll have to let me talk."

"But that's the way I talk and I'm the accused."

I fully expected that if I were permitted to set forth my human version of the Brownsville tragedies, no appeal would be required. But J. J. knew the courts and had no such hopes. He was still doubtful of any success before the lower tribunal, and was still unable to see my point, counting chiefly on technicalities to win the case. . . .

No less than thirty of the mothers of Brownsville had been subpoenaed by the prosecution, but about fifty arrived—some equipped with fruit, bread, pacifiers, and extra diapers, others distressed at having had to spend carfare, timid at the thought of being in court, hungry because no kosher food could be obtained near by. Nevertheless, all smiled and nodded at me reassuringly.

Formerly, a few women of wealth but of liberal tendencies had been actively concerned in the movement, but now some who were prominent socially were coming to believe on principle that birth control should not be denied to the masses. The subject was in the process of ceasing to be tagged as radical and revolutionary, and becoming admittedly human-itarian. . . .

It surprised me that in my trial the prosecution should be carried on so vehemently, because the prosecutor had little to prove. To me there seemed to be no argument at all; the last thing in my mind was to deny having given birth control advice. Certainly I had violated the letter of the law, but that was what I was opposing.

I grew more and more puzzled by the stilted language, the circumlocu-tions, the respect for precedent. These legal battles, fought in a curiously unreal world, intensified my defiance to the breaking point. I longed for a discussion in the open on merit and in simple, honest terms. . . . Ill health resulting from pregnancy caused by lack of its use might be construed as disease.

Then one by one the Brownsville mothers were called to the stand to answer the District Attorney. "Have you ever seen Mrs. Sanger before?"

"Yess. Yess, I know Mrs. Sanger."

"Where did you see her?"

"At the cleenic."

"Why did you go there?"

"To have her stop the babies."

The witness bowed sweet acknowledgment to me until she was peremp-torily commanded to address the court.

"Did you get this information?"

"Yess. Yess, dank you, I got it. It wass gut, too."

"Enough," the District Attorney barked, and called another.

Time after time they gave answers that were like nails to seal my doom, yet each thought she was assisting me.

J. J. saw how their testimony could be turned to our advantage.

He asked, "How many miscarriages have you had? How much sickness in your family? How much does your husband earn? The answers were seven, eight, nine dollars a week."

At last one woman more miserable and more poverty-stricken than the rest was summoned. "How many children have you?"

"Eight and three that didn't live."

"What does your husband earn?"

"Ten dollars a veek—ven he vorks."

Judge Freschi finally exclaimed, "I can't stand this any longer," and the court was adjourned over the week-end. . . .

J. J. had heard on reliable authority that if I were to change my plea to guilty, I could have a suspended sentence. To his mind freedom alone meant victory, and he urged me to accept it if it were offered. . . .

I sat listening to what seemed an interminable discussion between J. J. and Judge Freschi over whether the appeal were going to be prosecuted in a quick and orderly fashion, until I was nearly lulled to sleep. Suddenly my attention was caught by hearing J. J. declare that I would "promise not to violate the law."

My mind clicked. It was not in my program to bargain for freedom. J. J., knowing full well I would make no such promise, had planted himself in front of me so the court could not see my belligerent face. He was trying to act as a buffer and, at the same time, for fear of what I might say, to avoid having me summoned to the stand. I tried to peer around him, but he shifted from side to side, obscuring my view. I tugged on his coat like a badly brought up child, but he took no notice. Finally one of the judges interposed, "Your client wishes to speak to you, counselor." I could be ignored no longer, and was called. "Margaret Sanger, stand up."

History is written in retrospect, but contemporary documents must be consulted; therefore I have gone to the official records for the facts. After all, one courtroom is much like another, and the attitude of one justice not so dissimilar from that of another. I was combating a mass ideology, and the judges who were its spokesmen merged into a single voice, all saying, "Be good and we'll let you off." . . .

THE COURT: Very good. You have had your day in court; you advocated a cause, you were brought to the bar, you wanted to be tried here, you were judged, you didn't go on the stand and commit perjury in any sense, you took the facts and accepted them as true, and you are ready for judgment, even the worst. Now, we are prepared, however, under all the circumstances of this case, to be extremely lenient with you if you will tell us that you will respect this law and not violate it again. . . .

You have challenged the constitutionality of the law under consideration and the jurisdiction of this Court. When this is done in an orderly way no one can find fault. It is your right as a citizen. . . . Refusal to obey the law becomes an open defiance of the rule of the majority. While the law is in its present form, defiance provokes anything but reasonable consideration. The judgment of the Court is that you be confined to the Workhouse for the period of thirty days.

A single cry, "Shame!" was followed by a sharp rap of the gavel, and silence fell.

. . .

Sanger's contribution was not only personal. She organized conferences and raised funds, reaching out to a wide array of leaders in various professions who favored birth control, making a case in public opinion that aimed at legislative reform. Her supporters ran from mainstream medical practitioners to leaders of the American Socialist Party, such as Norman Thomas. At the sixth conference of Sanger's North American Birth Control League, held in 1925, Thomas gave a talk titled "Some Objections to Birth Control Considered." His arguments for birth control were entirely different from those of the conservatives.

Norman Thomas, "Some Objections to Birth Control Considered," in *Religious and Ethical Aspects of Birth Control*, edited by Margaret Sanger (New York, 1926), 44–50

It would be absurd to pretend that this short paper will be an adequate answer to all the objections that are raised to Birth Control. There are, for instance physiological and psychological questions that must be left to those with expert qualifications to which I do not pretend. Mine is the more modest but scarcely less necessary task of examining briefly certain objections to Birth Control more or less firmly believed or diligently inculcated among that large class of common people to which we non-experts belong.

[Religious and moral] objections are rationalized in various ways, but at the basis of them is the ancient sex taboo. In the course of time, in those regions and among those groups in which Christianity had its early successes, that taboo found expression in the general belief that sexual relations were per se unlovely and unclean. The highest ethical ideal was lifelong continence. Marriage was honorable, but only as a concession on the one hand to race propagation and on the other to the weakness of the flesh-witness the opinions of St. Paul. Later this view of sex crystallized in the definite emphasis on the holiness of celibacy. The Protestant Reformation denied the superior sanctity of celibacy without weakening the notion that the price of normal marital relations must be the willingness to have an indefinite number of children. In popular morality, the risk of having children, like the risk of contracting disease, was and is counted on as a mighty bulwark against illicit sexual relations.

When opposition to Birth Control derived from this way of looking at sex is rationalized, we have some strange results. Thus, there have been published statements attributed to Roman Catholic dignitaries to the effect that Birth Control is wrong because it hinders the entrance into this world of multitudes of souls and that such regulation should lie only within the providence of God. Obviously if Birth Control has this effect, so does continence, both within and without the marriage relation, and this doctrine of unrestricted procreation is strangely inconsistent on the lips of men who practice celibacy and preach continence. Another curious pronouncement was called to my attention only today. The mayor of Boston in an impassioned letter denouncing Birth Control, as opposed to all laws, secular and sacred, actually identifies it with abortion. Now abortion is the very thing that lack of modern Birth Control knowledge too often furthers and to denounce Birth Control as abortion is more than one might expect even from the politician who recently discovered, after endorsing the child labor amendment, that it had been made in Moscow!

But one may go farther and urge that there is no warrant for assuming that the sole legitimate end of sex relations is the procreation of children. Connected with the sex instinct in man is the development of art and fellowship and love. These things have for us the value of ends in themselves. When an instinct as strong as sex desire is deliberately restricted by husband and wife to those occasions on which it is proposed to bring children into the world, the consequences—save in exceptional cases—will be a morbid pre-occupation with sex and unwholesome psychological repressions. Without the possibility of Birth Control, the pitiful choice [is] beyond their strength to nourish and support, or a continual and rigorous denial of relations in themselves normal and beautiful. On the other hand Birth Control makes possible a creative morality and a conscious effort to bring into the world those who are indeed well born. . . .

I am so persuaded that Birth Control makes for a normal and happy married life, so convinced of its individual and social benefits, that I should argue that they outweigh any possible encouragement to illicit sex relations which a knowledge of Birth Control may bring. But I by no means believe that even temporarily Birth Control will substantially—to use the current phrase—already have the knowledge we deny to good women. There is no competent evidence that in Holland, for instance, where Birth

Control is legal, sex morals are worse or different than in countries of similar economic and climate conditions. Neither is there evidence of a dangerous refusal to have any children at all.

The second class of objections to Birth Control rises from our intense racial and national group consciousness. The white race, Europeans and Americans, we are told, or our own nation—whatever that nation may be—is endangered by practising Birth Control. Birth Control is something like disarmament—a good thing if effected by international agreement, but otherwise dangerous to us in both a military and economic sense. If we would not be overwhelmed by the "rising tide of color" we must breed against the world. If our nation is to survive, it must have more cannon and more babies as prospective food for the cannon.

I find it difficult to give this sort of objection the attention I suppose it deserves. It is bound up with a theory of national and racial supremacy that very literally menaces mankind with destruction. We are to breed not for peace but for war. We are to bring children into the world in order that they may be potential, if not actual soldiers. We are to deny mothers knowledge of Birth Control in order that sons whom they have borne in pain and travail may perish in the more horrible agony of trenches or battlefields by shells or poison gas. And all this to maintain a theory of national or racial superiority wholly unproved by sober science. Even the menace is in most cases exaggerated. It is, for instance, by no means proved that other races are actually increasing in numbers faster than we whites. Moreover it is we, not they who have been and are the aggressors.

Those who deplore the consequences of Birth Control in the interest of eugenics, or racial or national supremacy, have come to the field too late. The very groups they urge to produce more children than the alleged inferior stocks will not do it. If they did, their lowered economic status might make them seem inferior. They already know how to control births. Our present task is to make possible a similar knowledge and desire among the ignorant. Widespread Birth Control is an essential condition for the attainment of the desires of all those who, in the interests of eugenics, food, or peace seek an intelligent control of the quality and quantity of population.

· · ·

Sanger also turned to elite members of the medical profession to further her crusade. Their professionalism and contacts would shield the movement and her in a way that radicals such as Thomas could not. At the same time, she had to turn over the reins of the movement to the doctors if she wanted them to join her. In the following selection, a report on one of the medical conferences she ran suggests that leadership in her movement was shifting to these professionals.

"Up to the Doctors," *The Survey*, April 15, 1925, 73

Ten years ago the very idea of an international conference on birth control in New York city would have been unthinkable. Except to a few earnest propagandists and sociologists the term suggested only something rather daringly funny, even funnier than the activities of the "suffragettes" of those days. There was little public discussion of it except in the police courts, where Margaret Sanger bravely ignored the insults and innuendoes of judges, audience and reporters alike. Every hand seemed raised against her except for a few loyal followers, among them many of the weary mothers of Brownsville who had parked their baby carriages in rows outside the doors of her first clinic, closed by the police.

The opposite picture of the conference just concluded gives faith in the vitality of an idea backed by one determined person. For a week a distinguished group of professional men and women of widely differing interests has met in the auditorium of a New York hotel, listening to papers on various aspects of birth control by persons whose names are known the wide world over. There has been only one free public meeting; all the other sessions have been for groups who came and paid a conference fee not to hear propaganda or argument, but to learn of and contribute to an important sociological development.

The program listed members of the faculties of Amherst, New York University, Harvard, Cornell, Yale, Bryn Mawr, Columbia, Smith, the University of California, Syracuse and the University of Maine. It included such ranking physicians as Dr. William Allen Pusey, president of the American Medical Association; Dr. Alice Hamilton of the Harvard Medical School, Dr. Ira W. Wile, Mr. Max Schlapp, of the Postgraduate Medical School, Dr. Walter Timme, Dr. W. F. Robie, Dr. Rachelle Yarros of Hull House, and Dr. Aletta Jacobs, pioneer in her native Holland. It brought together the suggestions and criticism of a group of clergymen of churches both in and outside of New York; of sociologists and students of social problems such as Professor Ogburn of Columbia, Miriam Van Waters of the Juvenile Court of Los Angeles, Louis I. Owen Lovejoy of the National Child Labor Committee. The subjects of their papers were arranged in sessions headed Fecundity and Civilization, the Differential Birth Rate, Health of the Community, Economic Poverty and Child Labor, War and Population, Eugenics and

Welfare, Biological and Allied Problems, Sex and Reproduction, and Religious and Moral Factors.

The list of more than sixty foreign and American vice-presidents of the conference carries an equally brilliant roster of names. . . .

Through it all Mrs. Sanger smiled as quietly and as unconcerned as though she never had envisaged anything different from this focusing of all kinds of professional competence upon the subject which has been her life work. As Dr. Raymond Pearl of Johns Hopkins University declared: "This congress of leading scientific men and women from all over the world is also in large measure a tribute to the splendid work of Mrs. Margaret Sanger, the pioneer and leader of the birth control movement in America. Under difficulties and vicissitudes which would have completely disheartened a less courageous soul, she has kept up the fight and won a succession of victories which even a few years ago would have seemed impossible." . . .

A rapidly increasing professional interest and support was registered in the attendance at a meeting on contraceptive methods open only to licensed physicians, which jammed one hall, and necessitated an overflow meeting in another hotel, bringing together more than a thousand physicians, who acknowledged the interest and responsibility of the medical profession in birth control. . . .

Perhaps because birth control began as a lay movement the knowledge of its sociological implications has outrun progress in medical technique, so that there is great present need for a program of medical research and clinical trial. . . . Mrs. Sanger herself has been among the first to recognize this need. *The Survey* already has noted her offer, in accord with the generous and statesmanlike course of her ten year's campaign, to place the direction of the medical activities of the American Birth Control League in the hands of a representative medical group. Now it is up to the doctors. . . .

. . .

However successful Sanger's efforts might have been to sway an elite cadre of doctors, the dissemination of birth control information was still illegal. Mary Ware Dennett's Birth Control Laws *(1926) was a sober reminder that all Sanger's early efforts had still borne little fruit. In the first chapter of her book, Dennett outlined "The Situation," in her words, as she saw it.*

Mary Ware Dennett, *Birth Control Laws* (New York, 1926), 3–18

The actual situation under Federal and State law: not even parents can lawfully inform their married children about how to space their babies—no doctor can lawfully or adequately study the control of conception, present provisions of Federal law, scope of state laws, clinics under state laws— access to birth control information not only criminal but classed with obscenity-control of conception confused with abortion. . . . What if that principle were applied to some other scientific knowledge, making automobiles for instance?

It is a crime under the federal law for a mother to write to her daughter a letter such as this:

DAUGHTER DEAR:

It wrings my heart to know that you are so terribly worried. I have felt for a long time, that something was troubling you. You are absolutely right in your determination to know all there is to be known about how to have your babies when you want them and not otherwise. Now that your own doctor has failed to give you practicable advice, I realize more than ever that I should have raised heaven and earth to see to it that you had adequate information when you were first married. Somehow I blindly hoped that you would never have to go through what I did, that you would be sure to find out what I never properly knew in my married life, and that you would be spared the terror of living in fear that the love which brings you and your husband together should bring your babies so rapidly, that you can not possibly take care of them. I blame myself that I let my inhibitions stand in the way of finding help for you long ago, so that now you could help yourself.

But I will do my best to make up. There must be no more worry and uncertainty for you in this crisis. Now that he has lost his job and his health at the same time, you must be sure that no more babies are started for, say four years. I hope and believe that by that time you may be able to have your fourth child in safety. But until then you and he will need every atom of your vitality to make the little bank balance tide you over to better times.

Now here is help. (It makes my blood boil that your doctor should have been so helpless when you took your problem to him, but there is no use berating him, for it is probably not wholly his fault that he knows so little on this subject. The laws won't let him study the matter.) I am sending you a wonderfully clear explicit pamphlet which tells the best and simplest methods for regulating conception. It is written by Doctor — who has made a business of studying this problem, law, or no law, for over twenty-five years. The methods recommended in it are practically the same as those taught by the best authorities abroad.

I am not stopping to tell you how I got the pamphlet. But I was a "criminal" according to our State law when I got it. And I am a "criminal" again according to Federal law, now that I am mailing it to you. But I am willing to be that kind of a criminal a thousand times over if only I can at this late date make up for letting you go so long uninformed, and if only I can now put your poor tormented mind at rest.

With boundless love,

MOTHER.

For writing such a letter and for sending the pamphlet to which it refers, this mother could be sent to jail for five years and fined $5000. That she would not be discovered is probable. It is also likely that if discovered she would not be indicted. But that would be due, not to the law, but merely to the fact that the authorities are almost wholly negligent in enforcing the law. The federal law makes no exceptions whatever. It is a crime for anyone, even for the best of reasons and in the greatest need, to send or to receive by mail anything that tells "where, how or of whom" information may be secured as to how conception may be controlled. The number of unarrested "criminals" of the type of this mother is beyond knowledge or computation, but they are everywhere. Many of them could not tell exactly what the law is. . . .

First of all we have the federal law which affects the whole country. Then we have state laws in all the states but two, which either directly or by inference form a legal barrier between the people and this knowledge. In just half of the forty-eight states there are specific prohibitions. In all but two of the other half, the same prohibition is feasible under the obscenity laws, by virtue of the precedent of the Federal obscenity law and the obscenity laws of half the states, for it is in these obscenity laws that the prohibition of the circulation of contraceptives is found. . . .

Now as to the state laws. They are very similar in import and phraseology to the parent federal law . . . but they deal with other ways of circulating contraceptive knowledge and means than transportation by mail or express. The 24 states which have specific prohibitions, variously forbid publishing, advertising or giving the information. Fourteen States prohibit anyone to tell. (Fancy trying to enforce such a law!) In most of these states the statute is similar to that in the District of Columbia, which even forbids the telling of anything that "will be calculated to lead another" to apply any information to the prevention of conception, and also makes it a crime to have in one's possession any instructions to lend or give away. That is, the most ordinary channels for human relationship, private conversation and the sort of help one friend or relative naturally gives to another, become criminal where this subject is concerned. In several States private property and personal belongings can be searched by the authorities for "contraband" instructions. Colorado forbids anyone to bring contraceptive knowledge into the State. (The hold-up of traffic on the State line if that law were enforced, would be amazing to contemplate.) But Connecticut surely deserves the booby prize, for it has the grotesque distinction of being the one State to penalize the actual utilization of contraceptive information; in other words, the Connecticut law makes it a crime not only to find out how, but, actually to control conception. The enforcement of that law fairly staggers the imagination. What could have been in the minds of the legislators who passed it is a question. . . .

. . .

Most advocates of birth control denied that they favored abortion. Even doctors who called for open debate on birth control, or the legalization of birth control clinics and the dissemination of information on birth control, did not advocate abortion. Instead, they favored as a next step the expansion of the "therapeutic exception" to the abortion laws. One of them ventured a little further in an anonymous letter to the editor of The Nation.

"Abortions in the U.S.A.," *The Nation*, August 8, 1936, 167

Dear Sirs: . . . As a practicing physician of many years' experience in this country, especially among persons in poor circumstances, I have learned what doctors in similar practice usually learn, that effective contraception is too costly or requires too much effort on the part of the patient to be practiced by the great mass of people. As a result, conception occurs all too frequently. A very large percentage of women, unwilling for economic or other reasons to have a child, attempt to get rid of the pregnancy as speedily as possible.

Depending upon their circumstances, the women will either go to the midwife who in the most dangerous possible technical fashion will perform the abortion for from $5 to $10, or if they can afford it, will go to a so-called "private hospital," where the abortion is performed under sterile operating-room conditions with almost complete safety for the pregnant mother, for a fee of from $100 up.

Whereas 95 per cent and perhaps more of the medical profession will not perform abortions because of the fear of possible legal consequences or from moral or ethical reasons, there is always the remaining 5 per cent available, who will do the abortion for a price. And there are very few of the "ethical" 95 per cent who will not supply their patients, provided sufficient pressure is brought to bear, with the names and fees of one or more abortionists.

Abortions have become so common that a doctor who takes careful histories of his patients and who has their confidence will find that a large proportion of his married women patients have had one or more. Of course the average of abortions is somewhat higher for urban centers than for rural communities. I should estimate that at least 100 and probably more abortions are done annually in this community of 30,000 persons. So far as I know, there are not doctors in our community who now perform abortions, although a prominent physician did them until quite recently. But there are several doctors a few miles away who will perform them for fees of from $25 to $100. Incidentally, the ethical 95 per cent will not hesitate to attempt to induce an abortion by medication. And almost any doctor will tell you of cases he knows of, where the patient has died following "careless abortion" and nothing has been done about it. The average doctor unconsciously protects the murderers in his own profession.

I therefore regret very much that Russia has gone a step backward in doing away with abortions. I believe it would be far better if abortions were legalized in America, so that they might be done openly, with proper medical precautions, and by properly trained surgeons, rather than in the unclean, dangerous, furtive, and psychologically dangerous manner in which they are being done today.

A PRACTICING PHYSICIAN
New York State, July 23

. . .

A partial victory for Sanger and her medical allies came in 1936. It concerned the Comstock Act of 1873. The federal government appealed a decision from the U.S. District Court for the Southern District of New York, which dismissed a "libel" (a civil lawsuit arising out of the tariff law) brought against a physician for allegedly violating a section of the Tariff Act of 1930 designed to enforce the Comstock Act's provisions. The physician had received a package containing pessaries (the precursor to the vaginal diaphragm) for the purpose of trying them in her practice and giving her opinion as to their usefulness for contraceptive purposes. After the prosecution was dismissed in the federal district court, the government asked the court of appeals to reverse the lower court ruling and reinstitute the prosecution. The court refused, contending that changing mores should alter how courts interpreted out-of-date statutes.

United States v. One Package, 86 F. 2d 737
(Second Circuit Court of Appeals, 1936)

AUGUSTUS N. HAND, Circuit Judge

The United States filed this libel against a package containing 120 vaginal pessaries more or less, alleged to be imported contrary to section 305(a) of the Tariff Act of 1930. . . . From the decree dismissing the libel the United States has appealed. In our opinion the decree should be affirmed.

The claimant Dr. Stone is a New York physician who has been licensed to practice for sixteen years and has specialized in gynecology. The package containing pessaries was sent to her by a physician in Japan for the purpose of trying them in her practice and giving her opinion as to their usefulness for contraceptive purposes. She testified that she prescribes the use of pessaries in cases where it would not be desirable for a patient to undertake a pregnancy. The accuracy and good faith of this testimony is not questioned. The New York Penal Law which makes it in general a misdemeanor to sell or give away or to advertise or offer for sale any articles for the prevention of conception excepts furnishing such articles to physicians who may in good faith prescribe their use for cure or prevention of disease. . . . The witnesses for both the government and the claimant testified that the use of contraceptives was in many cases necessary for the health of women and that they employed articles of the general nature of the pessaries in their practice. There was no dispute as to the truth of these statements.

Section 305(a) of the Tariff Act of 1930 . . . provides that: "All persons are prohibited from importing into the United States from any foreign country *** [asterisks in origina] any article whatever for the prevention of conception or for causing unlawful abortion."

The question is whether physicians who import such articles as those involved in the present case in order to use them for the health of their patients are excepted by implication from the literal terms of the statute. Certainly they are excepted in the case of an abortive which is prescribed to save life, for section 305(a) of the Tariff Act only prohibits the importation of articles for causing "unlawful abortion." This was the very point decided in *Bours v. United States*, . . . declaring nonmailable "every article or thing designed, adapted, or intended for preventing conception or producing abortion, or for any indecent or immoral use," was held not to cover physicians using the mails in order to say that they will operate upon a patient if an examination shows the necessity of an operation to save life. . . .

The laws prohibiting the importing or transporting in interstate commerce of articles "designed, adapted, or intended for preventing conception, or producing abortion," all originated from the so-called Comstock Act of 1873 (17 Stat. 598), which was entitled "An Act for the Suppression of Trade in, and Circulation of, obscene Literature and Articles of immoral Use." . . .

All the statutes we have referred to were part of a continuous scheme to suppress immoral articles and obscene literature and should so far as possible be construed together and consistently. If this be done, the articles here in question ought not to be forfeited when not intended for an immoral purpose. . . .

It is true that in 1873, when the Comstock Act was passed, information now available as to the evils resulting in many cases from conception was most limited, and accordingly it is argued and the language prohibiting the sale or mailing of contraceptives should be taken literally and that Congress intended to bar the use of such articles completely. While we may assume that section 305(a) of the Tariff Act of 1930 . . . exempts only such articles as the act of 1873 excepted, yet we are satisfied that this statute, as well as all the acts we have referred to, embraced only such articles as Congress would have denounced as immoral if it had understood all the conditions under which they were to be used. Its design, in our opinion, was not to prevent the importation, sale, or carriage by mail of things which might intelligently be employed by conscientious and competent physicians for the purpose of saving life or promoting the well being of their patients. The word "unlawful" would make this clear as to articles for producing abortion. . . . The decree dismissing the libel is affirmed.

. . .

By the end of the 1930s, doctors who favored abortion in cases where a woman's physical or mental health seemed at stake focused their attention on expanding the availability of therapeutic abortions. In the next selection, Dr. Rigine K. Stix and public health expert Dorothy G. Wiehl reported the findings of a study funded by the Milbank Memorial Fund at the American Public Health Association annual meeting in 1937. Their conclusions went far beyond their statistical findings.

Rigine K. Stix and Dorothy G. Wiehl, "Abortion and the Public Health," *American Journal of Public Health* 28 (1938): 621–28 (tables and footnotes omitted)

Recent special studies of maternal mortality have shown that from one-fourth to one-third of all maternal deaths are associated with abortion.

These findings have stimulated wide interest in the problem of abortion from the point of view of the public health, and especially in the problem of the frequency with which abortion occurs. The question naturally arises whether abortions occur in a similarly large proportion of pregnancies, with a death rate approximately the same as that associated with other types of pregnancy termination, or whether these abortion deaths represent an abnormally high death rate for a small number of abortions. Obviously it is impossible to answer the question without having reliable information on which estimates of the number of abortions in the population as a whole can be based. Registration of provable terminations of pregnancy is not required in most states, and if required, as in New York City, they are very incompletely reported.

Recently several surveys have been undertaken by the Milbank Memorial Fund in which a physician or a nurse obtained complete pregnancy histories from women in their own homes. Two of the groups interviewed had been clients of birth control clinics, one in New York City, and the other in Cincinnati, Ohio. A third group consisted of an unselected sample of married women in New York City who had had a pregnancy which terminated within a few months of the interview. In each case the interviewer had the means of establishing a good contact with the surveyed case, either as a representative of the clinic from which the woman had sought advice or as a public health nurse interested in the problems of a recent delivery. Both the clinic groups and the survey group were selected with respect to overt fertility and the clinic groups showed an additional selection with respect to a special interest in the control of that fertility.

The outcome of pregnancies reported by the women interviewed in these three studies is compared with data from various other sources in Table I. For those groups for which information concerning the comparative prevalence of spontaneous, therapeutic and illegal abortions is available, there is a striking lack of variation in the incidence of involuntary abortion. In 6 of the 7 instances in which the proportion of pregnancies terminating in involuntary abortion is known, the variation is less than 2 per cent. The consistency of these figures suggests that an average involuntary abortion [miscarriage] rate of about 10 per cent of all pregnancies may be expected in any given population group and, therefore, with a known number of non-viable pregnancy terminations, the incidence of illegal abortions may be estimated with considerable accuracy.

Contrasted with the similarity of figures on involuntary abortion, there is a wide variation in the reported incidence of illegal abortion in these groups. The lowest incidence is reported by Pearl's group of multiparous patients in Chicago hospitals, and the highest by the group which attended the New York birth control clinic. Patients seeking advice on contraception in other cities had illegal abortion rates which were higher than those of women unselected with respect to an interest in limiting their families, but much lower than those reported by the New York clinic patients. Data for the non-clinic groups suggest that 5 per cent is a fair maximum estimate of the proportion of pregnancies terminated by illegal abortion among married white women. Higher estimates of the prevalence of illegal abortions have been based very largely on figures from the histories of women who attended the same New York birth control clinic for which data are given in Table I. This clinic group does not appear to be typical of either an average unselected group of urban married women or of clinic patients in other cities.

The per cent of pregnancies terminated by illegal abortion shows considerable variation with order of birth and income, and varies widely in these respects in the three groups studied. The variation by order of birth is contrasted with the lack of variation in spontaneous abortions by the same type of analysis in Figure I. Not only does the percentage of pregnancies terminated by illegal abortion vary widely in the three groups, but they show differing characteristics with respect to order of birth. The New York birth control clinic sample, like other samples from the same clinic, shows a marked rise in illegal abortion with increasing order of pregnancy. The Cincinnati birth control group shows a similar but much less marked rise up to the fourth pregnancy, after which the proportion of pregnancies illegally aborted tends to remain almost level. The same type of rise is observed in the New York City unselected group up to the third pregnancy. After the third pregnancy the percentage appears to drop, but the number of cases is too small to give dependable evidence on this point.

Variation of illegal abortions with family income is shown in Figure II. The variation is not so marked as that associated with increasing order of pregnancy, but the differences between the three survey groups persist. In both birth control clinic groups there is a rise in abortion rate associated with rise in income, while in the unselected New York City group, there is a rise only in one group, the poorest non-relief group. It appears from these analyses that the pressure of increasing pregnancies and certain economic and social pressures, while they appear to have no influence on the involuntary abortion rate, are important factors underlying the resort to voluntary induced abortion.

The total number of abortions occurring annually in New York City may be estimated on the basis of the ratio of abortions to live births reported in the unselected New York group. This estimate is probably quite accurate for spontaneous abortions and a minimum estimate for induced illegal abortions in New York City, estimated on this basis, is more than 20,000 annually, of which between 5,000 and 6,000 are illegally induced. Referring these figures to the classification of maternal deaths in the special study of deaths for 1930–1932 by the New York Academy of Medicine, the indicated risk of mortality for women in the first and second trimesters of pregnancy, exclusive of ectopic pregnancy [in which the fertilized egg does not leave the fallopian tube] and illegal abortion, is 7 per 1,000. The rate is almost exactly the same for women experiencing illegal abortion. This rate is slightly lower than the rates reported in several series of hospital cases. It is almost twice as high as the rate of 4 deaths per 1,000 confinements for women delivered in the third trimester of pregnancy.

From the point of view of the public health, prevention of abortion morbidity and mortality is the primary concern. What means of prevention can be devised? Spontaneous abortions may be prevented to some extent by careful management in cases in which the patient consults a physician in the early weeks of pregnancy. Taussig, in his text on abortion, has an excellent chapter outlining the measures which may be used both before and after conception. When abortion is inevitable, both morbidity and mortality can probably be reduced by conservative management and the avoidance of curettage whenever possible.

Theoretically all morbidity and mortality from illegal abortion is preventable and unnecessary. The phenomenon of a rapidly declining birth rate, however, is the expression of a widespread desire to limit the size of families. Population groups in the higher income brackets are enabled to limit the size of their families by the use of reliable contraceptives. For population groups of low income, however, where economic pressure and inadequate housing are most acute, reliable contraceptive methods are not at present readily available. In these groups abortion offers a means of family limitation when inadequate contraception fails. Increased economic security and more adequate housing may decrease the acuteness of the need for family limitation in these groups. The establishment of maternal health clinics, which would make reliable contraception more readily available, would be a more immediate and direct approach to the problem.

· · ·

Familiar with figures like those above and with patients who had suffered and died from self-abortions or the work of illegal and unsafe abortionists, obstetricians urged reform of the anti-abortion laws. On May 21, 1959, the mem-

bers of the American Law Institute discussed revision of its Model Penal Code *to expand the therapeutic exception in states' abortion laws. A tentative draft of the abortion reform written by Professor Louis B. Schwartz of the University of Pennsylvania Law School was voted up, and in 1962 it became part of the* Model Penal Code. *In striking fashion it differed from the vast majority of states' laws, but in some ways it did not. Note to whom the decision to abort a fetus is given.*

American Law Institute, *Model Penal Code*, section 230.3, Abortion (1962)

(1) *Unjustified Abortion.* A person who purposely and unjustifiably terminates the pregnancy of another otherwise than by a live birth commits a felony of the third degree or, where the pregnancy has continued beyond the twenty-sixth week, a felony of the second degree.

(2) *Justifiable Abortion.* A licensed physician is justified in terminating a pregnancy if he believes there is substantial risk that continuance of the pregnancy would gravely impair the physical or mental health of the mother or that the child would be born with grave physical or mental defect, or that the pregnancy resulted from rape, incest, or other felonious intercourse. All illicit intercourse with a girl below the age of 16 shall be deemed felonious for purposes of this subsection. Justifiable abortions shall be performed only in a licensed hospital except in case of emergency when hospital facilities are unavailable. [Additional exceptions from the requirement of hospitalization may be incorporated here to take account of situations in sparsely settled areas where hospitals are not generally accessible.] [Brackets in original.]

(3) *Physicians' Certificates; Presumption from Non-Compliance.* No abortion shall be performed unless two physicians, one of whom may be the person performing the abortion, shall have certified in writing the circumstances which they believe to justify the abortion. Such certificate shall be submitted before the abortion to the hospital where it is to be performed and, in the case of abortion following felonious intercourse, to the prosecuting attorney or the police. Failure to comply with any of the requirements of this Subsection gives rise to a presumption that the abortion was unjustified.

(4) *Self-Abortion.* A woman whose pregnancy has continued beyond the twenty-sixth week commits a felony of the third degree if she purposely terminates her own pregnancy otherwise than by a live birth, or if she uses instruments, drugs or violence upon herself for that purpose. Except as

justified under Subsection (2), a person who induces or knowingly aids a woman to use instruments, drugs or violence upon herself for the purpose of terminating her pregnancy otherwise than by a live birth commits a felony of the third degree whether or not the pregnancy has continued beyond the twenty-sixth week.

(5) *Pretended Abortion.* A person commits a felony of the third degree if, representing that it is his purpose to perform an abortion, he does an act adapted to cause abortion in a pregnant woman although the woman is in fact not pregnant, or the actor does not believe she is. A person charged with unjustified abortion under Subsection (1) or an attempt to commit that offense may be convicted thereof upon proof of conduct prohibited by this Subsection.

(6) *Distribution of Abortifacients.* A person who sells, offers to sell, possesses with intent to sell, advertises, or displays for sale anything specially designed to terminate a pregnancy, or held out by the actor as useful for that purpose, commits a misdemeanor, unless:

(a) the sale, offer or display is to a physician or druggist or to an intermediary in a chain of distribution to physicians or druggists; or

(b) the sale is made upon prescription or order of a physician; or

(c) the possession is with intent to sell as authorized in paragraphs (a) and (b); or

(d) the advertising is addressed to persons named in paragraph (a) and confined to trade or professional channels not likely to reach the general public.

(7) *Section Inapplicable to Prevention of Pregnancy.* Nothing in this Section shall be deemed applicable to the prescription, administration or distribution of drugs or other substances for avoiding pregnancy, whether by preventing implantation of a fertilized ovum or by any other method that operates before, at or immediately after fertilization.

· · ·

The shift in state laws was very slow in coming, despite the influence of the Model Penal Code *on other portions (for example, the insanity defense) in state penal codes. A few states, such as Georgia, did adopt a version of the* Model Penal Code *on abortion. Compare the first Georgia law on abortion, from 1876, with the law as revised in 1968. Note which of the recommendations the Georgia lawmakers omitted. Did either statute confer a "right to life" on the fetus?*

Georgia Sessions Laws, no. 130 (1876)

Sec. I. *Be it enacted, etc.*, That from and after the passage of this Act, the wilful killing of an unborn child, so far developed as to be ordinarily called "quick," by any injury to the mother of such child, which would be murder if it resulted in the death of such mother, shall be guilty of a felony, and punishable by death or imprisonment for life, as the jury trying the case may recommend.

Sec. II. *Be it further enacted*, That every person who shall administer to any woman pregnant with a child, any medicine, drug, or substance whatever, or shall use or employ any instrument or other means, with intent thereby to destroy such child, unless the same shall have been necessary to preserve the life of such mother, or shall have been advised by two physicians to be necessary for such purpose, shall, in case the death of such child or mother be thereby produced, be declared guilty of an assault with intent to murder.

Sec. III. *Be it further enacted*, That any person who shall wilfully administer to any pregnant woman any medicine, drug or substance, or anything whatever, or shall employ any instrument or means whatever, with intent thereby to procure the miscarriage or abortion of any such woman, unless the same shall have been necessary to preserve the life of such woman, or shall have been advised by two physicians to be necessary for that purpose, shall, upon conviction, be punished as prescribed in section 4310 of the Revised Code of Georgia.

Revised Criminal Code of Georgia, chapter 26-12, Abortion (1968)

26-1201. Criminal Abortion. Except as otherwise provided in section 26–1202, a person commits criminal abortion when he administers any medicine, drug or other substance whatever to any woman or when he uses any instrument or other means whatever upon any woman with intent to produce a miscarriage or abortion.

26-1202. Exception.

(a) Section 26-1201 shall not apply to an abortion performed by a physician duly licensed to practice medicine and surgery pursuant to Chapter 84-9 or 84-12 of the Code of Georgia of 1933, as amended, based upon his best clinical judgment that an abortion is necessary *because*:

(1) A continuation of the pregnancy would endanger the life of the pregnant woman or would seriously and permanently injure her health; or

(2) The fetus would very likely be born with a grave, permanent, and irremediable mental or physical defect; or

(3) The pregnancy resulted from forcible or statutory rape.

(b) No abortion is authorized or shall be performed under this section unless each of the following conditions is met:

(1) The pregnant woman requesting the abortion certifies in writing under oath and subject to the penalties of false swearing to the physician who proposes to perform the abortion that she is a bona fide legal resident of the State of Georgia.

(2) The physician certifies that he believes the woman is a bona fide resident of this State and that he has no information which should lead him to believe otherwise.

(3) Such physician's judgment is reduced to writing and concurred in by at least two other physicians duly licensed to practice medicine and surgery pursuant to Chapter 84-9 of the Code of Georgia of 1933, as amended, who certify in writing that based upon their separate personal medical examinations of the pregnant woman, the abortion is, in their judgment, necessary *because of one or more of the reasons enumerated above.*

(4) Such abortion is performed in a hospital licensed by the State Board of Health and accredited by the Joint Commission on Accreditation of Hospitals.

(5) The performance of the abortion has been approved in advance by a committee of the medical staff of the hospital in which the operation is to be performed. This committee must be one established and maintained in accordance with the standards promulgated by the Joint Commission on the Accreditation of Hospitals, and its approval must be by a majority vote of a membership of not less than three members of the hospital's staff; the physician proposing to perform the operation may not be counted as a member of the committee for this purpose.

(6) If the proposed abortion is considered necessary because the woman has been raped, the woman makes a written statement under oath, and subject to the penalties of false swearing, of the date, time and place of the rape and the name of the rapist, if known. There must be attached to this statement a certified copy of any report of the rape made by any law enforcement officer or agency and a statement by the solicitor general of the judicial circuit where the rape occurred or allegedly occurred that, according to his best information, there is probable cause to believe that the rape did occur.

(7) Such written opinions, statements, certificates, and concurrences are maintained in the permanent files of such hospital and are available at

all reasonable times to the solicitor general of the judicial circuit in which the hospital is located.

(8) A copy of such written opinions, statements, certificates, and concurrences is filed with the Director of the State Department of Public Health within 10 days after such operation is performed.

(9) All written opinions, statements, certificates, and concurrences filed and maintained pursuant to paragraphs (7) and (8) of this subsection shall be confidential records and shall not be made available for public inspection at any time.

(c) Any solicitor general of the judicial circuit in which an abortion is to be performed under this section, or any person who would be a relative of the child within the second degree of consanguinity, may petition the superior court of the county in which the abortion is to be performed for a declaratory judgment whether the performance of such abortion would violate any constitutional *or other legal rights of the fetus. Such solicitor general may also petition such court for the purpose of taking issue with compliance with the requirements of this section. The physician who proposes to perform the abortion and the pregnant woman shall be respondents. The petition shall be heard expeditiously and if the court adjudges that such abortion would violate the constitutional or other legal rights of the fetus, the court shall so declare and shall restrain the physician from performing the abortion.*

(d) If an abortion is performed in compliance with this section, the death of the fetus shall not give rise to any claim for wrongful death.

(e) Nothing in this section shall require a hospital to admit any patient under the provisions hereof for the purpose of performing an abortion, nor shall any hospital be required to appoint a committee such as contemplated under subsection (b) (5). A physician, or any other person who is a member of or associated with the staff of a hospital, or any employee of a hospital in which an abortion has been authorized, who shall state in writing an objection to such abortion on moral or religious grounds shall not be required to participate in the medical procedures which will result in the abortion, and the refusal of any such person to participate therein shall not form the basis of any claim for damages on account of such refusal or for any disciplinary or recriminatory action against such person. . . .

・ ・ ・

The Model Penal Code *and the Georgia statute did not define a "right" to an abortion or a "right" to life. Such a definition might have been implied in the*

U.S. Supreme Court's handling of an appeal of the Connecticut anti–birth control law, however. In 1965, the Court heard a suit by doctors and their patients seeking to practice birth control. The executive director of the Planned Parenthood League of Connecticut and its medical director had been convicted under Connecticut law for giving a married couple information and medical advice on how to prevent conception and prescribing a contraceptive device or material for the wife's use. The appellants claimed that the statute violated their federal constitutional rights.

Justice William O. Douglas wrote the opinion "of the Court," meaning that at least five of the judges subscribed to his reasoning and went along with the outcome. A number of the majority also wrote concurring opinions, stating additional reasons for joining with him in striking down the statute. Note to what extent it mattered to the Court that the couple seeking birth control assistance were married. On what constitutional grounds (where in the U.S. Constitution) did Douglas find the Connecticut law wanting? What name did he give to this fundamental right?

Griswold et al. v. Connecticut, 381 U.S. 479 (1965)

Mr. Justice Douglas delivered the opinion of the Court.

Appellant Griswold is Executive Director of the Planned Parenthood League of Connecticut. Appellant Buxton is a licensed physician and a professor at the Yale Medical School who served as Medical Director for the League at its Center in New Haven—a center open and operating from November 1 to November 10, 1961, when appellants were arrested.

They gave information, instruction, and medical advise to *married persons* as to the means of preventing conception. They examined the wife and prescribed the best contraceptive device or material for her use. Fees were usually charged, although some couples were serviced free.

The statutes whose constitutionality is involved in this appeal are §§53–32 and 5196 of the General Statutes of Connecticut (1958 rev.). The former provides: "Any person who uses any drug, medicinal article or instrument for the purpose of preventing conception shall be fined not less than fifty dollars or imprisoned not less than sixty days nor more than one year or be both fined and imprisoned." Section 54–196 provides: "Any person who assists, abets, counsels, causes, hires or commands another to commit any offense may be prosecuted and punished as if he were the principal offender."

The appellants were found guilty as accessories and fined $100 each, against the claim that the accessory statutes as so applied violated the

Fourteenth Amendment. The Appellate Division of the [state] Circuit Court affirmed. The [state] Supreme Court of Errors affirmed that judgement. . . .

Coming to the merits [the substantive legal basis of the decision as opposed to the initial procedural questions], we are met with a wide range of questions that implicate the Due Process Clause of the Fourteenth Amendment. . . . We decline that invitation . . . [to] sit as a super-legislature to determine the wisdom, need, and propriety of laws that touch economic problems, business affairs, or social conditions. This law, however, operates directly on an intimate relation of husband and wife and their physician's role in one aspect of that relation.

The association of people is not mentioned in the Constitution nor in the Bill of Rights. The right to educate a child in a school of the parent's choice—whether public or private or parochial—is also not mentioned. Nor is the right to study any particular subject or any foreign language. Yet the First Amendment has been construed to include certain of those rights.

In *NAACP v. Alabama*, 357 U.S. 449, 462, we protected the "freedom to associate and privacy in one's associations," noting that freedom of association was a peripheral First Amendment right. Disclosure of membership lists of a constitutionally valid association, we held, was invalid "as entailing the likelihood of a substantial restraint upon the exercise by petitioner's members of their right to freedom of association." *Ibid*. In other words, the First Amendment has a penumbra where privacy is protected from governmental intrusion. In like context, we have protected forms of "association" that are not political in the customary sense but pertain to the social, legal, and economic benefit of the members. . . .

The foregoing cases suggest that specific guarantees in the Bill of Rights have penumbras, formed by emanations from those guarantees that help give them life and substance. . . . Various guarantees create zones of privacy. The right of association contained in the penumbra of the First Amendment in its prohibition against the quartering of soldiers "in any house" in time of peace without the consent of the owner is another facet of that privacy. The Fourth Amendment explicitly affirms the "right of the people to be secure in their persons, houses, papers, and effects, against unreasonable searches and seizures." The Fifth Amendment in its Self-Incrimination Clause enables the citizens to create a zone of privacy which government may not force him to surrender to his detriment. The Ninth Amendment provides: "The enumeration in the Constitution, of certain rights, shall not be construed to deny or disparage others retained by the people."

The Fourth and Fifth Amendments were described in *Boyd v. United States*, 116 U.S. 616, 630, as protection against all governmental invasions "of the sanctity of a man's home and the privacies of life." We recently referred in *Mapp v. Ohio* . . . to the Fourth Amendment as creating a "right to privacy, no less important than any other right carefully and particularly reserved to the people." . . .

We have had many controversies over these penumbra rights of "privacy and repose." . . . These cases bear witness that the right of privacy which presses for recognition here is a legitimate one.

The present case, then, concerns a relationship lying within the zone of privacy created by several fundamental constitutional guarantees. And it concerns a law which, in forbidding the *use* of contraceptives rather than regulating their manufacturer or sale, seeks to achieve its goals by means having a maximum destructive impact upon that relationship. Such a law cannot stand in light of the familiar principle, so often applied by this Court, that a "governmental purpose to control or prevent activities constitutionally subject to state regulation may not be achieved by means which sweep unnecessarily broadly and thereby invade the area of protected freedoms." . . . Would we allow the police to search the sacred precincts of marital bedrooms for telltale signs of the use of contraceptives? The very idea is repulsive to the notions of privacy surrounding the marriage relationship.

We deal with a right of privacy older than the Bill of Rights—older than our political parties, older than our school system. Marriage is a coming together for better or worse, hopefully enduring, and intimate to the degree of being sacred. It is an association that promotes a way of life, not causes; a harmony in living, not political faiths; a bilateral loyalty, not commercial or social projects. Yet it is an association for as noble a purpose as any involved in our prior decisions.

Reversed.

. . .

In a concurring opinion, Justice Arthur Goldberg offered that the right of privacy might lie wholly and comfortably in the Ninth Amendment. If that were so, then a number of other rights not yet enunciated by the High Court or even sought by litigants might be found there as well.

Mr. Justice Goldberg, whom the Chief Justice and Mr. Justice Brennan join, concurring.

I agree with the Court that Connecticut's birth-control law unconstitutionally intrudes upon the right of marital privacy, and I join in its opinion and judgement. Although I have not accepted the view that "due process" as used in the Fourteenth Amendment incorporates all of the first eight Amendments . . . I do agree that the concept of liberty protects those personal rights that are fundamental, and is not confined to the specific terms of the Bill of Rights. My conclusion that the concept of liberty is not so restricted and that it embraces the right of marital privacy though that right is not mentioned explicitly in the Constitution is supported both by numerous decisions of this Court, referred to in the Court's opinion, and by the language and history of the Ninth Amendment. In reaching the conclusion that the right of marital privacy is protected, as being within the protected penumbra of specific guarantees of the Bill of Rights, the Court refers to the Ninth Amendment. . . . I add these words to emphasize the relevance of that Amendment to the Court's holding. . . .

This Court, in a series of decisions, has held that the Fourteenth Amendment absorbs and applies to the States those specifics of the first eight amendments which express fundamental personal rights. The language and history of the Ninth Amendment reveal that the Framers of the Constitution believed that there are additional fundamental rights, protected from governmental infringement, which exist alongside those fundamental rights specifically mentioned in the first eight constitutional amendments.

The Ninth Amendment reads, "The enumeration in the Constitution, of certain rights, shall not be construed to deny or disparage others retained by the people." The Amendment is almost entirely the work of James Madison. It was introduced in Congress by him and passed the House and Senate with little or no debate and virtually no change in language. It was proffered to quiet expressed fears that a bill of specifically enumerated rights could not be sufficiently broad to cover all essential rights and that the specific mention of certain rights would be interpreted as a denial that others were protected. . . .

While this Court has had little occasion to interpret the Ninth Amendment, "[i]t cannot be presumed that any clause in the constitution is intended to be without effect." In interpreting the Constitution, "real effect should be given to all the words it uses." The Ninth Amendment to the Constitution may be regarded by some as a recent discovery and may be forgotten by others, but since 1791 it has been a basic part of the Constitution which we are sworn to uphold. To hold that a right so basic and fundamental and so deep-rooted in our society as the right of privacy in marriage may be infringed because that right is not guaranteed in so many words by the first eight amendments to the Constitution is to ignore the Ninth Amendment and to give it no effect whatsoever. Moreover, a judicial construction that this fundamental right is not protected by the Constitution because it is not mentioned in explicit terms by one of the first eight amendments or elsewhere in the Constitution would violate the Ninth Amendment, which specifically states that "[t]he enumeration in the Constitution, of certain rights, shall not be construed to deny or disparage others retained by the people."

In determining which rights are fundamental, judges are not left at large to decide cases in light of their personal and private notions. Rather, they must look to the "traditions and [collective] conscience of our people" to determine whether a principle is "so rooted [there] . . . as to be ranked as fundamental." The inquiry is whether a right involved "is of such a character that it cannot be denied without violating those 'fundamental principles of liberty and justice which lie at the base of all our civil and political institutions.'" . . . "Liberty" also "gains content from the emanations of . . . specific [constitutional] guarantees" and "from experience with the requirements of a free society."

Although the Constitution does not speak in so many words of the right of privacy in marriage, I cannot believe that it offers these fundamental rights no protection. The fact that no particular provision of the Constitution situation explicitly forbids the State from disrupting the traditional relation of the family—a relation as old and as fundamental as our entire civilization—surely does not show that the Government was meant to have the power to do so. Rather, as the Ninth Amendment expressly recognizes, there are fundamental personal rights such as this one, which are protected from abridgement by the Government though specifically mentioned in the Constitution.

In a long series of cases this Court has held that where fundamental personal liberties are involved, they may not be abridged by the State simply on a showing that a regulatory statute has some rational relationship to the effectuation of a proper state purpose. . . . The law must be shown "necessary," and not merely "rationally related to the accomplishment of a permissible state policy."

Although the Connecticut birth-control law obviously encroaches upon a fundamental personal liberty, the State does not show that the law serves any "subordinating [state] interest which is compelling" or that it is "necessary . . . to the accomplishment of a permissible state policy." The State, at most, argues that there is some rational relationship between this statute and what is admittedly a legitimate subject of state concern—the discouraging of extra-marital relations. It says [that] preventing the use of birth-control devices by married persons helps prevent the indulgence by some in such extramarital relations. The rationality of this justification is dubious, particularly in light of the admitted widespread availability to all persons in the State of Connecticut, unmarried as well as married, of birth-control devices for the prevention of disease, as distinguished from the prevention of conception. . . . But, in any event, it is clear that the state interest in safeguarding marital fidelity can be served by a more discriminate tailored statute, which does not, like the present one, sweep unnecessarily broadly, reaching far beyond the evil sought to be dealt with and intruding upon the privacy of all married couples. . . . The State of Connecticut does have statutes, the constitutionality of which is beyond doubt, which prohibit adultery and fornication. . . . These statutes demonstrate that means for achieving the same basic purpose of protecting marital fidelity are available to Connecticut without the need to "invade the area of protected freedoms." . . .

Finally, it should be said of the Court's holding today that it in no way interferes with a State's proper regulation of sexual promiscuity or misconduct. . . .

· · ·

There were dissents in the case as well. Both Justice Hugo Black and Justice Potter Stewart were concerned, despite Douglas's reassurance, that the Court was setting itself up as a superlegislature and extending its purview under the Due Process Clause of the Fourteenth Amendment to cover every state law, even those, in the words of Stewart, that were "uncommonly silly." This was the old doctrine of "substantive due process" used by earlier courts to strike down progressive state legislation protecting workers. Justice John Marshall Harlan, who agreed that the statute must go, nevertheless worried, like Black and Stewart, that the logic of the majority opinion allowed the justices to roam "at large" through the Constitution seeking some basis for making new laws. For conservatives on the bench such as Harlan, resistance to such a vague yet potent addition to the panoply of constitutional protections as "privacy" was based on the fear that it had no limit. Harlan saw the right of married people to decide on the size of their families as part of an "ordered liberty" implicit in the Due Process Clause. But might it not be applied to homosexuality, pornography, or abortion? Such a prospect worried Justice Byron White, who had nevertheless agreed with the majority.

By the end of the 1960s, advocates of birth control had won nearly total victory over nineteenth-century laws and attitudes, and abortion law reformers had persuaded a few state legislatures to expand the "therapeutic exception" to the anti-abortion laws. In 1969, the American College of Obstetricians and Gynecologists, followed a year later by the American Medical Association, adopted "statements" supporting the ALI *Model Penal Code*. These, like the code, gave doctors the authority to decide when and if to perform abortions without fear of criminal prosecution. Their female patients, however, had no right to the abortion, nor did any of the "reform" enactments allow a woman to choose an abortion simply because she wanted one, whatever her circumstances.

At the same time as proponents of birth control celebrated their triumph in Connecticut and "reform" supporters savored the new Georgia law, feminists and their allies were mounting a different kind of campaign to secure the right to an abortion. They sought to make all abortions safe and legal for any woman who wished to terminate her pregnancy. They believed that the right to choose an abortion was part of a woman's fundamental autonomy and should be protected by the law, not based on the discretion of doctors or the leniency of legislatures.

CHAPTER 3

The "Right" to an Abortion

The rise of the "women's liberation" movement in the 1960s and 1970s led directly to the pro-choice approach to abortion rights. Women's advocacy groups seeking to end all criminal prosecution of abortion believed that a woman's reproductive career was a private matter, making the abortion rights crusade a natural centerpiece of the general agitation for women's equal rights in law.

The women's movement of the 1960s and 1970s starkly contrasted with the cult of domesticity and conformity that dominated family values in the 1950s. A general disillusionment with cold war ideology and increasing political turbulence during the Vietnam War era tutored a new generation of women's activists. In the cultural environment of protest, even women's magazines began to question the "myth of motherhood" and to publish articles extolling the "career woman." The introduction and wide use of oral contraceptives (colloquially called "the pill") and the loosening of some taboos surrounding premarital intercourse (popularly known as "the sexual revolution") paralleled the rise of women's liberation movements.

But it was women's own experiences, in particular the experience of having or not having an abortion, that directly influenced their views on abortion rights. In the early 1960s, abortion was not only illegal but also something that one simply did not discuss. "Getting caught" was the young woman's slang for becoming pregnant. The term had a moralistic tinge, as though women were paying for their sinfulness. Unmarried motherhood was not an option for "nice" girls. Neither was abortion, a word that one contemporary writer demanded be stricken from dictionaries.

Interviewed in the 1990s, women who matured in these years recalled that they did not talk about abortion. As one woman who had an abortion reported, when she told her mother, "she was completely silent for about five minutes. Then she went to bed for a few weeks. She never mentioned it again." Women recalled that they felt "soiled and filthy" after an illicit abortion.[1] One respondent confessed that she had become pregnant after a brief affair but could not get a therapeutic abortion. Alone and fearing that she could not take care of another child, she waited until her two small children had gone to bed, then she said she "used a knitting needle, and I probed and poked and tried to guide it into the right spot, but nothing seemed to happen that night, so I thought I'd failed. When I woke up the next morning there was blood all over the bed. So then I went to the hospital and this Jewish doctor took care of me, gave me a D & C [dilation and curettage—a technique for abortion]." Even the near-death event was shameful. "You know," she told the interviewer, "I've told almost no one about this because I felt it was such an idiotic thing to have done."[2]

In 1965, Patricia Tyson, young, black, unmarried, and pregnant, had a backroom abortion and nearly died as a result. She recalled many years later, "The worst thing about the experience for me was that the woman who'd done the abortion had said to me, after she'd put the tube in, 'If there are any problems, don't call me.' You felt like a piece of meat on the rack, you know? Nobody really cared about you. And that whole process was bad. You bled all over the place. . . . That was the worst part, that, and not being able to say it to anybody, acting like it didn't happen, not being able to talk about it, even among those individuals who knew."[3]

But a new ideology of women's liberation was already forming in the minds of feminists. At its core was the paramountcy of choice and individual autonomy. If choice was the model for law, then women should be free to choose to have or not have children. This new worldview of women and the law had abortion at its center and worked out from that center a rationale for the legitimacy of women's reproductive autonomy. Just as narrations of abortion experiences had the power to bond women to one another in consciousness-raising and liberation groups, so the logic of freedom of abortion provided a foundation for rethinking women's relations to men, to power, and to their own experience. Pro-choice abortion rights was thus an issue that the leaders of the women's movement hoped would empower women in a way that few other women's issues could. The search for equality with men raised important questions for women's liberation, but the struggle for freedom of access to a legal and safe abortion differed from such goals as equal pay for equal jobs. Abortion was an experience that only women could have, and as the leaders of the women's movement explained, abortion rights must thus be explained in the language of the legitimacy of differences rather than mere facial equality.

The pro-choice movement gained a number of victories in its first years. In the winter of 1970, three hundred women led by a group of feminist lawyers brought suit in the federal district court for the Southern District of New York against that state's anti-abortion laws. The state's law was one of

THE "RIGHT" TO AN ABORTION

the strictest in the nation, permitting therapeutic abortions only when the mother's life was in imminent danger, but a group of Roman Catholic physicians, Friends of the Fetus, with the church's hierarchy in support, had asked to intervene on the side of the state's law.[4] Then, unexpectedly, in 1970, the New York legislature passed and Governor Nelson Rockefeller signed a statute allowing abortion at will in the first trimester and obviating the need for the lawsuit. In Connecticut, women inspired by the New York movement filed their own suit, reaching out to a wide variety of women's groups for support. "We'd always start out with a personal story," Ann Hill, one of the group, recalled, echoing Margaret Sanger's unfulfilled desire when she found herself in court. In Connecticut, as in New York, abortion rights advocacy spurred women to pull together the disparate pieces of their lives under the law.[5]

Other challenges to criminal prosecutions of doctors for abortion were already moving forward in federal courts in Louisiana and Ohio. It was thus almost a matter of chance (along with hard work) that allowed two young Texas lawyers to bring the issues to the U.S. Supreme Court first. Sarah Weddington and Linda Coffee were looking for plaintiffs willing to challenge the Texas abortion laws. They found four and with them as plaintiffs brought a suit in the federal district court. The suit, *Roe v. Wade*, would become the centerpiece of the abortion/abortion rights controversy from the moment it was first decided by federal judges in Texas.

· · ·

In 1966, journalist Betty Friedan helped found an organization that women led and that had as its agenda women's issues, part of "a sex role revolution for men and women which will restructure all institutions: childrearing, education, marriage, the family, the architecture of the home, the practice of medicine, work, politics, the economy, religion, psychological theory, human sexuality, morality, and the very evolution of the [human] race."[6] The National Organization for Women (NOW) would become a leading sponsor of pro-choice initiatives. Its "Statement of Purpose" had in it a paragraph about childbearing and childrearing, but its tone reflected, in important ways, traditional views of women's roles.

NOW, "Statement of Purpose" (1966)

We believe that this nation has a capacity at least as great as other nations to innovate new social institutions which will enable women to enjoy true equality of opportunity and responsibility in society, without conflict with their responsibilities as mothers and homemakers. In such innovations, America . . . lags by decades behind many European countries. We do not accept the traditional assumption that a woman has to choose between marriage and motherhood, on the one hand, and serious participation in industry or the professions on the other. We question the present expectation that all normal women will retire from job or profession for ten or fifteen years, to devote their full time to raising children, only to reenter the job market at a relatively minor level. . . . Above all, we reject the assumption that these problems are the unique responsibility of each individual woman, rather than a basic social dilemma which society must solve. True equality of opportunity and freedom of choice for women requires such practical and possible innovations as a nationwide network of child-care centers, which will make it unnecessary for women to retire completely from society until their children are grown. . . .

. . .

Friedan's best-selling attack on male domination of women, the Feminine Mystique *(1962), had little to say about abortion explicitly, but in the following excerpt, the reader can grasp her views on it.*

Betty Friedan, *The Feminine Mystique* ### (1962; rev. ed., New York, 1984), 385–86

[In the 1960s,] women also had to confront their sexual nature, to deny or ignore it as earlier feminists has done. Society had to be restructured so that women, who happen to be the people who give birth, could make a human responsible choice whether or not—and when—to have children, and not be barred thereby from participating in society in their own right. This meant the right to birth control and safe abortion; the right to maternity leave and child-care centers if women did not want to retreat completely from adult society during the childbearing years; and the equivalent of a GI Bill for retraining if women chose to stay home with the children. For it seemed to me that most women would still choose to have children, though not so many if child rearing was no longer their only road to status and economic support—a vicarious participation in life.

. . .

Friedan's arguments made the most sense in the context of white, middle-class, educated women, although they were hardly limited to this audience. Congresswoman Shirley Chisholm of New York spoke to women of color about abortion in 1970 and explained why she felt she had to speak out on the subject.

Shirley Chisholm, *Unbought and Unbossed*
(Boston, 1970), 113–14

In August of 1969 I began to get calls from NARAL, the National Association for the Repeal of Abortion Laws, a new organization . . . looking for a national president. In the New York State Assembly, I had supported abortion reform bills . . . and this had apparently led NARAL to believe I would sympathize with its goal: complete repeal of all laws restricting abortion. As a matter of fact, when I was in the assembly, I had not been in favor of repealing all abortion laws . . . a step that would leave having or not having the operation entirely up to a woman and her doctor. The bills I had tried to help pass in Albany would only have made it somewhat easier for women to get therapeutic abortions in New York State. . . . But since that time I had been compelled to do some heavy thinking on the subject, mainly because of the experiences of several young women I knew. All had suffered permanent injuries at the hands of illegal abortionists. . . . It had begun to seem to me that the question was not whether the law should allow abortions. Experience shows that pregnant women who feel they have compelling reasons . . . will break the law, and even worse, risk injury and death, if they must get one. . . .

For me to take the lead in abortion repeal would be an even more serious step than for a white politician to do so, because there is a deep and angry suspicion among many blacks that even birth control clinics are a plot by the white power structure to keep down the numbers of blacks, and this opinion is even more strongly held by some in regard to legalizing abortions. But I do not know any black or Puerto Rican women who feel that way. . . .

The poor are more anxious about family planning than any other group. . . . The poor do not go to doctors or clinics except when they absolutely must; their medical ignorance is very great. . . . Botched abortions are the largest single cause of death of pregnant women in the United States, particularly among non-white women. . . . Such statistics convinced me that my instinctive feeling was right: a black woman legislator, far from avoiding the abortion question, was compelled to face it and deal with it.

• • •

Despite the rise of the women's movement and its focus on the right to an abortion, most states retained restrictive abortion laws. Texas's law on abor-

tion was in 1970 essentially the same as it had been in 1859, and Texas continued to prosecute abortionists under it.

Texas Penal Code, Title 15, chapter 9 (1970)

Article 1191. Abortion

If any person shall designedly administer to a pregnant woman or knowingly procure to be administered with her consent any drug or medicine, or shall use towards her any violence or means whatever externally or internally applied, and thereby procure an abortion, he shall be confined in the penitentiary not less than two nor more than five years; if it be done without her consent, the punishment shall be doubled. By "abortion" is meant that the life of the fetus or embryo shall be destroyed in the woman's womb or that a premature birth thereof be caused.

Art. 1192. Furnishing the means

Whoever furnishes the means for procuring an abortion knowing the purpose intended is guilty as an accomplice.

Art. 1193. Attempt at abortion

If the means used shall fail to produce an abortion, the offender is nevertheless guilty of an attempt to produce abortion, provided it be shown that such means were calculated to produce that result, and shall be fined not less than one hundred nor more than one thousand dollars.

Art. 1194. Murder in producing abortion

If the death of the mother is occasioned by an abortion so produced or by an attempt to effect the same it is murder.

Art. 1195. Destroying unborn child

Whoever shall during parturition of the mother destroy the vitality or life in a child in a state of being born and before actual birth, which child would otherwise have been born alive, shall be confined in the penitentiary for life or for not less than five years.

Art. 1196. By medical advice

Nothing in this chapter applies to an abortion procured or attempted by medical advice for the purpose of saving the life of the mother.

· · ·

Texas relied on this statute in prosecutions of defendants for performing or attempting to perform abortions. The worse cases, as in the nineteenth century, were those in which the pregnant woman died from the alleged ministrations of the abortionist. Still, there was always a conflict over the facts and, in the following case, over a disputed confession.

Sylvia Redman v. State, 162 Tex. Crim. 524 (1955)

BELCHER, J.

The offense is murder by attempted abortion; the punishment, confinement in the penitentiary for four years.

The state's testimony shows that the police identified a body as being that of Betty Ledel at a hospital and then went directly to appellant's clinic where appellant [Redman] told them that Betty Ledel was removed from her clinic a short time before their arrival.

Homicide Detective Howerton testified that during his investigation and prior to the arrest of appellant that "We asked her (appellant) *** [asterisks in original] what the purpose of Mrs. Ledel's visit was at the place and she said she had come to her some weeks prior to that—she thought she was pregnant and wanted something done about it; didn't want to have a child, and I asked her what occurred, and she said that she had inserted an instrument in her womb and injected air into her womb and I asked her where it occurred. *** She showed me the table that the woman was lying on, and that after she had injected the air into her womb with the instrument she became choky, couldn't get her breath. *** and she called an ambulance. I asked her what she did with the instruments she used in this case *** and (she) carried us to a garbage can where she had placed the instruments; she picked the lid up from the garbage can and I removed the instruments from the garbage can that she said she had used on this occasion." These instruments were identified and shown to be a pair of snips, a cannula, a syringe, and a speculum.

Witness Howerton further testified on cross-examination that appellant told him that the deceased thought she was pregnant, visited her on two or three occasions about ten days apart, and that if the deceased was pregnant, that she, appellant, didn't know it.

Dr. Fitzwilliam testified that he performed an autopsy on the body of the deceased which disclosed that the uterus was enlarged, filled with tissue of pregnancy, contained a small, live and normal embryo, which showed a six or seven week pregnancy; that he found evidence of air in the veins around the uterus, the heart, and in the veins and arteries leading to the brain; that the injection of air into the uterus of a pregnant woman would be highly dangerous and would likely cause a premature birth, and that the embryo here would probably have been expelled if the death of the deceased had not occurred, and that in his opinion air embolism caused deceased's death. On cross-examination, Dr. Fitzwilliam testified that the embryo appeared normal, but could have been dead for a few hours; and that there are no positive outward signs of pregnancy at six or seven weeks known to medical science.

The written confession of the appellant was introduced in evidence and contained the following: "*** About the 8th of October, 1954, a girl named Betty Ledel came to see me. She told me she thought she was pregnant. About a week over her time. And asked me if I could help her get rid of the baby. I told her the danger of everything and she said she was not afraid, I told her I would rather her to go somewhere else and have the baby stopped in twenty four hours, because my work is slow. I do it by shooting a little air up into the womb. (uterus) By going through the cervix into the uterus, where the embryo is carried. She told me she wanted me to do it. *** The first day she came to me, I shot a little air up into her uterus or womb. I used a syringe for air that's laying there on your desk, Mr. Cochran. I used a female speculum that's laying there too, Mr. Cochran, to open her vagina. I didn't know for sure she was pregnant. I have felt enough of them up inside the vagina to tell. After I shot the air up into her, I told her to come back every other day. She came back. Each time she came to see me, I pumped a little more air into her womb or uterus. Asking her if she could feel it. Sometimes she'd say, 'I do,' and sometimes she would say 'I don't feel it.' Yesterday morning, which was October 19, 1954, she came back to see me; she came in and I took her upstairs. I laid her on a table used for females. *** Then I inserted the speculum in her vagina to open it up, and then I put the cannula to the mouth of uterus—it is the cannula that I am holding here, Mr. Cochran, to the mouth of the uterus then I gave her about five syringes full of air through the cannula into the uterus. I asked her if she could feel it and she said not very much. And she looked up at me and said I feel choky, and then she passed out. I used artificial respiration. I picked her up in my arms and laid her on the floor. And I slung water at her to try to revive her, and then I had a lady downstairs to call an ambulance. The ambulance came and got her and took her to Harris Hospital. After this happened I called a friend and asked her what to do and she said throw all that stuff away. So I went upstairs to get the instruments that I had used, and I had just come downstairs when Mr. Howerton and Mr. Armstrong and another detective walked in. I told them I'd be with them in a minute and I kinda hid the instruments that I had used on Betty Ledel behind me, and I stepped into the back and put the instruments in a garbage can. Then I came back out to talk to Mr. Howerton and I admitted to him what I had done and he asked me what I had used on Betty Ledel, and I took him out (to) the garbage can and showed him exactly where I had hidden them and what I had used. He asked me if I had performed an abortion on her and I told him no, but I wasn't telling him the truth. And I gave these instruments to Mr. Howerton and Mr. Armstrong and the other detective. After she had told me that she felt choky, and after I laid her on the floor, I noticed she was bleeding from the vagina."

Appellant testifying in her own behalf stated that the deceased came to her about fourteen days before her death, and was run down physically, worried, and thought she was pregnant; that she examined her, found no indication of pregnancy, determined that she had a misplaced uterus for which she gave her about eight treatments by injecting air into the uterus which she said was the common method used by naturopaths for treating a misplaced uterus; that she told the deceased that air injections were dangerous to pregnant women and that if she was pregnant to go to another place, and that the deceased replied that she was not afraid. She testified that she hid the instruments at the suggestion of a friend. Appellant admitted, on cross-examination, that she voluntarily made and signed the statement introduced by the state, but testified that several of the matters contained therein were incorrect, that is, that the deceased did not "ask me if I could help her get rid of the baby" as therein set out, and the statement therein that she was not telling Howerton the truth when she told him that she had not performed an abortion on the deceased was incorrect because her statement about not telling him the truth referred to the money paid her by the deceased for treatments.

Drs. Bletner and Walker, naturopaths, testified that the injection of air was an accepted practice among naturopaths for treating a misplaced uterus, and that such treatment would not likely cause an abortion.

It was shown that the appellant had a license to practice naturopathy.

Appellant's motion for an instructed verdict on the ground that the state had failed to disprove the exculpatory portion of her confession which it had introduced in evidence, to wit: "I didn't know for sure that she was pregnant *** and she didn't feel pregnant" cannot be sustained because the appellant's testimony on the trial is in accord with said statements and the theory advanced in such statements and in her testimony was fairly submitted to the jury in the charge of the court. . . .

We conclude that the evidence offered by the state was sufficient to warrant the jury in resolving these issues of fact against the appellant.

· · ·

Texas was not alone in its legal or its moral posture; despite the few successes of the reform movement, notably in California, North Carolina, Hawaii, and Georgia, most state legislatures and courts still regarded abortion as a crime, abortionists as wicked, and women who sought abortions as weak or im-

moral. In 1968, a young lawyer named Roy Lucas offered an alternative to the "reform" of abortion law. It would become a vital source of ideas for the frontal attack on criminal abortion statutes, and he would become a leading pro-choice advocate.

Roy Lucas, "Federal Constitutional Limitations on the Enforcement and Administration of State Abortion Statutes," *North Carolina Law Review* 46 (1968): 730–78 (footnotes omitted)

Until recently, mishandled criminal abortions claimed the lives of an estimated ten thousand American women each year. The vast majority of these individuals were married—wives and mothers. Legal hospital abortions, on the other hand, presently account for the termination of only eight to nine thousand pregnancies yearly. This figure contrasts sharply with the probable one-quarter to two million annual illegal abortions performed within the United States. Such persistent flouting by citizens of laws written and enacted in the last century is the subject of increasing public controversy and discussion. It brings into focus sensitive issues of family planning and marital autonomy, church-state relations, subjective sexual taboos, and the mysteries of human procreation, life and death.

To date efforts at promoting or stifling abortion reform have focused on legislative action both in the United States and abroad. This article, however, examines the possibility of federal constitutional bases for invalidating state abortion restrictions.

The Mood for Reform

Increased public interest in the liberalization of abortion laws is evident in the currents of modern thought. In the sphere of family planning, many citizens today do not believe that a particular moral norm ought to be forced on all of a society unless the sacrifice in individual liberty of choice is offset by a significant societal benefit. This view, as applied to the abortion reform setting, necessarily further assumes that the value to be accorded to developing fetal tissue is a subjective moral choice that ought not to be dictated by the state. It is a premise widely shared, especially by those individuals whom rigid abortion laws most directly affect.

Outside of the continental United States, governmental authorities are less dictatorial in their demands on the pregnant woman. It was common knowledge that until recently abortion was available upon request in a clinical setting as near as San Juan, Puerto Rico, and in any number of towns and cities in Mexico. Japan is also becoming a center for aborting American women. In Japan abortion is legally available for a 15 dollar fee. Surgeons must obtain a special governmental license to perform the operation, and safe, hygienic conditions are virtually assured. This contrasts markedly with the extra-hospital setting of illegal abortion within the United States.

Several state legislatures have passed abortion reform bills, and the American Law Institute has proposed reform legislation as a part of the Model Penal Code. The American Medical Association supports the Code. In addition, the New York Civil Liberties Union has taken the position that: "A person is guilty of abortion [only] if he is not a duly licensed physician and intentionally terminates the pregnancy of another otherwise than by a live birth." Reform measures seek to transfer the power of family planning from the state back to the family and its physician. Further educational and reform activities have been undertaken by the California Committee for Therapeutic Abortion in San Francisco and the Association for the Study of Abortion in New York City, as well as numerous like organizations.

The chief thrust of reform urging has been to permit citizens—pregnant women, their husbands, their physicians—to decide for themselves when pregnancy ought to be terminated and to erect no state barrier to the carrying out of conclusions which these individuals privately reach. This approach does not force a single belief concerning the propriety of abortion on others who are unwilling to accept that belief. Those who equate abortion with sin or even murder are permitted to entertain their beliefs privately and act on them in their private spheres of influence. In contrast to this attitude of reform is that of the sole major organized body opposing all abortion reform . . . the Roman Catholic Church. Their position is ultimately detrimental to the health and well being of any woman who would choose to terminate her pregnancy. Moreover, rigid restrictions on permissible indications for abortion force physicians to refuse to treat pregnant patients according to their best medical judgement. The woman may then risk her life by resorting to an incompetent "butcher."

Modes of Reform

Abortion reform can take several routes. Statutory exceptions to the general prohibition are more typical of recent proposals. Other groups advocate the converse approach of general legal permission to terminate pregnancy, provided the woman consents and a licensed physician performs the operation. Supplementary to abortion reform are preventive measures designed better to inform large numbers of the citizenry concerning the availability of various contraceptives means. More extensive public sex education may be needed, as are greater facilities for seclusion for the unwed mother and further encouragement for adoption of unwanted children.

This article is chiefly concerned, however, with abortion reform by judicial interpretation, and the application of established constitutional concepts to the physician-patient relationship. Although interests at stake in the abortion controversy are diverse, subtle, novel, and sensitive the case appears ultimately to fit within the classical framework of governmental interference with important interests of individual liberty and to be capable of resolution in traditional constitutional terms.

The Physician's Interests

Present abortion statutes offer little guidance to physicians faced with sensitive problems brought to them by their patients. Most states offer no statutory guidelines to elucidate what constitutes a threat to the pregnant woman's life, and the distinction between a danger to health and probable danger to life is a nebulous one. In any given penumbra case the results reached by a large number of physicians may be no more than personal inclination—a poor basis for a decision of such immense importance to the woman. And, from the viewpoint of the physician, he must realize, that, in every case, "[t]he issue is whether a doctor should be sent to prison for performing an operation that he believes to be best for his patient. . . ."

As a matter of professional comity courts tend to stress the inherent competence of the medical profession for setting its own standards in a given community. . . . However, general medical opinion does not seem to exist, and if it did, the woman's rights might vary considerably from community to community depending on local taboos and the physician's willingness to undergo a judicial test of the relationship between his attitudes and those of his brethren. The bare fact of prosecution alone, coupled with pulpit denunciations, could wholly destroy a physician's practice and career regardless of the outcome of his case before a high tribunal. In effect, then, only crystal-clear statutory language is forthcoming or until a court establishes a woman's absolute legal right to abortion, the reputable physician can only turn his patient away, possibly knowing with certainty that she will seek a criminal abortionist who operates in secrecy under conditions endangering the woman's health and perhaps even her life. . . .

The Constitutional Issues

Existing abortion laws raise significant constitutional issues. The statutes sharply curtail a woman's freedom of choice in (1) planning her family size, (2) risking her physical or mental well being in carrying a pregnancy to term, (3) avoiding the birth of deformed child, and (4) bearing a child who is the product of rape or incest. Moreover, present abortion laws are (1) largely unenforced, (2) uncertain in their scope, (3) at odds with accepted medical standards, (4) discriminatory in effect, and (5) based upon the imposition by criminal sanction of subjective religious values of questionable social merit upon persons who do not subscribe to those values.

The constitutional issues implicit in the enactment and application of abortion laws have received scant judicial attention. Research discloses no significant test-case or other litigation attacking the constitutional power of a state to prohibit therapeutic abortion in circumstances not endangering the pregnant woman's life. Moreover, the literature of legal commentary appears to contain no in-depth examination of the constitutional issues which might be raised. Numerous reasons can be advanced for the absence of discussion and litigation on this point. Abortion, unlike contraception, remains a subject of intense taboo intertwined in the maze of political silence, religion, life, death, and sex. In the constitutional context it is a problem bearing few factual similarities to any decisions in the 150-year expanse of pre-*Griswold* history. And in theological circles, abortion is hardly a subject for light philosophical speculation—on the contrary, it typically evokes at the outset emotional charges of "murder" and "immorality" which generally are not conducive to a full investigation of underlying issues. . . .

Individual Immunities: Privacy and Choice

Of prime significance in any judicial challenge of abortion legislation is a convincing showing that the pregnant woman asserts an interest so fundamental and compelling that it outweighs the interest of the state in enforcing its value judgment that her pregnancy should continue to term. Time and circumstances, moreover, combine to inject unneeded emotionalism, sensitivity and taboo into the issues. . . .

A right to abortion by consent performed by a licensed physician can be strongly asserted in at least three related forms within the Bill of Rights and fourteenth amendment framework—first, as a fundamental right of marital privacy, human dignity, and personal autonomy reserved to the pregnant woman acting on the advice of a licensed physicians, second, as a penumbra right emanating from values embodied in the express provisions of the Bill of Rights themselves, or, third, as a necessary and altogether reasonable application of precedent, namely, *Griswold v. Connecticut*. . . .

The applicability of these principles to state abortion legislation will be at the heart of any effort by the medical profession to achieve abortion reform by challenging a state's authority to prohibit the termination of pregnancy when a woman so desires and her physician finds it necessary in his sound medical judgement.

From the viewpoint of many women, restrictive abortion legislation of any kind imposes a severe burden on female existence without corresponding benefit. . . .

The right to terminate her pregnancy shortly after conception may seem to a woman to be much more fundamental and of greater day-to-day importance in her life than the right to send her children to a private school, to associate with others for the advocacy of ideas, or to be free from racial discrimination in seeking an education. To secure an abortion may seem to her an infrequent, but necessary step when the exercises of her fundamental right to contraception has not been successful. It is an anomaly that a woman has absolute control over her personal reproductive capacities so long as she can successfully utilize contraceptives but that she forfeits this right when contraception fails. Clearly no government is permitted to compel the coming together of the egg and spermatozoon. Why then should the state sanctify the two cells after they have come together and accord them, over the woman's objection, all the rights of a human being in *esse*? If the logic behind present abortion laws were rigorously followed, abortion would be treated as murder punishable by death or life imprisonment, and perhaps a clearer focus would emerge. If an aborted woman and her physician were tried for "homicidal abortion," convicted, and sentenced to death, few would consider the result justifiable. It is a result, however, that follows from defining the fetus as a human being. No one holds full funeral services for the products of miscarriage. Certainly no one would suggest that a woman who miscarries regularly four weeks after each conception could be required by law to seek medical treatment to prevent future miscarriages, or otherwise be sentenced to death. The definition of a fetus as a "human being," is at odds with the view that conception is only one point in the transmission of life, not the beginning of it. It disregards the physical and developmental similarities between the embryo and the constituents which come together at conception. In the end the pregnant woman and her physician are required to abide by a religious belief which severely restricts their fundamental interests. Once it is recognized that present abortion laws represent an enforcement of dogma in which the state has no legitimate interest, the woman's right to choose for herself comes into clearer focus. . . .

THE "RIGHT" TO AN ABORTION

The Fetus' Claim to Due Process and Equal Protection

The fourteenth amendment to the United States Constitution requires that states accord "due process of law" and "equal protection of the laws" to *any person* within their respective jurisdictions and that "all *persons born or naturalized* in the United States, and subject to the jurisdiction thereof, are citizens of the United States and of the State wherein they reside (emphasis added)." Whether the living male and female reproductive cells (spermatozoon and ovum) constitute a "person" within the meaning of the fourteenth amendment before fertilization would seem to be fully settled in the negative. After conception, however, the initiation of growth toward eventual human status has prompted some observers to argue that a liberalized abortion law would deprive the fetus of that due process to which they silently assume it to be entitled. This claim is not developed with any seriousness in the literature and was not even mentioned in the extensive comments to the Model Penal Code's proposed abortion reform act. It can be dismissed by pointing out that the early fetus, similar in shape and functioning to the constituents which came together to form it, bears scarcely developed characteristics at the time abortion normally takes place. If life-transmission is recognized as a continuous process in which conception plays only the part of increasing and re-directing growth, contraception and abortion differ only in degree. Both are employed to prevent a birth several months in the future. Both "kill" living tissue, but only in the same sense that oral contraceptives cause the unfertilized egg to die at the end of each cycle. True, "an abortion kills something. The 'developing human organism,' which was alive and growing before the interruption of the pregnancy, is dead after it." The growth, however, is unlike the growth of a living child. . . .

State Police Power over Health, Welfare, and Morals

. . . Several grounds can be advanced as reasonable bases on which to rest state legislation which prohibits abortion except to protect the life of the pregnant woman. First, the state can urge that abortion statutes exist in part to protect pregnant women from the dangers of criminal abortionists and "quack" abortifacient home remedies. Second, a state may urge that an abortion prohibition acts as a reasonable deterrent to illicit intercourse—premarital or extramarital—by raising the stakes for such intercourse. The third and most significant claim is that state abortion acts protect a contingent interest in being born—an interest of the fetus, after conception and implantation in the womb. The third claim appears to be the chief distinction between the assertion of a fundamental right to use of contraceptives and the right to abortion when contraception fails. The first and second grounds for abortion statutes lack sufficient constitutional merit to warrant further examination.

The Vagueness Argument

State acts which prohibit abortion "without lawful justification" and "except to save the life of the mother" arguably can be challenged on grounds that they are so vague as to deprive a physician of that due process of law guaranteed him by the fourteenth amendment. . . . Disagreement is particularly sharp where an abortion is needed to protect the woman from severe damage to her physical or mental health, to avoid the products of incest or rape, or to prevent deformed births where contraception has failed. In these close cases a physician is frankly at the mercy of his colleagues and local prosecuting authorities. . . .

. . .

On March 6, 1970, Weddington and Coffee filed suit in federal court against the Texas anti-abortion law. By the time the case went to trial, plaintiffs in Weddington and Coffee's suit against the Texas law included Marsha and David King, a married couple who were afraid of another pregnancy for medical reasons. They became John and Mary Doe; it was typical for plaintiffs in these suits to use such legal pseudonyms as John Doe and Jane Roe. So long as the court was convinced that a real person was the plaintiff, they allowed the use of pseudonyms to protect the privacy of the plaintiff. Norma McCorvey, an unmarried waitress who was pregnant and wanted a safe and legal abortion, became Jane Roe. On March 19, 1970, lawyers Fred Bruner and Roy Merrill Jr. of Dallas asked permission to intervene (join) in the suit on behalf of their client, Dr. James Hallford. He had been indicted for performing an abortion on a woman who had contracted rubella. Although rubella causes birth defects, the abortion was not necessary to save the woman's life.

Coffee and Weddington asked the federal court sitting in the Northern District of Texas for a "declaratory judgment" (statement of law) that the Texas law was an unconstitutional violation of the plaintiffs' right to privacy under the First, Fourth, Fifth, Ninth, and Fourteenth Amendments. They also sought injunctive relief—an order from the court barring Texas from enforcing the statute against their clients. Injunctions were commands from courts to parties to do or not do something. Coffee and Weddington made their suit a "class action" so that, if they won, it would apply to everyone "similarly situated." The Federal Rules of Civil Procedure permitted class actions, and similar suits were common in civil rights cases.

Henry Wade, attorney for the city of Dallas, was the respondent (defendant, that is, the party being sued) in Roe *and its companion cases, and his office participated in defending the Texas law. The Texas Attorney General's Office also prepared a defense of the state law, based first on the concept that the fetus was a person from the moment of conception and the state had a duty to protect all human life. The second argument in defense of the law was that Roe had no suit because the law did not penalize the pregnant woman directly, nor was Mary Doe pregnant. In legal terms, there was no actual case or controversy for the court to decide. To counter the doctor's argument that the law was too vague, the defense asserted that the state law was quite precise. He knew he was violating it.*

Federal judges Irving L. Goldberg, Sarah T. Hughes, and W. M. Taylor Jr. hearing the case had three issues before them. The first was procedural: did the various plaintiffs have "standing" to bring to suit (were they in danger of harm from the statute), and did the federal court have jurisdiction over the matter at issue? The second issue was how to resolve the case, assuming affirmative answers to both parts of the first issue. The third issue was what remedy plaintiffs were entitled to if they should win on the merits of their legal arguments. They wanted both a declaration that the abortion right was protected by the federal Constitution and an injunction that Texas no longer enforce its criminal law on abortion.

Jane Roe v. Henry Wade, Defendant, v. James Hubert Hallford, M.D., Intervenor. John Doe and Mary Doe v. Henry Wade, 314 F. Supp. 1217 (U.S. District Court for the Northern District of Texas, 1970)

Goldberg, J.

Two similar cases are presently before the Court on motions for summary judgment pursuant to Rule 56 of the Federal Rules of Civil Procedure. The defendant in both cases is Henry Wade, District Attorney of Dallas County, Texas. In one action plaintiffs are John and Mary Doe, and in the other Jane Roe and James Hubert Hallford, M.D., intervenor. From their respective positions of married couple, single woman, and practicing physician, plaintiffs attack Articles 1191, 1192, 1193, 1194, and 1196 of the Texas Penal Code, hereinafter referred to as the Texas Abortion Laws. Plaintiffs allege that the Texas Abortion Laws deprive married couples and single women of the right to choose whether to have children, a right secured by the Ninth Amendment.

Defendant challenges the standing of each of the plaintiffs to bring this action. However, it appears to the Court that Plaintiff Roe and Plaintiff-intervenor Hallford occupy positions *vis-a-vis* the Texas Abortion Laws sufficient to differentiate them from the general public. . . . Plaintiff Roe filed her portion of the suit as a pregnant woman wishing to exercise the asserted constitutional right to choose whether to bear the child she was carrying. Intervenor Hallford alleged in his portion of the suit that, in the course of daily exercise of his duty as a physician and in order to give his patients access to what he asserts to be their constitutional right to choose whether to have children, he must act so as to render criminal liability for himself under the Texas Abortion Laws a likelihood. Dr. Hallford further alleges that Article 1196 of the Texas Abortion Laws is so vague as to deprive him of warning of what produces criminal liability in that portion of his medical practice and consultations involving abortions. . . .

Each plaintiff seeks as relief, *first*, a judgment declaring the Texas Abortion Laws unconstitutional on their face and, *second*, an injunction against their enforcement. The nature of the relief requested suggests the order in which the issues presented should be passed upon. . . .

Defendants have suggested that this Court should abstain from rendering a decision on plaintiffs' request for a declaratory judgment. . . . "It is the duty of a federal court to decide the federal question when presented to it. Any other course would impose expense and long delay upon the litigants without hope of its bearing fruit." . . .

On the merits, plaintiffs argue as their principal contention that the Texas Abortion Laws must be declared unconstitutional because they deprive single women and married couples of their right, secured by the Ninth Amendment, to choose whether to have children. We agree.

The essence of the interest sought to be protected here is the right of choice over events which, by their character and consequences, bear in a fundamental manner on the privacy of individuals. The manner by which such interests are secured by the Ninth Amendment is illustrated by the concurring opinion of Mr. Justice Goldberg in *Griswold v. Connecticut*. . . .

Relative sanctuaries for such "fundamental" interests have been established for the family, the marital couple, and the individual.

Freedom to choose in the matter of abortions has been accorded the status of a "fundamental" right in every case coming to the attention of this Court where the question has been raised.

"The fundamental right of the woman to choose whether to bear children follows from the Supreme Court's and this court's repeated acknowledgment of a 'right of privacy' or 'liberty' in matters related to marriage, family, and sex." . . .

Since the Texas Abortion Laws infringe upon plaintiffs' fundamental right to choose whether to have children, the burden is on the defendant to demonstrate to the satisfaction of the Court that such infringement is necessary to support a compelling state interest. The defendant has failed to meet this burden.

To be sure, the defendant has presented the Court with several compelling justifications for state presence in the area of abortions. These include the legitimate interests of the state in seeing to it that abortions are performed by competent persons and in adequate surroundings. Concern over abortion of the "quickened" fetus may well rank as another such interest. The difficulty with the Texas Abortion Laws is that, even if they promote these interests, they far outstrip these justifications in their impact by prohibiting *all* abortions except those performed "for the purpose of saving the life of the mother."

It is axiomatic that the fact that a statutory scheme serves permissible or even compelling state interests will not save it from the consequences of unconstitutional overbreadth. . . . While the Ninth Amendment right to choose to have an abortion is not unqualified or unfettered, a statute designed to regulate the circumstances of abortions must restrict its scope to compelling state interests. There is unconstitutional overbreadth in the Texas Abortion Laws because the Texas Legislature did not limit the scope of the statutes to such interests. On the contrary, the Texas statutes, in their monolithic interdiction, sweep far beyond any areas of compelling state interest.

Not only are the Texas Abortion Laws unconstitutionally overbroad, they are also unconstitutionally vague. The Supreme Court has declared that "a statute which either forbids or requires the doing of an act in terms so vague that men of common intelligence must necessarily guess at its meaning and differ as to its application violates the first essential of due process of law." Under this standard the Texas statutes fail the vagueness test.

The Texas Abortion Laws fail to provide Dr. Hallford and physicians of his class with proper notice of what acts in their daily practice and consultation will subject them to criminal liability. . . .

It is apparent that there are grave and manifold uncertainties in the application of Article 1196. How *likely* must death be? Must death be certain if the abortion is not performed? Is it enough that the woman could not undergo birth without an ascertainably higher possibility of death than would normally be the case? What if the woman threatened suicide if the abortion was not performed? How *imminent* must death be if the abortion is not performed? Is it sufficient if having the child will shorten the life of the woman by a number of years? These questions simply cannot be answered.

The grave uncertainties in the application of Article 1196 and the consequent uncertainty concerning criminal liability under the related abortion statutes are more than sufficient to render the Texas Abortion Laws unconstitutionally vague in violation of the Due Process Clause of the Fourteenth Amendment.

We come finally to a consideration of the appropriateness of plaintiffs' request for injunctive relief. Plaintiffs have suggested in oral argument that, should the Court declare the Texas Abortion Laws unconstitutional, that decision would of itself warrant the issuance of an injunction against state enforcement of the statutes. However, the Court is of the opinion that it must abstain from granting the injunction.

Clearly, the question whether to abstain concerning an injunction against the enforcement of state criminal laws is divorced from concerns of abstention in rendering a declaratory judgment. . . . The strong reluctance of federal courts to interfere with the process of state criminal procedure was reflected in Dombrowski v. Pfister, 380 U.S. 479. . . .

"[The] Court has recognized that federal interference with a State's good faith administration of its criminal laws is peculiarly inconsistent with our federal framework. It is generally to be assumed that state courts and prosecutors will observe constitutional limitations as expounded by this Court, and that the mere possibility of erroneous initial application of constitutional standards will usually not amount to the irreparable injury necessary to justify a disruption of orderly state proceedings." . . .

We therefore conclude that we must abstain from issuing an injunction against enforcement of the Texas Abortion Laws. . . .

It is therefore ordered, adjudged and decreed that: (1) the complaint of John and Mary Doe be dismissed; (2) the Texas Abortion Laws are declared void on their face for unconstitutional overbreadth and for vagueness; (3) plaintiffs' application for injunction be dismissed.

• • •

Weddington and Coffee were not satisfied with the district court's refusal to enjoin Texas from enforcing its abortion law. Nor was the state happy with the court's declaratory judgment that its law was unconstitutional. Both sides went to work to prepare an appeal to higher federal courts. In the end, the U.S. Supreme Court agreed to hear to the case. Presentation of such cases requires both a statement of the Court's jurisdiction and then a written brief laying out the grounds for the appeal. In their brief for the U.S. Supreme Court, lawyers for Roe tried to find a right to abortion in a variety of constitutional provisions. What were these? What policy (i.e., social and other extralegal) considerations did they mention? How did they answer the argument that personhood began with conception?

Appellants' brief in *Roe v. Wade*, no. 70-18, U.S. Supreme Court, 1971 (ready access: *Landmark Briefs*, 75:57–226, excerpted)

The personal right to care for and protect one's health in the manner one deems best has been honored by legislatures, except as to measures necessary to check widespread disease and except for the intrusion of restrictive contraception, abortion, and sterilization laws.

Although this Court has not expressly delineated a right to seek health care, the importance of such care has been recognized and the existence of such a right suggested. In *United States v. Vuitch*, 402 U.S. 62 (1971), this Court reaffirmed society's expectation that patients receive "such treatment as is necessary to preserve their health." In this Court's invalidation of Connecticut's proscription against contraception, Justice [Byron] White noted that statute's intrusion upon "access to medical assistance . . . in respect to proper methods of birth control." The existence of other types of state statutes, not under constitutional attack, which affect matters of personal health does not negate the right asserted here. In contrast to laws which intrude upon the protection of personal health, statutes which prescribe working conditions have an indirect, positive impact on the person's well-being. None intrude so far as the . . . compulsory pregnancy asserted here. . . . Similarly, laws prescribing requisites for medical practice are designed to assure qualified practitioners, not to impose upon a citizen's person.

. . . Policy statements of national and international organizations indicate a pervasive recognition of the right to seek health care. . . .

Congress, in passing the comprehensive health planning act of 1966, took a similar position: "[T]he fulfillment of our national purpose depends on promoting and assuring the highest level of health attainable for every person, in an environment which contributes positively to healthful individual and family living. . . ."

Abortion is an accepted medical procedure for terminating pregnancy.

. . . *Amici* medical organizations recognize the acceptability of abortion, as their policy statements indicate; they draw no distinction between abortion and other medical procedures.

The Texas abortion law effectively denies appellants Roe and Doe access to health care. Jane Roe was forced to bear a pregnancy to term though an abortion would have involved considerably less risk to her health. . . . Physicians who would otherwise be willing to perform an abortion in clinical surroundings are deterred by the fear of prosecution. Since appellant Roe could not afford to travel elsewhere to secure a safe abortion, to avoid continuation of pregnancy she would have been forced to resort to an unskilled layman and accept all the health hazards attendant to such a procedure. Even had she been able to travel out of state, the time required to make financial and travel arrangements would have entailed greater health risks inherent in later abortions. . . .

Recognition of the sanctity of the marital relationship has resulted in recognition of a right of marital privacy or as the *Griswold* decision states, "notions of privacy surrounding the marriage relationship" . . . and of rights attendant to the marital state. Protection has been extended to such rights as the rights to marry and have offspring because of their fundamental nature, even though such rights are not expressly enumerated in the Bill of Rights. These decisions support the proposition that there is a sphere of marital privacy and that important interests associated with marriage and the family are, and should be, protected from arbitrary government intrusion. . . .

Associated with the right to marry is the right to bear children, if one chooses, without arbitrary governmental interference. This Court unanimously held that the right to have offspring is a "constitutionally protected human right." . . .

Griswold reaffirms these privacy concepts, and makes it clear that a husband and wife are constitutionally privileged to control the size and spacing of their family at least by contraception.

Taken together, the[se] . . . decisions illustrate that the constitution protects certain privacy and family interests from governmental intrusion unless a compelling justification exists for the legislation. The right of a family to determine whether to have additional children, and to terminate a pregnancy in its early stages if a negative decision is reached, is such a right and is fully entitled to protection.

The number and spacing of children obviously have a profound impact upon the marital union. Certainly the members of this Court know from personal experience the emotional and financial expenditures parenthood demands. For those couples who are less fortunate financially and especially for those who are struggling to provide the necessities of life, additional financial responsibilities can be economically disastrous. For families who require two incomes for economic survival, the pregnancy can be ruinous since the wife will generally have to resign her job. In many other situations, such as where husband and wife are working to put themselves through school, pregnancy at a particular time can present a crisis.

Pregnancy can be a significant added problem in marriages. The added pressures of prospective parenthood can be "the last straw." This Court has previously upheld the right to use contraceptives to avoid unwanted pregnancy. . . .

In addition to rights associated with marital privacy, an overlapping body of precedent extends significant constitutional protection to the citizen's sovereignty over his or her own physical person. . . .

This right, like all rights, does have some limitations. . . . Nonetheless, absent a compelling justification, one is entitled to personal autonomy.

In family matters relating to child rearing and procreation, the Court has recognized and sustained individual rights on a constitutional plane. . . .

Pregnancy obviously does have an overwhelming impact on the woman. The most readily observable impact of pregnancy, of course, is that of carrying the pregnancy for nine months. Additionally there are numerous more subtle but no less drastic impacts.

Without the right to respond to unwanted pregnancy, a woman is at the mercy of possible contraceptive failure, particularly if she is unable or unwilling to utilize the most effective measures. Failure to use contraceptives effectively, if pregnancy ensues, exacts an exceedingly high price. . . .

When pregnancy begins, a woman is faced with a governmental mandate compelling her to serve as an incubator for months and then as an ostensibly willing mother for up to twenty or more years. She must often forego further education or a career and often must endure economic and social hardships. Under the present law of Texas she is given no other choice. Continued pregnancy is compulsory, unless she can persuade the authorities that she is potentially suicidal or that her life is otherwise endangered. Texas Penal Code, arts. 1191–1194, 1196 (1961). The law impinges severely upon her dignity, her life plan and often her marital relationship. The Texas abortion law constitutes an invasion of her privacy with irreparable consequences. Absent the right to remedy contraceptive failure, other rights of personal and marital privacy are largely diluted. . . .

The decisions of this Court which implicitly recognize rights of marital and personal privacy have been followed by state and federal Court decisions expressly holding the decision of abortion to be within the sphere of constitutionally protected privacy.

That there is a fundamental constitutional right to abortion was the conclusion of the Court below in the instant case. . . .

That view has been shared by a number of other Courts which have considered the question and have affirmed that this is a fundamental right.
. . .

Without the ability to control their reproductive capacity, women and couples are largely unable to control determinative aspects of their lives and marriages. If the concept of "fundamental rights" means anything, it must surely include the right to determine when and under what circumstances to have children. . . .

The First, Ninth and Fourteenth Amendments protect the right of every citizen to follow any lawful calling, business, or profession he may choose, subject only to rational regulation by the state as necessary for the protection of legitimate public interests. . . . In reviewing legislation affecting the medical profession, Courts have particularly respected the knowledge and skill necessary for medical practice, the broad professional discretion necessary to apply it, and the concomitant state interest in guaranteeing the quality of medical practitioners. . . .

Similarly, Courts have been alert to protect medical practice from rash or arbitrary legislative interference. . . .

Most recently, this Court, in *United States v. Vuitch*, 102 U.S. 62 (1971), recognized that "doctors are encouraged by society's expectations . . . and by their own professional standards to give their patients such treatment as is necessary to preserve their health." . . . The *Vuitch* decision went on to construe the term health to encompass "psychological as well as physical health," and "the state of being sound in body or mind."

Here, the practice of medicine clearly includes the treatment of pregnancy and conditions associated with it. However, the Texas statute prohibits physicians from administering the appropriate remedy to preserve the patient's health or well-being. Physicians are not required to forego the right to make medically sound judgments and to act upon them with respect to any other human disease or condition. With appropriate consents they may administer electric shock therapy, excise vital organs, perform prefrontal lobotomies and take any other drastic action they believe indicated. They are not indictable for these actions. However, obstetricians and gynecologists who are asked to abort their patients for sound medical reasons risk a prison sentence if they do so. The statute severely infringes their practice and seriously compromises their professional judgments. . . .

. . . The statute in question here does not protect the public from un-qualified practitioners. . . . Rather the statute applies to laymen and physi-cians alike. Indeed, it endangers patients' health by unduly confining doc-tors' exercise of medical judgment. . . .

As argued above, the Texas abortion laws infringe privacy rights here as much as the Connecticut statute did in *Griswold*. As in that case, the com-pelling interest test is the proper standard for reviewing the Texas statute. . . . The physical and psychological harm caused by the statute fully war-rants a demonstration of compelling justification to sustain it.

Here, the availability of adultery and fornication statutes to enforce strictures on sexual behavior, the absence of any distinctions based on gestation period in the abortion statute, and its blanket application to gynecologists and laymen alike suggest classifications which are overly broad. To meet these constitutional objections, the state must show that a less restrictive statute will not effectuate any compelling interests it can establish. . . .

Medical abortion is a safe and simple procedure when performed during the early stages of pregnancy; indeed, it is safer than childbirth. This fact alone vitiates any contention that the statute here serves a public health interest. Numerous state and federal Courts have taken notice of this fact and concurred that no health rationale supports a statute like the one here. . . .

Moreover, no concern for mental health justifies the statute, for it does not permit abortion even if a woman's mental health is threatened. Such a view is untenable for the additional reason that abortion is a procedure without clinically significant psychiatric sequel.

Additional data reveal that statutes like the one here actually *create* "a public problem of pandemic proportions" by denying women the oppor-tunity to seek safe medical treatment. Severe infection, permanent sterility, pelvic disease, and other serious complications accompany the illegal abor-tions to which women are driven by law like this one.

Any notion that less restrictive abortion laws would produce excessive demands on medical resources and thereby endanger public health also is unfounded. The experience in New York City after one year under an elec-tive abortion law dispels any such fears:

New York City has accounted for the lion's share of abortions in the State and has been a resource for woman all over the country. Nevertheless, the catastrophe many foresaw a year ago failed to materialize: we have been able to serve our residents as well as substantial numbers of out-of-state women, and, most important, we are serving women safely. (Chase, "Twelve Month Report on Abortions in New York City" [Health Services Administration, City of New York, June 29, 1971]).

The absence of a public health problem accompanying less restrictive abortion is indicated by comparative mortality rates: for the first eleven months of operation, the mortality for abortion in New York City is approximately equal to that of tonsillectomy in the United States.

Against this background of medical fact, there is no support whatever for the suggestion that public health is an interest protected by this statute. . . .

No evidence exists that limited access to abortion curtails promiscuity, nor is it conceivable that such a correlation could exist. The widespread availability of contraception would seem to be a more significant factor. In any event, from the physician's standpoint, a patient is no less worthy of medical care simply because she has unfortunately conceived out of wedlock. . . .

As counsel for appellee admitted during oral argument [in the district court], "the State only has one interest and that is the protection of the life of the unborn child." . . . The question then becomes whether this interest is sufficiently compelling to overcome the couple's or woman's fundamental right to privacy or autonomy. In this regard it is revealing to examine other aspects of the State's attitude toward the fetus. Such an inquiry reveals that only in the area of abortion does the State exhibit an interest in the fetus or treat it as having legal personality.

An unborn fetus is not a "human being" and killing a fetus is not murder or any other form of homicide. "Homicide" in Texas is defined as "the destruction of the life of one human being by the act, agency, procurement, or culpable omission of another," 2A Tex. Pen. Code art. 1201 (1961). Since the common law definition of "human being" is applicable, a fetus neither born nor in the process of birth is not a "human being" within the meaning of those words as they appear in the homicide statute. . . .

The State does not require that a pregnant woman with a history of spontaneous abortion go into seclusion in an attempt to save the pregnancy. No pregnant woman having knowingly engaged in conduct which she reasonably could have foreseen would result in injury to the fetus (such a skiing in late pregnancy) has ever been charged with negligent homicide.

No formalities of death are observed regarding a fetus of less than five months gestation. Property rights are contingent upon being born alive. There has never been a tort recovery in Texas as the result of injury to a fetus not born alive. No benefits are given prior to birth in situations, such as workman's compensation, where benefits are normally allowed for "children."

Appellants realize that the fact that states have failed in most instances to protect the rights of the fetus does not automatically mean that a state would not have a compelling interest in doing so. One assumes that if a state had never enacted a statute prohibiting theft, a constitutional right to steal would not necessarily follow. However, the traditional subjects of legislation which bear upon individual liberty have, of necessity, always guided our notions of what the state may or may not do. The fact that the fetus has only been protected in the area of abortion, and not even then when the mother's life is in danger or she performs the abortion herself, together with the strong evidence that abortion laws were passed in response to the dangers of surgery, makes out a strong case for a traditional right of the mother to abort the fetus which was only taken away for her own protection. This converse is that the state has no *traditional* interest in protection of the fetus. . . .

It is sometimes argued that scientific discoveries show that human life exists in the fetus. Scientific studies in embryology have greatly expanded our understanding of the process of fertilization and development of the fetus and studies relating to the basic elements of life have shown that life is not only present in the fertilized egg, sperm and ova but that each cell contains elements which could conceivably constitute the beginning of a new human organism. Such studies are significant to science but only confuse the problem of defining human life. . . .

Thus science only leads to a worse quandary. . . . Obviously if one goes far enough back along the continuum of human development one encounters the existence of sub-microscopic double-helix molecules which have human life potential. When does something become human? . . .

The question than becomes not one of destroying or preserving potential, but one of who should make the decision. Obviously some decisions are better left to a representative process since individual decisions on medical facilities, wars, or the release of a convict would tend toward the chaotic. It is our contention that the decision on abortion is exactly the opposite. A representative or majority decision making process has led to chaos. Indeed, in the face of two difficult, unresolvable choices to destroy life potential in either a fetus or its host the choice can only be left to one of the entities whose potential is threatened.

• • •

The state (referred to as "the appellees") had, in one sense, an easier task than the appellants. Its anti-abortion law was well established over time, reflected state laws over much of the country, and seemed to be related to the idea of protecting the mother as well as the fetus. At the same time, the state had to overcome the district court's decision and the right of privacy established by Griswold. What kinds of evidence did the state introduce to prove that the fetus was a human life? Did the medical evidence bolster the religious argument, stand outside it, or provide an alternative to a religious definition of the beginning of life? Why could the appellees not rely on a religious definition of life's beginning? How did the appellees rebut the appellants' constitutional arguments?

Appellees' brief in *Roe* (figures 1–11, pictures of fetuses, omitted) (ready access: *Landmark Briefs*, 75:227–96, excerpted)

. . . THE CONSTITUTION OF THE UNITED STATES DOES NOT GUARANTEE A WOMAN THE RIGHT TO ABORT AN UNBORN FETUS.

One must recognize the interest of a husband and wife in preserving their conjugal relations from state interference, an interest which, in *Griswold v. Connecticut*, (1965), was found to be violated by Connecticut's statute forbidding the use of contraceptives. This law interfered with the most private aspect of the marital relation, sexual intercourse, making it criminal for a couple to engage in sexual intercourse when using contraceptives. In contrast, the usual statute restricting abortions does not affect the sexual relations of a couple except under some circumstances and only for a limited time. Prevention of abortion does not entail, therefore, state interference with the right of marital intercourse, nor does enforcement of the statute require invasions of the conjugal bedroom.

Assuming arguendo [for the sake of argument] that there are other marital rights the state must respect, may it then be urged that the rights of marital privacy include the freedom of a married couple to raise and educate a child they do not want, or commit infanticide, incest, engage in pandering and the like? Family privacy, like personal privacy, is highly valued, but not absolute. . . . The family may not practice polygamy, may not prohibit schooling for a child, or prohibit the child's labor, or expose the community or a child to communicable disease. . . . Proponents of abortion-on-demand assert that anti-abortion laws unlawfully intrude into the privacy of the physician-patient relationship. They assume necessarily that the doctor treating a pregnancy owes an obligation of good medical care to only one patient, the pregnant woman. . . . Appellants' contentions of intrusion upon physician-patient relationship are not self-sustaining and must be associated with or connected to a violation of some basic right. . . .

Personal privacy is an exalted right but, as in marital privacy, it has never been regarded as absolute. A person may be subjected to a "stop and frisk" though it constitutes an intrusion upon his person, or a person may be required to submit to a vaccination, and a blood sample may forcibly be extracted from the body of an individual arrested for suspicion of driving while intoxicated. A woman has been required to submit to a blood transfusion necessary to preserve her life in order that her small child shall not be left without a mother. The "right to privacy" is a highly cherished right—however one which is nowhere expressly mentioned in the Constitution of the United States or its amendments. Numerous examples in tort and criminal law indicate the right to privacy is a relative right. A woman cannot in privacy, even though she harms no other person, legally utilize or even possess certain forbidden drugs, such as LSD or heroin. . . .

When the "right of privacy" is attached to an "express right" such as the "right of freedom of religion" a very strong constitutional basis exists for upholding the "right—except when in conflict with the most basic and fundamental of all rights—the right to life." . . .

The crux of the moral legal debate over abortion is, in essence, the right of the woman to determine whether or not she should bear a particular child versus the right of the child to life. The proponents of liberalization of abortion laws speak of the fetus as "a blob of protoplasm" and feel it has no right to life until it has reached a certain stage of development. On the other hand, the opponents of liberalization maintain the fetus is human from the time of conception, and so interruption of pregnancy cannot be justified from the time of fertilization. It most certainly seems logical that from the stage of differentiation, after which neither twinning nor recombination will occur, the fetus implanted in the uterine wall deserves respect as a human life. If we take the definition of life as being said to be present when an organism shows evidence of individual animate existence, then from the blastocyst stage the fetus qualifies for respect. It is alive because it has the ability to reproduce dying cells. It is human because it can be distinguished from other non-human species, and once implanted in the uterine wall it requires only nutrition and time to develop into one of us.

The recent recognition of autonomy of the unborn child has led to the development of new medical specialties concerning the unborn child from the earliest stages of the pregnancy. Modern obstetrics has discarded the unscientific concept that the child in the womb is but tissue of the mother. . . .

Yet the attack on the Texas statute assumes this discredited scientific concept . . . completely ignoring the development of the human being in the mother's womb. . . .

It is our task in the next subsections to show how clearly and conclusively modern science—embryology, fetology, genetics, perinatology, all of biology—establishes the humanity of the unborn child. We submit that the data not only shows the constitutionality of the Texas legislature's effort to save the unborn from indiscriminate extermination, *but in fact suggests a duty to do so*. We submit also that no physician who understands this will argue that the law is vague, uncertain or overbroad for he will understand that the law calls upon him to exercise his art for the benefit of his *two patients*: mother *and* child.

From conception the child is a complex, dynamic, rapidly growing organism. By a natural and continuous process the single fertilized ovum will, over approximately nine months, develop into the trillions of cells of the newborn. The natural end of the sperm and ovum is death unless fertilization occurs. At fertilization a new and unique being is created which, although receiving one-half of its chromosomes from each patient, it really unlike either.

About seven to nine days after conception, when there are already several hundred cells of the new individual formed, contact with the uterus is made and implantation begins. Blood cells begin at 17 days and a heart as early as 18 days. This embryonic heart which begins as a simple tube starts irregular pulsations at 24 days, which, in about one week, smooth into a rhythmic contraction and expansion. It has been shown that the ECG on a 23 mm embryo (7.5 weeks) presents the existence of a functionally complete cardiac system and the possible existence of a myo-neurol or humoral regulatory mechanism. . . .

Commencing at 18 days the developmental emphasis is on the nervous system even though other vital organs, such as the heart, are commencing development at the same time. Such early development is necessary since the nervous system integrates the action of all other systems. By the end of the 20th day the foundation of the child's brain, spinal cord and entire nervous system will have been established. . . .

The baby's eyes begin to form at 19 days. By the end of the first month the foundation of the brain, spinal cord, nerves and sense organs is completely formed. By 28 days the embryo has the building blocks for 40 pairs of muscles situated from the base of its skull to the lower end of its spinal column. . . .

By the beginning of the second month the unborn child, small as it is, looks distinctly human. Yet, by this time the child's mother is not even aware that she is pregnant. . . .

At the end of the first month the child is about ¼ of an inch in length. At

30 days the primary brain is present and the eyes, ears and nasal organs have started to form. . . .

Earliest reflexes begin as early as the 42nd day. The male penis begins to form. The child is almost ½ inch long and cartilage has begun to develop. . . .

The new body not only exists, it also functions. The brain in configuration is already like the adult brain and sends out impulses that coordinate the function of the other organs. The brain waves have been noted at 43 days. The heart beats sturdily. The stomach produces digestive juices. The liver manufactures blood cells and the kidney begins to function by extracting uric acid from the child's blood. The muscles of the arms and body can already be set in motion.

After the eighth week no further primordia will form; everything is *already* present that will be found in the full term baby. . . .

From this point until adulthood, when full growth is achieved somewhere between 25 and 27 years, the changes in the body will be mainly in dimension and in gradual refinement of the working parts. . . .

In the third month, the child becomes very active. By the end of the month he can kick his legs, turn his feet, curl and fan his toes, make a fist, move this thumb, bend his wrist, turn his head, squint, frown, open his mouth, press his lips tightly together. He can swallow and drinks the amniotic fluid that surrounds him. Thumb sucking is first noted at this age. The first respiratory motions move fluid in and out of his lungs with inhaling and exhaling respiratory movements. . . .

The twelfth week brings a whole new range of responses. The baby can now move his thumb in opposition to his fingers. He now swallows regularly. He can pull up his upper lip; the initial step in the development of the sucking reflex. By the end of the twelfth week, the quality of muscular response is altered. It is no longer marionette-like or mechanical—the movements are now graceful and fluid, as they are in the newborn. The child is active and the reflexes are becoming more vigorous. All this is before the mother feels any movement. . . .

The baby sleeps and wakes just as it will after birth. When he sleeps he invariably settles into his favorite position called his "lie." Each baby has a characteristic lie. When he awakens he moves about freely in the buoyant fluid turning from side to side, and frequently head over heel. Sometimes his head will be up and sometimes it will be down. He may sometimes be aroused from sleep by external vibrations. He may wake up from a loud tap on the tub when his mother is taking a bath. A loud concert or the vibrations of a washing machine may also stir him into activity. The child hears and recognizes his mother's voice before birth. Movements of the mother, whether locomotive, cardiac or respiratory, are communicated to the child. . . . Quickening is only a relative concept which depends upon the sensitivity of the mother, the position of the placenta, and the size of the child. . . .

Whatever personal right of privacy a pregnant woman may have with respect to the disposition and use of her body must be balanced against the personal right of the unborn child to life. . . .

If it be true the compelling state interest in prohibiting or regulating abortion did not exist at one time in the stage of history, under the result of the findings and research of modern medicine, a different legal conclusion can now be reached. . . .

· · ·

Joining both sides in the appeal were "amici curiae" (literally "friends of the court" who supported one side or the other). By permission of the court, individuals or groups who have an interest in the outcome of the adjudication but are not parties to it may apply to submit briefs on the issues. By the time the case was accepted by the Supreme Court, almost a year after it was decided in the lower federal court, these friends of the court had rallied to the respective sides in the suit.

Briefs of amici curiae in support of the Texas law were filed by Gary K. Nelson, attorney general of Arizona; Robert K. Killian, attorney general of Connecticut; Ed W. Hancock, attorney general of Kentucky; Clarence A. H. Meyer, attorney general of Nebraska; and Vernon B. Romney, attorney general of Utah, all states with similar laws to that of Texas. In addition, the Association of Texas Diocesan Attorneys, Americans United for Life, the National Right to Life Committee, and Women for the Unborn, all Roman Catholic–sponsored advocacy groups, filed to defend the state's protection of the potential life and to express their view that legally, life began with conception. The American College of Obstetricians and Gynecologists and other groups of doctors filed briefs in support of the plaintiffs, as did the Planned Parenthood Federation of America Inc. and the National Legal Program on Health Problems of the Poor. The American Association of University Women, the California Committee to Legalize Abortion, and the National Organization for Women filed briefs to argue that the abortion rights question was a women's rights issue.

The briefs of amici came from perspectives so far apart that their arguments did not overlap in any way. The first of the friends of the court briefs that follows was prepared and submitted by a coalition of women's groups. In the brief, enforced completion of a pregnancy was likened to slavery, and the authors of the brief spend much time criticizing the roles of women in a society without choice. Note the use of the term "conceptus" for the fetus.

Brief in support of appellants by the California Committee to Legalize Abortion, the South Bay Chapter of the National Organization for Women, Zero Population Growth Inc., in *Roe* (ready access: *Landmark Briefs*, 75:649–86, excerpted)

Despite the numerous issues involved in these cases, this brief will address itself only to one, so as to avoid repetition of the arguments presented by appellants by other briefs of *amici curiae*. We believe that the time is ripe for this Court to announce that the laws which restrict or regulate abortion as a special procedure violate the Thirteenth Amendment by imposing involuntary servitude without due conviction for a crime.

Although the Texas abortion laws permit abortion only in the single instance where the mother's life would be saved and the Georgia laws permit abortion in certain additional categories, both, in the view of Amici, involve rights of unwillingly pregnant women that make it appropriate to treat the particular issue, to which this brief addresses itself, as being the same in both cases. . . .

The Thirteenth Amendment to the Constitution provides: Neither slavery nor involuntary servitude, except as a punishment for crime whereof the party shall have been duly convicted, shall exist within the United States, or any place subject to their jurisdiction.

The Amendment, by its very language, prohibits both slavery *and* involuntary servitude, and requires due conviction of a crime as a condition precedent to all forms of involuntary servitude regardless of racial contexts. . . .

Application of the Amendment has never been limited to its contexts. . . .

The Thirteenth Amendment prohibits many forms of compulsory labor, *i.e.*, involuntary servitude of all kinds. As defined by this Court, involuntary servitude is "a condition of enforced compulsory service of one to another."

Laws compelling personal service in liquidation of a debt or other obligation are null and void as violations of the Thirteenth Amendment. . . .

As conditions and values change, constitutional language takes on new meanings, because constitutional concepts are not static, "not shackled to the political theory of a particular era." . . . The Thirteenth Amendment, as revived by this Court with new force in *Jones v. Mayer*, 392 U.S. 409 (1968) reconsidered the early interpretation of the Amendment. . . .

In *Jones v. Mayer, supra*, this Court was not reluctant to recognize within the Thirteenth Amendment the "promise of freedom," turning the focus again from what the Amendment prohibits to what it guarantees, a broader principle of freedom from compulsory service of one person to another. . . .

It is the purpose of this brief to show that anti-abortion laws, which force an unwillingly pregnant woman to continue pregnancy to term, are a form of involuntary servitude without the justification of serving any current national or public need. . . .

Pregnancy is not a mere inconvenience. "The physical and functional alterations of pregnancy involve all the body systems," displacing body parts, depleting the body of its necessary elements and changing its chemical balance.

The pregnant woman's body is in a state of constant service, providing warmth, nutrients, oxygen and waste disposal for the support of the conceptus. These activities are always to the detriment of the woman's body. They are performed for the benefit of the conceptus alone unless an interest of the pregnant woman is also served thereby, that is, unless the pregnant woman defines the pregnancy as wanted.

During pregnancy, enlargement of the uterus within the abdominal cavity displaces and compresses the other abdominal contents including the heart, lungs and gastro-intestinal tract. The resulting pressure has a direct effect on circulation of the blood and increase in venous pressure, sometimes leading to irreversible varicose veins and hemorrhoids and, with predictable frequency, to disabling thrombophlebitis. The gastro-intestinal tract experiences functional interference causing constipation and displacement of the urinary tract, thus urinary tract infections occur in six to seven per cent of all pregnant women and such infections, in turn, lead to kidney infections. During the second and third months, bladder irritability is quite constant. Tearing and over-stretching of the muscles of the pelvic floor occurs frequently during delivery, causing extensive and irreparable damage to the pelvic organs and their supporting connections. Surgery is often required to return these organs to position. Bladder control may be permanently lost. The weight of the contents of the uterus causes sacroiliac strain accompanied by pain and backache, with the effects of the pressure being felt as far as the outermost extremities of the woman's body. The weight causes such pressure on the cervical spine as to result in numbness, tingling and proprioceptive acuity reduction in the hands. . . .

At least 40 per cent of pregnant women have symptomatic edema, distorting the hands, face, ankles and feet. A woman's lungs respire 45 per cent more air than normal in an attempt to obtain the needed oxygen, but oxygen absorbed is less than normal despite the extra effort of the crowded lungs. . . .

Amici ask this Court to consider the lack of options open to the pregnant woman at this time of onset of her pregnancy. . . .

Contraceptives are never foolproof. Any act of intercourse between a fertile man and woman constitutes some risk of conception, no matter what contraceptives are used. . . .

Under the present state of contraceptive failure, a woman does not have the option of remaining free of pregnancy by making careful use of contraceptives. She is at some risk in using the most effective methods of contraception available.

The average married woman expects to bear two to three children, yet coitus takes place between a couple married during the period of the woman's reproductive years (age 18 to 43) an average of 2,535 times. The frequency of coitus stated in the Kinsey Report [on human sexuality] is average behavior between married couples. If the woman wishes to remain free of pregnancy once her desired family size is reached, her only sure method of remaining so free of pregnancy is complete abstinence from sexual intercourse. If she embarks on such a course, will the law uphold her decision?

A wife has no legal power to refuse to participate in the intimacies of married life. If she refuses her husband's forced attentions, there is no law to intervene in her behalf. She cannot charge her husband with rape. Indeed, if a married woman attempts to practice abstinence, the laws of most states treat her behavior as a denial of the marital right of the husband. Some jurisdictions construe refusal of sexual relations as desertion and thus ground for divorce. . . . In some other jurisdictions, desertion is held to occur upon cessation of sexual relations notwithstanding that the spouses continue to take meals together, converse and in other ways behave as husband and wife. In some other states in which cruelty is a ground, such refusal constitutes cruelty, giving the husband cause for divorce. In the states now recognizing "no-fault" divorce, or dissolution of marriage, the husband no longer needs to plead or prove specific grounds; his dissatisfaction is thus acceptable as sufficient cause for dissolving the marriage.

Under present law, a married woman has two choices: she can attempt to refuse to fulfill the sexual obligations of the marriage and thus risk termination of her marriage; or she can participate in normal marital relations and risk unwanted pregnancy and childbirth. With a choice of either alternative, she risks the consequence of a legally imposed penalty. . . .

The women who bear children and the medical experts who assist them testify that pregnancy and childbearing are indeed labor. The fact that many women enter into such labor voluntarily and joyfully does not alter the fact that other women, under other circumstances, find childbearing too arduous, become pregnant through no choice of their own, and are then forced to complete the pregnancy to term by compulsion of state laws prohibiting voluntary abortion.

It is the purpose of the Thirteenth Amendment to prohibit a relationship in which one person or entity limits the freedom of another person. In the absence of a compelling state interest or due conviction for a crime, the state's forcing the pregnant woman through unwanted pregnancy to full term is a denial of her Thirteenth Amendment right to be free from "a condition of enforced compulsory service of one to another." This is the very essence of involuntary servitude in which the personal service of one person is "disposed of or coerced for another's benefit." . . .

Even if the position were accepted, *arguendo*, that the fetus is a "person" or "potential person," such recognition of the fetus would not provide the state with a compelling interest to justify encroachment upon the pregnant woman's possession and free control of her own person. . . . Yet the laws prohibiting and regulating abortion, unlike all other laws in respect of persons, compel this pregnant woman to breathe, process food and donate blood for the sustenance of another human entity, either fully or partially developed. In no other instance does the law compel one individual to donate his/her bodily force to another individual. In no other instance does the law give another human—even a fully developed human—a right to life beyond that which the person himself can sustain. . . .

The very language of the Thirteenth Amendment prohibits subjection to involuntary servitude "except as punishment for crime whereof the party shall have been duly convicted." Yet, the state's subjection of an unwilling woman to the continued pregnancy and childbearing compelled by anti-abortion law is accomplished without defining her substantive crime or providing her with due process in proving her guilt and inflicting her punishment. . . .

What is the woman's crime? Substantive due process requires that it be clearly defined, not vague, not arbitrary. Is her crime that of having engaged in a sexual relationship? If the relationship occurred within marriage, the woman was compelled by virtue of her married state to submit to her husband. Even if the pregnancy may have occurred as the result of some prohibited non-marital sexual conduct (according to due proof), an anti-abortion law punishing such conduct would be overbroad and beyond the competence of the state. Is her crime that of failing in knowledge of, access to, or effectiveness of contraceptives? Such crime has not been defined by the state. . . .

. . .

The second amicus brief could not have been more different from the one above. It was prepared and submitted by the National Right to Life Committee and based the case for the Texas law on the fact that the state must protect the life of the fetus because it was already a human being. Note the reference to the "child" in the womb.

Brief in support of appellees by Americans United for Life in *Roe* (ready access: *Landmark Briefs*, 75:502–6)

Americans United for Life is a national, non-sectarian, educational organization of citizens who affirm the sacredness of all human life from conception to natural death. . . . It is a particular purpose of Americans United for Life to promote a wider application of constitutional rights to children in the womb. It is this purpose which gives Americans United for Life an interest in this appeal. For this appeal involves the issue of whether the child in the womb is entitled to the protection of constitutional rights in the specific situation where his abortion is sought where it is not necessary to save the life of the mother. . . .

The aspect of this case argued in this brief involves the Equal Protection Clause of the Fourteenth Amendment to the Constitution of the United States and Articles 1191, 1192, 1193, 1194 and 1196 of the Texas Penal Code. The specific portion of the Fourteenth Amendment involved reads as follows: "No state shall . . . deny to any person within its jurisdiction the equal protection of the laws." The pertinent provisions of the Texas Penal Code forbid abortion where it is not necessary to save the life of the mother; they are set forth verbatim in the briefs of appellant and appellee. . . .

The child in the womb is a person within the meaning of the Equal Protection Clause of the Fourteenth Amendment. The Equal Protection Clause forbids classifications of law that are arbitrary, capricious or unreasonable. To allow the child in the womb to be killed by abortion, where it is not necessary to save the life of his mother, would be to subject him to arbitrary, capricious and unreasonable classification. This is so because he is in fact a living human being and his young age and his situation do not provide a sufficient basis for a legal determination that he be subject to death where older human beings are not so subject. Enforcement of the statute in question should not be enjoined since such an injunction would allow the child in the womb to be killed by abortion where it is not necessary to save the life of his mother. It would therefore deprive him of the equal protection of the laws. . . .

The child in the womb meets these criteria of personhood under the Equal Protection Clause. He is human, he lives and he has his being. That is, he is a living human being. As the highest court of New Jersey [in 1960] summarized the state of scientific knowledge, "Medical authorities have long recognized that child is in existence from the moment of conception."

The character of the child in the womb as a person is clearly recognized in the law of torts [civil wrongs]. . . . It is significant that a majority of courts, keeping pace with advancing scientific knowledge, now hold that even a stillborn child may maintain a wrongful death action where his death was caused by a prenatal injury. . . .

A similar trend can be seen in the law of property. . . . The law of property has long recognized the rights of the child in the womb for purposes which affect the property rights of that child. . . .

When the property rules of the English common law were adopted by American courts the same approach was taken. . . .

Indeed, there is authority for the proposition that the child in the womb will be regarded as in existence even where it is against his interest to do so.

For purposes of equity, too, the law has recognized the existence of the child in the womb. An unborn child, for example, can compel his father to provide him support. . . . He can compel his mother to undergo a blood transfusion for his benefit, even where such transfusion is forbidden by the mother's religious beliefs. . . . The court held that the child's right to live outweighed even the mother's right to the free exercise of her religion. . . .

Even if one somehow does not concede that the child in the womb is a living human being, one ought at least to give him the benefit of the doubt. Our law does not permit the execution, or imprisonment under sentence, of a criminal unless his guilt of the crime charged is proven beyond a reasonable doubt. The innocent child in the womb is entitled to have us resolve in his favor any doubts we may feel as to his living humanity and his personhood.

· · ·

The final words in the National Right to Life Committee brief suggested its deep-rootedness in the concept of a Christian soul. That soul alone would explain why the fetus was "innocent"—a moral and religious term rather than a scientific one, and a perspective entirely lacking from the brief of the appellants. As it sat to hear the appeals in *Roe*, the High Court thus faced two entirely different conceptions of rights, life, and liberty.

NOTES

1. These stories appear in Brett Harvey, ed., *The Fifties: A Women's Oral History* (New York, 1993), 21, 22, 27, 28.

2. Ibid., 41.

3. Patricia Tyson quoted in *The Choices We Made: 26 Women and Men Speak Out about Abortion*, edited by Angela Bonavoglia (New York, 2001), 113.

4. Susan Brownmiller, *In Our Time: Memoir of a Revolution* (New York, 1999), 102–35.

5. Amy Kesselman, "Women versus Connecticut: Conducting a Statewide Hearing on Abortion," in *Abortion Wars: A Half Century of Struggle, 1950–2000*, edited by Rickie Salinger (Berkeley, 1998), 42–68.

6. Friedan's account of these events appears in her *It Changed My Life: Writings on the Women's Movement*, rev. ed. (Cambridge, Mass., 1998), 156–65, 192–202.

. . .

Roe v. Wade before the High Court

Roe v. Wade had the company of other abortion cases making their way toward the U.S. Supreme Court in 1971. Of the other cases on appeal, one from Georgia also caught the attention of the justices. In *Doe v. Bolton* abortion rights advocates were challenging a "reform" statute with a much broader therapeutic exception than Texas allowed. The federal district court panel in Georgia had struck down the statute for much the same reasons as the federal district court panel in Texas, and both sides in *Doe* appealed to the High Court for the same reasons as both sides in *Roe*.

In the meantime, another doctor prosecuted for performing an abortion in Texas had appealed his case to the state supreme court. The state supreme court upheld the prosecution, ignoring the federal district court ruling in *Roe*. In *Thompson v. State* (1971), the court held that "the State of Texas has a compelling interest to protect fetal life" and that the state's law was not in violation of the federal Constitution. What was more, the state court insisted that the definition of human life was for the state legislature and not the federal courts to determine. The physician's abortion conviction was affirmed.

Thus the federal court's refusal to enjoin Texas from prosecuting doctors under its law had become a live issue—just as plaintiffs in *Roe* had feared. Moreover, the Texas authorities' defiance of the federal court ruling raised the specter of massive resistance by southern state legislatures and courts to federal court orders in desegregation and other civil rights, a defiance that had infuriated the High Court. The abortion rights cases would thus touch more than abortion and women's rights issues. They raised questions of federalism (federal government–state government relations) and separation of powers among the branches of government (legislatures versus courts).

Roe v. Wade and *Doe v. Bolton* were argued before the Supreme Court twice, once in December 1971 and again in the fall of 1972. The oral arguments in the first case pitted Weddington against lawyers representing the state. Margie Pitts Hames, who represented Doe in the district court, argued the appeal for appellants. Georgia's deputy attorney general, Dorothy T. Beasley, reargued the cause for appellees.

The task of writing the Supreme Court opinion in both *Roe* and *Doe* was assigned to Justice Harry Blackmun of Minnesota. He was relatively new to the Court, and this was his first major drafting task. Although in the "conference," the twice-a-week meeting of the justices to discuss the cases, the majority seemed to favor affirming the lower court rulings in both cases, the grounds for the affirmance would make a huge difference in the way the decision affected all concerned parties.

Justice Blackmun's opinion for the Court was long in coming and did not satisfy all of his colleagues. Although he had been pressed by two of his supporters on the Court, Justices William Brennan and William O. Douglas, to ground the opinion in fundamental Fourteenth Amendment rights, Blackmun was still strongly influenced by the stances taken in preceding years by the American Medical Association and by his own work in the library of the Mayo Clinic, a leading medical center. He had represented the clinic when he was in private practice and had great respect for its medical staff. His opinion in *Roe* rested as much on medical grounds as on constitutional doctrine, as he developed a balancing test for when the state could regulate or even bar abortions (later called the "trimester formula") based on the stages of fetal development.

. . .

When the Supreme Court accepts a case for hearing, oral arguments before the justices on the briefs submitted by the parties are scheduled. These arguments are limited to one hour per case (thirty minutes for each side) and can be dramatic as well as instructive. The justices may hint at their stance through the kinds of questions they ask or the way they respond to the oral arguments. They certainly gave some clues in this oral argument.

Sarah Weddington, oral argument in *Roe v. Wade*, December 13, 1971 (ready access: *Landmark Briefs*, 75:782–96, excerpted)

Mr. Chief Justice Burger: We will hear argument in No. 18, *Roe* against *Wade*.

Mrs. Weddington, you may proceed whenever you're ready.

MRS. WEDDINGTON: Mr. Chief Justice, and may it please the court:

The instant case is a direct appeal from a decision of the United States District Court for the Northern District of Texas. The court declared the

Texas abortion law to be unconstitutional for two reasons: First, that the law was impermissibly based; and, second, that it violated a woman's right to continue or terminate a pregnancy.

Although the court granted declaratory relief, the court denied appellant's request for injunctive relief. The Texas law in question permits abortions to be performed only in instances where it is for the purpose of saving the life of the woman.

The case originated with the filing of two separate complaints, the first being filed on behalf of Jane Roe, an unmarried pregnant girl; and the second being filed on behalf of James and Mary Doe, a married couple. Jane Roe, the pregnant woman, had gone to several Dallas physicians seeking an abortion, but had been refused care because of the Texas law. She filed suit on behalf of herself and all those women who have in the past—at that present time—or in the future would seek termination of a pregnancy. In her affidavit she did state some of the reasons that she desired an abortion at the time she sought one. But, contrary to the contentions of appellee, she continued to desire the abortion. And it was not only at the time she sought the abortion that her desire was to terminate the pregnancy. . . .

Since the time of the lower court ruling, the District Attorney in Texas has said that he considers the Federal court decision there not to be binding. And we do have a letter from him—the first thing in our Appendix to the brief—stating that he will continue to prosecute. So the doctors in Texas, even with the Federal decision, and even after the *Vuitch* decision, do not feel free to perform abortions. And, instead, 728 women in the first nine months after the decision went to New York for an abortion. Texas women are coming here. It's so often the poor and the disadvantaged in Texas who are not able to escape the effect of the law. Certainly there are many Texas women who are affected because our doctors still feel uncertain about the impact of the law, even in light of the *Vuitch* decision.

THE COURT: Well then, Mrs. Weddington, of course you make many additional constitutional attacks upon the Texas statute. . . .

MRS. WEDDINGTON: Yes, Your Honor, we do. . . .

THE COURT: Could they [pregnant women seeking abortions], under Texas law, be charged as accomplices or as co-conspirators, or anything like that?

MRS. WEDDINGTON: No, we have express Texas cases. In one situation, *Woodrow v. State*, an 1880 case, the woman had taken a potion to induce abortion, and the Texas court specifically said that the woman is guilty of no crime, even in that situation. And, that in fact she is the victim of our law. . . .

THE COURT: You have three plaintiffs here representing a class, as I gather?

MRS. WEDDINGTON: Yes, sir.

THE COURT: One, an unmarried pregnant woman; two, a married couple—and the doctor told them that it would be injurious to the wife's health to have a child, and also injurious to her health to use the most efficient form of birth control; and, then third, is a physician who is under indictment, or was, at the time of this complaint.

MRS. WEDDINGTON: The physician intervened after the order was entered granting Jane Roe a three judge court. And he intervened, again, asking only that future prosecution under the law be enjoined. . . . As to— there is an allegation that the question is moot since the woman [Jane Roe-Norma McCorvey] has now had—has carried the pregnancy to term. And I think it is important to realize that there are several important aspects in which this case differs from the case that the Court might usually be presented.

First, the case is different in the nature of the interest which is involved, and in the extent to which personal determination is undermined by this statute—the effect that it has on women. Second, it is unique in the type of injury that is presented. Certainly there are some injuries that can be compensated, and most last over a sufficient period of time for the courts to litigate the interest. But in this case, a progressing pregnancy does not suspend itself in order to give the courts time to act. Certainly Jane Roe brought her suit as soon as she knew she was pregnant. As soon as she had sought an abortion, and been denied, she came to Federal court. She came on behalf of a class of women. And I don't think there's any question but that women in Texas continue to desire abortions, and to seek them outside our State. There was an absence of any other remedy, and without the ability to litigate her claim—as a pregnant woman who came seeking relief and who was affected by the time required by the Federal process; not because of any infirmity in her own attempt to litigate her interests—this will, in fact, be a case certainly presenting a substantial Federal question, and yet evading review in the future.

I think the third way in which it is unique is, as I stated, the fact that this is the only forum available to these women. They have no other way to litigate their interests.

THE COURT: Does that mean that there is no possibility of getting a declaratory judgment under Texas law?

MRS. WEDDINGTON: Yes, Your Honor. Declaratory judgements in the State of Texas are limited to the situation where property rights are involved. And we also have a very unusual situation in Texas, where we have two concurrent jurisdictions, one the civil and one the criminal. And even—there are some cases which indicate that our State Supreme Court would not have the ability to mandamus any of the criminal prosecution officers because the Texas Court of Criminal Appeals has jurisdiction as to all criminal matters in the State of Texas. So, even if the woman had been able to bring a declaratory judgment—which she couldn't—she couldn't have gotten any sort of relief against future prosecutions. And it was exactly the absence of the court granting an injunction against future prosecutions which has resulted in the irreparable injuries these women have suffered.

In Texas, the woman is the victim. The State cannot deny the effect that this law has on the women in Texas. Certainly there are problems regarding even the use of contraception. Abortion now, for a woman, is safer than childbirth. In the absence of abortions—or, legal medically safe abortions—women often resort to the illegal abortions, which certainly carry risks of death, all the side effects such as severe infections, permanent sterility, all the complications that result. And, in fact, if the woman is unable to get either a legal abortion or an illegal abortion in our State, she can do a self-abortion, which is certainly, perhaps, by far the most dangerous. And that is no crime. . . .

Texas, for example, it appears to us, would not allow any relief at all, even in situations where the mother would suffer perhaps serious physical and mental harm. There is certainly a great question about it. If the pregnancy would result in the birth of a deformed or defective child, she has no relief. Regardless of the circumstances of conception, whether it was because of rape, incest, whether she is extremely immature, she has no relief.

I think it's without question that pregnancy to a woman can completely disrupt her life. Whether she's unmarried; whether she's pursuing an education; whether she's pursuing a career; whether she has family problems; all of the problems of personal and family life, for a woman, are bound up in the problem of abortion.

For example, in our State there are many schools where a woman is forced to quit if she becomes pregnant. In the City of Austin that is true. A woman, if she becomes pregnant, and if in high school, must drop out of [the] regular education process. And that's true of some colleges in our State. In the matter of employment, she often is forced to quit at an early point in her pregnancy. She has no provision for maternity leave. She has—she cannot get unemployment compensation under our laws, because the laws hold that she is not eligible for employment, being pregnant, and therefore is eligible for no unemployment compensation. At the same time, she can get no welfare to help her at a time when she has no unemployment compensation and she's not eligible for any help in getting a job to provide for herself.

There is no duty for employers to rehire women if they must drop out to carry a pregnancy to term. And, of course, this is especially hard on the many women in Texas who are heads of their own households and must provide for their already existing children. And, obviously, the responsibility of raising a child is a most serious one, and at times an emotional investment that must be made, cannot be denied.

So, a pregnancy to a woman is perhaps one of the most determinative aspects of her life. It disrupts her body. It disrupts her education. It disrupts her employment. And it often disrupts her entire family life. And we feel that, because of the impact on the woman, this certainly—in as far as there are any rights which are fundamental—is a matter which is of such fundamental and basic concern to the woman involved that she should be allowed to make the choice as to whether to continue or to terminate her pregnancy.

I think the question is equally serious for the physicians of our State. They are seeking to practice medicine in what they consider the highest methods of practice. We have affidavits in the back of our brief from each of the heads of public—of heads of obstetrics and gynecology departments from each of our public medical schools in Texas. And each of them points out that they were willing and interested to immediately begin to formulate methods of providing care and services for women who are pregnant and do not desire to continue the pregnancy. They were stopped cold in their efforts, even with the declaratory judgement, because of the DA's position that they would continue to prosecute.

THE COURT: Mrs. Weddington, so far on the merits, you've told us about the important impact of this law, and you made a very eloquent policy argument against it. And I trust you are going to get to what provisions of the Constitution you rely on. Sometimes the Court—we would like to, sometimes—but we cannot here be involved simply with matters of policy, as you know.

MRS. WEDDINGTON: Your Honors, in the lower court, as I'm sure you're aware, the court held that the right to determine whether or not to continue a pregnancy rested upon the Ninth Amendment—which, of course, reserves those rights not specifically enumerated to the Government, to the people. I think it is important to note, in a law review article recently submitted to the Court and distributed among counsel by Professor Cyril Means, Jr., entitled "The Phoenix of Abortional Freedom," that at the time the Constitution was adopted there was no common law prohibition against abortions; that they were available to the women of this country.

Certainly, under the *Griswold* decision, it appears that the members of the Court in that case were obviously divided as to the specific constitutional framework of the right which they held to exist in the *Griswold* decision. I'm a little reluctant to say what the Court was not in agreement on. I do feel that it is—that the Ninth Amendment is an appropriate place for the freedom to rest. I think the Fourteenth Amendment is equally an appropriate place, under the rights of persons to life, liberty, and the pursuit of happiness. I think that in as far as "liberty" is meaningful, that liberty to these women would mean liberty from being forced to continue the unwanted pregnancy.

THE COURT: You're relying, in essence, in this branch of the argument simply on the due process clause, equal protection clause of the Fourteenth Amendment?

MRS. WEDDINGTON: We had originally brought this suit alleging both the due process clause, equal protection clause, and the Ninth Amendment, and a variety of others.

THE COURT: And anything else that might obtain.

MRS. WEDDINGTON: Yeah, right.

Since that District Court found that right to reside in the Ninth Amendment, we pointed our attention in the brief to that particular aspect of the Constitution. But I think we would not presume—I do feel that in-so-much as members of the Court have said that the Ninth Amendment applies to rights reserved to the people, and those which were most important—and certainly this is—that the Ninth Amendment is the appropriate place insofar as the Court has said that life, liberty, and the pursuit of happiness involve the most fundamental things of people; that this matter is one of these most fundamental matters. I think, in as far as the Court has said that there is a penumbra that exists to encompass the entire purpose of the Constitution, I think one of the purposes of the Constitution was to guarantee to individuals the right to determine the course of their own lives. Insofar as there was, perhaps, no compelling state interest—and we allege there is none in this case—that, there again, that the right fits within the framework of the previous decisions of this Court.

THE COURT: What is the asserted State interest? Is there any legislative history on this statute?

MRS. WEDDINGTON: No, sir, Your Honor. No, sir, there is not. The only legislative history, of course, is that which is found in other states—which as been pointed out to the Court before—and, as Professor Means points out again, that these statutes were adopted for the health of the mother. Certainly, the Texas courts have referred to the woman as being the victim, and they have never referred to anyone else as being the victim.

Concepts have certainly changed. I think it's important to realize that in Texas self-abortion is no crime. The woman is guilty of no crime, even though she seeks out the doctor; even though she consents; even though she participates; even though she pays for the procedures. She, again, is guilty of no crime whatsoever. . . .

Obviously, in our State, the offense is not murder. It is an abortion, which carries a significantly lesser offense. . . . Even though the State, in its brief, points out the development of the fetus in an eight-week period, the same States does not require any death certificate, or any formalities of birth. The product of such a conception would be handled merely as a pathological specimen.

THE COURT: And the statute doesn't make any distinctions based upon at what period of pregnancy the abortion is performed?

MRS. WEDDINGTON: No, Your Honor. There is no time limit or indication of time, whatsoever. So I think—

THE COURT: Well, do you make any distinctions?

MRS. WEDDINGTON: No, sir. I do—I feel that the question of a time limit is not strictly before the Court, because of the nature of the situation in which the case is handled. Certainly I think, as a practical matter though, most of the states that do have some time limit indicated still permit abortions beyond the time limit for specified reasons, usually where the health of the mother is involved.

THE COURT: What's your constitutional position there?

MRS. WEDDINGTON: As to a time limit—

THE COURT: What about whatever clause of the Constitution you rest on—Ninth Amendment, due process, the general pattern penumbra—will that take you right up to the time of birth?

MRS. WEDDINGTON: It is our position that the freedom involved is that of a woman to determine whether or not to continue a pregnancy. Obviously I have a much more difficult time saying that the State has no interest in late pregnancy.

THE COURT: Why? What is that?

MRS. WEDDINGTON: I think that's more the emotional response to a late pregnancy, rather than it is any constitutional—

THE COURT: Emotional response by whom?

MRS. WEDDINGTON: I guess by persons considering the issue outside the legal context. I think, as far as the State—

THE COURT: Well, do you or don't you say that the constitutional—

MRS. WEDDINGTON: I would say the constitutional—

THE COURT: —right you insist on reaches up to the time of birth, or—

MRS. WEDDINGTON: The Constitution, as I read it, and as interpreted and as documented by Professor Means, attaches protection to the person at the time of birth. Those persons born are citizens. The enumeration clause, we count those people who are born. The Constitution, as I see it, gives protection to people after birth. . . .

THE COURT: All right, then I come back again. If we're left only with the ladies' action, are you suggesting that the declaratory relief they already obtained was not enough, because that doesn't help terminate the pregnancy?

MRS. WEDDINGTON: Because they are still subject to the irreparable injury, and have no adequate State remedy. And, if they are not able to continue to litigate their interest in this situation, any time there was any prosecution pending against anyone in the State, at any point in the appeal—for example, the *Thompson* case was filed in 1968. It's been decided now in our State courts. It's on appeal, or it will be appealed here, I think. And, certainly if they cannot litigate their interests while there is a prosecution pending against the doctor, they will—in many instances where a statute—

THE COURT: Well, I suppose the answer is that if there's a prosecution against the doctor, there's not going to be any doctor that's going to be available. Is that it?

MRS. WEDDINGTON: Yes. They cannot even decide to take the risk for themselves under the declaratory judgment. They must rely on another person to take that risk. But, certainly, the doctor raised not only his own rights, but the rights of his patients. And those same patients are suffering the same sort of irreparable injury that the original plaintiffs are suffering. . . .

THE COURT: Does the Texas law in other areas of the law give rights to unborn children—in the areas of trusts, estates and wills, or any of the other—

MRS. WEDDINGTON: No, Your Honor, only—only if they are born alive. We have—the Supreme Court of Texas recently has held in one case that there is an action for prenatal injuries at any stage prior to birth, but only upon the condition that it must be born alive. The same is true of our property law. The child must be born alive. And I think there is a distinction between those children which are ultimately born; and I think it is appropriate to give them retroactive rights. But I think that's a completely different question from whether or not they had rights at the time they were still in the womb. . . .

MR. CHIEF JUSTICE BURGER: Thank you, Mrs. Weddington.

Jay Floyd, representing the state of Texas, followed Weddington to the table in front of the Supreme Court bench. He was hobbled by his own state's refusal to accept the ruling of the federal district court and by his own personal attitude toward the "women's argument" that Weddington had made at the outset of her oral presentation.

Jay Floyd, oral argument on behalf of appellee in *Roe* (ready access: *Landmark Briefs*, 75:796–806)

MR. FLOYD: Mr. Chief Justice, may it please the Court:

It's an old joke, but when a man argues against two beautiful ladies like this, they are going to have the last word.

Before I proceed to the original issue in this case—which was the propriety of the trial court grant, or denying of injunctive relief—I would like to bring to the Court's attention some grave matters concerning what has been referred to as the standing of the parties. The couple involved: they were a married couple—childless married couple. The only matter—evidence, or whatever, in the record concerning their contentions is contained in their first amended original petition. That is, that the woman would have difficulty if she became pregnant in carrying a child to childbirth. Further, that they were unprepared for parenthood.

We submit to the Court that their cause of action is strictly based upon conjecture. Will they continue the marriage? Will her health improve? Will the man be, at some time in the future, prepared or unprepared for parenthood? There is no fear of prosecution by Mary Doe. . . .

As to the unmarried pregnant female, a unique situation arises in: Is her action now moot [because she is no longer pregnant]? Of course if moot, there is no case or controversy.

THE COURT: It's a class action, wasn't it?

MR. FLOYD: It was a class action.

THE COURT: Surely you would—I suppose we could almost take judicial notice of the fact that there are, at any given time, unmarried pregnant females in the State of Texas.

MR. FLOYD: Yes, Your Honor. I would say that the only thing that would uphold her standing would be—or eliminate the mootness issue—would be whether or not this is a class action on her part. Yes, Your Honor.

The record that came up to this Court contains the amended petition of Jane Roe, an unsigned alias affidavit, and that is all. She alleges that she was pregnant on April the 10th, 1970, which is some 21 months ago. Now I think that it is—it has been recognized by the appellant's counsel that she is no longer pregnant. This Court has consistently held that the time of determination of mootness is when the hearing is before the Court. That is, the case can become moot from the hearing in the trial court until the time it reaches this Court. . . .

THE COURT: How do you suggest, if you're right, how do you—what procedure would you suggest for any pregnant female in the State of Texas ever to get any judicial consideration of this constitutional claim?

MR. FLOYD: Your Honor, let me answer your question with a statement, if I may. I do not believe it can be done. There are situations in which, of course as the Court knows, no remedy is provided. Now I think she makes her choice prior to the time she becomes pregnant. That is the time of the choice. It's like, more or less, the first three or four years of our life we don't remember anything. But, once a child is born, a woman no longer has a choice, and I think pregnancy then terminates that choice. That's when.

THE COURT: Maybe she makes her choice when she decides to live in Texas.

[Laughter] [Brackets in original.]

MR. FLOYD: May I proceed?

There is no restriction on moving. . . .

THE COURT: What is Texas' interest? What is Texas' interest in the statute?

MR. FLOYD: Mr. Justice, the *Thompson* case, which as been cited to the Court—*Thompson* v. *State*—the Court of Criminal Appeals did not decide the issue of privacy. It was not before the court; or, the right of choice issue. The . . . State Court, Court of Criminal Appeals, held that the State had a compelling interest because of the protection of fetal life—of fetal life protection. They recognized the humanness of the embryo, or the fetus, and they said we have an interest in protecting fetal life.

Whether or not that was the original intent of the statute, I have no idea.

THE COURT: Yet, Texas does not attempt to punish a woman who herself performs an abortion of herself.

MR. FLOYD: That is correct, Your Honor. And the matter has been brought to my attention: Why not punish for murder, since you are destroying what you—or what has been said to be a human being? I don't know, except that I will say this. As medical science progresses, maybe the law will progress along with it. Maybe at one time it could be possible, I suppose, statutes could be passed. Whether or not that would be constitutional or not, I don't know.

THE COURT: But we're dealing with the statute as it is. There's no state, is there, that equates abortion with murder? Or is there?

MR. FLOYD: There is none, Your Honor, except one of our statutes that if the mother dies, that the doctor shall be guilty of murder. . . .

THE COURT: The Texas statute covers the entire period of pregnancy?

MR. FLOYD: Yes, it does, Mr. Justice.

THE COURT: You're saying, in answer to my brother [Justice Thurgood] Marshall's question—what is the interest of the State in this litigation; or, even, what is its purpose, its societal purpose—your answer was, I think, relying on your opinion, the most recent opinion of the Court of Criminal Appeals in Texas, it was the protection of fetal life?

MR. FLOYD: Yes, sir.

THE COURT: And I think you also said that that was not, perhaps, its original purpose.

MR. FLOYD: Well, I'm not sure of that. I—

THE COURT: Well, it may be rather important. In a constitutional case of this kind, it becomes quite vital, sometimes, to rather precisely identify what the asserted interest of the state is. . . .

MR. FLOYD: . . . The protection of the mother, at one time, may still be the primary—but the policy considerations, Mr. Justice, would seem to me to be for the State legislature to make a decision.

THE COURT: Certainly that's true. Policy questions are for legislative and executive bodies, both in the State and Federal Governments. But we have here a constitutional question. And, in deciding it, it's important to know what the asserted interest of the State is in the enactment of this legislation.

MR. FLOYD: . . . I speak personally, if I may—I would think that even when this statute was first passed, there was some concern for the unborn fetus. . . .

THE COURT: Well, I can't quite square that most recent pronouncement with the earlier decisions of the Texas Court, that refer to the mother as the victim. Can you?

MR. FLOYD: . . . I don't think the courts have come to the conclusion that the unborn has full juristic rights—not yet. Maybe they will. I don't know. I just don't feel like they have, at the present time.

THE COURT: In the first few weeks of pregnancy?

MR. FLOYD: Sir?

THE COURT: In the first few weeks of pregnancy?

MR. FLOYD: At any time, Mr. Justice. We make no distinctions in our statute.

THE COURT: You make no distinctions whether there's life there or not?

MR. FLOYD: We say there is life from the moment of impregnation.

THE COURT: And do you have any scientific data to support that?

MR. FLOYD: Well we begin, Mr. Justice, in our brief, with the development of the human embryo, carrying it through the development of the fetus from about seven to nine days after conception.

THE COURT: Well, what about six days?

MR. FLOYD: We don't know.

THE COURT: But the statute goes all the way back to one hour?

MR. FLOYD: . . . Mr. Justice, there are unanswerable questions in this field. . . .

MR. FLOYD: Thank you.

When does the soul come into the unborn—if a person believes in a soul—I don't know. . . .

There are allegations of First Amendment rights being violated. However, I feel there is no merit—this statute does not establish any religion; nor does it prohibit anyone from practicing of any part of any religious group. . . .

As far as the freedom over one's body is concerned, this is not absolute. . . .

Now there is nothing in the United States Constitution concerning birth, contraception, or abortion. Now, the appellee does not disagree with the appellants' statement that a woman has a choice. But, as we have previously mentioned, we feel that this choice is left up to the woman prior to the time she becomes pregnant. This is the time of the choice. . . .

THE COURT: Texas doesn't grant any exemption in the case of a rape, where the woman's pregnancy has resulted from rape—either statutory or otherwise—does it?

MR. FLOYD: There is nothing in our statute about that.

Now, the procedure—

THE COURT: And such a woman wouldn't have had a choice, would she?

MR. FLOYD: The procedure—and now I'm telling the Court something that's outside the record—as I understand, the procedure when a woman is brought in after a rape, is to try to stop whatever has occurred, immediately, by the proper procedure in the hospital. Immediately she's taken there, if she reports it immediately. But no, there is nothing in the statute. . . .

MR. CHIEF JUSTICE BURGER: Mr. Floyd, your time is consumed. . . . Thank you, Mrs. Weddington. Thank you, Mr. Floyd.

This case is submitted.

With two new justices, Louis Powell and William Rehnquist, added to the Court and Justice Harry Blackmun, who was writing the opinion, asking for more time, Chief Justice Burger scheduled a second round of oral argument for Wednesday, October 11, 1972. In the next selection, Sarah Weddington recalled how she prepared for it and how it transpired.

Sarah Weddington, *A Question of Choice* (New York, 1992), 134–37

I did not know what I could say during a second presentation that would be more persuasive than the arguments I had presented during the first. I would be busy in the Fall, campaigning for myself [for the Texas legislature] and other Democratic candidates and trying to elect a pro-choice president. For weeks before the first argument I had done nothing but prepare for those thirty minutes; now squeezing in preparation time would be difficult. . . .

Linda [Coffee] and I had a deadline of September 15 to submit a short supplementary brief. . . . We reported that since the [federal] district court [in Texas] had not granted injunctive relief and so had refused to tell the [Texas] district attorney not to prosecute doctors who performed abortions, Texas physicians were still refusing to perform them. During the last nine months of 1971, a total of 1,658 women from Texas had gone to New York to obtain abortions. We mentioned that the American Bar Association House of Delegates had approved a Uniform Abortion Act, which would allow termination of pregnancy up to twenty weeks; abortion was also allowed thereafter for reasons such as rape, incest, fetal deformity, and endangerment of the mental or physical health of the woman. We cited the Rockefeller Commission on Population Growth and the American Future, which had recommended that the matter of abortion be left to the conscience of the individual concerned. . . .

Another section of the brief stressed, yet again, the fact that Texas had never treated the fetus as having the rights and dignity of a person. . . .

I set aside a few days to review and prepare for argument. . . .

The day after we arrived in D.C. the others went sightseeing while I worked on the case. I spent the morning of the tenth in the Supreme Court library, during the afternoon I participated in a moot court organized by Harriet Pilpel [counsel for the Planned Parenthood Federation of America] and Cyril Means [a New York Law School professor] for Margie Pitts Hames [counsel for Jane Doe in *Doe v. Bolton*] and me. . . . Many of the attorneys who had filed amicus briefs were present at this session to help plan strategy. Frank Susman, a well-known St. Louis attorney who was handling a challenge of the Missouri anti-abortion laws . . . also participated. Harriet commented that [a *New York Times* reporter] had suggested some members of the Court felt little sympathy with a pregnant woman, but could sympathize with the doctor; she wondered whether we should stress the medical aspects more. . . .

We considered what I should do if a justice tried to back me into a corner and get me to say things I did not want to say. The most time was spent on the subject of when life beings. We knew it would come up at the hearing. Obviously, life began once billions of years ago and has been a continuum ever since. But there are various key points of development: conception, implantation, quickening, viability, and birth, for example. The Court seemed uncomfortable with my prior [oral] argument that birth was the peg at which *legal rights* should attach, and that "when life begins" is an individual leap of faith that one can prove; people tend to say "I believe." But we could find no substantial legal peg for maintaining that rights began prior to birth. . . .

Inside, the physical grandeur of the courtroom still inspired a sense of awe in me, but this time there was no electricity to the hearing. I was expecting frequent interruptions from the justices, but there were few. When the justices did speak, it seemed it was primarily to ask if they had heard a certain word correctly or to finish my sentences. Their lack of response made me nervous, whereas the intensity of the first hearing had calmed me.

. . .

There were a few key exchanges in the second round of oral argument among Weddington, her new opponent, Texas assistant attorney general Robert Flowers, and the justices. These indicated the basic lines of division that would appear throughout the later debate over Roe.

Sarah Weddington and Robert Flowers, oral argument in *Roe*, October 11, 1972 (ready access: *Landmark Briefs*, 75:808–18)

MR. CHIEF JUSTICE BURGER: We will hear argument first of No. 70-18, *Roe* against *Wade*.

Mrs. Weddington, you may proceed whenever you're ready. . . .

MRS. WEDDINGTON: We have all the contradictions in the statute, and the way so many things that just don't make sense. If the statute was adopted for that purpose [the purpose of protecting unborn life], for example, why is the woman guilty of no crime? If the statute was adopted for that purpose, why is it that the penalty for abortion is determined by whether or not you have the woman's consent?

THE COURT: Regardless of the purpose for which the statute was originally enacted, or the purpose which keeps it on the books in Texas today, you would agree, I suppose, that one of the important factors that has to be considered in this case is what rights, if any, does the unborn fetus have?

MRS. WEDDINGTON: That's correct.

There have been two cases decided since the September 13th [1971] argument that expressly hold that a fetus has no constitutional right—one being *Byrn* v. *New York*; the other being the *Magee-Women's Hospital* case. In both situations, persons sought to bring that very question to the Court: does a fetus—in the one instance *Bryn* was a challenge to the New York Revised Statutes. The other was a situation where a person sought to prevent Magee-Women's Hospital from allowing further abortions to be done in that hospital. And, in both cases, it was held that the fetus had no constitutional rights.

Several of the briefs before this Court would also argue that this Court . . . which has allowed abortions to continue in the District of Columbia—certainly the Court would not have made that kind of decision if it felt there were any ingrained rights of the fetus within the Constitution.

There is also, of course—

THE COURT: Well, is it critical to your case that the fetus not be a person under the due process clause?

MRS. WEDDINGTON: It seems to me that it is critical, first, that we prove this is a fundamental interest on behalf of the woman, that it is a constitutional right. And, second—

THE COURT: Well, yes. But about the fetus?

MRS. WEDDINGTON: Okay.

And, second, that the State has no compelling State interest. And the State is alleging a compelling State interest in—

THE COURT: Yes. But I'm just asking you, under the Federal Constitution, is the fetus a person, for the protection of due process?

MRS. WEDDINGTON: All of the cases—the prior history of this statute—the common law history would indicate that it is not. The State has shown no—

THE COURT: Well, what about—would you lose your case if the fetus was a person?

MRS. WEDDINGTON: Then you would have a balancing of interest.

THE COURT: Well, you say you have anyway, don't you?

MRS. WEDDINGTON: Excuse me?

THE COURT: You have anyway, don't you? You're going to be balancing the rights of the mother against the rights of the fetus.

MRS. WEDDINGTON: It seems to me that you do not balance constitutional rights of one person against mere statutory rights of another.

THE COURT: You think a State interest, if it's only a statutory interest, or a constitutional interest under the State law, can never outweigh a constitutional right?

MRS. WEDDINGTON: I think—it would seem to me that—

THE COURT: So all talk of compelling State interest is beside the point. It can never be compelling enough.

MRS. WEDDINGTON: If the State could show that the fetus was a person under the Fourteenth Amendment, or under some other Amendment, or part of the Constitution, then you would have the situation of trying—you would have a State compelling interest which, in some instances, can outweigh a fundamental right. This is not the case in this particular situation.

THE COURT: Do you make any distinction between the first month, and ninth month of gestation?

MRS. WEDDINGTON: Our statute does not.

THE COURT: Do you, in your position in this case?

MRS. WEDDINGTON: We are asking, in this case, that the Court declare the statute unconstitutional; the State having proved no compelling interest at all.

There are some states that now have adopted time limits. Those have not yet been challenged. And, perhaps that question will be before this Court. Even those statutes, though, allow exceptions. Well New York, for example, says an abortion is lawful up to 24 weeks. But, even after the 24 weeks it is still lawful where there's rape or incest; where the mother's mental or physical health is involved. In other words, even after that period, it's not a hard and fast cutoff.

THE COURT: Then it's the weighing process that Mr. Justice White was referring to. Is that your position?

MRS. WEDDINGTON: The legislature, in that situation, engaged in the weighing process. And it seems to me that is has not yet been determined whether the State has the compelling interest to uphold even that kind of relation. But that's really not before the Court in this particular case. We have no time limit. There is no indication in Texas that any would be applied at any future date. You know, we just don't know that. . . .

THE COURT: Well, do I get from this, then, that your case depends primarily on the proposition that the fetus has no constitutional rights?

MRS. WEDDINGTON: It depends on saying that the woman has a fundamental constitutional right; and that the State has not proved any compelling interest for regulation in the area. Even if the Court, at some point, determined the fetus to be entitled to constitutional protection, you would still get back into the weighing of one life against another.

THE COURT: That's what's involved in this case? Weighing one life against another?

MRS. WEDDINGTON: No, Your Honor. I say that would be what would be involved, if the facts were different and the State could prove that there was a "person" for the constitutional right.

THE COURT: Well, if—if it were established that an unborn fetus is a person, with the protection of the Fourteenth Amendment, you would have almost an impossible case here, would you not?

MRS. WEDDINGTON: I would have a very difficult case. . . .

THE COURT: Could Texas constitutionally, in your view, declare that—by statute, that the fetus is a person, for all constitutional purposes, after the third month of gestation?

MRS. WEDDINGTON: I do not believe that the State legislature can determine the meaning of the Federal Constitution. It is up to this Court to make that determination. . . .

MR. CHIEF JUSTICE BURGER: Mr. Flowers?

MR. FLOWERS: Mr. Chief Justice, and may it please the Court:

. . . It is impossible for me to trace, within my allocated time, the development of the fetus from the date of conception to the date of its birth. But it is the position of the State of Texas that, upon conception, we have a human being; a person, within the concept of the Constitution of the United States, and that of Texas, also.

THE COURT: Now how should that question be decided? Is it a legal question? A constitutional question? A medical question? A philosophical question? Or, a religious question? Or what is it?

MR. FLOWERS: Your Honor, we feel that it could be best decided by a legislature, in view of the fact that they can bring before it the medical testimony—the actual people who do the research. But we do have—

THE COURT: So then it's basically a medical question?

MR. FLOWERS: From a constitutional standpoint, no, sir. I think it's fairly and squarely before this Court. We don't envy the Court for having to make this decision.

THE COURT: Do you know any case, anywhere, that's held that an un-born fetus is a person within the meaning of the Fourteenth Amendment?

MR. FLOWERS: No, sir. We can only go back to what the framers of our Constitution had in mind.

THE COURT: Well, these weren't the framers that wrote the Fourteenth Amendment. It came along much later.

MR. FLOWERS: No, sir. I understand. But the Fifth Amendment—under the Fifth Amendment, no one shall be deprived of the right to life, liberty, and property, without due process of law.

THE COURT: Yes. But then the Fourteenth Amendment defines "person" as somebody who's born, doesn't it?

MR. FLOWERS: I'm not sure about that, sir. I—

THE COURT: All right. Any person born, or naturalized in the United States.

MR. FLOWERS: Yes, sir.

THE COURT: It doesn't—that's not the definition of a "person," but that's the definition of a "citizen."

MR. FLOWERS: Your Honor, it's our position that the definition of a person is so basic, it's so fundamental, that the framers of the Constitution had not even set out to define it. We can only go to what the teachings were at the time the Constitution was framed. We have numerous listings in the brief by Mr. Joe Witherspoon—a professor at the University of Texas—that there to trace back what was in their mind when they had the "person" con-cept, when they drew up the Constitution. He quoted Blackstone here in 1765, and he observed in his *Commentaries* that: "Life. This right is inherent by nature in every individual, and exists even before the child is born." . . .

THE COURT: Mr. Flowers, when you quote Blackstone, is it not true that in Blackstone's time abortion was not a felony?

MR. FLOWERS: That's true, Your Honor. But my point there was to see the thinking of the framers of the Constitution, from the people they learned from, and the general attitudes of the times.

THE COURT: Well, I think—I'm just wondering if there isn't basic incon-sistency there. And let me go back to something else that you said. Is it . . . true that the medical profession itself is not in agreement as to when life begins?

MR. FLOWERS: I think that's true, sir. But, from a layman's standpoint, medically speaking, we would say that at the moment of conception from the chromosomes, every potential that anybody in this room has is present —from the moment of conception.

THE COURT: But then you're speaking of potential of right.

MR. FLOWERS: Yes, sir.

THE COURT: With which everyone can agree.

MR. FLOWERS: On the seventh day, I think that the heart, in some form, starts beating. On the 20th day, practically all the facilities are there that you and I have, Your Honor. . . .

THE COURT: Well, if you're correct that the fetus is a person, then . . . the State would have great trouble permitting an abortion, would it?

MR. FLOWERS: Yes, sir.

THE COURT: In any circumstances?

MR. FLOWERS: It would, yes, sir.

THE COURT: To save the life of a mother, or her health, or anything else?

MR. FLOWERS: Well, there would be the balancing of the two lives, and I think that—

THE COURT: Well, what would you choose? Would you choose to kill the innocent one, or what?

MR. FLOWERS: Well, in our statute, the State did choose that way, Your Honor. . . .

Gentlemen, we feel that the concept of a fetus being within the concept of a person, within the framework of the United States Constitution and the Texas Constitution, is an extremely fundamental thing.

THE COURT: Of course, if you're right about that, you can sit down, you've won your case.

MR. FLOWERS: Your Honor—

THE COURT: Except insofar as, maybe, the Texas abortion law presently goes too far in allowing abortions.

MR. FLOWERS: Yes, sir. That's exactly right. We feel that this is the only question, really, that this Court has to answer. We have a—

THE COURT: Do you think the case is over for you? You've lost your case, then, if the fetus or the embryo is not a person? Is that it?

MR. FLOWERS: Yes, sir, I would say so. . . .

THE COURT: You see, that's the reason I asked you at the beginning, within what framework should this question be decided? Should it be a theological one—

MR. FLOWERS: Yes, sir.

THE COURT: —a philosophical one, or a medical one. Or, that we could find here dealing with—

MR. FLOWERS: I think, Your Honor, that the Court—

THE COURT: —the judicial meaning of it.

MR. FLOWERS: I wish I could answer that. I believe that the Court must take these—the medical research—and apply it to our Constitution the best they can. I said I'm without envy of the burden that the Court has. I think that possibly we have an opportunity to make one of the worst mistakes here that we've ever made, from the—I'm sorry.

THE COURT: But there's no medical testimony that backs up your statement that it goes from inception, is there? . . .

Is there any medical testimony of any kind that says that a fetus is a person at the time of inception?

MR. FLOWERS: The date of conception until the day of—yes, sir. . . .

THE COURT: . . . I want you to give me a medical, recognizable medical writing of any kind that says that at the time of conception the fetus is a person.

MR. FLOWERS: I do not believe that I could give that to you, without researching through the briefs that have been filed in this case, Your Honor. I'm not sure that I could give it to you after research. . . .

THE COURT: I didn't think so.

MR. FLOWERS: You're entirely right there. But I find no way that I know that any court or any legislature or any doctor anywhere can say that here is the dividing line. Here is not a life; and here is a life, after conception. Perhaps it would be better left to that legislature. There they have the facilities to have some type of medical testimony brought before them, and the opinion of the people who are being governed by it.

THE COURT: Well, if you're right that an unborn fetus is a person, then you can't leave it to the legislature to play fast and loose dealing with that person. In other words, if you're correct, in your basic submission that an unborn fetus is a person, then abortion laws such as that which New York has are grossly unconstitutional, isn't it?

MR. FLOWERS: That's right, yes.

THE COURT: Allowing the killing of people.

MR. FLOWERS: Yes, sir. . . .

MR. CHIEF JUSTICE BURGER: Thank you, Mrs. Weddington. Thank you, Mr. Flowers.

The case is submitted.

. . .

In their twice-a-week "conference" to discuss the cases before them, the Supreme Court justices present their views in descending order of seniority, with the chief justice speaking first. The notes on the conferences after the two oral hearings in Roe *were preserved in the notes of Justices William O. Douglas and William Brennan. The notes suggest the issues that most concerned each justice and how, at the outset of deliberations, the justices saw those issues.*

The Supreme Court in Conference, 1940–1985, edited by Del Dickson (New York, 2001), 804–12

CONFERENCE OF DECEMBER 16, 1971

[CHIEF JUSTICE] BURGER: Jane Roe is unmarried and pregnant. She does not claim health problems—she just doesn't want the baby. This is a class action. Another petitioner, the doctor, is under indictment. The married couple have no children, but might suffer if she had any. The district court dismissed the marrieds for lack of standing, but gave Jane Roe standing and a declaratory judgment holding the act unconstitutional. The doctor also got standing and declaratory relief. Injunctive relief was denied. As to the doctor, the act was held too vague. As to the doctor, the district court should have restrained itself. *Vuitch* [an earlier case in which the Supreme Court found a D.C. abortion statute not vague or overboard] disposes of his due process claim. *Younger* [an earlier case in which the Court declined to order injunctive relief in a state's criminal proceeding] forecloses the doctor's relief, and he has no standing on behalf of the women. As to the married couple, their interests are too speculative for standing. The unmarried girl, Jane Roe, has standing. She can't be prosecuted if the state gives her no remedy. Texas has no declaratory relief. Abstention [the federal court staying out of the matter] would be dubious. On mootness, Jane Roe still has standing, although she gave birth. She still represents a class. There is no *Younger* problem as to Roe. The declaratory judgment without an injunction is tantamount to a mere advisory opinion. So she is entitled to an injunction if the statute is unconstitutional. The balance here is between the state's interest in protecting fetal life and a woman's interest in not having children. Does an unmarried woman also represent married women? If so, what of a husband's interest where he won't consent? But I can't find the Texas statute unconstitutional, although it is certainly archaic and obsolete. There is nothing vague about it. Doctors in Texas perform abortions to protect the health of the mother. The law is not enforced as to rape and incest. Rule 23 and class are not treated by district court.

DOUGLAS: The Texas abortion statute is unconstitutional. This is basically a medical and psychiatric problem. The law is vague and unclear. It gives a licensed physician no immunity for good faith abortions. There is no standard for doctors—the law is too vague at that level. This statute goes only part way. All parties have standing to get a declaration of rights, irrespective of injunctions. A declaratory judgment does not collide with *Younger*. I reverse [the lower federal court refusal to issue the injunction].

BRENNAN: The Texas act does not allow an abortion even for a twelve-year-old. Jane Roe has standing. The act is infirm. Perhaps she was raped. I am willing to say that the law is "vague." Declaratory relief is O.K. . . . I would go beyond what the district court did. I reverse. All parties have standing. I would reverse on standing and affirm in other aspects.

STEWART: Standing is not important. Issues of standing ought not confuse this if we agree that the unmarried girl has standing to get a judgment on the merits. She clearly has standing. . . . The married couple probably has standing. The district court did not have to issue an injunction on the merits—it was not an error in not entering an injunction. I agree with Bill Douglas on the merits. I reverse.

WHITE: I agree with Potter on all of the preliminaries, but I take the other side on the merits. They want the right to get rid of a child apart from health reasons. They want us to say that women have this choice under the Ninth Amendment—a privacy argument. Does the state have the police power to protect a fetus that has life in it as opposed to the desire of the mother? I am not at rest on the merits.

STEWART: The state can legislate in this field. They can require that only doctors can do this, they can decide that after a certain period of pregnancy that women can't have abortions, and so forth.

MARSHALL: I'll go along with Douglas and Brennan, but the time problem concerns me. I do not see what interest the state has in abortion in the early stages after conception, but why can't a state prohibit abortions after a certain stage? If a fetus comes out breathing and you kill it, it is murder. "Liberty" covers almost any right to have things done to your body. I would turn on this "liberty" under the Fourteenth Amendment as a constitutional base. I affirm.

BLACKMUN: On standing, Roe has it. It is then irrelevant whether the married couple of the doctor have it. *Samuels* bars the doctor. On the merits, can a state outlaw all abortions? If you accept fetal life, there is a strong argument that it can. If there is life from conception on, the state could ban all abortions unless the right of mother to life and health are opposed to the fetus. There are opposing interests—the right of the mother to life and mental and physical health, the right of parents in case of rape, by the state in case of incest. There is no absolute right to do what you will with your body. Jane Roe has Fourteenth Amendment rights here. This statute is a poor statute. It does not go as far as it should in some respects, and at the same time it also impinges too far on her Ninth Amendment rights. It is over-narrow. The Texas act does not go far enough to protect doctors. It impinges on Jane Roe's constitutional rights. I would affirm on the declaratory judgment. I could go so far as to grant an injunction. The

Texas and Georgia laws are in good contrast. Georgia has fine statute. The district court ruined the statute in Georgia.

[On] *Doe v. Bolton*[:]

BURGER: We don't have to worry about standing if any one of the plaintiffs has standing. The district court said that only Mary Doe had standing. If she has standing, then relief can be granted to all. I think that there was standing as to the pregnant girl. She was twenty-seven weeks pregnant. I do not agree with this carving up of the statute by the three-judge court. The district court should have abstained. The state has a duty to protect fetal life at some stage, but we are not confronted with that question here. No reasons were given for striking parts of the act. The district court made a poor statute out of a good statute. I would hold this act constitutional. It has more limitations than the Texas one.

DOUGLAS: This is a much better statute than Texas's. I don't know how this statute operates. Is it weighted on the side of only those who can afford this? What about the poor? I am inclined to remand to the district court for a hearing on whether in operation the system is discriminatory.

MARSHALL: In urban centers the scheme may work, but in rural areas there are no Negro doctors. I agree with Bill Douglas.

BRENNAN: The act may not cover all the situations where a doctor might order an abortion. The district court did not deal with Bill Douglas' problem or with the veto power that two doctors have over one. I would not reach the point that the Ninth Amendment right is absolute. The district court is right on (a) and (b), but I think that the rest is bad. I will affirm as far as it goes, and would go further to strike down the three-doctor thing as too restrictive.

STEWART: I agree with Bill Brennan.

WHITE: It is a hard case. The state can protect the unborn child. This plaintiff had no problem getting the case reviewed. There is no burdensome procedure. The state has the power to declare abortions illegal. I think that the state has struck the right balance here, and I reverse [the lower federal court's declaratory judgment that the statute was unconstitutional].

MARSHALL: I affirm. I am in between Bill Douglas and Bill Brennan.

BLACKMUN: Medically, this statute is perfectly workable. The doctor has standing here, too. On procedure, the residence requirement does not bother me. The right to cross-examine the doctor is a spurious one. I see this kind of act operating well in a rural area of Minnesota. Some cases are borderline, and doctors like the security of a joint board. I would like to see an opinion that recognizes the opposing interest of fetal life and the mother's interest in health and happiness. This act strikes a balance that is good. Some of these boards operate without cost to the patient. I would be perfectly willing to paint some standards and remand for findings on Bill Douglas's points—does it operate to deny equal protection by discriminating against the poor? I am sympathetic to psychiatric people. We should try to provide standards.

WHITE: Equal protection for those on medicare is a real issue, and I am willing to have a hearing. I am not sure, however, that equal protection is here.

[DOUGLAS: *In summary:* Douglas, Brennan, Stewart, and Marshall agreed that a state abortion law could require all abortions to be performed by a licensed physician, that a woman's psychological problems, as well as her health problems, must be considered and that some period must be prescribed protecting fetal life.]

CONFERENCE OF OCTOBER 13, 1972

Roe v. Wade & Doe v. Bolton

BURGER: The statute is bad in Texas. It is too restrictive, but I am not sure on whether it fails for vagueness. But a state cannot by criminal statute restrict abortions to save a life. I reverse. On the Georgia case, the act is much more complex. The state has a right to legislate in this area. Many operations are more serious than abortions. Is there a fetal life that is entitled to protection? In *Vuitch* we gave some standards. Fetal life is entitled to protection at some point.

DOUGLAS: I reverse on Texas. I agree with the Chief Justice. I also agree with Harry in his memo, modifying the three-judge court judgments.

BRENNAN: I am with Harry on his memo.

STEWART: I am in the same position as last term, but I think that a fetus should not be declared a person. The Connecticut and New York cases both deal with it. A fetus is not a person, although that does not mean that a fetus has no right or can't be given them by the state. I cannot say that the Texas law is vague in light of *Vuitch*. I like John Newman's reasoning in his opinion for the three-judge court in the Connecticut case. I cannot rest on the Ninth Amendment at all. This is a Fourteenth Amendment right, as John Harlan said in *Griswold*. Defining "person" is a constitutional question, not a theological one.

WHITE: What is a woman's right? It is in the Fourteenth Amendment. In

Georgia, a woman has rights—life, liberty, and health are included. We should not hold that a fetus is a "person" for purposes of the Fourteenth Amendment. But this does not end the case. We have to weigh state interests against constitutional rights. Some state interests, whether constitutional or not, can override federal rights. Some federal rights are overriden by state laws—e.g., some First Amendment rights. I am not going to second guess state legislatures in striking the balance in favor of abortion laws.

On weighing the rights of the mother versus the fetus, there is an overbreadth problem in these cases. Would personal convenience of the mother be sufficient? I think not. Unless you can say that there is no conceivable reason that the state can refute, I don't see how we can strike these statutes down on their face. So these acts are not void on their faces. Why can't a state at least require, after a certain period of gestation, no abortion but only a caesarian operation for women who rest solely on convenience? No women in these cases assert an injury to life or health. I affirm in the Georgia case. On Texas, I pass. I would not go on vagueness in Texas.

MARSHALL: In Texas, a woman who aborts herself is in the clear. No doctor would perform an abortion when the case is an advanced one. I agree on the fetus point. I would reverse in Texas. I affirm in part in Georgia.

BLACKMUN: I stand by what I wrote last term. I have not changed from where I was last Spring.

[DOUGLAS: He recites a Minneapolis paper saying our vote was 5-2 later term, with Burger putting the measure in for reargument.] [Brackets in original.] I would prefer to make the Georgia case the lead case. I have revised both the Texas and Georgia opinions of last term. I stand by jurisdiction. The direct appeal is here, and there is standing both by the wife and by the doctors. The case is not moot. I want to put in the history of abortion [in my opinion for the Court]. I rest on the Fourteenth, not the Ninth Amendment. There is a point where other interests are at stake, where the state can regulate.

I would hold invalid the requirement of JCAH [panel of doctors] approval. I would do away with the licensed hospital requirement, although states can have abortions performed in a licensed facility. The residence requirement goes too far. Requiring the approval of many doctors is bad. The Texas act is vague. Vagueness is not involved in Georgia. *Vuitch* can be reconciled. Texas, since last spring, has upheld the Texas act. I will demolish the Texas act, but I will make Georgia the leading opinion. If the Texas act falls, abortion laws in a majority of our states will fall. We might hold the mandate for awhile—I want to avoid complete disorganization.

POWELL: I am basically in accord with Harry's position, except that I am concerned about allowing doctors to rely on economic or other factors except as related to health. I think that Texas should be the lead case, and I would not go on vagueness grounds but on basic grounds.

BLACKMUN: I would be willing to bypass the vagueness issue and put the Texas and Georgia cases in that order.

REHNQUIST: I agree with Byron.

· · ·

As Justice Blackmun prepared his opinion, he paid special attention to the views of leading medical authorities. Not only were the views of these men and women represented in the amicus briefs, but the American Medical Association (AMA) had also gone on record in 1970 favoring deference to the doctor-patient relationship in allowing abortion in the early stages of pregnancy, reversing many years of limiting abortion to cases in which the health of the woman was at stake.

AMA House of Delegates, *Proceedings*, June 1970, 220

Whereas, Abortion, like any other medical procedure, should not be performed when contrary to the best interests of the patient since good medical practice requires due consideration for the patient's welfare and not mere acquiescence to the patient's demand; and

Whereas, The standards of sound clinical judgment, which, together with informed patient consent should be determinative according to the merits of each individual case; therefore be it

RESOLVED, That abortion is a medical procedure and should be performed only by a duly licensed physician and surgeon in an accredited hospital acting only after consultation with two other physicians chosen because of their professional competency and in conformance with standards of good medical practice and the Medical Practice Act of his State; and be it further

RESOLVED, That no physician or other professional personnel shall be compelled to perform any act which violates his good medical judgment. Neither physician, hospital, nor hospital personnel shall be required to perform any act violative of personally-held moral principles. In these circumstances good medical practice requires only that the physician or other professional personnel withdraw from the case so long as the withdrawal is consistent with good medical practice.

The Principles of Medical Ethics of the AMA do not prohibit a physician from performing an abortion that is performed in accordance with good medical practice and under circumstances that do not violate the laws of the community in which he practices.

In the matter of abortions, as of any other medical procedure, the Judicial Council becomes involved whenever there is alleged violation of the Principles of Medical Ethics as established by the House of Delegates.

· · ·

The AMA position found a prominent place in Blackmun's opinion; one may ask if he was too much influenced by the professional interests of doctors, as opposed to women's claims or the argument of the state. Note that Blackmun was concerned with fundamental rights derived from the Due Process Clause of the Fourteenth Amendment. States could pass laws limiting those fundamental rights when the state could establish its "compelling interest" in such limitations. The justices of the Supreme Court had already developed a "test" for such interests based upon a "strict scrutiny" of the statute.

Roe et al. v. Wade, 410 U.S. 113 (1973)

Mr. Justice Blackmun delivered the opinion of the Court.

This Texas federal appeal and its Georgia companion, *Doe* v. *Bolton* . . . present constitutional challenges to state criminal abortion legislation. The Texas statutes under attack here are typical of those that have been in effect in many States for approximately a century. The Georgia statutes, in contrast, have a modern cast and are a legislative product that, to an extent at least, obviously reflects the influences of recent attitudinal change, of advancing medical knowledge and techniques, and of new thinking about an old issue.

We forthwith acknowledge our awareness of the sensitive and emotional nature of the abortion controversy, of the vigorous opposing views, even among physicians, and of the deep and seemingly absolute convictions that the subject inspires. One's philosophy, one's experiences, one's exposure to the raw edges of human existence, one's religious training, one's attitudes toward life and family and their values, and the moral standards one establishes and seeks to observe, are all likely to influence and to color one's thinking and conclusions about abortion.

In addition, population growth, pollution, poverty, and racial overtones tend to complicate and not to simplify the problem.

Our task, of course, is to resolve the issue by constitutional measurement, free of emotion and of predilection. We seek earnestly to do this, and, because we do, we have inquired into, and in this opinion place some emphasis upon, medical and medical-legal history and what that history reveals about man's attitudes toward the abortion procedure over the centuries. . . . The Texas statutes that concern us here make it a crime to "procure an abortion," as therein defined, or to attempt one, except with respect to "an abortion procured or attempted by medical advice for the purpose of saving the life of the mother." Similar statutes are in existence in a majority of the States. . . .

Roe alleged that she was unmarried and pregnant; that she wished to terminate her pregnancy by an abortion "performed by a competent, licensed physician, under safe, clinical conditions"; that she was unable to get a "legal" abortion in Texas because her life did not appear to be threatened by the continuation of her pregnancy; and that she could not afford to travel to another jurisdiction in order to secure a legal abortion under safe conditions. She claimed that the Texas statutes were unconstitutionally vague and that they abridged her right of personal privacy, protected by the First, Fourth, Fifth, Ninth, and Fourteenth Amendments. By an amendment to her complaint Roe purported to sue "on behalf of herself and all other women" similarly situated.

James Hubert Hallford, a licensed physician, sought and was granted leave to intervene in Roe's action. In his complaint he alleged that he had been arrested previously for violations of the Texas abortion statutes and that two such prosecutions were pending against him. He described conditions of patients who came to him seeking abortions, and he claimed that for many cases he, as a physician, was unable to determine whether they fell within or outside the exception recognized by Article 1196 [of the Texas law]. He alleged that, as a consequence, the statutes were vague and uncertain, in violation of the Fourteenth Amendment, and that they violated his own and his patients' rights to privacy in the doctor-patient relationship and his own right to practice medicine, rights he claimed were guaranteed by the First, Fourth, Fifth, Ninth, and Fourteenth Amendments.

John and Mary Doe, a married couple, filed a companion complaint to that of Roe. They also named the District Attorney as defendant, claimed like constitutional deprivations, and sought declaratory and injunctive relief. . . .

A. *Jane Roe*. Despite the use of the pseudonym, no suggestion is made that Roe is a fictitious person. For purposes of her case, we accept as true, and as established, her existence; her pregnant state, as of the inception of her suit in March 1970 and as late as May 21 of that year when she filed an alias affidavit with the District Court; and her inability to obtain a legal abortion in Texas.

Viewing Roe's case as of the time of its filing and thereafter until as late as May, there can be little dispute that it then presented a case or controversy and that, wholly apart from the class aspects, she, as a pregnant single woman thwarted by the Texas criminal abortion laws, had standing to challenge those statutes. . . .

The appellee notes, however, that the record does not disclose that Roe was pregnant at the time of the District Court hearing on May 22, 1970, or on the following June 17 when the court's opinion and judgment were filed. . . . The usual rule in federal cases is that an actual controversy must exist at stages of appellate or certiorari review, and not simply at the date the action is initiated. . . . But when, as here, pregnancy is a significant fact in the litigation, the normal 266-day human gestation period is so short that the pregnancy will come to term before the usual appellate process is complete. If that termination makes a case moot, pregnancy litigation seldom will survive much beyond the trial stage, and appellate review will be effectively denied. Our law should not be that rigid. . . .

B. *Dr. Hallford*. The doctor's position is different. . . . Although he stated that he has been arrested in the past for violating the State's abortion laws, he makes no allegation of any substantial and immediate threat to any federally protected right that cannot be asserted in his defense against the state prosecutions. . . . The District Court erred when it granted declaratory relief to Dr. Hallford instead of refraining from so doing. . . .

C. *The Does*. In view of our ruling as to Roe's standing in her case, the issue of the Does' standing in their case has little significance. The claims they assert are essentially the same as those of Roe, and they attack the same statutes. . . . Their alleged injury rests on possible future contraceptive failure, possible future pregnancy, possible future unpreparedness for parenthood, and possible future impairment of health. Any one or more of these several possibilities may not take place and all may not combine. In the Does' estimation, these possibilities might have some real or imagined impact upon their marital happiness. But we are not prepared to say that the bare allegation of so indirect an injury is sufficient to present an actual case or controversy. . . .

The principal thrust of appellant's attack on the Texas statutes is that they improperly invade a right, said to be possessed by the pregnant woman, to choose to terminate her pregnancy. Appellant would discover this right in the concept of personal "liberty" embodied in the Fourteenth Amendment's Due Process Clause; or in personal, marital, familial, and sexual privacy said to be protected by the Bill of Rights or its penumbras, see *Griswold* v. *Connecticut* . . . or among those rights reserved to the people by the Ninth Amendment. . . .

It is . . . apparent that at common law, at the time of the adoption of our Constitution, and throughout the major portion of the 19th century, abortion was viewed with less disfavor than under most American statutes currently in effect. Phrasing it another way, a woman enjoyed a substantially broader right to terminate a pregnancy than she does in most States today. At least with respect to the early stage of pregnancy, and very possibly without such a limitation, the opportunity to make this choice was present in this country well into the 19th century. Even later, the law continued for some time to treat less punitively an abortion procured in early pregnancy.

. . . The anti-abortion mood prevalent in this country in the late 19th century was shared by the medical profession. Indeed, the attitude of the profession may have played a significant role in the enactment of stringent criminal abortion legislation during that period. . . .

Except for periodic condemnation of the criminal abortionist, no further formal AMA action took place until 1967. In that year, the Committee on Human Reproduction urged the adoption of a stated policy of opposition to induced abortion, except when there is "documented medical evidence" of a threat to the health or life of the mother, or that the child "may be born with incapacitating physical deformity or mental deficiency," or that a pregnancy "resulting from legally established statutory or forcible rape or incest may constitute a threat to the mental or physical health of the patient." . . . This recommendation was adopted by the House of Delegates. . . .

On June 25, 1970, the House of Delegates adopted preambles and most of the resolutions proposed by the reference committee. The preambles emphasized "the best interests of the patient," "sound clinical judgment," and "informed patient consent," in contrast to "mere acquiescence to the patient's demand." The resolutions asserted that abortion is a medical procedure that should be performed by a licensed physician in an accredited hospital only after consultation with two other physicians and in conformity with state law, and that no party to the procedure should be required to violate personally held moral principles. . . .

. . . The Constitution does not explicitly mention any right of privacy. In a line of decisions, however, going back perhaps as far as . . . 1891, the Court has recognized that a right of personal privacy, or a guarantee of certain areas or zones of privacy, does exist under the Constitution. . . . This right of privacy, whether it be founded in the Fourteenth Amendment's concept of personal liberty and restrictions upon state action, as we feel it is, or, as the District Court determined, in the Ninth Amendment's reservation of rights to the people, is broad enough to encompass a woman's decision whether or not to terminate her pregnancy.

The detriment that the State would impose upon the pregnant woman by denying this choice altogether is apparent. Specific and direct harm medically diagnosable even in early pregnancy may be involved. Maternity, or additional offspring, may force upon the woman a distressful life and future. Psychological harm may be imminent. Mental and physical health may be taxed by child care. There is also the distress, for all concerned, associated with the unwanted child, and there is the problem of bringing a child into a family already unable, psychologically and otherwise, to care for it. In other cases, as in this one, the additional difficulties and continuing stigma of unwed motherhood may be involved. All these are factors the woman and her responsible physician necessarily will consider in consultation.

. . . On the basis of elements such as these, appellant and some *amici* argue that the woman's right is absolute and that she is entitled to terminate her pregnancy at whatever time, in whatever way, and for whatever reason she alone chooses. With this we do not agree.

Appellant's arguments that Texas either has no valid interest at all in regulating the abortion decision, or no interest strong enough to support any limitation upon the woman's sole determination, are unpersuasive. The Court's decisions recognizing a right of privacy also acknowledge that some state regulation in areas protected by that right is appropriate. As noted above, a State may properly assert important interests in safeguarding health, in maintaining medical standards, and in protecting potential life. At some point in pregnancy, these respective interests become sufficiently compelling to sustain regulation of the factors that govern the abortion decision. The privacy right involved, therefore, cannot be said to be absolute. . . .

We, therefore, conclude that the right of personal privacy includes the abortion decision, but that this right is not unqualified and must be considered against important state interests in regulation. . . .

Where certain "fundamental rights" are involved, the Court has held that regulation limiting these rights may be justified only by a "compelling state interest," . . . and that legislative enactments must be narrowly drawn to express only the legitimate state interests at stake.

The appellee and certain *amici* argue that the fetus is a "person" within the language and meaning of the Fourteenth Amendment. In support of this, they outline at length and in detail the well-known facts of fetal development. If this suggestion of personhood is established, the appellant's case, of course, collapses, for the fetus' right to life would then be guaranteed specifically by the Amendment. The appellant conceded as much on reargument. On the other hand, the appellee conceded on reargument that no case could be cited that holds that a fetus is a person within the meaning of the Fourteenth Amendment. . . .

. . . All this, together with our observation, *supra*, that throughout the major portion of the 19th century prevailing legal abortion practices were far freer than they are today, persuades us that the word "person," as used in the Fourteenth Amendment, does not include the unborn. . . .

The pregnant woman cannot be isolated in her privacy. She carries an embryo and, later, a fetus, if one accepts the medical definitions of the developing young in the human uterus. . . . The situation therefore is inherently different from marital intimacy, or bedroom possession of obscene material, or marriage, or procreation, or education. . . . As we have intimated above, it is reasonable and appropriate for a State to decide that at some point in time another interest, that of health of the mother or that of potential human life, becomes significantly involved. The woman's privacy is no longer sole and any right of privacy she possesses must be measured accordingly. . . .

In areas other than criminal abortion, the law has been reluctant to endorse any theory that life, as we recognize it, begins before live birth or to accord legal rights to the unborn except in narrowly defined situations and except when the rights are contingent upon live birth. . . .

In view of all this, we do not agree that, by adopting one theory of life, Texas may override the rights of the pregnant woman that are at stake. We repeat, however, that the State does have an important and legitimate interest in preserving and protecting the health of the pregnant woman . . . and that it has still *another* important and legitimate interest in protecting the potentiality of human life. These interests are separate and distinct. Each grows in substantiality as the woman approaches term and, at a point during pregnancy, each becomes "compelling."

With respect to the State's important and legitimate interest in the health of the mother, the "compelling" point, in the light of present medical knowledge, is at approximately the end of the first trimester. This is so because of the now-established medical fact . . . that until the end of the first trimester mortality in abortion may be less than mortality in normal childbirth. It follows that, from and after this point, a State may regulate the abortion procedure to the extent that the regulation reasonably relates to the preservation and protection of maternal health. Examples of permissible state regulation in this area are requirements as to the qualifications of the person who is to perform the abortion; as to the licensure of that person; as to the facility in which the procedure is to be performed, that is, whether it must be a hospital or may be a clinic or some other place of less-than-hospital status; as to the licensing of the facility; and the like. This means, on the other hand, that, for the period of pregnancy prior to this "compelling" point, the attending physician, in consultation with his patient, is free to determine, without regulation by the State, that, in his medical judgment, the patient's pregnancy should be terminated. If that decision is reached, the judgment may be effectuated by an abortion free of interference by the State.

With respect to the State's important and legitimate interest in potential life, the "compelling" point is at viability. This is so because the fetus then presumably has the capability of meaningful life outside the mother's womb. State regulation protective of fetal life after viability thus has both logical and biological justifications. If the State is interested in protecting fetal life after viability, it may go so far as to proscribe abortion during that period, except when it is necessary to preserve the life or health of the mother.

Measured against these standards, Art. 1196 of the Texas Penal Code, in restricting legal abortions to those "procured or attempted by medical advice for the purpose of saving the life of the mother," sweeps too broadly. The statute makes no distinction between abortions performed early in pregnancy and those performed later, and it limits to a single reason, "saving" the mother's life, the legal justification for the procedure. The statute, therefore, cannot survive the constitutional attack made upon it here. . . .

. . .

By contrast, Justice Rehnquist, with whom Justice White agreed, based his dissent upon doctrinal grounds—a theory that the Constitution should be read strictly and that the Court should not be inventing new rights that did not appear in the language of the Constitution. At the same time, one must wonder if this strict construction of the Constitution was intended as a general way to read it or was a way here to protect the interests of states against the intrusion of the federal government.

Mr. Justice Rehnquist dissenting.

The Court's opinion brings to the decision of this troubling question both extensive historical fact and a wealth of legal scholarship. While the opinion thus commands my respect, I find myself nonetheless in fundamental disagreement with those parts of it that invalidate the Texas statute in question, and therefore dissent.

The Court's opinion decides that a State may impose virtually no restriction on the performance of abortions during the first trimester of pregnancy. Our previous decisions indicate that a necessary predicate for such an opinion is a plaintiff who was in her first trimester of pregnancy at some time during the pendency of her lawsuit. While a party may vindicate his own constitutional rights, he may not seek vindication for the rights of others. . . . The Court's statement of facts in this case makes clear, however, that the record in no way indicates the presence of such a plaintiff. We know only that plaintiff Roe at the time of filing her complaint was a pregnant woman; for aught that appears in this record, she may have been in her *last* trimester of pregnancy as of the date the complaint was filed.

Nothing in the Court's opinion indicates that Texas might not constitutionally apply its proscription of abortion as written to a woman in that stage of pregnancy. Nonetheless, the Court uses her complaint against the Texas statute as a fulcrum for deciding that States may impose virtually no restrictions on medical abortions performed during the *first* trimester of pregnancy. In deciding such a hypothetical lawsuit, the Court departs from the longstanding admonition that it should never "formulate a rule of constitutional law broader than is required by the precise facts to which it is to be applied." . . .

Even if there were a plaintiff in this case capable of litigating the issue which the Court decides, I would reach a conclusion opposite to that reached by the Court. I have difficulty in concluding, as the Court does, that the right of "privacy" is involved in this case. Texas, by the statute here challenged, bars the performance of a medical abortion by a licensed physician on a plaintiff such as Roe. A transaction resulting in an operation such as this is not "private" in the ordinary usage of that word. Nor is the "privacy" that the Court finds here even a distant relative of the freedom from searches and seizures protected by the Fourth Amendment to the Constitution, which the Court has referred to as embodying a right to privacy. . . .

If the Court means by the term "privacy" no more than that the claim of a person to be free from unwanted state regulation of consensual transactions may be a form of "liberty" protected by the Fourteenth Amendment, there is no doubt that similar claims have been upheld in our earlier decisions on the basis of that liberty. . . . But that liberty is not guaranteed absolutely against deprivation, only against deprivation without due process of law. The test traditionally applied in the area of social and economic legislation is whether or not a law such as that challenged has a rational relation to a valid state objective. . . .

The Due Process Clause of the Fourteenth Amendment undoubtedly does place a limit, albeit a broad one, on legislative power to enact laws such as this. If the Texas statute were to prohibit an abortion even where the mother's life is in jeopardy, I have little doubt that such a statute would lack a rational relation to a valid state objective under the test. . . . But the Court's sweeping invalidation of any restrictions on abortion during the first trimester is impossible to justify under that standard, and the conscious weighing of competing factors that the Court's opinion apparently substitutes for the established test is far more appropriate to a legislative judgment than to a judicial one. . . .

The fact that a majority of the States reflecting, after all, the majority sentiment in those States, have had restrictions on abortions for at least a century is a strong indication, it seems to me, that the asserted right to an abortion is not "so rooted in the traditions and conscience of our people as to be ranked as fundamental." . . . Even today, when society's views on abortion are changing, the very existence of the debate is evidence that the "right" to an abortion is not so universally accepted as the appellant would have us believe. . . .

For all of the foregoing reasons, I respectfully dissent.

. . .

In Doe v. Bolton, *Justice Blackmun again delivered the opinion of the Court, in which Chief Justice Burger and Justices Douglas, Brennan, Stewart, Marshall, and Powell joined. Chief Justice Burger and Justice Douglas filed concurring (agreeing with the judgment of the Court but providing alternative legal grounds for that judgment) opinions. Justice White filed a dissenting opinion in which Justice Rehnquist joined. Justice Rehnquist filed a separate dissenting opinion as well. Note what Blackmun had to say about the difference between the two states' laws.*

Doe et al. v. Bolton, Attorney General of Georgia, 410 U.S. 179 (1973)

Mr. Justice Blackmun delivered the opinion of the Court.

In this appeal, the criminal abortion statutes recently enacted in Georgia are challenged on constitutional grounds. . . . In *Roe* v. *Wade*, we today have struck down, as constitutionally defective, the Texas criminal abortion statutes that are representative of provisions long in effect in a majority of our States. The Georgia legislation, however, is different and merits separate consideration.

The statutes in question are patterned upon the American Law Institute's Model Penal Code. The new Georgia provisions replaced statutory law that had been in effect for more than 90 years. . . . The predecessor statute paralleled the Texas legislation considered in *Roe* v. *Wade, supra,* and made all abortions criminal except those necessary "to preserve the life" of the pregnant woman. The new statutes have not been tested on constitutional grounds in the Georgia state courts.

. . . Section 26-1202 (a) [of the new Georgia law] . . . removes from §1201's definition of criminal abortion, and thus makes noncriminal, an abortion "performed by a physician duly licensed" in Georgia when, "based upon his best clinical judgment . . . an abortion is necessary because: (1) A continuation of the pregnancy would endanger the life of the pregnant woman or would seriously and permanently injure her health; or (2) The fetus would very likely be born with a grave, permanent, and irremediable mental or physical defect; or "(3) The pregnancy resulted from forcible or statutory rape."

Section 26-1202 also requires, by numbered subdivisions of its subsection (b), that, for an abortion to be authorized or performed as a noncriminal procedure, additional conditions must be fulfilled . . . residence of the woman in Georgia; . . . reduction to writing of the performing physician's medical judgment that an abortion is justified for one or more of the reasons specified by §26-1202 (a), with written concurrence in that judgment by at least two other Georgia-licensed physicians, based upon their separate personal medical examinations of the woman; performance of the abortion in a hospital licensed by the State Board of Health and also accredited by the Joint Commission on Accreditation of Hospitals; advance approval by an abortion committee of not less than three members of the hospital's staff; certifications in a rape situation; and maintenance and confidentiality of records. . . . There is also a provision giving a hospital the right not to admit an abortion patient and giving any physician and any hospital employee or staff member the right, on moral or religious grounds, not to participate in the procedure. . . .

Our decision in *Roe* . . . establishes that . . . Doe presents a justiciable controversy and has standing to maintain the action. . . . We conclude . . . that the physician-appellants, who are Georgia-licensed doctors consulted by pregnant women, also present a justiciable controversy and do have standing despite the fact that the record does not disclose that any one of them has been prosecuted, or threatened with prosecution, for violation of the State's abortion statutes. The physician is the one against whom these criminal statutes directly operate in the event he procures an abortion that does not meet the statutory exceptions and conditions. The physician-appellants, therefore, assert a sufficiently direct threat of personal detriment. They should not be required to await and undergo a criminal prosecution as the sole means of seeking relief. . . . Whether, in the words of the Georgia statute, "an abortion is necessary" is a professional judgment that the Georgia physician will be called upon to make routinely.

We agree with the District Court . . . that the medical judgment may be exercised in the light of all factors—physical, emotional, psychological, familial, and the woman's age—relevant to the well-being of the patient. All these factors may relate to health. This allows the attending physician the room he needs to make his best medical judgment. And it is room that operates for the benefit, not the disadvantage, of the pregnant woman.

The appellants next argue that the District Court should have declared unconstitutional three procedural demands of the Georgia statute: (1) that the abortion be performed in a hospital accredited by the Joint Commission on Accreditation of Hospitals[;] (2) that the procedure be approved by the hospital staff abortion committee; and (3) that the performing physician's judgment be confirmed by the independent examinations of the patient by two other licensed physicians. The appellants attack these provisions not only on the ground that they unduly restrict the woman's right of privacy, but also on procedural due process and equal protection grounds. The physician-appellants also argue that, by subjecting a doctor's individual medical judgment to committee approval and to confirming consultations, the statute impermissibly restricts the physician's right to practice his profession and deprives him of due process. . . .

This is not to say that Georgia may not or should not, from and after the end of the first trimester, adopt standards for licensing all facilities where abortions may be performed so long as those standards are legitimately related to the objective the State seeks to accomplish. . . .

The second aspect of the appellants' procedural attack relates to the hospital abortion committee and to the pregnant woman's asserted lack of access to that committee. . . . We see nothing in the Georgia statute that explicitly denies access to the committee by or on behalf of the woman. If the access point alone were involved, we would not be persuaded to strike down the committee provision on the unsupported assumption that access is not provided.

Appellants attack the discretion the statute leaves to the committee. The most concrete argument they advance is their suggestion that it is still a badge of infamy "in many minds" to bear an illegitimate child, and that the Georgia system enables the committee members' personal views as to extramarital sex relations, and punishment therefor, to govern their decisions. . . .

Viewing the Georgia statute as a whole, we see no constitutionally justifiable pertinence in the structure for the advance approval by the abortion committee. With regard to the protection of potential life, the medical judgment is already completed prior to the committee stage, and review by a committee once removed from diagnosis is basically redundant. We are not cited to any other surgical procedure made subject to committee approval as a matter of state criminal law. The woman's right to receive medical care in accordance with her licensed physician's best judgment and the physician's right to administer it are substantially limited by this statutorily imposed overview. . . .

The third aspect of the appellants' attack centers on the "time and availability of adequate medical facilities and personnel." It is said that the system imposes substantial and irrational roadblocks and "is patently unsuited" to prompt determination of the abortion decision. Time, of course, is critical in abortion. Risks during the first trimester of pregnancy are admittedly lower than during later months.

It should be manifest that our rejection of the accredited-hospital requirement and, more important, of the abortion committee's advance approval eliminates the major grounds of the attack based on the system's delay and the lack of facilities. There remains, however, the required confirmation by two Georgia-licensed physicians in addition to the recommendation of the pregnant woman's own consultant (making under the statute, a total of six physicians involved, including the three on the hospital's abortion committee). We conclude that this provision, too, must fall.

The appellants attack the residency requirement of the Georgia law as violative of the right to travel. . . . We do not uphold the constitutionality of the residence requirement. It is not based on any policy of preserving state-supported facilities for Georgia residents, for the bar also applies to private hospitals and to privately retained physicians. There is no intimation, either, that Georgia facilities are utilized to capacity in caring for Georgia residents. Just as the Privileges and Immunities Clause, Const. Art. IV, §2, protects persons who enter other States to ply their trade . . . so must it protect persons who enter Georgia seeking the medical services that are available there. . . . A contrary holding would mean that a State could limit to its own residents the general medical care available within its borders. This we could not approve.

The last argument on this phase of the case is one that often is made, namely, that the Georgia system is violative of equal protection because it discriminates against the poor. The appellants do not urge that abortions should be performed by persons other than licensed physicians, so we have no argument that because the wealthy can better afford physicians, the poor should have nonphysicians made available to them. The appellants acknowledged that the procedures are "nondiscriminatory in . . . express terms" but they suggest that they have produced invidious discriminations. . . . We have set aside the accreditation, approval, and confirmation requirements, however, and with that, the discrimination argument collapses in all significant aspects. . . .

. . .

Justice Byron White had not signed on to Roe, *and in his dissent to* Doe *he spelled out his objections to both majority opinions. Justice Rehnquist agreed with Justice White. There is a moral undertone in the opinion that is not hard to find. Do such moral views belong in judicial readings of the Constitution? Did the majority in* Roe *also read their morality into the law?*

Mr. Justice White, with whom Mr. Justice Rehnquist joins, dissenting.

At the heart of the controversy in these cases are those recurring pregnancies that pose no danger whatsoever to the life or health of the mother but are, nevertheless, unwanted for any one or more of a variety of reasons —convenience, family planning, economics, dislike of children, the embarrassment of illegitimacy, etc. The common claim before us is that for any one of such reasons, or for no reason at all, and without asserting or claiming any threat to life or health, any woman is entitled to an abortion at her request if she is able to find a medical advisor willing to undertake the procedure.

The Court for the most part sustains this position: During the period prior to the time the fetus becomes viable, the Constitution of the United States values the convenience, whim, or caprice of the putative mother more than the life or potential life of the fetus; the Constitution, therefore, guarantees the right to an abortion as against any state law or policy seeking to protect the fetus from an abortion not prompted by more compelling reasons of the mother.

With all due respect, I dissent. I find nothing in the language or history of the Constitution to support the Court's judgment. The Court simply fashions and announces a new constitutional right for pregnant mothers and, with scarcely any reason or authority for its action, invests that right with sufficient substance to override most existing state abortion statutes. The upshot is that the people and the legislatures of the 50 States are constitutionally disentitled to weigh the relative importance of the continued existence and development of the fetus, on the one hand, against a spectrum of possible impacts on the mother, on the other hand. As an exercise of raw judicial power, the Court perhaps has authority to do what it does today; but in my view its judgment is an improvident and extravagant exercise of the power of judicial review that the Constitution extends to this Court.

The Court apparently values the convenience of the pregnant mother more than the continued existence and development of the life or potential life that she carries. Whether or not I might agree with that marshaling of values, I can in no event join the Court's judgment because I find no constitutional warrant for imposing such an order of priorities on the people and legislatures of the States. In a sensitive area such as this, involving as it does issues over which reasonable men may easily and heatedly differ, I cannot accept the Court's exercise of its clear power of choice by interposing a constitutional barrier to state efforts to protect human life and by investing mothers and doctors with the constitutionally protected right to exterminate it. This issue, for the most part, should be left with the people and to the political processes the people have devised to govern their affairs. . . .

. . .

In *Roe* and *Doe* the Court had confronted what seemed to White to be a conflict between women's rights and the rights of the "unborn." Although the majority refused to couch its decision in this way, regarding the beginning of life as a question not appropriate for the Court to determine, many of those who heard the announcement of the Court's opinion saw the cases in precisely this fashion. No sooner were the decisions announced, than abortion and abortion rights disputes returned to Justice White's conundrum.

CHAPTER 5

. . .

Regulating and Funding Abortions

The decisions in *Roe* and *Doe* hit the public like bombshells. Women's rights advocates were surprised at the scope of their victory, and many doctors hailed the decisions as landmarks in the drive for the medical profession's authority. Roman Catholic and other religious spokesmen, as well as many social conservatives, rejected both the reasoning and the outcome of the cases. President Richard Nixon spoke out against the decisions, but other politicians supported them. In time politicians' stands on *Roe* and abortion rights would become a "litmus test" for some voters. Street demonstrations by both sides became commonplace.

Leading the initial opposition to *Roe* in public was the Roman Catholic hierarchy. In 1869 Pope Pius IX had prohibited all abortions. The papacy renewed its opposition in a 1968 encyclical. On March 1, 1971, John Joseph Cardinal Carberry, archbishop of St. Louis, had sent a pastoral letter to the parishes in Missouri. It read, in part, "Reverend and Dear Father: A bill has now been introduced into the Missouri legislature to liberalize Missouri's anti-abortion laws. . . . We want our legislators and all Missouri citizens to know the affront to God and the attack on human life that we feel these laws present. Of special importance in this campaign is the understanding of our own Catholic people and other people of good will who oppose virtually unrestricted abortion."[1] A brochure had been prepared by the conference of bishops of Missouri, which was to be made available to all parishioners. From 1966 to 1973, the Family Life Bureau of the National Conference of Catholic Bishops kept watch on the reform efforts in states and helped prepare statements for Catholic clergy warning against the immorality of abortion. The hierarchy ordered the more than six hundred Catholic hospitals in the country not to allow its doctors, whether they wanted to or not, to perform abortions. As one director of the leading Catholic pro-life organization reported with pride, "The only reason we have a movement [against abortion] in this nation is because of the Catholic people and the Catholic Church."[2]

In 1973 the National Conference of Catholic Bishops (NCCB) called for the formation of "grassroots pro-life organizations" and underwrote a National Right to Life Committee to coordinate local and national protests against *Roe*. In the same year, Monsignor Robert Lynch organized the National Committee for a Human Life Amendment to be funded through a one-cent-per-Catholic assessment each year. Although the Roman Catholic laypersons were divided on the issue (by one estimate Roman Catholic women constituted over 25 percent of those who sought abortions after *Roe*) and some liberal Roman Catholic spokesmen saw a danger in making the abortion issue the leading public question addressed by the church, Reverend Edward Bryce, the head of the Committee for Pro-Life Activities of the NCCB, told an interviewer in 1978 that the conference saw abortion as an issue that mobilized opinion within the church.[3]

Joining the Catholic Church in the battle against legalized abortion were a number of evangelical Protestant leaders. Ministers such as Jerry Falwell decided that *Roe* was "a terrible decision" and that it would lead to a "disaster" for the American family. Falwell later recalled that "hoping that would be enough, I began to preach regularly against abortion, calling it 'America's national sin.' I compared abortion to Hitler's 'final solution' for the Jews and the Court's decision to letting loose a 'biological holocaust' upon our nation." Falwell had previously argued that preachers should not become political figures or take "political action." After *Roe* he found himself "calling for all-out involvement by the Christian community."[4]

In the political arena, politicians who shared the anti-abortion views of Cardinal Carberry and Jerry Falwell began to work for legislative curtailment of *Roe*. While much of the impetus for regulation of abortion came from the states, some members of Congress almost immediately expressed their opposition to the terms of *Roe*. In Congress, eight days after the decision in *Roe* was announced, Maryland representative Lawrence Hogan introduced a draft amendment to the Constitution to make the fetus a "person" under the Fourteenth Amendment. Fetal life (and legal rights) were to begin with conception. New York senator James F. Buckley introduced a constitutional amendment to reverse *Roe* the next day. Within three years, more than fifty differently worded amendments to ban or cut back on abortion had reached the floor of Congress. During the 1976 legislative session, Henry Hyde, an Illinois Republican congressman, sought to amend the Health, Education, and Welfare appropriations bill by banning all federal funding for abortions or abortion counseling. President Nixon had barred funding abortions unless they were a medical necessity; Hyde's amendment would have barred all aid to abortion for any reason, in effect going beyond even Texas's old statute. President Gerald Ford vetoed the

Hyde Amendment, but it was passed over his veto. President Jimmy Carter accepted its terms, as did President Ronald Reagan, who favored a constitutional amendment barring abortion funding.

At the same time, such states as Connecticut and Pennsylvania opted to deny the use of federal Medicaid funds for abortion at any stage of the pregnancy unless one or more doctors certified in writing that the abortion was necessary to save the life or health of the mother, or the fetus was likely to have crippling birth defects, or the pregnancy was the result of a rape or incest that had been reported to the police. The same states used federal Medicaid funds for prematernity and maternity care for the indigent, in effect favoring continued pregnancy over abortion.

Anti-abortion state politicians also sought to undermine *Roe* by imposing limitations on when and where an abortion could be performed, as well as the means by which a woman seeking an abortion might be convinced to forgo it. From 1974 to 1986, the Court heard a number of cases from states and localities concerning such restrictions, sharply dividing over their constitutionality.

. . .

No sooner had the Blackmun opinions appeared than jurists and law teachers began to grade them. Much of the scholarly commentary, even from those who supported the idea of choice and opposed discrimination based on gender, was critical. One of the leading examples of that literature was Yale law professor John Hart Ely's essay excerpted below. On what alternative grounds does Ely hint the right to choice should have rested?

John Hart Ely, "The Wages of Crying Wolf: A Comment on *Roe v. Wade*," *Yale Law Journal* 82 (1973): 920–49 (footnotes omitted)

In *Roe v. Wade*, decided January 22, 1973, the Supreme Court—Justice Blackmun speaking for everyone but Justices White and Rehnquist—held unconstitutional Texas's (and virtually every other state's) criminal abortion statute. . . .

A number of fairly standard criticisms can be made of *Roe*. A plausible narrower basis of decision, that of vagueness, is brushed aside in the rush toward broader ground. The opinion strikes the reader initially as a sort of guidebook, addressing questions not before the Court and drawing lines with an apparent precision one generally associates with a commissioner's regulations. On closer examination, however, the precision proves largely illusory. Confusing signals are emitted, particularly with respect to the nature of the doctor's responsibilities and the permissible scope of health regulations after the first trimester. The Court seems, moreover, to get carried away on the subject of remedies: Even assuming the case can be made for an unusually protected constitutional right to an abortion, it hardly seems necessary to have banned during the first trimester *all* state regulation of the conditions under which abortions can be performed.

By terming such criticisms "standard," I do not mean to suggest they are unimportant, for they are not. But if they were all that was wrong with *Roe*, it would not merit special comment.

Let us not underestimate what is at stake: Having an unwanted child can go a long way toward ruining a woman's life. And at bottom *Roe* signals the Court's judgment that this result cannot be justified by any good that anti-abortion legislation accomplishes. This surely is an understandable conclusion—indeed it is one with which I agree—but ordinarily the Court claims no mandate to second-guess legislative balances, at least not when the Constitution has designated neither of the values in conflict as entitled to special protection. But even assuming it would be a good idea for the Court to assume this function, *Roe* seems a curious place to have begun. . . . Whether anti-abortion legislation cramps the life style of an unwilling mother more significantly than anti-homosexuality legislation cramps the life style of a homosexual is a close question. But even granting that it does, the *other* side of the balance looks very different. For there is more than simple societal revulsion to support legislation restricting abortion: abortion ends (or if it makes a difference, prevents) the life of a human being other than the one making the choice.

The Court's response here is simply not adequate. It agrees, indeed it holds, that after the point of viability (a concept it fails to note will become even less clear than it is now as the technology of birth continues to develop) the interest in protecting the fetus is compelling. Exactly what is the magic moment is not made clear: Viability, as the Court defines it, is achieved some six to twelve weeks after quickening. (Quickening is the point at which the fetus begins discernibly to move independently of the mother and the point that has historically been deemed crucial—to the extent *any* point between conception and birth has been focused on.) But no, it is *viability* that is constitutionally critical: the Court's defense seems to mistake a definition for a syllogism.

With respect to the State's important and legitimate interest in potential life, the "compelling" point is at viability. This is so because the fetus then presumably has the capacity of meaningful life outside the mother's womb.

With regard to why the state cannot consider this "important and legitimate interest" prior to viability, the opinion is even less satisfactory. The discussion begins sensibly enough: The interest asserted is not necessarily tied to the question whether the fetus is "alive," for whether or not one calls it a living being, it is an entity with the potential for (and indeed the likelihood of) life. But all of arguable relevance that follows are arguments that fetuses (a) are not recognized as "persons in the whole sense" by legal doctrine generally and (b) are not "persons" protected by the Fourteenth Amendment.

To the extent they are not entirely inconclusive, the bodies of doctrine to which the Court adverts respecting the protection of fetuses under general legal doctrine tend to undercut rather than support its conclusion. And the argument that fetuses (unlike, say, corporations) are not "persons" under the Fourteenth Amendment fares little better. The Court notes that most constitutional clauses using the word "persons"—such as the one outlining the qualifications for the Presidency—appear to have been drafted with postnatal beings in mind. (It might have added that most of them were plainly drafted with *adults* in mind, but I suppose that wouldn't have helped.) . . .

The canons of construction employed here are perhaps most intriguing when they are contrasted with those invoked to derive the constitutional right to an abortion. But in any event, the argument that fetuses lack constitutional rights is simply irrelevant. For it has never been held or even asserted that the state interest needed to justify forcing a person to refrain from an activity, *whether or not that activity is constitutionally protected,* must implicate either the life or the constitutional rights of another person. Dogs are not "persons in the whole sense" nor have they constitutional rights, but that does not mean the state cannot prohibit killing them: It does not even mean the state cannot prohibit killing them in the exercise of the First Amendment right of political protest. Come to think of it, draft cards aren't persons either.

Thus even assuming the Court ought generally to get into the business of second-guessing legislative balances, it has picked a strange case with which to begin. Its purported evaluation of the balance that produced antiabortion legislation simply does not meet the issue: That the life plans of the mother must, not simply may, prevail over the state's desire to protect the fetus simply does not follow from the judgment that the fetus is not a person. Beyond all that, however, the Court has no business getting into that business.

Were I a legislator I would vote for a statute very much like the one the Court ends up drafting. I hope this reaction reflects more than the psychological phenomenon that keeps bombardiers sane—the fact that it is some-how easier to "terminate" those you cannot see—and am inclined to think it does: that the mother, unlike the unborn child, has begun to imagine a future for herself strikes me as morally quite significant. But God knows I'm not *happy* with that resolution. Abortion is too much like infanticide on the one hand, and too much like contraception on the other, to leave one comfortable with any answer; and the moral issue it poses is as fiendish as any philosopher's hypothetical. . . .

Compared with men, very few women sit in our legislatures, a fact I believe should bear some relevance—even without an Equal Rights Amendment—to the appropriate standard of review for legislation that favors men over women. But *no* fetuses sit in our legislatures. Of course they have their champions, but so have women. The two interests have clashed repeatedly in the political arena, and had continued to do so up to the date of the opinion, generating quite a wide variety of accommodations. By the Court's lights virtually all of the legislative accommodations had unduly favored fetuses; by its definition of victory, women had lost. Yet in every legislative balance one of the competing interests loses to some extent; indeed usually, as here, they both do. . . .

Of course a woman's freedom to choose an abortion is part of the "liberty" the Fourteenth Amendment says shall not be denied without due process of law, as indeed is anyone's freedom to do what he wants. But "due process" generally guarantees only that the inhibition be procedurally fair and that it have some "rational" connection—though plausible is probably a better word—with a permissible governmental goal. What is unusual about *Roe* is that the liberty involved is accorded a far more stringent protection, so stringent that a desire to preserve the fetus's existence is unable to overcome it—a protection more stringent, I think it fair to say, than that the present Court accords the freedom of the press explicitly guaranteed by the First Amendment. What is frightening about *Roe* is that this super-protected right is not inferable from the language of the Constitution, the framers' thinking respecting the specific problem in issue, any general value derivable from the provisions they included, or the nation's governmental structure. Nor is it explainable in terms of the unusual political impotence of the group judicially protected vis-à-vis the interest that legislatively prevailed over it. . . .

* * *

Law professor (later judge and then Supreme Court justice) Ruth Bader Ginsburg had her own concerns about the constitutional basis for Blackmun's opinion in Roe. *Although as a lawyer she had won a number of landmark suits for equality for women and favored the abortion right, she did not think much of Justice Blackmun's formula. In a lecture titled "Some Thoughts on Autonomy and Equality in Relation to* Roe v. Wade" *presented at the University of North Carolina School of Law on April 6, 1984, she laid out her concerns and an alternative line of reasoning on which to base the right to choose.*

Ruth Bader Ginsberg, "Some Thoughts on Autonomy and Equality in Relation to *Roe v. Wade*," *North Carolina Law Review* 63 (January 1985): 375–84 (footnotes omitted)

These remarks contrast two related areas of constitutional adjudication: gender-based classification and reproductive autonomy. . . . The two areas are intimately related in this practical sense: the law's response to questions subsumed under these headings bears pervasively on the situation of women in society. Inevitably, the shape of the law on gender-based classification and reproductive autonomy indicates and influences the opportunity woman will have to participate as men's full partners in the nation's social, political, and economic life.

Doctrine in the two areas, however, has evolved in discrete compartments. The High Court has analyzed classification by gender under an equal protection/sex discrimination rubric; it has treated reproductive autonomy under the substantive due process/personal autonomy headline not expressly linked to discrimination against woman. The Court's gender classification decisions overturning state and federal legislation, in the main, have not provoked large controversy; the Court's initial 1973 abortion decision, *Roe v. Wade*, on the other hand, became and remains a storm center. *Roe v. Wade* sparked public opposition and academic criticism, in part, I believe, because the Court ventured too far in the change it ordered and presented an incomplete justification for its action. . . .

In 1971 . . . over a year before *Roe v. Wade*, I visited a neighboring institution to participate in a conference on women and the law. I spoke then of the utility of litigation attacking official line-drawing by sex. My comments focused on the chance in the 1970s that courts, through constitutional adjudication, would aid in evening out the rights, responsibilities, and opportunities of women and men. I did not mention the abortion cases then on the dockets of several lower courts—I was not at that time or any other time thereafter personally engaged in reproductive-autonomy litigation. Nonetheless, the most heated questions I received concerned abortion.

The questions were pressed by black men. The suggestion, not thinly veiled, was that legislative reform and litigation regarding abortion might have less to do with individual autonomy or discrimination against women than with restricting population growth among oppressed minorities. The strong word "genocide" was uttered more than once. It is a notable irony that, as constitutional law in this domain has unfolded, women who are not poor have achieved access to abortion with relative ease; for poor women, however, a group in which minorities are disproportionately represented, access to abortion is not markedly different from what it was in pre-*Roe* days. . . .

In the 1970s overt sex-based classification fell prey to the Burger Court's intervention. Men could not be preferred to women for estate administration purposes, the Court declared in the pivotal *Reed v. Reed* decision. Married women in the military could not be denied fringe benefits—family housing and health care allowances—accorded married men in military service, the High Court held in *Frontiero v. Richardson*. Social security benefits, welfare assistance, and workers' compensation secured by a male's employment must be secured, to the same extent, by a female's employment the Supreme Court ruled in a progression of cases. . . . Girls are entitled to the same parental support as boys, the Supreme Court stated in *Stanton v. Stanton*. . . .

Roe v. Wade, in contrast to decisions involving explicit male/female classification, has occasioned searing criticism of the Court, over a decade of demonstrations, a stream of vituperative mail addressed to Justice Blackmun (the author of the opinion), annual proposals for overruling *Roe* by constitutional amendment, and a variety of measures in Congress and state legislatures to constrain or curtail the decision. In 1973, when *Roe* issued, abortion law was in a state of change across the nation. There was a distinct trend in the states, noted by the Court, "toward liberalization of abortion statutes." Several states had adopted the American Law Institute's Model Penal Code approach setting out grounds on which abortion could be justified at any stage of pregnancy; most significantly, the Code included as a permissible ground preservation of the woman's physical or mental health. Four states—New York, Washington, Alaska, and Hawaii—permitted physicians to perform first-trimester abortions with virtually no restrictions. This movement in legislative arenas bore some resemblance to the law revision activity that eventually swept through the states establishing no-fault divorce as the national pattern.

The Texas law at issue in *Roe* made it a crime to "procure an abortion" except "by medical advice for the purpose of saving the life of the mother." It was the most extreme prohibition extant. The Court had in close view . . .

a 1965 precedent, *Griswold v. Connecticut,* holding inconsistent with personal privacy, somehow sheltered by due process, a state ban on the use of extending *Griswold* to strike down a state prohibition on sales of contraceptives except to married persons by prescription. . . . The Court had already decided *Reed v. Reed,* recognizing the arbitrariness in the 1970s of a once traditional gender-based classification, but it did not further pursue that avenue in *Roe.* . . .

I earlier observed that, in my judgment, *Roe* ventured too far in the change it ordered. The sweep and detail of the opinion stimulated the mobilization of a right-to-life movement and an attendant reaction in Congress and state legislatures. In place of the trend "toward liberalization of abortion statutes" noted in *Roe,* legislatures adopted measures aimed at minimizing the impact of the 1973 rulings, including notification and consent requirements, prescriptions for the protection of fetal life, and bans on public expenditures for poor women's abortions.

Professor Paul Freund explained where he thought the Court went astray in *Roe,* and I agree with his statement. The Court properly invalidated the Texas proscription, he indicated, because "[a] law that absolutely made criminal all kinds and forms of abortion could not stand up; it is not a reasonable accommodation of interests." If *Roe* had left off at that point and not adopted what Professor Freund called a "medical approach," physicians might have been less pleased with the decision, but the legislative trend might have continued in the direction in which it was headed in the early 1970s. . . .

I commented at the outset that I believe the Court presented an incomplete justification for its action. Academic criticism of *Roe,* charging the Court with reading its own values into the due process clause, might have been less pointed had the Court placed the woman alone, rather than the woman tied to her physician, at the center of its attention. . . .

I do not pretend that, if the Court had added a distinct sex discrimination theme to its medically oriented opinion, the storm *Roe* generated would have been less furious. I appreciate the intense divisions of opinion on the moral question and recognize that abortion today cannot fairly be described as nothing more than birth control delayed. The conflict, conceived, is not simply one between a fetus' interests and a woman's interests, narrowly conceived, nor is the overriding issue state versus private control of a woman's body for a span of nine months. Also in the balance is a woman's autonomous charge of her full life's course. . . .

Roe, I believe, would have been more acceptable as a judicial decision if it had not gone beyond a ruling on the extreme statute before the Court.

The political process was moving in the early 1970s, not swiftly enough for advocates of quick, complete change, but majoritarian institutions were listening and acting. Heavy-handed judicial intervention was difficult to justify and appears to have provoked, not resolved, conflict. . . .

Overall, the Court's *Roe* position is weakened, I believe, by the opinion's concentration on a medically approved autonomy idea, to the exclusion of a constitutionally based sex-quality perspective. I understand the view that for political reasons the reproductive autonomy controversy should be isolated from the general debate on equal rights, responsibilities, and opportunities for women and men. I expect, however, that organized and determined opposing efforts to inform and persuade the public on the abortion issue will continue through the 1980s. In that process there will be opportunities for elaborating in public forums the equal-regard conception of women's claims to reproductive choice uncoerced and unsteered by government.

. . .

The first of the abortion regulatory cases came from the state of Missouri, and in the coming years, Missouri would provide many of the test cases. When Roe *was decided, advocates for abortion rights had already brought a suit against a Missouri law criminalizing the performance of abortions. The federal courts resolved that suit according to the rule laid down in* Roe. *The next year, strongly supported by the right-to-life movement within the Roman Catholic Church, the Missouri legislature passed a new abortion regulation statute. The state's 1974 act did not on its face deny women access to legal and safe abortions, but it placed some burdens on physicians performing the procedures and even more on poor women who could not afford to pay for abortions. Can it be read as an end run around* Roe?

"An Act relating to Abortion with Penalty Provisions and Emergency Clause," *Missouri Statutes*, June 14, 1974

Be it enacted by the General Assembly of the State of Missouri, as follows:

Section 1. It is the intention of the general assembly of the state of Missouri to reasonably regulate abortion in conformance with the decisions of the Supreme Court of the United States.

Section 2. Unless the language or context clearly indicates a different meaning is intended, the following words or phrases for the purpose of this act shall be given the meaning ascribed to them: . . .

"Viability," that stage of fetal development when the life of the unborn child may be continued indefinitely outside the womb by natural or artificial life supportive systems. . . .

Section 3. No abortion shall be performed prior to the end of the first twelve weeks of pregnancy except:

(1) By a duly licensed, consenting physician in the exercise of his best clinical medical judgment.

(2) After the woman, prior to submitting to the abortion, certifies in writing her consent to the abortion and that her consent is informed and freely given and is not the result of coercion.

(3) With the written consent of the woman's spouse, unless the abortion is certified by a licensed physician to be necessary in order to preserve the life of the mother.

(4) With the written consent of one parent or person in loco parentis of the woman if the woman is unmarried and under the age of eighteen years, unless the abortion is certified by a licensed physician as necessary in order to preserve the life of the mother.

Section 4. No abortion performed subsequent to the first twelve weeks of pregnancy shall be performed except where the provisions of section 3 of this act are satisfied and in a hospital.

Section 5. No abortion not necessary to preserve the life or health of the mother shall be performed unless the attending physician first certifies with reasonable medical certainty that the fetus is not viable.

Section 6. (1) No person who performs or induces an abortion shall fail to exercise that degree of professional skill, care and diligence to preserve the life and health of the fetus which such person would be required to exercise in order to preserve the life and health of any fetus intended to be born and not aborted. Any physician or person assisting in the abortion who shall fail to take such measures to encourage or to sustain the life of the child, and the death of the child results, shall be deemed guilty of manslaughter and upon conviction shall be punished as provided in Section 559.140, RSMo [revised statutes of Missouri]. Further, such physician or other person shall be liable in an action for damages as provided in Section 537.080, RSMo.

(2) Whoever, with intent to do so, shall take the life of a premature infant aborted alive, shall be guilty of murder of the second degree.

(3) No person shall use any fetus or premature infant aborted alive for any type of scientific, research, laboratory or other kind of experimentation either prior to or subsequent to any abortion procedure except as necessary to protect or preserve the life and health of such premature infant aborted alive.

Section 7. In every case where a live born infant results from an attempted abortion which was not performed to save the life or health of the mother, such infant shall be an abandoned ward of the state under the jurisdiction of the juvenile court wherein the abortion occurred, and the mother and father, if he consented to the abortion, of such infant, shall have no parental rights or obligations whatsoever relating to such infant, as if the parental rights had been terminated pursuant to section 211.411, RSMo. The attending physician shall forthwith notify said juvenile court of the existence of such live born infant.

Section 8. Any woman seeking an abortion in the state of Missouri shall be verbally informed of the provisions of section 7 of this act by the attending physician and the woman shall certify in writing that she has been so informed.

Section 9. The general assembly finds that the method or technique of abortion known as saline amniocentesis whereby the amniotic fluid is withdrawn and a saline or other fluid is inserted into the amniotic sac for the purpose of killing the fetus and artificially inducing labor is deleterious to maternal health and is hereby prohibited after the first twelve weeks of pregnancy.

Section 10(1) Every health facility and physician shall be supplied with forms promulgated by the Division of Health, the purpose and function of which shall be the preservation of maternal health and life by adding to the sum of medical knowledge through the compilation of relevant maternal health and life data and to monitor all abortions performed to assure that they are done only under and in accordance with the provisions of the law. . . .

(3) All information obtained by physician, hospital, clinic or other health facility from a patient for the purpose of preparing reports to the Division of Health under this section or reports received by the Division of Health shall be confidential and shall be used only for statistical purposes. Such records, however, may be inspected and health data acquired by local, state, or national public health officers.

Section 11. All medical records and other documents required to be kept shall be maintained in the permanent files of the health facility in which the abortion was performed for a period of seven years.

Section 12. Any practitioner of medicine, surgery, or nursing, or other health personnel who shall willfully and knowingly do or assist any action made unlawful by this act shall be subject to having his license, application for license, or authority to practice his profession as a physician, surgeon, or nurse in the state of Missouri rejected or revoked by the appropriate state licensing board. . . .

Section A. Because of the necessity for immediate state action to regulate abortions to protect the lives and health of citizens of this state, this act is deemed necessary for the immediate preservation of the public health, welfare, peace and safety, and is hereby declared to be an emergency act within the meaning of the constitution, and this act shall be in full force and effect upon its passage and approval. . . .

. . .

Doctors, along with a clinic providing abortion counseling, sought injunctive and declaratory relief against the Missouri abortion statute in Planned Parenthood v. Danforth, *which arrived at the High Court in 1976. Justice Blackmun prepared the majority opinion. In it, he made some concessions to the statute and declared parts of it unconstitutional. A separate question, and one that would figure in all of the regulatory cases that followed, was whether an entire law should fall because portions of it were flawed.*

Planned Parenthood of Central Missouri et al. v. Danforth, Attorney General of Missouri, et al., 428 U.S. 52 (1976)

Mr. Justice Blackmun delivered the opinion of the Court.

This case is a logical and anticipated corollary to *Roe* v. *Wade* and *Doe* v. *Bolton*, for it raises issues secondary to those that were then before the Court. Indeed, some of the questions now presented were forecast and reserved [i.e., explicitly mentioned but not resolved] in *Roe* and *Doe*. . . .

In June 1974, somewhat more than a year after *Roe* and *Doe* had been decided, Missouri's 77th General Assembly . . . impose[d] a structure for the control and regulation of abortions in Missouri during all stages of pregnancy. . . .

Our primary task, then, is to consider each of the challenged provisions of the new Missouri abortion statute in the particular light of the opinions and decisions in *Roe* and in Doe. . . .

It is true that *Doe* and *Roe* clearly establish that the State may not restrict the decision of the patient and her physician regarding abortion during the first stage of pregnancy. Despite the fact that apparently no other Missouri statute, with the exceptions referred to, requires a patient's prior written consent to a surgical procedure, the imposition by §3(2) of such a requirement for termination of pregnancy even during the first stage, in our view, is not in itself an unconstitutional requirement. The decision to abort, indeed, is an important, and often a stressful one, and it is desirable and imperative that it be made with full knowledge of its nature and consequences. The woman is the one primarily concerned, and her awareness of the decision and its significance may be assured, constitutionally, by the State to the extent of requiring her prior written consent. . . .

Section 3(3) requires the prior written consent of the spouse of the woman seeking an abortion during the first 12 weeks of pregnancy, unless "the abortion is certified by a licensed physician to be necessary in order to preserve the life of the mother." . . . The appellees [i.e., the state of Missouri] defend §3(3) on the ground that it was enacted in the light of the General Assembly's "perception of marriage as an institution," . . .

The appellants, on the other hand, contend that §3(3) obviously is designed to afford the husband the right unilaterally to prevent or veto an abortion, whether or not he is the father of the fetus, and that this not only violates *Roe* and *Doe* but is also in conflict with other decided cases. . . . They also refer to the situation where the husband's consent cannot be obtained because he cannot be located. . . . In *Roe* and *Doe* we specifically reserved decision on the question whether a requirement for consent by the father of the fetus, by the spouse, or by the parents, or a parent, of an unmarried minor, may be constitutionally imposed. We now hold that the State may not constitutionally require the consent of the spouse, as is specified under §3(3) of the Missouri Act, as a condition for abortion during the first 12 weeks of pregnancy. . . . The State cannot "delegate to a spouse a veto power which the state itself is absolutely and totally prohibited from exercising during the first trimester of pregnancy."

We recognize, of course, that when a woman, with the approval of her physician but without the approval of her husband, decides to terminate her pregnancy, it could be said that she is acting unilaterally. The obvious fact is that when the wife and the husband disagree on this decision, the view of only one of the two marriage partners can prevail. Inasmuch as it is the woman who physically bears the child and who is the more directly and immediately affected by the pregnancy, as between the two, the balance weighs in her favor.

Section 3(4) requires, with respect to the first 12 weeks of pregnancy, where the woman is unmarried and under the age of 18 years, the written consent of a parent or person *in loco parentis* unless, again, "the abortion is certified by a licensed physician as necessary in order to preserve the life of the mother." It is to be observed that only one parent need consent.

The appellees defend the statute in several ways. They point out that the law properly may subject minors to more stringent limitations than are permissible with respect to adults. . . . Missouri law, it is said, "is replete with provisions reflecting the interest of the state in assuring the welfare of minors." . . . The appellants, in their turn, emphasize that no other Missouri statute specifically requires the additional consent of a minor's parent for medical or surgical treatment, and that in Missouri a minor legally may consent to medical services for pregnancy (excluding abortion), venereal disease, and drug abuse. . . .

We agree with appellants . . . that the State may not impose a blanket provision, such as §3(4), requiring the consent of a parent or person *in loco parentis* as a condition for abortion of an unmarried minor during the first 12 weeks of her pregnancy. Just as with the requirement of consent from the spouse, so here, the State does not have the constitutional authority to give a third party an absolute, and possibly arbitrary, veto over the decision of the physician and his patient to terminate the patient's pregnancy, regardless of the reason for withholding the consent. . . . Constitutional rights do not mature and come into being magically only when one attains the state-defined age of majority. Minors, as well as adults, are protected by the Constitution and possess constitutional rights. . . .

It is difficult . . . to conclude that providing a parent with absolute power to overrule a determination, made by the physician and his minor patient, to terminate the patient's pregnancy will serve to strengthen the family unit. Neither is it likely that such veto power will enhance parental authority or control where the minor and the nonconsenting parent are so fundamentally in conflict and the very existence of the pregnancy already has fractured the family structure. . . . We emphasize that our holding that §3(4) is invalid does not suggest that every minor, regardless of age or maturity, may give effective consent for termination of her pregnancy. . . .

Section 9 of the statute prohibits the use of saline amniocentesis, as a method or technique of abortion, after the first 12 weeks of pregnancy. . . . The statute imposes this proscription on the ground that the technique "is deleterious to maternal health," and places it in the form of a legislative finding. Appellants challenge this provision on the ground that it operates to preclude virtually all abortions after the first trimester. This is so, it is claimed, because a substantial percentage, in the neighborhood of 70% according to the testimony, of all abortions performed in the United States after the first trimester are effected through the procedure of saline amniocentesis. Appellants stress the fact that the alternative methods of hysterotomy and hysterectomy are significantly more dangerous and critical for the woman than the saline technique; they also point out that the mortality rate for normal childbirth exceeds that where saline amniocentesis is employed. Finally, appellants note that the perhaps safer alternative of prostaglandin instillation, suggested and strongly relied upon by the appellees, at least at the time of the trial, is not yet widely used in this country.

We held in *Roe* that after the first stage, "the State, in promoting its interest in the health of the mother, may, if it chooses, regulate the abortion procedure in ways that are reasonably related to maternal health." . . . The State, through §9, would prohibit the use of a method which the record shows is the one most commonly used nationally by physicians after the first trimester and which is safer, with respect to maternal mortality, than even continuation of the pregnancy until normal childbirth. Moreover, as a practical matter, it forces a woman and her physician to terminate her pregnancy by methods more dangerous to her health than the method outlawed. . . . As such, it does not withstand constitutional challenge. . . .

Sections 10 and 11 of the Act impose recordkeeping requirements for health facilities and physicians concerned with abortions irrespective of the pregnancy stage. . . . On the one hand, maintenance of records indeed may be helpful in developing information pertinent to the preservation of maternal health. On the other hand, as we stated in *Roe*, during the first stage of pregnancy the State may impose no restrictions or regulations governing the medical judgment of the pregnant woman's attending physician with respect to the termination of her pregnancy. . . . Recordkeeping and reporting requirements that are reasonably directed to the preservation of maternal health and that properly respect a patient's confidentiality and privacy are permissible. . . .

Section 6(1) requires the physician to exercise the prescribed skill, care, and diligence to preserve the life and health of the *fetus*. It does not specify that such care need be taken only after the stage of viability has been reached. As the provision now reads, it impermissibly requires the physician to preserve the life and health of the fetus, whatever the stage of pregnancy. . . .

. . .

The dissenters in Roe *and* Doe *found all parts of the Missouri law acceptable. They were joined by Chief Justice Burger, who had joined the majority in* Roe. *Did the dissenters actually believe that the statute fit the* Roe *formula, or was the dissent an occasion to develop a deeper rationale for overturning* Roe?

Mr. Justice White, with whom the Chief Justice and Mr. Justice Rehnquist join, concurring in part and dissenting in part.

In *Roe v. Wade*, this Court recognized a right to an abortion free from state prohibition. The task of policing this limitation on state police power is and will be a difficult and continuing venture in substantive due process. However, even accepting *Roe v. Wade*, there is nothing in the opinion in that case and nothing articulated in the Court's opinion in this case which justifies the invalidation of four provisions of [the Missouri act]. . . . Accordingly, I dissent, in part [i.e., Justice White agreed with the Court in upholding the other provisions of the law]. . . .

The State is not—under §3(3)—delegating to the husband the power to vindicate the *State's* interest in the future life of the fetus. It is instead recognizing that the husband has an interest of his own in the life of the fetus which should not be extinguished by the unilateral decision of the wife. It by no means follows, from the fact that the mother's interest in deciding "whether or not to terminate her pregnancy" outweighs the *State's* interest in the potential life of the fetus, that the husband's interest is also outweighed and may not be protected by the State. A father's interest in having a child—perhaps his only child—may be unmatched by any other interest in his life. . . . It is truly surprising that the majority finds in the United States Constitution, as it must in order to justify the result it reaches, a rule that the State must assign a greater value to a mother's decision to cut off a potential human life by abortion than to a father's decision to let it mature into a live child. Such a rule cannot be found there, nor can it be found in *Roe* v. *Wade*. These are matters which a State should be able to decide free from the suffocating power of the federal judge, purporting to act in the name of the Constitution. . . .

Section 3(4) requires that an unmarried woman under 18 years of age obtain the consent of a parent or a person *in loco parentis* as a condition to an abortion. Once again the Court strikes the provision down in a sentence. . . . The Court rejects the notions that the *State* has an interest in strengthening the family unit, or that the *parent* has an "independent interest" in the abortion decision, sufficient to justify §3(4) and apparently concludes that the provision is therefore unconstitutional. But the purpose of the parental-consent requirement is not merely to vindicate any interest of the parent or of the State. The purpose of the requirement is to vindicate the very right created in *Roe* v. *Wade*, the right of the pregnant woman to decide "whether *or not* to terminate her pregnancy." . . . Missouri is entitled to protect the minor unmarried woman from making the decision in a way which is not in her own best interests, and it seeks to achieve this goal by requiring parental consultation and consent. This is the traditional way by which States have sought to protect children from their own immature and improvident decisions. . . .

. . .

From 1965 onward, using Medicaid money, the federal government provided funds for states to spend on health care for their citizens. Beginning in 1970,

these funds had underwritten the expenses of hundreds of birth control coun-
seling and family planning centers. The next selection comes from the House
of Representatives debate of June 24, 1976, on the Hyde Amendment to bar all
funding for abortion from the appropriation for the Department of Health,
Education, and Welfare. Debates over legislation in Congress are different
from majority and dissenting opinions by members of a court, but the dispute
over federal funding for abortions paralleled the division of opinion on the
High Court in important ways. Representative Henry Hyde opposed the Roe
decision, as did those who supported his amendment. Opponents of the
amendment did not comment on Roe *directly, however.*

"The Hyde Amendment," *Congressional Record—House*, June 24, 1976, 20410–12

Mr. HYDE. Mr. Chairman, I offer an amendment.

The Clerk read as follows:

Amendment offered by Mr. Hyde: On page 36, after line 9, add the fol-lowing new section: "Sec. 209. None of the fund appropriated under this Act shall be used to pay for abortions or to promote or encourage abortions."

Mr. HYDE. Mr. Chairman, this amendment may stimulate a lot of debate —but it need not—because I believe most Members know how they will vote on this issue.

Nevertheless, there are those of us who believe it is to the everlasting shame of this country that in 1973 approximately 800,000 legal abortions were performed in this country—and so it is fair to assume that this year over a million human lives will be destroyed because they are inconvenient to someone.

The unborn child facing an abortion can best be classified as a member of the innocently inconvenient and since the pernicious doctrine that some lives are more important than others seems to be persuasive with the pro-abortion forces, we who seek to protect that most defenseless and innocent of human lives—the unborn—seek to inhibit the use of Federal funds to pay for and thus encourage abortion as an answer to the human and compel-ling problem of an unwanted child.

We are all exercised at the wanton killing of the porpoise, the baby seal. We urge big game hunters to save the tiger, but we somehow turn away at the specter of a million human beings being violently destroyed because this great society does not want them.

And make no mistake, an abortion is violent.

I think in the final analysis, you must determine whether or not the unborn person is human. If you think it is animal or vegetable then, of course, it is disposable like an empty beer can to be crushed and thrown out with the rest of the trash.

But medicine, biology, embryology, say that growing living organism is not animal or vegetable or mineral—but it is a human life.

And if you believe that human life is deserving of due process of law—of equal protection of the laws—then you cannot in logic and conscience help fund the execution of these innocent defenseless human lives.

If we are to order our lives by the precepts of animal husbandry, then I guess abortion is an acceptable answer. If we human beings are not of a higher order than animals then let us save our pretentious aspirations for a better and more just world and recognize this is an anthill we inhabit and there are no such things as ideals or justice of morality.

Once conception has occurred a new and unique genetic package has been created, not a potential human being, but a human being with potential. For 9 months the mother provides nourishment and shelter, and birth is no substantial change, it is merely a change of address.

We are told that bringing an unwanted child into the world is an obscene act. Unwanted by whom? Is it too subtle a notion to understand it is more important to be a loving person than to be one who is loved. We need more people who are capable of projecting love.

We hear the claim that the poor are denied a right available to other women if we do not use tax money to fund abortions.

Well, make a list of all the things society denies poor women and let them make the choice of what we will give them.

Don't say "poor woman, go destroy your young, and we will pay for it."

An innocent, defenseless human life, in a caring and humane society deserves better than to be flushed down a toilet or burned in an incinerator.

The promise of America is that life is not just for the privileged, the planned, or the perfect.

Mr. MYERS of Pennsylvania. Mr. Chairman, will the gentleman yield [give up the floor]?

Mr. HYDE. I yield to the gentleman from Pennsylvania.

Mr. MYERS of Pennsylvania. Mr. Chairman, I support the gentleman's amendment. I think the basic question is, as the gentleman has put it, if we believe that human lives, in fact, are the objects which are being disposed of in plastic bags in the abortion clinics, then we certainly have a responsibility to protect them from the use of Federal funds to destroy them.

Mr. Chairman, I respect the gentleman for coming to the floor with the issue.

Mr. SNYDER. Mr. Chairman, will the gentleman yield?

Mr. HYDE. I yield to the gentleman from Kentucky.

Mr. SNYDER. Mr. Chairman, I want to associate myself with the gentleman in the well [of the House chamber] and commend the gentleman for his initiative in offering this amendment. I support it.

Mr. FLOOD. Mr. Chairman, I rise in opposition to the amendment.

Mr. Chairman, I would like the attention of the Members on this. I will tell them why. Nobody, but nobody in this room, has a better right to be standing here this minute on this subject, and everybody knows this, than the gentleman from Pennsylvania that is talking to the House now.

Mr. Chairman, everybody knows my position for many years with respect to abortion. I believe it is wrong, with a capital "W." It violates the most basic rights, the right of the unborn child, the right to life.

It is for that reason that I have supported for many, many years constitutional amendments which would address this very serious matter, and the Members know it. So, what am I doing down here now? Well, I will tell you. I oppose this amendment, and I will tell you why. Listen. This is blatantly discriminatory; that is why.

The Members do not like that? Of course they do not. It does not prohibit abortion. No, it does not prohibit abortion. It prohibits abortion for poor people. That is what it does. That is a horse of a different rolling stone. That is what it does. It does not require any change in the practice of the middle-income and the upper-income people. Oh, no. They are able to go to their private practitioners and get the service done for a fee. But, it does take away the option from those of our citizens who must rely on medicaid —and other public programs for medical care.

Now abortion. Mr. Chairman, abortion is not an economic issue; not at all. The morality—all right, the morality of abortion is no different for a poor family—the morality of abortion is no different for a poor family than it is for a rich family. Is that right? Of course: a standard of morality is a standard.

To accept—now, this is coming from me—to accept this amendment, the right of this country to impose on its poor citizens, impose on them a morality which it is not willing to impose on the rich as well, we would not dare do that. That is what this amendment does. To me, the choice is clear. Listen: A vote for this amendment is not a vote against abortion. It is a vote against poor people. That is what it is, as plain as the nose on your face.

This is not the place, on an appropriation bill, to address that kind of issue. This is not. Mr. Chairman, this is an appropriation bill. This is not a constitutional amendment.

I urge my colleagues to reject this amendment.

Mr. GUYER . . . Mr. Chairman, this issue has all but become threadbare, largely due to the fact that we cannot get action from the proper committee to really correct the wrong by a constitutional amendment that would solve the problem totally and properly. In the meantime, I think that children should have a bill of rights, which the law has indicated. They have legal rights, they have human rights, they have civil rights, they have property rights and they have divine rights. What a woman does with her body is her own business.

What she does with the body of somebody else is not her business.

I think that we here should go on record as safeguarding that most precious commodity, the gift of little children from God, who have a right to live. . . .

Ms. ABZUG . . . Mr. Chairman, the issue confronting this body is whether it will conduct itself with respect for the normal processes in which we engage and for which we were sent here. The issue being discussed here today is irrelevant, nongermane, and inappropriate as it relates to this measure, because the relief that is being sought by those who have a very particular point of view cannot be accomplished by this amendment.

This amendment is a cruel amendment, as was very ably pointed out by the chairman of the subcommittee presenting this appropriation bill. The passage of this amendment will not overcome the fact that every survey and every poll in this country show that a majority of people support the Supreme Court decision.

This is not to say that I and others who support the Supreme Court decision and the right of privacy that is protected therein do not respect the right of others to differ with us. We do respect the right of those who take an opposite point of view to differ with us on this subject. As a matter of fact, people like myself probably have more contact with those who differ on this subject than those who claim to represent them in the House. They understand our differences, and they had and we understand that there is a right to differ with a decision. Still, there must be an understanding that those who differ as a matter of conscience or religious belief have no right to impose their views on others who also wish to exercise their rights in their own way.

The implementation of this amendment or an amendment like this, if agreed to in this House, will mean only one thing, and that will be, as was pointed out by the subcommittee chairman, to deny to some people the rights the majority have in this country.

The fact is that most of the women who would be denied medicaid for the purpose of obtaining an abortion would be forced to carry unwanted pregnancies to term.

I have sat here all day and listened to the enormous concern that the Members of this House have expressed about increasing the budget. Well, the cost to the Government for the fiscal year, after implementation of this particular section in the public assistance area, would be between $450 million and $565 million. That is what those who seek to impose this irrelevant legislation upon an appropriation bill will cost this country—$450 million to $565 million. But it will not achieve the objective that they seek, namely, to create a law that says abortions are not permitted, because those same abortions will continue.

These abortions will continue, but under much more difficult conditions. Up to 25,000 cases involving serious medical complications from self-induced abortions would result, and the hospital costs involved would be anywhere from $375 to $2,000 per patient. And some will die—and you can calculate the social cost of that.

Language in the HEW bill restraining abortion is not a neutral position. By refusing medicaid reimbursement for abortions performed on poor women, the Government is de facto putting itself in the position of countenancing abortion for those who can pay for it but denying it to others who cannot. That would be clearly a discriminatory action, one which may result in legal action against the Government, if not indeed against this Congress itself.

Mr. Chairman, it seems to me that we have a form of relief. If this Congress wants to change the law of the Supreme Court, then . . . it should do so by appropriate procedures. There are hearings taking place in the Judiciary Committee. There have been extensive hearings on amendments which seek to reverse the decision of the Supreme Court. That is the proper and the orderly method in which we should proceed, and that is the path that should be taken by those who wish indeed to put an end to the Supreme Court decision. We should not act in this improper, disorderly way of attempting to put legislation in an appropriation bill. This will not solve the problem.

Hearings have taken place in the Judiciary Committee. That is what was wanted. Petitions were circulated in this House demanding that there be hearings.

I see the chairman of the Committee on the Judiciary here. He has indeed held these hearings.

Some say that is not enough and there are individuals who seek only to reflect their own point of view in this lawless and inappropriate way; and not the point of view of the majority who seek to distort the legislative process; and who seek to deprive the poor person, who always carries the burden of discrimination now once again.

Mr. Chairman, I hope the Members of this House will not take this improper action. The committee has to act. It will act. We can then proceed lawfully. . . .

Mr. KOCH. Mr. Chairman, I am opposed to the Hyde amendment. And I believe even those who are opposed to the Supreme Court decision allowing abortion as a constitutional right are not for this all encompassing amendment. This amendment would deny an abortion even to a woman whose very life would be lost without the abortion. I cannot believe that the Members here would be so heartless. I urge a no vote.

. . .

In Maher v. Roe *(1977) from Connecticut,* Beal v. Doe *(1977) from Pennsylvania, and* Poelker v. Doe *(1977) involving a municipal regulation from St. Louis, Missouri, Justices Louis Powell and Potter Stewart and Chief Justice Warren Burger from the* Roe *majority had joined Justices White, John Paul Stevens, and Rehnquist in upholding laws that denied funding abortions at any stage of the pregnancy. Powell, writing for the majority, concluded that a constitutionally protected right against state interference to seek an abortion was not the same as a constitutional mandate that states or other local government agencies would pay for abortions. Nor was a government's preference for birth over abortion barred by* Roe*. Justices William Brennan, Harry Blackmun, and Thurgood Marshall dissented, claiming to see in the denial of funding for abortion a blatant and cynical purpose to defeat* Roe *by making abortion difficult to obtain. The fact that all three states involved had stringent anti-abortion laws before* Roe *may have influenced the dissenters' views. In the last of the funding cases,* Harris v. McRae *(1980), Justice Potter Stewart wrote for himself and Justices White, Powell, and Rehnquist and for the chief justice.*

Harris, Secretary of Health and Human Services, v. McRae et al., 448 U.S. 297 (1980)

Mr. Justice Stewart delivered the opinion of the Court.

This case presents statutory [i.e., interpretation of a congressional act] and constitutional [i.e., interpretation of the federal Constitution] questions concerning the public funding of abortions under Title XIX of the Social Security Act, commonly known as the "Medicaid" Act, and recent annual Appropriations Acts containing the so-called "Hyde Amendment." The statutory question is whether Title XIX requires a State that participates in the Medicaid program to fund the cost of medically necessary abortions for which federal reimbursement is unavailable under the Hyde Amendment. The constitutional question, which arises only if Title XIX imposes no such requirement, is whether the Hyde Amendment, by denying public funding for certain medically necessary abortions, contravenes the liberty or equal protection guarantees of the Due Process Clause of the Fifth Amendment, or either of the Religion Clauses of the First Amendment. . . .

Since September 1976, Congress has prohibited—either by an amendment to the annual appropriations bill for the Department of Health, Education, and Welfare or by a joint resolution—the use of any federal funds to reimburse the cost of abortions under the Medicaid program except under certain specified circumstances. This funding restriction is commonly known as the "Hyde Amendment," after its original congressional sponsor, Representative Hyde. . . .

The plaintiffs . . . sought to enjoin the enforcement of the funding restriction on abortions. They alleged that the Hyde Amendment violated the First, Fourth, Fifth, and Ninth Amendments of the Constitution insofar as it limited the funding of abortions to those necessary to save the life of the mother, while permitting the funding of costs associated with childbirth. . . .

After a lengthy trial [in the federal district court], which inquired into the medical reasons for abortions and the diverse religious views on the subject, the District Court . . . concluded that the Hyde Amendment, though valid under the Establishment Clause, violates the equal protection component of the Fifth Amendment's Due Process Clause and the Free Exercise Clause of the First Amendment. . . . The court concluded that the Hyde Amendment violates the equal protection guarantee because, in its view, the decision of Congress to fund medically necessary services generally but only certain medically necessary abortions serves no legitimate governmental interest. As to the Free Exercise Clause of the First Amendment, the court held that insofar as a woman's decision to seek a medically necessary abortion may be a product of her religious beliefs under certain Protestant and Jewish tenets, the funding restrictions of the Hyde Amendment violate that constitutional guarantee as well. . . .

The doctrine of *Roe v. Wade*, the Court held in *Maher*, "protects the woman from unduly burdensome interference with her freedom to decide whether to terminate her pregnancy," such as the severe criminal sanctions at issue in *Roe v. Wade*, or the absolute requirement of spousal consent for an abortion challenged in *Planned Parenthood of Central Missouri v. Danforth*. . . .

But the constitutional freedom recognized in *Wade* [i.e., *Roe v. Wade*] and its progeny, the *Maher* Court explained, did not prevent Connecticut from making "a value judgement favoring childbirth over abortion, and . . . implement[ing] that judgement by the allocation of public funds."

The Court in *Maher* noted that its description of the doctrine recognized in *Wade* and its progeny signaled "no retreat" from those decisions. In explaining why the constitutional principle recognized in *Wade* and later cases—protecting a woman's freedom of choice—did not translate into a constitutional obligation of Connecticut to subsidize abortions, the Court cited the "basic difference between direct state interference with a protected activity . . ." [and a mandate to support that activity]. Thus, even though the Connecticut regulation favored childbirth over abortion by means of subsidization of one and not the other, the Court in *Maher* concluded that the regulation did not impinge on the constitutional freedom recognized in *Wade* because it imposed no governmental restriction on access to abortions.

The Hyde Amendment, like the Connecticut welfare regulation at issue in *Maher*, places no governmental obstacle in the path of a woman who chooses to terminate her pregnancy, but rather, by means of unequal subsidization of abortion and other medical services, encourages alternative activity deemed in the public interest. The present case does differ factually from *Maher* insofar as that case involved a failure to fund non-therapeutic abortions, whereas the Hyde Amendment affects a significant interest not present or asserted in *Maher*—the interest of a woman in protecting her health during pregnancy—and because that interest lies at the core of the personal constitutional freedom recognized in *Wade*, the present case is constitutionally different from *Maher*. It is the appellees' view that to the extent that the Hyde Amendment withholds funding for certain medically necessary abortions, it clearly impinges on the constitutional principle recognized in *Wade*.

But, regardless of whether the freedom of a woman to choose to terminate her pregnancy for health reasons lies at the core or the periphery of the due process liberty recognized in *Wade*, it simply does not follow that a woman's freedom of choice carries with it a constitutional entitlement to the financial resources to avail herself of the full range of protected choices. . . . The fact remains that the Hyde Amendment leaves an indigent woman with at least the same range of choice in deciding whether to obtain a medically necessary abortion as she would have had if Congress had chosen to subsidize no health care costs at all. We are thus not persuaded that the Hyde Amendment impinges on the constitutionally protected freedom of choice recognized in *Wade*.

The appellees also argue that the Hyde Amendment contravenes rights secured by the Religion Clauses of the First Amendment. It is the appellees' view that the Hyde Amendment violates the Establishment Clause because it incorporates into law the doctrines of the Roman Catholic Church concerning the sinfulness of abortion and the time at which life commences. Moreover, insofar as a woman's decision to seek a medically necessary abortion may be a product of her religious beliefs under certain Protestant and Jewish tenets, the appellees assert that the funding limitations of the Hyde Amendment impinge on the freedom of religion guaranteed by the Free Exercise Clause.

It is well settled that "a legislative enactment does not contravene the Establishment Clause if it has a secular legislative purpose, if its principal or primary effect neither advances nor inhibits religion, and if it does not foster an excessive governmental entanglement with religion." . . . Although neither a State nor the Federal Government can constitutionally "pass laws which aid one religion, aid all religions, or prefer one religion over another," . . . it does not follow that a statute violates the Establishment Clause because it "happens to coincide or harmonize with the tenets of some or all religions." . . . The Hyde Amendment, as the District Court noted, is as much a reflection of "traditionalist" values towards abortion, as it is an embodiment of the views of any particular religion. . . . The remaining question then is whether the Hyde Amendment is rationally related to a legitimate governmental objective. It is the Government's position that the Hyde Amendment bears a rational relationship to its legitimate interest in protecting the potential life of the fetus. We agree.

• • •

The three dissenting opinions in Harris *were concerned with the way in which the federal funding ban affected poor women. This issue had been raised even before* Roe *was decided, and in* Roe *the majority had explicitly dodged it. Were these concerns about policy rather than constitutionality and thus better left to legislatures? Note how the dissenters changed the use of the word "burden" from its application in the majority opinion.*

Mr. Justice Brennan, with whom Mr. Justice Marshall and Mr. Justice Blackmun join, dissenting.

REGULATING AND FUNDING ABORTIONS

. . . I . . . express my continuing disagreement with the Court's mis-characterization of the nature of the fundamental right recognized in *Roe v. Wade*, and its misconception of the manner in which that right is in-fringed by federal and state legislation withdrawing all funding for medically necessary abortions.

Roe v. Wade held that the constitutional right to personal privacy encom-passes a woman's decision whether or not to terminate her pregnancy. *Roe* and its progeny established that the pregnant woman has a right to be free from state interference with her choice to have an abortion—a right which, at least prior to the end of the first trimester, absolutely prohibits any governmental regulation of that highly personal decision. The proposition for which these cases stand thus is not that the State is under an affirmative obligation to ensure access to abortions for all who may desire them; it is that the State must refrain from wielding its enormous power and influ-ence in a manner that might burden the pregnant woman's freedom to choose whether to have an abortion. The Hyde Amendment's denial of public funds for medically necessary abortions plainly intrudes upon this constitutionally protected decision, for both by design and in effect it serves to coerce indigent pregnant women to bear children that they would otherwise elect not to have.

When viewed in the context of the Medicaid program to which it is appended, it is obvious that the Hyde Amendment is nothing less than an attempt by Congress to circumvent the dictates of the Constitution and achieve indirectly what *Roe v. Wade* said it could not do directly. . . .

The Court's contrary conclusion is premised on its belief that "[t]he financial constraints that restrict an indigent woman's ability to enjoy the full range of constitutionally protected freedom of choice are the product not of governmental restrictions on access to abortions, but rather of her indigence." Accurate at this statement may be, it reveals only half the picture. For what the Court fails to appreciate is that it is not only simply the woman's indigence that interferes with her freedom of choice, but the combination of her own poverty and the Government's unequal subsidiza-tion of abortion and childbirth.

A poor woman in the early stages of pregnancy confronts two alterna-tives: she may elect either to carry the fetus to term or to have an abortion. In the abstract, of course, this choice is hers alone, and the Court rightly observes that the Hyde Amendment "places no governmental obstacle in the path of a woman who chooses to terminate her pregnancy." But the reality of the situation is that the Hyde Amendment has effectively re-moved this choice from the indigent woman's hands. By funding all of the expenses associated with childbirth and none of the expenses incurred in terminating pregnancy, the Government literally makes an offer that the indigent woman cannot afford to refuse. It matters not that in this instance the Government has used the carrot rather than the stick. What is critical is the realization that as a practical matter, many poverty-stricken women will choose to carry their pregnancy to term simply because the Government provides funds for the associated medical services, even though these same women would have chosen to have an abortion if the Government had also paid for that option, or indeed if the Government had stayed out of the picture altogether and had defrayed the costs of neither procedure. . . .

Mr. Justice Marshall, dissenting.

Three years ago, in *Maher v. Roe* (1977), the Court upheld a state program that excluded non-therapeutic abortions from a welfare program that generally subsidized the medical expenses incidental to pregnancy and childbirth. At that time, I expressed my fear "that the Court's decisions will be an invitation to public officials, already under extraordinary pressure from well-financed and carefully orchestrated lobbying campaigns, to approve more such restrictions" on governmental funding for abortion. . . .

That fear has proved justified. Under the Hyde Amendment, federal funding is denied for abortions that are medically necessary and that are necessary to avert severe and permanent damage to the health of the mother. The Court's opinion studiously avoids recognizing the undeniable fact that for women eligible for Medicaid—poor women—denial of a Medicaid-funded abortion is equivalent to denial of legal abortion altogether. By definition, these women do not have the money to pay for an abortion themselves. If abortion is medically necessary and a funded abortion is unavailable, they must resort to back-alley butchers, attempt to induce an abortion themselves by crude and dangerous methods, or suffer the serious medical consequences of attempting to carry the fetus to term. Because legal abortion is not a realistic option for such women, the predictable result of the Hyde Amendment will be a significant increase in the number of poor women who will die or suffer significant health damage because of an inability to procure necessary medical services. . . .

Mr. Justice Stevens, dissenting.

The consequences of today's opinion—consequences to which the Court seems oblivious—are not difficult to predict. Pregnant women denied the funding necessary to procure abortions will be restricted to two alternatives. First, they can carry the fetus to term—even though that route may result in severe injury or death to the mother, the fetus, or both. If that course appears intolerable, they can resort to self-induced abortions or attempt to obtain illegal abortions—not because bearing a child would be inconvenient, but because it is necessary in order to protect their health. The result will not be to protect their health. The result will not be to protect what the Court describes as "the legitimate governmental objective of protecting potential life," but to ensure the destruction of both fetal and maternal life. . . . In my view, it is only be blinding itself to that other world that the Court can reach the result it announces today. . . .

· · ·

Not only did states attempt to regulate abortion, cities with municipal hospital systems also weighed in. An Akron, Ohio, ordinance passed by the city in February 1978 had a preamble stating as a matter of law that the fetus was a being in life from conception.

Akron (Ohio) Ordinance no. 160-1978

WHEREAS, it is the finding of Council that there is no point in time between the union of sperm and egg, or at least the blastocyst stage and the birth of the infant at which point we can say the unborn child is not a human life, and that the changes occurring between implantation, a six-weeks embryo, a six-month fetus, and a one-week-old child, or a mature adult are merely stages of development and maturation; and

WHEREAS, traditionally the physician has been responsible for the welfare of both the pregnant woman and her unborn child, and that while situations of conflict may arise between a pregnant woman's health interests and the welfare of her unborn child, the resolution of such conflicts by inducing abortion in no way implies that the physician has an adversary relationship towards the unborn child; and

WHEREAS, Council therefore wishes to affirm that the destruction of the unborn child is not the primary purpose of abortion and that consequently Council recognizes a continuing obligation on the part of the physician towards the survival of a viable unborn child where this obligation can be discharged without additional hazard to the health of the pregnant woman; and

WHEREAS, Council, after extensive public hearings and investigations concludes that enactment of this ordinance is a reasonable and prudent action which will significantly contribute to the preservation of the public life, health, safety, morals, and welfare.

The Akron, Ohio, ordinance included a list of restrictions and requirements that would become the standard for many other localities and states. Under it, all abortions performed after the first trimester of pregnancy were to be performed in a hospital; it prohibited a physician from performing an abortion on an unmarried minor under the age of fifteen unless he obtained the consent of one of her parents or unless the minor obtained an order from a court having jurisdiction over her that the abortion be performed; it required that the attending physician inform his or her patient of the status of her pregnancy, the development of her fetus, the date of possible viability, the physical and emotional complications that may result from an abortion, and the availability of agencies to provide her with assistance and information with respect to birth control, adoption, and childbirth and also inform her of the particular risks associated with her pregnancy and the abortion technique to be employed; it prohibited a physician from performing an abortion until twenty-four hours after the pregnant woman signed a consent form; and it required physicians performing abortions to ensure that fetal remains were disposed of in a "humane and sanitary manner." A violation of the ordinance was punishable as a misdemeanor.

Abortion providers suspected that the underlying purpose of the ordinance was to deter all women from gaining abortions, and they turned to the federal courts to gain permanent injunctions against the imposition of the ordinance. The new president, Ronald Reagan, sent Solicitor General Rex Lee to the oral argument to support the Akron ordinance. Justice Powell wrote for the majority an opinion of the Court in which Chief Justice Burger and Justices Brennan, Marshall, Blackmun, and Stevens joined. Justice O'Connor dissented, with an opinion that Justices White and Rehnquist joined. Note as you read the opinion the importance of the standard of review the Court decides to apply to the ordinance. Is it to be "strict scrutiny" (required of all statutes that seem to deny a "fundamental right") or "rational basis" (that the statute's provisions have a rational relation to a permissible goal) test, the latter much more permissive of such legislation but applicable only when no fundamental constitutional right is at stake?

City of Akron v. Akron Center for Reproductive Health, Inc., et al., 462 U.S. 416 (1983)

JUSTICE POWELL delivered the opinion of the Court.

In this litigation we must decide the constitutionality of several provisions of an ordinance enacted by the city of Akron, Ohio, to regulate the performance of abortions. . . . Today . . . the dissenting opinion rejects the basic premise of *Roe* and its progeny. The dissent stops short of arguing flatly that *Roe* should be overruled. Rather, it adopts reasoning that, for all practical purposes, would accomplish precisely that result. The dissent states that "[even] assuming that there is a fundamental right to terminate pregnancy in some situations," the State's compelling interests in maternal health and potential human life "are present *throughout* pregnancy." . . .

The existence of these compelling interests turns out to be largely unnecessary, however, for the dissent does not think that even one of the numerous abortion regulations at issue imposes a sufficient burden on the "limited" fundamental right . . . to require [the use of the standard of] heightened scrutiny. . . . The dissent therefore would hold that a requirement that all abortions be performed in an acute-care, general hospital does not impose an unacceptable burden on the abortion decision. It requires no great familiarity with the cost and limited availability of such hospitals to appreciate that the effect of the dissent's views would be to drive the performance of many abortions back underground free of effective regulation and often without the attendance of a physician.

In sum, it appears that the dissent would uphold virtually any abortion regulation under a rational-basis test. It also appears that even where heightened scrutiny is deemed appropriate, the dissent would uphold virtually any abortion-inhibiting regulation because of the State's interest in preserving potential human life. . . . This analysis is wholly incompatible with the existence of the fundamental right recognized in *Roe* v. *Wade*. . . .

We think it prudent, however, to retain *Roe*'s identification of the beginning of the second trimester as the approximate time at which the State's interest in maternal health becomes sufficiently compelling to justify significant regulation of abortion. We note that the medical evidence suggests that until approximately the end of the first trimester, the State's interest in maternal health would not be served by regulations that restrict the manner in which abortions are performed by a licensed physician. . . . The *Roe* trimester standard thus continues to provide a reasonable legal framework for limiting a State's authority to regulate abortions. Where the State adopts a health regulation governing the performance of abortions during the second trimester, the determinative question should be whether there is a reasonable medical basis for the regulation. . . . This does not mean that a State never may enact a regulation touching on the woman's abortion right during the first weeks of pregnancy. Certain regulations that have no significant impact on the woman's exercise of her right may be permissible where justified by important state health objectives. . . .

In the District Court plaintiffs sought to demonstrate that this hospitalization requirement has a serious detrimental impact on a woman's ability to obtain a second-trimester abortion in Akron and that it is not reasonably related to the State's interest in the health of the pregnant woman. . . . We reaffirm today, that a State's interest in health regulation becomes compelling at approximately the end of the first trimester. The existence of a compelling state interest in health, however, is only the beginning of the inquiry. The State's regulation may be upheld only if it is reasonably designed to further that state interest. . . . If it appears that during a substantial portion of the second trimester the State's regulation "[departs] from accepted medical practice," regulation may not be upheld simply because it may be reasonable for the remaining portion of the trimester. Rather, the State is obligated to make a reasonable effort to limit the effect of its regulations to the period in the trimester during which its health interest will be furthered. . . . There can be no doubt that . . . [the] second-trimester hospitalization requirement places a significant obstacle in the path of women seeking an abortion. A primary burden created by the requirement is additional cost to the woman. . . .

We turn next to . . . the provision prohibiting a physician from performing an abortion on a minor pregnant woman under the age of 15 unless he obtains "the informed written consent of one of her parents or her legal guardian" or unless the minor obtains "an order from a court having jurisdiction over her that the abortion be performed or induced." . . . The relevant legal standards are not in dispute. The Court has held that "the State may not impose a blanket provision . . . requiring the consent of a parent or person *in loco parentis* as a condition for abortion of an unmarried minor." . . . Under these decisions, it is clear that Akron may not make a blanket determination that *all* minors under the age of 15 are too immature to make this decision or that an abortion never may be in the minor's best interests without parental approval. . . .

The Akron ordinance provides that no abortion shall be performed except "with the informed written consent of the pregnant woman . . . given freely and without coercion." . . . Furthermore, "in order to insure that the consent for an abortion is truly informed consent," the woman must be "orally informed by her attending physician" of the status of her pregnancy, the development of her fetus, the date of possible viability, the physical and emotional complications that may result from an abortion, and the availability of agencies to provide her with assistance and information with respect to birth control, adoption, and childbirth. . . . In addition, the attending physician must inform her "of the particular risks associated with her own pregnancy and the abortion technique to be employed . . . [and] other information which in his own medical judgment is relevant to her decision as to whether to have an abortion or carry her pregnancy to term." . . . The validity of an informed consent requirement thus rests on the State's interest in protecting the health of the pregnant woman. . . . This does not mean, however, that a State has unreviewable [by a court] authority to decide what information a woman must be given before she chooses to have an abortion. It remains primarily the responsibility of the physician to ensure that appropriate information is conveyed to his patient, depending on her particular circumstances. *Danforth*'s recognition of the State's interest in ensuring that this information be given will not justify abortion regulations designed to influence the woman's informed choice between abortion or childbirth. . . .

Viewing the city's regulations in this light, we believe that §1870.06(B) [of the ordinance] attempts to extend the State's interest in ensuring "informed consent" beyond permissible limits. First, it is fair to say that much of the information required is designed not to inform the woman's consent but rather to persuade her to withhold it altogether. Subsection (3) requires the physician to inform his patient that "the unborn child is a human life from the moment of conception," a requirement inconsistent with the Court's holding in *Roe* v. *Wade* that a State may not adopt one theory of when life begins to justify its regulation of abortions. Moreover, much of the detailed description of "the anatomical and physiological characteristics of the particular unborn child" required by subsection (3) would involve at best speculation by the physician. And subsection (5), that begins with the dubious statement that "abortion is a major surgical procedure" and proceeds to describe numerous possible physical and psychological complications of abortion, is a "parade of horribles" intended to suggest that abortion is a particularly dangerous procedure. . . .

The Akron ordinance prohibits a physician from performing an abortion until 24 hours after the pregnant woman signs a consent form. . . . We find that Akron has failed to demonstrate that any legitimate state interest is furthered by an arbitrary and inflexible waiting period. There is no evidence suggesting that the abortion procedure will be performed more safely. Nor are we convinced that the State's legitimate concern that the woman's decision be informed is reasonably served by requiring a 24-hour delay as a matter of course. . . .

The Akron ordinance requires physicians performing abortions to "insure that the remains of the unborn child are disposed of in a humane and sanitary manner." The Court of Appeals found that the word "humane" was impermissibly vague as a definition of conduct subject to criminal prosecution. The court invalidated the entire provision. . . . We affirm this judgment. . . .

. . .

Justices White and Rehnquist supported the Akron ordinance using familiar arguments. Justice Sandra Day O'Connor, new to the Court, phrased her grounds for dissent in a different way from those of her colleagues. What was Justice O'Connor's formula, and did it spell the end of the constitutionally protected right to an abortion or merely replace the trimester formula with another, more workable formulation?

Justice O'Connor, with whom Justice White and Justice Rehnquist join, dissenting.

In *Roe* v. *Wade* the Court held that the "right of privacy . . . founded in the Fourteenth Amendment's concept of personal liberty and restrictions upon state action . . . is broad enough to encompass a woman's decision whether or not to terminate her pregnancy." The parties in these cases have not asked the Court to re-examine the validity of that holding and the court below did not address it. Accordingly, the Court does not re-examine its previous holding.

Nonetheless, it is apparent from the Court's opinion that neither sound constitutional theory nor our need to decide cases based on the application of neutral principles can accommodate an analytical framework that varies according to the "stages" of pregnancy, where those stages, and their concomitant standards of review, differ according to the level of medical technology available when a particular challenge to state regulation occurs. The Court's analysis of the Akron regulations is inconsistent both with the methods of analysis employed in previous cases dealing with abortion, and with the Court's approach to fundamental rights in other areas. Our recent cases indicate that a regulation imposed on "a lawful abortion 'is not unconstitutional unless it unduly burdens the right to seek an abortion.'"

. . . In my view, this "unduly burdensome" standard should be applied to the challenged regulations throughout the entire pregnancy without reference to the particular "stage" of pregnancy involved. If the particular regulation does not "unduly [burden]" the fundamental right, *Maher, supra,* at 473, then our evaluation of that regulation is limited to our determination that the regulation rationally relates to a legitimate state purpose. . . .

The trimester or "three-stage" approach adopted by the Court in *Roe,* and, in a modified form, employed by the Court to analyze the regulations in these cases, cannot be supported as a legitimate or useful framework for accommodating the woman's right and the State's interests. The decision of the Court today graphically illustrates why the trimester approach is a completely unworkable method of accommodating the conflicting personal rights and compelling state interests that are involved in the abortion context. . . .

As the Court indicates today, the State's compelling interest in maternal health changes as medical technology changes, and any health regulation must not "depart from accepted medical practice." . . . It is not difficult to see that despite the Court's purported adherence to the trimester approach adopted in *Roe*, the lines drawn in that decision have now been "blurred" because of what the Court accepts as technological advancement in the safety of abortion procedure. . . . It is even more difficult to believe that this Court, without the resources available to those bodies entrusted with making legislative choices, believes itself competent to make these inquiries and to revise these standards every time the American College of Obstetricians and Gynecologists (ACOG) or similar group revises its views about what is and what is not appropriate medical procedure in this area. Indeed, the ACOG Standards on which the Court relies were changed in 1982 after trial in the present cases. Before ACOG changed its Standards in 1982, it recommended that all mid-trimester abortions be performed in a hospital. . . . As today's decision indicates, medical technology is changing, and this change will necessitate our continued functioning as the Nation's "*ex officio* medical board with powers to approve or disapprove medical and operative practices and standards throughout the United States." *Planned Parenthood of Central Missouri* v. *Danforth*, 428 U.S. 52, 99 (1976) (White, J., concurring in part and dissenting in part).

. . . The *Roe* framework, then, is clearly on a collision course with itself. As the medical risks of various abortion procedures decrease, the point at which the State may regulate for reasons of maternal health is moved further forward to actual childbirth. As medical science becomes better able to provide for the separate existence of the fetus, the point of viability is moved further back toward conception. . . .

. . .

Pennsylvania was the second state, after Missouri, determined to test the limits of the Roe *doctrine. The Abortion Control Act of 1974, for example, denied state funding for "unneeded and unnecessary" abortions (including those sought in the first trimester) and required spousal and parental consent. In 1982, a broad-spectrum right-to-life movement had emerged, and its lead-*

ers created the Pennsylvania Pro-Life Federation. They helped elect two governors, Richard Thornburgh and Robert Casey, the former a Republican and the latter a Democrat, who shared one important stance: they were opposed to abortion rights.

Thornburgh signed the 1982 Abortion Control Act, which reintroduced the 1974 provisions in addition to introducing some new ones. The state of Pennsylvania had added to the list of physicians' duties the determination of the viability of the fetus; the preparation of a report (which could be "copied" but was not a public record) of personal information on the patient; and the insistence on a second physician at the procedure, not to protect the health of the mother but to take control of the "child" (the language in the statute, which the Court quoted) and make every effort to save it if possible. Violation of this last requirement was a felony. Although the statute provided that a doctor's oath that he acted in good faith to save the mother or that the fetus could not be saved was a defense to the charge, doctors who did not want to be placed in the precarious position of losing a license or having to defend against a felony charge brought suit against the law.

The Supreme Court decided Thornburgh v. American College of Obstetricians and Gynecologists in 1986. Justice Blackmun wrote the opinion of the Court.

Thornburgh, Governor of Pennsylvania, et al. v. American College of Obstetricians and Gynecologists et al., 476 U.S. 747 (1986)

Justice Blackmun delivered the opinion of the Court.

. . . In the years since this Court's decision in *Roe*, States and municipalities have adopted a number of measures seemingly designed to prevent a woman, with the advice of her physician, from exercising her freedom of choice. *Akron* is but one example. But the constitutional principles that led this Court to its decisions in 1973 still provide the compelling reason for recognizing the constitutional dimensions of a woman's right to decide whether to end her pregnancy. . . . The States are not free, under the guise of protecting maternal health or potential life, to intimidate women into continuing pregnancies. Appellants claim that the statutory provisions before us today further legitimate compelling interests of the Commonwealth. Close analysis of those provisions, however, shows that they wholly subordinate constitutional privacy interests and concerns with maternal health in an effort to deter a woman from making a decision that, with her physician, is hers to make. . . .

The report required . . . is detailed and must include, among other things, identification of the performing and referring physicians and of the facility or agency; information as to the woman's political subdivision and State of residence, age, race, marital status, and number of prior pregnancies; the date of her last menstrual period and the probable gestational age; the basis for any judgment that a medical emergency existed; the basis for any determination of nonviability; and the method of payment for the abortion. The report is to be signed by the attending physician. . . .

Despite the fact that §3214(e)(2) provides that such reports "shall not be deemed public records," within the meaning of the Commonwealth's "Right-to-Know Law" . . . each report "shall be made available for public inspection and copying within 15 days of receipt in a form which will not lead to the disclosure of the identity of any person filing a report." Similarly, the report of complications, required by §3214(h), "shall be open to public inspection and copying." A willful failure to file a report required under §3214 is "unprofessional conduct" and the noncomplying physician's license "shall be subject to suspension or revocation." §3214(i)(1). The scope of the information required and its availability to the public belie any assertions by the Commonwealth that it is advancing any legitimate interest. . . . The reports required under the Act before us today go well beyond the health-related interests that served to justify the Missouri reports under consideration in *Danforth*.

Pennsylvania would require, as Missouri did not, information as to method of payment, as to the woman's personal history, and as to the bases for medical judgments. The Missouri reports were to be used "only for statistical purposes." . . . They were to be maintained in confidence, with the sole exception of public health officers. . . . The required Pennsylvania reports, on the other hand, while claimed not to be "public," are available nonetheless to the public for copying. Moreover, there is no limitation on the use to which the Commonwealth or the public copiers may put them. The elements that proved persuasive for the ruling in *Danforth* are absent here. The decision to terminate a pregnancy is an intensely private one that must be protected in a way that assures anonymity. . . .

Section 3210(c) n15 requires that a second physician be present during an abortion performed when viability is possible. The second physician is to "take control of the child and . . . provide immediate medical care for the child, taking all reasonable steps necessary, in his judgment, to preserve the child's life and health." Violation of this requirement is a felony of the third degree. . . .

While the Missouri statute [challenged in *Danforth*] . . . was worded sufficiently to imply an emergency exception, Pennsylvania's statute contains no such comforting or helpful language and evinces no intent to protect a woman whose life may be at risk. . . .

It is clear that the Pennsylvania Legislature knows how to provide a medical-emergency exception when it chooses to do so. . . . We necessarily conclude that the legislature's failure to provide a medical-emergency exception in §3210(c) was intentional. All the factors are here for chilling the performance of a late abortion, which, more than one performed at an earlier date, perhaps tends to be under emergency conditions. . . .

. . .

The justices routinely circulate drafts of their intended opinions, so Justice White had already seen an earlier version of the majority opinion when he prepared his dissent. He supported all of the Pennsylvania provisions and rebutted Blackmun's arguments.

Justice White, with whom Justice Rehnquist joins, dissenting.

Today the Court carries forward the "difficult and continuing venture in substantive due process," *Planned Parenthood of Central Missouri* v. *Danforth*, 428 U.S. 52 (1976) (WHITE, J., dissenting), that began with the decision in *Roe* v. *Wade*, and has led the Court further and further afield in the 13 years since that decision was handed down. I was in dissent in *Roe* v. *Wade* and am in dissent today. . . . Indeed, in my view, our precedents in this area, applied in a manner consistent with sound principles of constitutional adjudication, require reversal of the Court of Appeals [which had struck down the Pennsylvania law] on the ground that the provisions before us are facially constitutional.

The rule of *stare decisis* [literally "let the decision stand," a basic doctrine of common-law courts] is essential if case-by-case judicial decision-making is to be reconciled with the principle of the rule of law, for when governing legal standards are open to revision in every case, deciding cases becomes a mere exercise of judicial will, with arbitrary and unpredictable results. But *stare decisis* is not the only constraint upon judicial decision-making. Cases—like this one—that involve our assumed power to set aside on grounds of unconstitutionality a state or federal statute representing the democratically expressed will of the people call other considerations into play.

Because the Constitution itself is ordained and established by the people of the United States, constitutional adjudication by this Court does not, in theory at any rate, frustrate the authority of the people to govern themselves through institutions of their own devising and in accordance with principles of their own choosing. But decisions that find in the Constitution principles or values that cannot fairly be read into that document usurp the people's authority, for such decisions represent choices that the people have never made and that they cannot disavow through corrective legislation. For this reason, it is essential that this Court maintain the power to restore authority to its proper possessors by correcting constitutional decisions that, on reconsideration, are found to be mistaken. . . . *Stare decisis* did not stand in the way of the Justices who, in the late 1930's, swept away constitutional doctrines that had placed unwarranted restrictions on the power of the State and Federal Governments to enact social and economic legislation. . . . Nor did *stare decisis* deter a different set of Justices, some 15 years later, from rejecting the theretofore prevailing view that the Fourteenth Amendment permitted the States to maintain the system of racial segregation [in *Brown* v. *Board of Education*]. In both instances, history has been far kinder to those who departed from precedent than to those who would have blindly followed the rule of *stare decisis*. . . .

In my view, the time has come to recognize that *Roe* v. *Wade*, no less than the cases overruled by the Court in the decisions I have just cited, "departs from a proper understanding" of the Constitution and to overrule it. . . .

If the woman's liberty to choose an abortion is fundamental . . . it is not because any of our precedents (aside from *Roe* itself) command or justify that result; it can only be because protection for this unique choice is itself "implicit in the concept of ordered liberty" or, perhaps, "deeply rooted in this Nation's history and tradition." It seems clear to me that it is neither. The Court's opinion in *Roe* itself convincingly refutes the notion that the abortion liberty is deeply rooted in the history or tradition of our people, as does the continuing and deep division of the people themselves over the question of abortion. As for the notion that choice in the matter of abortion is implicit in the concept of ordered liberty, it seems apparent to me that a free, egalitarian, and democratic society does not presuppose any particular rule or set of rules with respect to abortion. And again, the fact that many men and women of good will and high commitment to constitutional government place themselves on both sides of the abortion controversy strengthens my own conviction that the values animating the Constitution do not compel recognition of the abortion liberty as fundamental. In so denominating that liberty, the Court engages not in constitutional interpretation, but in the unrestrained imposition of its own, extraconstitutional value preferences. . . .

The majority's opinion evinces no deference toward the State's legitimate policy. Rather, the majority makes it clear from the outset that it simply disapproves of any attempt by Pennsylvania to legislate in this area. The history of the state legislature's decade-long effort to pass a constitutional abortion statute is recounted as if it were evidence of some sinister conspiracy. . . . The majority, however, seems to find it necessary to respond by changing the rules to invalidate what before would have seemed permissible. The result is a decision that finds no justification in the Court's previous holdings, departs from sound principles of constitutional and statutory interpretation, and unduly limits the State's power to implement the legitimate (and in some circumstances compelling) policy of encouraging normal childbirth in preference to abortion. . . .

The decision today appears symptomatic of the Court's own insecurity over its handiwork in *Roe* v. *Wade* and the cases following that decision. Aware that in *Roe* it essentially created something out of nothing and that there are many in this country who hold that decision to be basically illegitimate, the Court responds defensively. Perceiving, in a statute implementing the State's legitimate policy of preferring childbirth to abortion, a threat to or criticism of the decision in *Roe* v. *Wade*, the majority indiscriminately strikes down statutory provisions that in no way contravene the right recognized in *Roe*. I do not share the warped point of view of the majority, nor can I follow the tortuous path the majority treads in proceeding to strike down the statute before us. I dissent.

. . .

There the matter stood—with a sharply divided Court mirroring a sharply divided nation. But abortion and abortion rights cases continued to arrive at the High Court, and new appointments to the Court meant that the tide might turn at any time against *Roe*. Chief Justice Burger had stepped down in 1986, and President Ronald Reagan, who opposed *Roe*, wanted and got Senate confirmation of Justice Rehnquist as chief justice. He was a strong opponent of abortion rights. His place as associate justice was taken by Antonin Scalia, a former professor, judge, and Republican political appointee whose opposition to *Roe* was relentless. The last of the Reagan appointees to the Court was Anthony Kennedy, who replaced Powell in 1988. A conservative in many matters, his position on abortion was unclear. On the Supreme Court, he seemed to fit nicely into the emerging conservative majority. But would he join Scalia, Rehnquist, and O'Connor in rejecting *Roe*'s trimester test? Would he also vote to overturn *Roe*? The future of abortion rights seemed to rest with him and other new appointments to the bench.

NOTES

1. The full text of the letter appears in Cynthia Gorney, *Articles of Faith: A Frontline History of the Abortion Wars* (New York, 1998), 182–83.

2. Quoted in N. E. H. Hull and Peter Charles Hoffer, *Roe v. Wade: The Abortion Rights Controversy in American History* (Lawrence, Kans., 2001), 185.

3. Ibid., 186.

4. Jerry Falwell, *Strength for the Journey: An Autobiography* (New York, 1987), 336, 337, 342.

CHAPTER 6

Nineteen Eighty-Nine: A Year of Decision

By the end of the 1980s, an unbiased observer might have concluded that the legal rights of women in the law were not as tenuous as they had been two decades before. Provisions of the Civil Rights Act of 1964 laid the groundwork for women's admission to higher education and professional programs. Titles of the act also mandated athletic opportunities for women. Despite the failure of the Equal Rights Amendment to gain ratification, suits brought by feminist legal scholars and litigators had made sexual harassment into a justiciable cause of civil action in the federal courts, preventing employers and fellow workers from turning the workplace into a hostile environment for the working woman. Businesses and educational institutions adopted sexual harassment codes that helped men and women report, mediate, and reduce harassment on the job. The women's movement had identified the abused spouse as a victim in a crime that was as hidden as abortion and had made the "battered wife" a widely recognized figure in the law. Suits for equal pay for equal work and for pension, medical leave, and other long-neglected inequities in employment law gained women a measure of financial equality. Women also gained jobs through affirmative action programs when the employer had a long history of discriminating against women.

At the same time, and perhaps as a result of the legal changes, a backlash against women who challenged traditional views of women's roles was building. In the flagship issue for the women's movement—abortion law reform—the backlash seemed on the verge of triumph. A constitutionally based fundamental right to an abortion in the early stages of a pregnancy had barely survived for the past decade. In the High Court, burdensome state regulations had fallen, but the majority had dwindled from seven to five. State and federal medical care providers did not have to fund abortions. With the Reagan appointments, the dissenters in *Akron* and *Thornburgh* could reasonably expect to triumph.

Under Justice O'Connor's "undue burden" test, the state's interest in protecting potential human life justified regulation of abortion from the first moment of conception. The choice of ending a pregnancy was no longer a fundamental right. It was a small step from this position for the High Court to return control of abortion to the state legislatures and Congress.

Roe owed its survival thus far in part to the doctrine of stare decisis, the principle that courts should not lightly overturn well-established precedents, but Justices Rehnquist, White, and Scalia agreed that the Court had decided *Roe* wrongly in the first place and wanted it reversed. If *Roe* went down, however, its constitutional underpinnings in the right to privacy could be exposed to attack, endangering *Griswold*. This was not acceptable to Justice Kennedy. In his statement to the Senate Judiciary Committee during hearings on his appointment, he made clear that the Constitution provides for "protection of a value that we call privacy."[1]

It appeared at the time that 1989 would be the year of decision. Certainly the year was filled with momentous events for the future of abortion services and abortion rights. In the second week of the new year, the High Court agreed to hear *Webster v. Reproductive Health Services*, another effort by the majority in the Missouri state legislature to regulate abortion practices. In 1986, Missouri had passed the third generation of its anti-abortion laws. The new statute included twenty provisions, seven of which, based on right-to-life lobbyists' models (the very same models that were adopted in the city of Akron and struck down by the Court in 1983 in *Planned Parenthood v. Ashcroft*), were openly designed to discourage abortion. There was a preamble to the act labeled a "finding" by the legislature that the "life of each human being begins at conception" and "unborn children have protectable interests in life, health, and well-being." William Webster, the state's attorney general, conceded in the oral argument that the preamble did not violate *Roe*, for the findings neither served any right nor imposed any duty.

The next provision required that all abortions after the sixteenth week be performed in hospitals. This created a problem for both doctors and their patients given a third provision that no public hospital or public hospital worker was to take part in an abortion and no public hospital was to expend funds on abortions. The former limitation had already been struck down by the Court. The latter was upheld.

The next set of provisions applied to all abortion clinics as well as to public facilities—a series of rules forbidding doctors from advising anyone to have an abortion, that an abortion was available, or that one might be advisable, even if the pregnancy was in trouble. This was part of the legislatively scripted "informed consent" that the doctor was required to read to the patient and the patient was required to sign, although again such scripts had been rejected by the Court in *Akron* and *Thornburgh*.

A final provision required doctors to ascertain, through a series of tests, whether a fetus was viable. This was unobjectionable in itself, but for opponents of the Missouri law, the means were not. The High Court had already ruled that the state could not dictate to a doctor which tests were to be used to determine fetal age, but Missouri required its physicians to determine lung size, and the only sure test for lung size, amniocentesis, was both expensive and dangerous to the mother and the fetus. The state seemed to be telling doctors that it was more important to determine the viability of the fetus than to insure the health of the woman patient and that the potentially viable fetus was the doctor's primary patient until proven otherwise.

State legislatures are subject to the rulings of the Supreme Court, and the Missouri legislature knew the Court's views on all of these provisions years before it passed its revised abortion law. But the state legislators also knew that the composition of the Court had changed and persistence might pay off with a pro-life majority on the Court. Some pro-choice advocates likened Missouri's inclusion of regulatory provisions already struck down by the Court to southern state legislatures' "massive resistance" to the end of segregation ordered in *Brown v. Board of Education* (1954). At the same time, pro-life advocates regarded *Roe* the way that antislavery forces perceived *Dred Scott v. Sandford* (1857), the Supreme Court decision that announced that slavery was legal in all territories of the United States. They claimed that overturning *Roe* would be a democratic as well as moral step.

Doctors and nurses who worked at the Truman Memorial Hospital and two clinic providers of abortions sought declaratory and injunctive relief to prevent the act from going into effect. By the time the case came to the Supreme Court, advocates on both sides had geared themselves for public action. Operation Rescue, a loose national confederation of local anti-abortion groups, staged demonstrations in the District of Columbia, and the National Right to Life Committee joined in the publicity campaign. In January 1989, sixty-five thousand pro-life marchers filled the streets of the District. Three months later, abortion rights advocates staged their own march, attracting half a million pro-choice supporters to the Capitol steps and the Mall. Seventy-eight amici submitted briefs, twenty more than in any previous case. One of the briefs in favor of upholding the circuit court rested heavily on the work of historian James Mohr, and it had gained support from 286 other historians. The majority of the amici, however, called for reversal of the lower courts' decisions, and public support for the right to an abortion had slipped from over 70 percent to 60 percent (though the same polls showed that only 9 percent of the respondents thought abortion should always be illegal).

The oral arguments in *Webster* were familiar in most ways—the statute's provisions were hardly new—but they featured one striking novelty. Charles Fried, the departing solicitor general, appeared by special permission and on behalf of the outgoing Reagan administration asked the Court to overturn *Roe*. He did not want the Court to roll back all privacy rights—he did not challenge *Griswold*—but rather "to pull this one thread." Frank Susman, speaking for the doctors and the other plaintiffs, replied that in his experience, when one pulled one thread, the whole garment unraveled. He continued, "When you have an issue that is so divisive and so emotional and so personal, and so intimate, it must be left as a fundamental right to the individual to make that choice." Speaking both as an advocate for one side and as a long-time observer of the abortion rights wars, Susman continued, "The very debate that went on outside this morning, outside this building, and has gone on in various towns and communities across our nation is the same debate that every woman who becomes pregnant and doesn't wish to be pregnant has with herself."[2]

In the end, the Court split on the case. The decision in *Webster* was widely reported, and veteran political and legal commentators all over the country weighed in with their assessment of its meaning. They noted that in July, the Louisiana legislature would pass a resolution calling for the reimposition of criminal penalties for all abortions. In a special session that met on October 10, the Florida legislature called for similar step. But the news was not all bad for abortion rights advocates. The Florida legislators rejected eight anti–abortion rights bills, and on October 11, the House of Representatives in Washington, D.C., voted to extend Medicaid funding to cover abortions when the woman was raped or incest was alleged. President George Bush, who in 1980 had been a supporter of abortion rights, vetoed the liberalized bill, but in Virginia and New Jersey, pro–abortion rights candidates won their gubernatorial contests. In November, abortion rights demonstrators took to the streets, but in Pennsylvania, the state legislature once again passed stringent restrictions on abortion. These would, in time, come to the Court.

· · ·

The religious implications of the Missouri law were readily apparent. There were sixty-seven self-identified religious groups that submitted amicus briefs in Webster. *The religious debate revolved not only around the First Amend-*

ment question of establishment of a religion but also around theological questions of when human life (or "ensoulment") began. Some religious groups submitting briefs believed that the key question was not scientific but moral. To counter the appearance of a monolithic Catholic opposition to abortion rights, a number of Catholic women joined in a brief supporting Roe *on religious grounds.*

Brief in support of appellees by Catholics for a Free Choice, Chicago Catholic Women, National Coalition of American Nuns, et al. in *Webster v. Reproductive Health Services*, 492 U.S. 490 (1989) (ready access: Lexis, 1988 U.S. Briefs 605, excerpted)

. . . Amici are individuals and organizations of persons of the Catholic faith who are committed to principles of religious liberty and constitutional privacy. The religious and moral beliefs and values of amici, which are deeply rooted in Catholic theology, include the beliefs that the abortion decision is a highly personal one made in the exercise of conscience, informed by an individual's religious and moral teachings and values, and that the individual woman's conscience is the final arbiter of any abortion decision. Amici recognize that other religious faiths permit, counsel and even mandate abortion in some circumstances. Amici strongly believe that a woman's decision about childbearing must be free of government burden, interference or coercion.

Amici believe that freedom of religious belief and conscience are protected by the constitutional doctrines of religious liberty and privacy which mandate invalidation of Sec. 1.205 [the preamble to the act]. The United States Constitution, as consistently interpreted by this Court, expressly denies to civil government the power to decide what is correct in debates over moral or religious values.

Amici strongly oppose reconsideration or overruling of *Roe v. Wade*. . . .

There is no constant teaching in Catholic theology on the commencement of personhood. At the core of the Roman Catholic belief system are the tenets that the question of personhood is spiritual, not scientific, and that personhood commences upon the infusion of the soul into the body. For many centuries Catholic theologians, including Thomas Aquinas, held that infusion of the soul is possible only when the embryo begins to show human form, i.e., a point after conception. Today [there is] a diversity [of] opinion among committed Catholics on the subject of abortion.

Catholic tradition teaches probabilism as a method of moral decision-making. The teaching of Aquinas and others, and the scientific evidence regarding fetal development provide "good and solid reasons" for believing that the early embryo is not ensouled and thus not a person. These views are solidly rooted in Catholic theology and deeply held. Further, Catholic tradition and theology teach that on issues involving moral decision-making the conscience of the individual is supreme, and that once a conscientious decision is reached persons must be permitted to act in accordance with his or her conscience, especially on religious matters.

From 1140 through 1869 Canon law "distinguished between the unensouled and the ensouled fetus in its treatment of the gravity of abortion and the penalties to be imposed." . . .

The Vatican II commission which developed a statement on prenatal life expressly refused to define the point of ensoulment for purposes of the abortion discussion. Acknowledging the canonical and theological history summarized above, the Sacred Congregation for the Doctrine of the Faith stated: "This declaration expressly leaves aside the question of the moment when the spiritual soul is infused. There is not a unanimous tradition on this point and authors are in disagreement. For some it dates from the first instant, for others it could not at least precede nidation." Sacred Congregation for the Doctrine of the Faith, Declaration on Abortion (1975).

There is not now and never has been an infallible proclamation on abortion. . . .

Those who proclaim that Sec. 1.205 is reflective of the clear and constant teaching of the Roman Catholic Church ignore, insult or are unaware of the historical data and Catholic tradition set forth above.

Today a diversity of opinion exists among committed Catholics on the subject of abortion. . . . Many Catholic philosophers and theologians still hold with Aquinas' position on delayed animation. . . .

Sec. 1.205, in ascribing full personhood status to the conceptus, embryo and fetus would require Catholics to act in a manner which is contrary to their religious teachings. It had been widely accepted Catholic teaching over the centuries that embryos and fetuses which lack human shape or form may not be baptized, because those entities do not possess a soul. . . . It is not Catholic practice to hold funerals after miscarriages.

The search for truth on subjects of moral importance is a dynamic process in the Catholic Church. Declarations of the Church hierarchy, even by the Pope, on moral issues are not infallible. Moreover, the content of Church teaching on moral issues involving serious claims of liberty and life change over time as a result of argument and reflection and no position should be taken as final. Popes from 650 through 1866 issued affirmations of the moral justification of slavery. Today that is not an approved or acceptable moral teaching. Similarly, for many years Popes issued opinions permitting castration of boys for religious choirs. That, too, is a practice not considered morally correct today. . . .

Dissent, from even authoritative teaching, and debate on issues of moral significance is part of the tradition of the Catholic Church. Theologian Charles Curran notes that such debate is part of a dynamic process which has seen authoritative teaching change and corrections made in errors of moral judgment: "[I]n specific moral judgments on complex matters one cannot hope to attain a degree of certitude that excludes the possibility of error." . . . Just as the Church cannot hope to correct errors in moral judgment without the debate and dissent which is part of its tradition, the civil government must allow the possibility of different moral and scientific truths by permitting free exchange of ideas and the exercise of conscience. . . .

The morality of abortion is a subject of "respectable debate" within the Catholic Church just as it is within the society at large. . . . For Catholics the question of abortion is a matter of conscience to be resolved by reference to theology, church tradition and individual contemplation and prayer. Further, Catholic teaching is that once a conscientious decision has been reached a person must be permitted to act in a manner consistent with the dictates of conscience. . . .

· · ·

Much of the persuasive power of the Catholic women's brief arose from the fact that its signers were women speaking to what they saw as a women's issue. But pro-choice voices were not the only women's voices raised in the briefs. While the Catholic women offered a theological case, the Feminists for Life brief rested on firsthand accounts.

Brief in support of appellants by Feminists for Life of America et al. in *Webster* (ready access: Lexis, 1988 U.S. Briefs 605, excerpted)

Feminists for Life of America (FFLA), Women Exploited by Abortion of Greater Kansas City (WEBA), the National Association of Pro-Life Nurses, Let Me Live, and the Elliot Institute for Social Services Research file this brief. . . . These organizations, having seen the adverse physical and psychological effects of abortion on women, oppose the continued deregulation of the lucrative abortion industry, advocate the development of non-violent alternatives to crisis pregnancies and seek an end to the exploitation of women and the widespread destruction of preborn children which characterizes the current state of abortion on demand. . . .

The decisions of the United States Supreme Court in *Roe v. Wade* and its progeny have been based upon the assumption that legal abortion is safe and beneficial to women. Many women who have had legal abortions, and who are purportedly the beneficiaries of the Court's abortion rulings maintain that the very heart of the decision in *Roe*—"safe, legal abortion" is a myth, and that women are being exploited at the hands of the lucrative, unregulated private abortion industry which has developed in the sixteen years since *Roe*. . . .

Many women are seeking recompense for injuries sustained through legal abortion. Some have recovered large sums in malpractice suits against abortion profiteers, only to see those responsible for their injuries continue to victimize yet more women and girls, unhampered by any regulatory authority. Others who have brought actions for abortion deaths and injuries do not recover anything because the courts have determined that their deaths and injuries were caused not by a physician's malpractice, but are due to the inherent dangers of induced abortion, whether the procedure is legal or illegal.

Many aborted women have reported that their concerns about the potential dangers of abortion, or the ambivalence they expressed regarding the prospect of having their child killed, were simply dismissed as "irrational" by "counselors" who downplay the medical risks of abortion, and evade any real discussion of fetal characteristics or alternatives to abortion.

The self-serving silence of the abortion industry regarding the dangers to women of induced abortion has been bolstered by the Court's decisions holding that a physician may in his or her own discretion withhold information regarding the particular medical risks of abortion and other information relevant to an informed decision on the part of the woman considering an abortion. Abortion is the only medical procedure known to Amici with respect to which the normal requirements for informed consent prior to undergoing a medical procedure are suspended.

There is ample evidence in the medical studies and public health statistics cited herein that the unfettered right of abortion on demand foisted upon our society by the Court and by abortion advocates is a public health disaster the proportions of which we are just beginning to uncover. . . .

However, studies and statistics cannot adequately describe the tragedy of the abortion establishment's exploitation of women—only the families of abortion's victims and the surviving victims themselves can adequately describe the pain they have endured. Therefore, Amici have lodged with the Court a volume containing the testimonies of abortion's victims. . . .

Their stories speak for themselves. . . .

Sue Liljenberg, who was a teenager when she obtained a "safe, legal" abortion, had no immediate physical complications. The passing years have revealed the self-destructive behavior and sterility that are the price she paid for exercising her "right to choose."

> . . . I'm a victim of abortion and, even if it takes until my last breath, I must be heard. When I was 17 I found myself in a crisis pregnancy. . . . When I went to the local family planning clinic, I sought guidance and wanted to know what I could do about my situation. I wanted a helping hand. When I walked into the clinic, I trusted the nurses and doctors, and thought they were concerned about my health enough to help me make a decision, not make my decision for me.
>
> Only one solution was strongly recommended that day. When I questioned the development of my baby, I was told it wasn't a baby yet, and that it looked like a tadpole. Since that day I have learned differently. . . . I was told that abortion was simple and safe and that I could go and live the rest of my life and have children when I was in a position to provide for them. I heard no scientific facts that day, only biased opinions. I was not told what abortion itself could do to me in the years to come, only that it was "safe and simple." I was not told that I would abuse myself with alcohol, try to kill myself, develop an eating disorder, and have terrible dreams. Worst of all, I was not told that I might never have another child. It has been 14 years since my "safe and simple" abortion and I have never been able to have another child. (Letter from Sue Liljenberg to Sen. Gordon Humphrey, dated June 6, 1986)

Can it be doubted that a young woman who was told she could have the children she wanted "someday," and yet will never hold her own child in her arms, is harmed irrevocably by abortion on demand? What about the impact of abortion upon her physical, psychological and emotional health?

Another woman, Elaine Blakely of Hunstville, Alabama, describes the "safe, legal" abortion she had in 1976:

> I am a woman who was exploited by abortion ten years ago. My abortion was free, legal and by no means performed in a "back alley" facility. In fact, the abortion facility was recommended by Planned Parenthood. Since I was not working at the time, Planned Parenthood happily gave

me a "free pass" for the abortion. I didn't even have to pay for the abortion. At the Kansas City abortion clinic, I was given a pelvic exam. . . . Contrary to what I was told, the abortion hurt very much and it led to severe complications. The "doctor" who performed my abortion perforated my uterus, cut an artery, and traumatized my colon. The doctor left me alone there with the "counselors" and one "nurse" for one and a half hours. After all of the other patients had left the abortion facility, I was rushed by ambulance to a hospital across the state line for observation and blood transfusions. The ambulance rushed me to the hospital with lights flashing and sirens blaring in an attempt to save my life. The complaint that back alley abortions kill girls must be seen in light of the fact that girls are dying today from LEGAL abortions. In order to save my life, a few hours later a hysterectomy was performed at the Kansas City, Missouri, hospital. I am telling you this because I am an adult. I was misled into believing it was a simple procedure with no complications. Since then I have had eighty percent of my colon removed. (Letter to Gordon Humphrey from Elaine Blakely dated August 5, 1986)

Are Sue Liljenberg, Elaine Blakely and tens of thousands of women who have also suffered the physical and psychological and emotional trauma of legal abortion entitled to protection of their "health" by State legislatures or are their lives and health expendable in the quest for unfettered abortion on demand? . . .

The common thread which runs through almost all testimonies of aborted women who have suffered psychological trauma and/or physical injury as a result of decisions such as *Akron* and *Thornburgh*, is the sense of anger and betrayal when they discover that they were not told of the possible consequences of a decision to abort, and often were fed outright lies when asking questions regarding the procedure, particularly when the questions involved fetal developmental characteristics. . . .

· · ·

Members of Congress also insisted on being heard in Webster. *Not only did these elected officials' briefs indicate how strongly they felt, but the fact that they filed briefs suggests that they did not see the separation of powers (legislators sticking to legislation) as curtailing their advocacy of judicial positions. How odd it would have been if the justices of the Supreme Court or sitting federal judges had come into Congress to lobby for statutes or appointees! One wonders also if the signers would have said the same about precedent if* Roe *had favored the Texas law.*

Brief in support of appellees by Howard Metzenbaum, Bob Packwood, Barbara Mikulski, Don Edwards, Bill Green, Patricia Schroeder, Olympia Snowe, et al. in *Webster* (ready access: Lexis, 1988 U.S. Briefs 605, excerpted)

Members of Congress are sworn to uphold the Constitution of the United States and have an interest in the outcome of this case as members of a coordinate branch of government committed to the preservation of the rule of law. This brief is submitted in the conviction that the interpretation of individual liberties espoused by the Executive Branch is fundamentally at odds with the Constitution, and with the judiciary's role as a principled and independent guardian of constitutional liberties. Moreover, Amici have an institutional interest in the stability of constitutional precedent. Overruling *Roe v. Wade* would threaten the repose of the nation.

When public sentiment is most sharply divided, the independence of the judiciary is vital. It is precisely the task of this Court to insulate individual rights from the changing winds of politics. As members of a coordinate branch of government, Amici would find themselves in an untenable position with respect to their own responsibilities, both to uphold the Constitution and to urge their constituents and fellow citizens to accept the decisions of the Supreme Court, were a widespread perception to arise that the constitutional protection of rights depends merely on changing political events and the accident of new appointments to the Court. Fundamental rights cannot be subject to the cycles of changing political opinion if the Constitution is to represent the rule of law.

As members of Congress we are concerned that the overruling of *Roe v. Wade* would criminalize conduct that is now constitutionally protected, resulting in a sudden and unprecedented problem of non-compliance with individual state criminal laws. Congress is ill-equipped to design a national response to this problem. Nor can Congress remedy the patchwork of state regulations that will result in burdensome and inequitable treatment of women based on income and, in all likelihood, race. Our respect for the rule of law, along with our recognition of the problems of law enforcement and equality in the administration of justice, lead us to urge this Court to place great weight on stare decisis with regard to *Roe v. Wade*. . . .

The practical consequences of overruling *Roe v. Wade* would be far-reaching. Criminalizing abortions will not eliminate them. Since illegal abortions would become commonplace, as was the case before state abortion prohibitions were deemed unconstitutional in 1973, overruling *Roe v. Wade* would criminalize the conduct of otherwise law-abiding citizens, as well as their physicians and others who assist them. Massive non-compliance can only foster a disrespect for the rule of law. Women with access to money will be able to travel to those states where abortion is legal, replicating the interstate traffic before the liberalizing of divorce laws. Driving abortions underground, or forcing women to travel to have one, will have a particularly cruel and disparate impact on poor women, who consist disproportionately of racial minorities.

Nor would overruling *Roe v. Wade* diminish the controversy that surrounds the issue of abortion; on the contrary, by shifting the controversy to the political arena, abortion can be expected to be a dominant issue in every legislative election, and in every contest where judges are elected. This Court has effectively adjusted the contours of the right recognized in *Roe v. Wade*; while the Court's decisions have been criticized and praised by both sides of the controversy, the process has taken the usual course that follows from the unambiguous enunciation of a right not hitherto established. That process should not be abandoned to the harsh arena of divisive single-issue politics. . . .

Nor have there been any factual developments since 1973 to undermine the conclusion of *Roe v. Wade* that, prior to the point when a fetus possesses physical qualities to enable it to survive if separated from the womb, no compelling state interest exists for depriving a woman of her right to procreative choice. The recognition of that right has facilitated the movement of women toward full and equal participation in American life. Denying that right would re-impose on this discrete segment of our population a burden that had been lifted by this Court sixteen years ago. . . .

· · ·

Another group of members of Congress supported the Missouri regulations. There were no women in the group. What did they say about the impact of the Roe *decision? Who did they think should have legal control over abortion?*

Brief in support of appellants by Christopher H. Smith, Alan B. Mollohan, John H. Danforth, et al. in *Webster* (ready access: Lexis, 1988 U.S. Briefs 605, excerpted)

The amici, Members of Congress and Senators, have substantial interests in the disposition of this appeal. Congress has enacted broad restrictions on the funding of abortion, which have been upheld by this Court. . . . The decision of the court of appeals, if upheld, could adversely impact the ability of Congress to maintain such restrictions. Furthermore, among the questions accepted for review by this Court is whether *Roe v. Wade* should be reconsidered or reversed. Congress is interested in this question, as it affects the correct interpretation of the Fourteenth Amendment's protections of the right to life and of due process under law, as well as the fundamental balance between legislative authority and judicial review under the federal Constitution. . . .

Stare decisis, a doctrine of diminished importance in the field of constitutional law, provides no basis for declining to reverse the multiple errors of *Roe v. Wade*. More than 100 times, this Court has corrected itself on constitutional questions and overturned prior case law. The reasons for this self-correction—the difficulty of addressing constitutional error through amendment or legislation; the primacy of the text of the constitution over the interpretations placed upon it; and the inappropriateness of the nation's highest tribunal perpetuating constitutional error—apply with special force to *Roe*. Moreover, the interests furthered by stare decisis are not served by adherence to *Roe*. The doctrines of *Roe* have caused great instability and unpredictability in the law, such that reversal is necessary to restore an appropriate balance.

Reversal of *Roe* would also be consistent with past willingness to admit error. This Court has corrected decisions which, like *Roe*, have misinterpreted the "liberty" clause of the Fourteenth Amendment to place an undue strait-jacket on legislative authority. And it has renounced the role of "super-legislature," sitting in judgment on the wisdom of state statutes. Doctrines on which long-standing social institutions and conventions were established have been overturned, as have doctrines on which scores of criminal convictions were predicated. The overturning of such decisions has often caused change, some of it disruptive. But it has also returned to the political branches of government their rightful authority to respond to the pressing moral and social issues at the root of such change. *Roe*, contrary to this tradition, has usurped the legislative function, and exacerbated the social turmoil over abortion.

Roe also merits reversal because it erroneously removed the protections of the Fourteenth Amendment, intended to embrace "all human beings," from the unborn. The humanity of the unborn cannot be debated in light of current medical technology, nor can the uniqueness of each individual unborn life be called into question. Redress of this error is imperative.

Finally, although this Court has shown an appropriate reluctance to reverse constitutional decisions where a less severe remedy is available, this case does not counsel such a cautious approach. The decision of the court of appeals illustrates the extent to which *Roe* has been utilized to frustrate even the most modest efforts to protect unborn life in general, and the viable unborn in particular. This opinion, unfortunately, typifies the application of *Roe* by the federal courts. *Roe* is constitutional error of the most radical variety, and the traditions of this Court call for such error to be dispatched without ambiguity. . . .

. . . The growing polarization over *Roe* within this Court, and within society, confirm the assessment of legal scholars that many of these holdings were in error. It is wrong to propogate such a decision unless, under renewed scrutiny, the reasoning of *Roe* withstands the arguments made against it. Unless independent grounds exist for affirming *Roe*, stare decisis alone stands as no impediment to reversal. . . .

. . . Political activity, scholarly analysis, and public opinion also reject the hypothesis that *Roe* is settled law. Since *Roe*, nearly 900 separately numbered resolutions relating to abortion have been introduced into Congress. Over 300 are joint resolutions seeking Constitutional amendments that would overturn *Roe*. Congress has also acted broadly to remove direct federal financial support for abortion. Moreover, a 1988 Presidential proclamation declared the unborn to be protected under the Constitution, and directed the executive branch to carry out actions and programs consistent with that declaration.

The strongest evidence of a popular rejection of the abortion right created in *Roe* is seen in the vast number of state legislative actions and public referenda designed to limit or regulate the performance of abortions. During the 1988 elections, public referenda in Michigan, Arkansas, and Colorado affirmed restrictions on abortion, and in Arkansas, granted rights to the unborn under the state constitution. During the years since *Roe*, state legislatures from all regions have enacted hundreds of laws regulating abortion. At least 23 state legislatures have sent memorials requesting Congress to propose an anti-abortion amendment to the Constitution, and 19 state legislatures have passed petitions to convene a constitutional convention to propose a human life amendment to the Constitution. The democratic branches of government, therefore, have not accepted or endorsed *Roe*.

• • •

In the conference after oral argument on April 28, 1992, the Court was divided over both the Missouri rules and the fate of Roe. *Chief Justice Rehnquist assigned to himself the writing of the opinion for the majority, which he delivered on July 3, 1989.*

Webster, Attorney General of Missouri, et al. v. Reproductive Health Services et al., 492 U.S. 490 (1989)

Chief Justice Rehnquist announced the judgment of the Court and delivered the opinion of the Court with respect to Parts I, II-A, II-B, and II-C, and an opinion with respect to Parts II-D and III, in which Justice White and Justice Kennedy join.

Decision of this case requires us to address four sections of the Missouri Act: (a) the preamble; (b) the prohibition on the use of public facilities or employees to perform abortions; (c) the prohibition on public funding of abortion counseling; and (d) the requirement that physicians conduct viability tests prior to performing abortions. . . .

The Act's preamble, as noted, sets forth "findings" by the Missouri Legislature that "[t]he life of each human being begins at conception," and that "[u]nborn children have protectable interests in life, health, and well-being." . . . The Act then mandates that state laws be interpreted to provide unborn children with "all the rights, privileges, and immunities available to other persons, citizens, and residents of this state," subject to the Constitution and this Court's precedents. . . . In invalidating the preamble, the Court of Appeals relied on this Court's dictum that "'a State may not adopt one theory of when life begins to justify its regulation of abortions.'" . . . It rejected Missouri's claim that the preamble was "abortion-neutral," and "merely determine[d] when life begins in a nonabortion context, a traditional state prerogative." . . .

The State contends that the preamble itself is precatory and imposes no substantive restrictions on abortions, and that appellees therefore do not have standing to challenge it. . . . Appellees, on the other hand, insist that the preamble is an operative part of the Act intended to guide the interpretation of other provisions of the Act. . . .

In our view, the Court of Appeals misconceived the meaning of the *Akron* dictum, which was only that a State could not "justify" an abortion regulation otherwise invalid under *Roe* v. *Wade* on the ground that it embodied the State's view about when life begins. Certainly the preamble does not by its terms regulate abortion or any other aspect of appellees' medical practice. . . .

It will be time enough for federal courts to address the meaning of the preamble should it be applied to restrict the activities of appellees in some concrete way. . . .

Section 188.210 provides that "[i]t shall be unlawful for any public employee within the scope of his employment to perform or assist an abortion, not necessary to save the life of the mother," while §188.215 makes it "unlawful for any public facility to be used for the purpose of performing or assisting an abortion not necessary to save the life of the mother." The Court of Appeals held that these provisions contravened this Court's abortion decisions. . . . We take the contrary view. . . .

Nothing in the Constitution requires States to enter or remain in the business of performing abortions. Nor, as appellees suggest, do private physicians and their patients have some kind of constitutional right of access to public facilities for the performance of abortions. . . . It is difficult to see how any procreational choice is burdened by the State's ban on the use of its facilities or employees for performing abortions. . . .

Section 188.029 of the Missouri Act provides: "Before a physician performs an abortion on a woman he has reason to believe is carrying an unborn child of twenty or more weeks gestational age, the physician shall first determine if the unborn child is viable by using and exercising that degree of care, skill, and proficiency commonly exercised by the ordinarily skillful, careful, and prudent physician engaged in similar practice under the same or similar conditions. In making this determination of viability, the physician shall perform or cause to be performed such medical examinations and tests as are necessary to make a finding of the gestational age, weight, and lung maturity of the unborn child and shall enter such findings and determination of viability in the medical record of the mother."

As with the preamble, the parties disagree over the meaning of this statutory provision. The State emphasizes the language of the first sentence, which speaks in terms of the physician's determination of viability being made by the standards of ordinary skill in the medical profession. . . . Appellees stress the language of the second sentence, which prescribes such "tests as are necessary" to make a finding of gestational age, fetal weight, and lung maturity. . . .

We must first determine the meaning of §188.029 under Missouri law. . . . We think the viability-testing provision makes sense only if the second sentence is read to require only those tests that are useful to making subsidiary findings as to viability. If we construe this provision to require a physician to perform those tests needed to make the three specified findings *in all circumstances*, including when the physician's reasonable professional judgment indicates that the tests would be irrelevant to determining viability or even dangerous to the mother and the fetus, the second sentence of §188.029 would conflict with the first sentence's *requirement* that a physician apply his reasonable professional skill and judgment. It would also be incongruous to read this provision, especially the word "necessary," to require the performance of tests irrelevant to the expressed statutory purpose of determining viability. . . .

Stare decisis is a cornerstone of our legal system, but it has less power in constitutional cases, where, save for constitutional amendments, this Court is the only body able to make needed changes. . . . We think the *Roe* trimester framework falls into that category.

In the first place, the rigid *Roe* framework is hardly consistent with the notion of a Constitution cast in general terms, as ours is, and usually speaking in general principles, as ours does. The key elements of the *Roe* framework—trimesters and viability—are not found in the text of the Constitution or in any place else one would expect to find a constitutional principle. Since the bounds of the inquiry are essentially indeterminate, the result has been a web of legal rules that have become increasingly intricate, resembling a code of regulations rather than a body of constitutional doctrine. . . .

In the second place, we do not see why the State's interest in protecting potential human life should come into existence only at the point of viability, and that there should therefore be a rigid line allowing state regulation after viability but prohibiting it before viability. . . .

Justice Blackmun takes us to task for our failure to join in a "great issues" debate as to whether the Constitution includes an "unenumerated" general right to privacy as recognized in cases such as *Griswold* v. *Connecticut* . . . and *Roe*. But *Griswold* v. *Connecticut*, unlike *Roe*, did not purport to adopt a whole framework, complete with detailed rules and distinctions, to govern the cases in which the asserted liberty interest would apply. As such, it was far different from the opinion, if not the holding, of *Roe* v. *Wade*, which sought to establish a constitutional framework for judging state regulation of abortion during the entire term of pregnancy. That framework sought to deal with areas of medical practice traditionally subject to state regulation, and it sought to balance once and for all by reference only to the calendar the claims of the State to protect the fetus as a form of human life against the claims of a woman to decide for herself whether or not to abort a fetus she was carrying. . . .

Justice Blackmun also accuses us, *inter alia*, of cowardice and illegitimacy in dealing with "the most politically divisive domestic legal issue of our time." There is no doubt that our holding today will allow some governmental regulation of abortion that would have been prohibited. . . . But the goal of constitutional adjudication is surely not to remove inexorably "politically divisive" issues from the ambit of the legislative process, whereby the people through their elected representatives deal with matters of concern to them. The goal of constitutional adjudication is to hold true the balance between that which the Constitution puts beyond the reach of the democratic process and that which it does not. We think we have done that today. . . .

. . .

Justice O'Connor's refusal to join in any opinion overturning Roe *reduced the number of justices that Rehnquist could muster to overturn* Roe *to four members of the Court.*

Justice O'Connor, concurring in part and concurring in the judgment.

Nothing in the record before us or the opinions below indicates that subsections 1(1) and 1(2) of the preamble to Missouri's abortion regulation statute will affect a woman's decision to have an abortion. . . . Justice Stevens asserts that any possible interference with a woman's right to use such postfertilization contraceptive devices would be unconstitutional under *Griswold* v. *Connecticut*, and our subsequent contraception cases. . . . It may be correct that the use of postfertilization contraceptive devices is constitutionally protected by *Griswold* and its progeny, but, as with a woman's abortion decision, nothing in the record or the opinions below indicates that the preamble will affect a woman's decision to practice contraception. . . . I agree with the Court, therefore, that all of these intimations of unconstitutionality are simply too hypothetical to support the use of declaratory judgment procedures and injunctive remedies in this case.

Similarly, it seems to me to follow directly from our previous decisions concerning state or federal funding of abortions . . . that appellees' facial challenge to the constitutionality of Missouri's ban on the utilization of public facilities and the participation of public employees in the performance of abortions not necessary to save the life of the mother . . . cannot succeed. . . . There may be conceivable applications of the ban on the use of public facilities that would be unconstitutional. . . .

In its interpretation of Missouri's "determination of viability" provision . . . the plurality [here the chief justice and Justices Kennedy, White, and Scalia] has proceeded in a manner unnecessary to deciding the question at hand. . . . The plurality is quite correct: "the viability-testing provision makes sense only if the second sentence is read to require only those tests that are useful to making subsidiary findings as to viability," and, I would add, only those examinations and tests that it would not be imprudent or careless to perform in the particular medical situation before the physician.

Unlike the plurality, I do not understand these viability testing requirements to conflict with any of the Court's past decisions concerning state regulation of abortion. Therefore, there is no necessity to accept the State's invitation to reexamine the constitutional validity of *Roe* v. *Wade*. . . .

It is clear to me that requiring the performance of examinations and tests useful to determining whether a fetus is viable, when viability is possible, and when it would not be medically imprudent to do so, does not impose an undue burden on a woman's abortion decision. On this ground alone I would reject the suggestion that §188.029 as interpreted is unconstitutional. . . .

· · ·

Justice Scalia concurred in the result but was unhappy that Roe *had not been reversed. He thus concurred with the chief justice's opinion upholding all of the provisions but wanted to go further.*

Justice Scalia, concurring in part and concurring in the judgment.

I join Parts I, II-A, II-B, and II-C of the opinion of the Court. As to Part II-D, I share Justice Blackmun's view, *post*, at 556, that it effectively would overrule *Roe* v. *Wade*, 410 U.S. 113 (1973). I think that should be done, but would do it more explicitly. Since today we contrive to avoid doing it, and indeed to avoid almost any decision of national import, I need not set forth my reasons, some of which have been well recited in dissents of my colleagues in other cases. . . .

The outcome of today's case will doubtless be heralded as a triumph of judicial statesmanship. It is not that, unless it is statesmanlike needlessly to prolong this Court's self-awarded sovereignty over a field where it has little proper business since the answers to most of the cruel questions posed are political and not juridical—a sovereignty which therefore quite properly, but to the great damage of the Court, makes it the object of the sort of organized public pressure that political institutions in a democracy ought to receive. . . .

The real question, then, is whether there are valid reasons to go beyond the most stingy possible holding today. It seems to me there are not only valid but compelling ones. Ordinarily, speaking no more broadly than is absolutely required avoids throwing settled law into confusion; doing so today preserves a chaos that is evident to anyone who can read and count. Alone sufficient to justify a broad holding is the fact that our retaining control, through *Roe*, of what I believe to be, and many of our citizens recognize to be, a political issue, continuously distorts the public perception of the role of this Court. We can now look forward to at least another

Term with carts full of mail from the public, and streets full of demonstrators, urging us—their unelected and life-tenured judges who have been awarded those extraordinary, undemocratic characteristics precisely in order that we might follow the law despite the popular will—to follow the popular will. Indeed, I expect we can look forward to even more of that than before, given our indecisive decision today. And if these reasons for taking the unexceptional course of reaching a broader holding are not enough, then consider the nature of the constitutional question we avoid: In most cases, we do no harm by not speaking more broadly than the decision requires. Anyone affected by the conduct that the avoided holding would have prohibited will be able to challenge it himself and have his day in court to make the argument. Not so with respect to the harm that many States believed, pre-*Roe*, and many may continue to believe, is caused by largely unrestricted abortion. That will continue to occur if the States have the constitutional power to prohibit it, and would do so, but we skillfully avoid telling them so. Perhaps those abortions cannot constitutionally be proscribed. That is surely an arguable question, the question that reconsideration of *Roe* v. *Wade* entails. But what is not at all arguable, it seems to me, is that we should decide now and not insist that we be run into a corner before we grudgingly yield up our judgment. The only sound reason for the latter course is to prevent a change in the law—but to think that desirable begs the question to be decided. . . .

Justice O'Connor would nevertheless uphold the law because it "does not impose an undue burden on a woman's abortion decision." This conclusion is supported by the observation that the required tests impose only a marginal cost on the abortion procedure, far less of an increase than the cost-doubling hospitalization requirement invalidated in *Akron*. . . . The fact that the challenged regulation is less costly than what we struck down in *Akron* tells us only that we cannot decide the present case on the basis of that earlier decision. It does not tell us whether the present requirement is an "undue burden," and I know of no basis for determining that this particular burden (or any other for that matter) is "due." One could with equal justification conclude that it is not. To avoid the question of *Roe* v. *Wade*'s validity, with the attendant costs that this will have for the Court and for the principles of self-governance, on the basis of a standard that offers "no guide but the Court's own discretion" . . . merely adds to the irrationality of what we do today.

Of the four courses we might have chosen today—to reaffirm *Roe*, to overrule it explicitly, to overrule it *sub silentio* [in silence], or to avoid the question—the last is the least responsible. . . .

Justice Blackmun's dissent conveyed his sense of dismay that Roe *might soon be overturned. In it, Justices Brennan and Marshall concurred.*

Justice Blackmun, dissenting.

. . . Today, *Roe* v. *Wade* . . . and the fundamental constitutional right of women to decide whether to terminate a pregnancy, survive but are not secure. Although the Court extricates itself from this case without making a single, even incremental, change in the law of abortion, the plurality and Justice Scalia would overrule *Roe* (the first silently, the other explicitly) and would return to the States virtually unfettered authority to control the quintessentially intimate, personal, and life-directing decision whether to carry a fetus to term. Although today, no less than yesterday, the Constitution and the decisions of this Court prohibit a State from enacting laws that inhibit women from the meaningful exercise of that right, a plurality of this Court implicitly invites every state legislature to enact more and more restrictive abortion regulations in order to provoke more and more test cases, in the hope that sometime down the line the Court will return the law of procreative freedom to the severe limitations that generally prevailed in this country before January 22, 1973. Never in my memory has a plurality announced a judgment of this Court that so foments disregard for the law and for our standing decisions.

Nor in my memory has a plurality gone about its business in such a deceptive fashion. At every level of its review, from its effort to read the real meaning out of the Missouri statute, to its intended evisceration of precedents and its deafening silence about the constitutional protections that it would jettison, the plurality obscures the portent of its analysis. With feigned restraint, the plurality announces that its analysis leaves *Roe* "undisturbed," albeit "modif[ied] and narrow[ed]." . . . But this disclaimer is totally meaningless. The plurality opinion is filled with winks, and nods, and knowing glances to those who would do away with *Roe* explicitly, but turns a stone face to anyone in search of what the plurality conceives as the scope of a woman's right under the Due Process Clause to terminate a pregnancy free from the coercive and brooding influence of the State. The simple truth is that *Roe* would not survive the plurality's analysis, and that the plurality provides no substitute for *Roe*'s protective umbrella.

I fear for the future. I fear for the liberty and equality of the millions of women who have lived and come of age in the 16 years since *Roe* was decided. I fear for the integrity of, and public esteem for, this Court.

I dissent. . . .

Had the plurality read the statute as written, it would have had no cause to reconsider the *Roe* framework. As properly construed, the viability-testing provision does not pass constitutional muster under even a rational-basis standard, the least restrictive level of review applied by this Court. . . . By mandating tests to determine fetal weight and lung maturity for every fetus thought to be more than 20 weeks gestational age, the statute requires physicians to undertake procedures, such as amniocentesis, that, in the situation presented, have no medical justification, impose significant additional health risks on both the pregnant woman and the fetus, and bear no rational relation to the State's interest in protecting fetal life. As written, §188.029 is an arbitrary imposition of discomfort, risk, and expense, furthering no discernible interest except to make the procurement of an abortion as arduous and difficult as possible. Thus, were it not for the plurality's tortured effort to avoid the plain import of §188.029, it could have struck down the testing provision as patently irrational irrespective of the *Roe* framework. . . .

The plurality opinion is far more remarkable for the arguments that it does not advance than for those that it does. The plurality does not even mention, much less join, the true jurisprudential debate underlying this case: whether the Constitution includes an "unenumerated" general right to privacy as recognized in many of our decisions, most notably *Griswold v. Connecticut* and *Roe*, and, more specifically, whether, and to what extent, such a right to privacy extends to matters of childbearing and family life, including abortion. . . . These are questions of unsurpassed significance in this Court's interpretation of the Constitution, and mark the battleground upon which this case was fought, by the parties, by the United States as *amicus* on behalf of petitioners, and by an unprecedented number of *amici*. On these grounds, abandoned by the plurality, the Court should decide this case. . . .

Finally, the plurality asserts that the trimester framework cannot stand because the State's interest in potential life is compelling throughout pregnancy, not merely after viability. The opinion contains not one word of rationale for its view of the State's interest. This "it-is-so-because-we-say-so" jurisprudence constitutes nothing other than an attempted exercise of brute force; reason, much less persuasion, has no place. . . .

The . . . [plurality] standard completely disregards the irreducible minimum of *Roe*: the Court's recognition that a woman has a limited fundamental constitutional right to decide whether to terminate a pregnancy. That right receives no meaningful recognition in the plurality's written opinion. Since, in the plurality's view, the State's interest in potential life is compelling as of the moment of conception, and is therefore served only if abortion is abolished, every hindrance to a woman's ability to obtain an abortion must be "permissible." . . .

It is impossible to read the plurality opinion[,] and especially its final paragraph, without recognizing its implicit invitation to every State to enact more and more restrictive abortion laws, and to assert their interest in potential life as of the moment of conception. All these laws will satisfy the plurality's nonscrutiny, until sometime, a new regime of old dissenters and new appointees will declare what the plurality intends: that *Roe* is no longer good law. . . .

For today, at least, the law of abortion stands undisturbed. For today, the women of this Nation still retain the liberty to control their destinies. But the signs are evident and very ominous, and a chill wind blows.

* * *

Justice Stevens also wrote an opinion. It focused on one part of the law and offered a strong reading of the First Amendment's requirements on religious neutrality.

Justice Stevens, concurring in part and dissenting in part.

My interpretation of the plain language is supported by the structure of the statute as a whole, particularly the preamble, which "finds" that life "begins at conception" and further commands that state laws shall be construed to provide the maximum protection to "the unborn child at every stage of development." . . . I agree with the District Court [that issued an injunction against the enforcement of the law] that "[o]bviously, the purpose of this law is to protect the potential life of the fetus, rather than to safeguard maternal health." . . . A literal reading of the statute tends to accomplish that goal. . . . I am satisfied that the Court of Appeals, as well as the District Court, correctly concluded that the Missouri Legislature meant exactly what it said in the second sentence of §188.029. I am also satisfied, for the reasons stated by Justice Blackmun, that the testing provision is manifestly unconstitutional. . . .

Indeed, I am persuaded that the absence of any secular purpose for the legislative declarations that life begins at conception and that conception occurs at fertilization makes the relevant portion of the preamble invalid under the Establishment [of religion] Clause of the First Amendment to the Federal Constitution. . . . The preamble, an unequivocal endorsement of a religious tenet of some but by no means all Christian faiths, serves no identifiable secular purpose. That fact alone compels a conclusion that the statute violates the Establishment Clause. . . .

My concern can best be explained by reference to the position on this issue that was widely accepted by the leaders of the Roman Catholic Church for many years. The position is summarized in a report, entitled "Catholic Teaching on Abortion," prepared by the Congressional Research Service of the Library of Congress. It states in part: "The disagreement over the status of the unformed as against the formed fetus was crucial for Christian teaching on the soul. It was widely held that the soul was not present until the formation of the fetus 40 or 80 days after conception, for males and females respectively. Thus, abortion of the 'unformed' or 'inanimate' fetus (from *anima*, soul) was something less than true homicide, rather a form of anticipatory or quasi-homicide. This view received its definitive treatment in St. Thomas Aquinas and became for a time the dominant interpretation in the Latin Church. . . ."

If a state legislature were to enact a statute prefaced with a "finding" that female life begins 80 days after conception and male life begins 40 days after conception, I have no doubt that this Court would promptly conclude that such an endorsement of a particular religious tenet is violative of the Establishment Clause. . . .

In fact, if one rescinds the theological concept of ensoulment—or one accepts St. Thomas Aquinas' view that ensoulment does not occur for at least 40 days—a State has no greater secular interest in protecting the potential life of an embryo that is still "seed" than in protecting the potential life of a sperm or an unfertilized ovum. . . .

Bolstering my conclusion that the preamble violates the First Amendment is the fact that the intensely divisive character of much of the national debate over the abortion issue reflects the deeply held religious convictions of many participants in the debate. The Missouri Legislature may not inject its endorsement of a particular religious tradition into this debate. . . .

. . .

The response to the decision in the media was as polarized as the debate over abortion rights itself. Like the justices, the contributors to the public debate looked ahead to predict the fate of Roe. *But the journalists and the people they interviewed saw the issue in political rather than purely legal terms. Tom Wicker, the* New York Times *editor who authored the next selection, saw the disagreements on the Court as reflecting political as well as legal currents.*

Tom Wicker, "Abortion and the G.O.P.,"
New York Times, July 7, 1989

Despite loud cries of triumph and tragedy, the Supreme Court in Missouri v. Webster made no change whatever in abortion law or in a woman's constitutional right to choose an abortion.

What the Court may have done, however, is to contribute to a political burden too heavy for the Republican Party to bear.

As for the substance of the abortion ruling, Justice Blackmun pointed out in his dissent: "The Court extricates itself from this case without making a single, even incremental change in the law of abortion."

Or as Justice Scalia, partially concurring, wrote: "Today we contrive to avoid overturning Roe v. Wade, and indeed to avoid almost any decision of national import."

It also may have been too quickly assumed—even by Justice Blackmun—that the Court put itself in position to overturn Roe v. Wade, explicitly or implicitly, in its next term. My colleague Anthony Lewis, closely examining the various opinions, found numerous "constraints and hesitations" plausibly suggesting that even this Court is not willing to go that far. Justice Scalia, who expressly favors overturning Roe, apparently agrees. "What will it take," he asked in rather despairing terms, "to permit us to reach that fundamental question?" He does not appear to have a majority for his purpose and remarked unhappily that the various opinions in the Missouri case show that Roe v. Wade can never be "entirely brought down."

The politics of the issue is another matter. Anti-abortion forces interpreted the ruling as a victory and quickly prepared Missouri-like restrictions for various state legislatures. Pro-choice leaders—wisely having planned to proclaim anything short of an endorsement of Roe as a disaster for women—are effectively polarizing the issue on that emotional line.

The anti-abortion position is identified with and has been pushed by the Republicans, with some individual exceptions. Party leaders like Ronald Reagan and George Bush strongly advocated that position, not least to placate the powerful right wing of their party; now that right wing will hold Republicans to what may prove to have been a Faustian political bargain, starting with those anti-abortion statutes in state legislatures.

Democrats—again with some individual exceptions—are closely associated with pro-choice arguments. Already, in this year's major elections, following the claims of the two sides in the Missouri case, a clear party lineup has emerged. In the New York City mayoral election, the favored Republican, Rudolph Giuliani, has been thrown on the defensive; but

Mayor Koch, a Democrat, has announced that he'll put up $7 million for abortions the Federal or state governments won't finance.

In New Jersey, the Democratic gubernatorial candidate, James Florio, quickly restated his support for abortion rights; his Republican opponent, Jim Courter, backed the Missouri decision. In Virginia, Gov. Gerald Baliles, a Democrat, strongly endorsed a woman's right to choose an abortion; the Democratic candidate to succeed him, Douglas Wilder, probably will have to take a similar stand. The Democrats can only be strengthened, perhaps now but especially for the long term, by the identification of their party with women's independence, privacy and right to choose—in effect, its identification with women.

If the Supreme Court should go on to overturn Roe v. Wade, and thus a woman's right to make her own decision about abortion, the Republicans would have a real problem—a national problem—whatever the near-term results in some legislatures. They would then be forced, in fear of alienating the right and splitting their party, to defend Federal power to intervene in the most private decisions of women's and families' lives. That seems sure to widen the "gender gap" that already favors Democrats.

Only 1 in 10 Americans believes abortion is murder, and should be prohibited—though 6 of 10 tell polltakers they consider it immoral. More significant politically, polls show that 3 of every 4 Americans believe that abortion is a choice a woman has a right to make for herself. Generations have become accustomed to that right, since Roe v. Wade in 1973, and will not lightly accept its abolition or restraint.

When more and more women are working, including wives who must supplement family income, limitations on the right to choose abortion will be seen as repressing a woman's economic as well as her personal freedom. A party seen as having helped to bring about such repression is likely to find that it has paid too high a price for the support of its right wing.

· · ·

By the end of the year, the political fallout was still not clear. Political commentators in the media continued to speculate. But the tone of the speculation was more measured, as much "spin control" as prognostication. Elaine Kamarck's piece for Newsday, *a Long Island paper, tracked the impact of the* Webster *decision on the political races that fall.*

Elaine Ciulla Kamarck, "The Abortion Dilemma:
The Pols Shift with the Wind as the Abortion Fight Evolves,"
Newsday, December 21, 1989

BEFORE LAST JULY, there was no more surefire way of putting a male candidate in a bad mood than to sit him down and make him think about abortion. Well, what a difference one Supreme Court case and two election campaigns make.

In the wake of the Supreme Court's decision in the Webster case and following the governor's races in Virginia and New Jersey, the candidates of 1990 are scrambling to define themselves before the next election year begins in earnest. This has prompted a flurry of "clarifications," "reassurances" and some downright conversation. In what must be viewed as a serious setback to the opponents of legalized abortion, all the changes going on are in the direction of protecting legal abortions. There are no new converts to the ranks of the right-to-lifers.

In the pre-Webster days, candidates tried to avoid having a position on abortion; if they did have one, it was likely to be short, vague and to sound something like this: "Uh-mmm-yes-that-is-a-serious-and-sensitive-issue-we-have-here. But the real issue is education." So it was a real surprise to me to call up a series of campaign offices and talk to male press secretaries who were enthusiastic about spelling out their candidate's long and solid record protecting a woman's right to choose.

Gina Glantz, a well-known national political consultant who now consults for NARAL (National Abortion Rights Action League), illustrates the change as follows: "It used to be when candidates got a check from NARAL there would be a debate within the campaign on whether to accept it because it would have to show up on the financial report. Now I get called by candidates asking if they can get a check, even a small one, from NARAL."

As the pro-abortion rights movement among politicians picks up, candidates fall into two broad groups, the "converts" and the "clarifiers." The converts are former right-to-lifers who have made a 180-degree turnaround; the clarifiers are those who, for one reason or another, never had to take a very public stand on the issue and are now "clarifying" their position in order to reassure the newly mobilized pro-abortion rights forces that they will protect legalized abortions.

One of the best known converts is Ohio Attorney General Anthony Celebrezze, a strong candidate for the Democratic nomination for governor. In Celebrezze's earlier races, he had run with the endorsements of Ohio's right-to-life groups, but on Dec. 2, he went before a packed news conference to present a six-page position paper that announced, in effect, that he had changed his mind.

Despite the charges of political opportunism, the Celebrezze conversion was a class act. He did not try to disguise his change of heart or dance around the issue. He carefully distinguished between his own beliefs and what he believed was the proper role of the state in this matter and came down on the side of protecting a woman's right to choose until the time the fetus is medically viable. He also ended up supporting public funding of abortion.

In Florida, the leading contender for the Democratic gubernatorial nomination is Rep. Bill Nelson—a "clarifier." He has been pro–abortion rights but has voted against public funding for abortions. He now says that he is in favor of public funding in the cases of rape, incest, where the mother's life is in danger or where a fetus is severely damaged. Nelson has the advantage of running against Gov. Bob Martinez, whose recent attempt to pass restrictive abortion legislation in the wake of the Webster case failed.

Frank Bellotti, a former Massachusetts attorney general running for the Democratic nomination for governor, has also had to "clarify" his position. As attorney general, he never had to take a position on abortion. Now Bellotti, a Roman Catholic and the father of 12, whose wife is a member of a right-to-life group, is encountering some trouble convincing people that he is in favor of a woman's right to choose. His problem is compounded by the fact that his strongest opponent is Lt. Gov. Evelyn Murphy, who made abortion rights an early and visible issue.

In Texas, Attorney General Jim Mattox, a candidate for the Democratic gubernatorial nomination, has a similar problem. Mattox has a strong pro–abortion rights record and filed an amicus brief before the Supreme Court on that side of the Webster case. But on this issue he has an uphill battle against Treasurer Ann Richards, a favorite of the feminist and pro-abortion rights community.

In Iowa, the leading contender for the Democratic nomination is Attorney General Tom Miller. Miller opposes abortion except in cases of rape, incest or a threat to the life of the mother. But in a recent interview with the largest paper in the state, Miller said that, as governor, he would propose only one piece of legislation on abortion: legislation on parental notification. The headline "Miller: I Wouldn't Seek Ban" that ran in the Nov. 5 *Des Moines Register*, is the best example so far of someone who is trying to "clarify" without "converting."

The temptation is great to dismiss all this conversion and clarification as sheer political opportunism. But something else seems to be at work here. Now that candidates have been forced to think about this issue, they are realizing that, as Celebrezze put it, the states "cannot turn back the clock twenty years on the question of abortion."

. . .

Another way to gauge public opinion—in effect coming from the bottom up rather than from the top down (telling people what to believe)—was to administer public opinion polls. The Chicago Tribune *regularly does these on a variety of issues. The validity of the returns depends in part on matters entirely outside the scope of the questions (for example, on how representative the sample of respondents was). In the following article, the paper reported the results of a poll on the abortion issue, taken at the end of the year.*

Barbara Brotman, "Voters Firmly in Middle on Key Abortion Issues," *Chicago Tribune*, December 26, 1989

Most Illinois voters take a middle-of-the-road stance on abortion, a new *Tribune* poll has found. Few voters believe that abortion should be outlawed or that it should be legal under any circumstance.

The majority fall into a middle ground, approving abortion in some cases and opposing it in others.

Fifty-four percent of those polled said that abortion should be legal, but with restrictions on the reasons that women could obtain them.

Only 16 percent of the state's residents believe abortion should be completely outlawed, and only 23 percent said it should be legal without any restriction.

The poll showed substantial support for outlawing abortions if the woman or parents cannot afford the child or if the woman is unmarried, two of the most common reasons women give for seeking abortions.

And it showed that voters were deeply disturbed by the 1.5 million abortions performed in the U.S. every year. Fifty-eight percent said that more restrictions are needed to reduce the number of abortions.

The poll revealed, as have similar national polls, a fundamental dichotomy between private morality and public policy. Even those who believe abortion is wrong are often unwilling to outlaw it for other people.

While only 16 percent would outlaw abortion, 48 percent said abortion is wrong, and 63 percent of those who believe it is wrong said that abortion is sometimes the only choice in a bad situation.

Polls have shown that even people who believe abortion is wrong are loath to make it illegal. For example, 57 percent of respondents in a *Los Angeles Times* poll in March, 1988, said abortion is the same as murder. But 74 percent also said that "abortion is a decision that has to be made by every woman for herself."

Fifty-four percent of those polled by the *Tribune* said abortions should be forbidden if sought because the woman or parents could not afford to raise the child.

Sixty-eight percent of women who got abortions in 1987 said they did so partly because they could not afford a baby, according to the Alan Guttmacher Institute, a research organization that studies reproductive health issues.

Fifty percent of Illinois residents said abortion should be forbidden if sought because a woman is unmarried. Fifty-one percent of women who got abortions in 1987 said they did so partly because they wanted to avoid single parenthood, the Guttmacher Institute survey found.

Thirty-one percent said abortion should be forbidden if the fetus shows physical or mental abnormalities.

The *Tribune* poll found strong support for limiting the point in pregnancy at which a woman could seek an abortion. Only 13 percent of those polled said abortion should be legal after the first three months of pregnancy.

Even those who said abortion should be legal without any restrictions largely supported such limits. Forty-eight percent said abortion should be permitted only until the first, second or third month of pregnancy. Only 31 percent said abortion should be legal until some point in the second or third trimester.

Abortion is legal at any point in pregnancy. Ninety-one percent of abortions take place in the first trimester, according to the Guttmacher Institute.

Twenty percent of all those polled said they had no opinion on the point during pregnancy at which abortion should not be permitted, indicating considerable uncertainty over the point at which life begins—a central issue to the abortion debate.

The *Tribune* poll found considerable support for viability testing at any time during pregnancy.

Fifty-two percent of those polled said that abortions should be allowed only after tests showed the fetus could not survive outside the womb.

Even 49 percent of those who said they favored legal abortion under any circumstance said abortions should be permitted only after such viability testing.

Some of those who said abortion should always be illegal made exceptions for certain circumstances.

Sixty-four percent of them would permit abortion to save the life of the woman. Thirty-six percent would allow it in cases of rape or incest.

Seventy-five percent of those polled by the *Tribune* said a parent should be notified before a girl under 18 can get an abortion. Forty-three percent said abortions should require the consent of the father of the fetus.

Fifty-eight percent said more restrictions are needed to reduce the number of abortions.

The widespread support for abortion restrictions in the *Tribune* poll and other surveys offers ammunition to abortion opponents pushing to narrow the circumstances in which women may get abortions.

The U.S. Supreme Court, in its Webster v. Reproductive Health Services decision on July 3, allowed states for the first time since 1973 to impose restrictions on abortion.

Abortion foes in some states, including Illinois, hope to pass restrictive laws.

Fifty percent of those polled said they opposed the use of public funds to pay for abortions. Of those who approved of abortion under any circumstance, 29 percent said public funds should not be used.

Of those who believed abortion should always be illegal, 15 percent approved of the use of public funds.

Opponents of abortion under any circumstances tended to have lower incomes and be less educated than abortion supporters.

Support for legal abortion with no restrictions was strongest in Cook County and weakest outside of Cook County. For example, while 28 percent of Cook County residents approved of legal abortion in all circumstances, only 19 percent of those outside of Cook County did so.

Blacks and whites largely mirrored the statewide results.

Whites were somewhat more likely than blacks to take the middle-ground position of supporting abortion with some restrictions, and blacks were more likely than whites to say they had no opinion on the issue. . . .

. . .

While the political pundits tried to prognosticate, individuals who had dedicated at least a part of their lives to the abortion and abortion rights struggles over the past year revealed that, for them, the issue was still moral.

Eileen McNamara, "Taking Stock of the Struggle: Abortion—An American Divide," *Boston Globe*, December 31, 1989

If there was one moment when the renewed national abortion battle was joined, it was on Jan. 9, when the U.S. Supreme Court agreed to review a restrictive Missouri law.

Both sides agreed that the law, which the court would uphold six months later in Webster v. Reproductive Health Services, was a pivotal test of a woman's right to end an unwanted pregnancy.

Since that constitutional guarantee was established in 1973 in Roe v. Wade, it has been besieged by those whose moral certitude was abetted by public ambivalence about abortion.

But when the justices agreed to hear the Webster case, the times seemed tailored for retrenchment. The court's newly-constituted conservative majority was buttressed by a federal bench reshaped by Ronald Reagan.

By agreeing to reconsider the role of the states in abortion policy, the court set the stage for political upheaval that is shaping the 1990 elections and forcing reexamination of fundamental definitions of life and privacy.

The story of what happened this year and what lies ahead is best told by some of those in the middle of one of the most contentious debates in recent American social history.

The controversy has involved many combatants: social activists, lawyers, politicians and the women who this year found their personal decisions part of an acrimonious public debate.

The Activists

KATE MICHELMAN: "I THINK THERE IS A SERIOUS LIKELIHOOD THAT ROE WILL BE DISMANTLED."

Kate Michelman traces her commitment to unfettered access to abortion to that moment nearly 20 years ago when she learned, on the heels of her husband's request for a divorce, that she was expecting their fourth child.

Still reeling from the announcement that he had fallen in love with another woman, she was shocked anew to learn that she could not terminate the pregnancy without the permission of a panel of doctors and the man who had just walked out on her.

What she felt at the time was a sense of powerlessness. Today, on her office wall at the National Abortion Rights Action League in Washington[,] is a photograph of Eleanor Roosevelt underscored by her observation, "No one can make you feel inferior without your consent."

Consent. Choice. Empowerment. Watchwords of the struggle Michelman has led as the executive director of the abortion rights league for the last four years, no year as critical as the one now ending.

Since the court signaled its willingness to reexamine the Roe vs. Wade decision in the Webster case, the league's membership has almost doubled, to 350,000, and revenues have almost tripled, to $11.9 million. Michelman has crisscrossed the country a dozen times, given hundreds of speeches and recruited thousands of volunteers.

She is exhausted but not nearly as discouraged as she was a year ago.

"I campaigned for Dukakis for six weeks before that election, and people just did not believe the court would ever change its position on Roe or that George Bush would be active on the issue," she said. "On Jan. 9, when they took Webster, we knew we were in trouble." From that point, Michelman kept a packed overnight bag handy, for a life lived in motel rooms more often than in the 17th-century Pennsylvania farmhouse she and her second husband share. "NARAL is 20 years old. We've always been steady-as-you-go," she said of the organization recognized as the political arm of the abortion rights movement. "We've had moments in the spotlight—the 1981 fight against a human life amendment in Congress, the 1987 fight against the nomination of Robert Bork," an Appeals Court judge, to the US Supreme Court. "But nothing like this."

This year, the league hired media consultants, ran focus groups, bought mailing lists. "We've run this like a political campaign: very intense. It's hard to capture how it feels out there, knowing you are responsible for speaking to people's hearts and minds if you want to activate them.

"I feel accountable. Travel is so tiring. Yet every time I go somewhere I hear the women's stories, and I remember that this is what it is about."

The stories she hears are seldom as simple as the slogans the league has popularized, she conceded, but complexity and ambiguity are subtleties the abortion rights movement cannot afford right now. "We needed to narrow the focus to broaden our support," she said. "After the court said, 'You can't count on us anymore,' we had to make the preservation of this right vital. There is a danger, and I'm always struggling with it, that we will not articulate the broader issues because we are so focused on the right to this one medical procedure."

She is heartened by last month's political victories but worried that they could prove ephemeral.

"I think there is a serious likelihood that Roe will be dismantled. If not this term, next term. If not next term, the term after that," she predicted. "As we do this work, precinct by precinct, we have to build a network with that in mind. We might need to pass a federal statute or a constitutional amendment guaranteeing a woman's right to choose. Otherwise we are going to be forever putting out fires."

Chances of passing such a statute are remote in the current Congress, which failed to override four abortion-related presidential vetoes in the fall. But Michelman, whose persistence got her that abortion 20 years ago, said the league will just work harder to elect a more sympathetic Congress. "None of these fights is easy, but we're in it for the long haul," she said.

BISHOP VAUGHAN: "AKIN TO THE GERMAN BISHOPS IN
THE FACE OF HITLER'S CONCENTRATION CAMPS."

The auxiliary bishop of the Roman Catholic Archdiocese of New York once confined his resistance to abortion to the occasional condemnatory sermon in St. Patrick's Church, his parish church in Newburgh, N.Y.

But that was before he became a jailbird.

An unlikely lawbreaker, Bishop Austin B. Vaughan is a member of Operation Rescue, the antiabortion group that blocks the doors of clinics in an effort to prevent some of the 1.5 million abortions performed in the United States each year.

"I had to be pushed and dragged into action," said the bishop, whose criminal record now includes two brief jail terms for trespass. "I finally got involved when I was challenged by the simple statements of Joan Andrews, who calls abortion the murder of her brothers and sisters, and Randy Terry, who asks why, if you believe it is murder, you don't act to stop it."

Joan Andrews, Randall Terry and Bishop Vaughan represent a dramatic tactical shift in the antiabortion movement. Frustrated over the last several years by the failure of well-financed groups such as the National Right to Life Committee to turn the tide through persuasion, these activists embraced civil disobedience and direct action.

Andrews, arrested more than 120 times and convicted 17 times on misdemeanor charges, served 31 months of a 5-year sentence in a Florida jail for invading a Pensacola abortion clinic. She was released late last year on a clemency order.

Terry, a former used car dealer and evangelical preacher, now runs Operation Rescue from an Atlanta jail, where he is serving a two-year term stemming from clinic protests. For Vaughan, the leap from pulpit to jail cell was an uneasy one, but once made, the decision felt preordained, he said.

"The only hesitation I might have had was the thought that maybe these people would be a bunch of kooks," he said. "Well, they aren't kooks. And being in jail is no more a sign of defeat than was the crucifixion."

Vaughan, one of four U.S. bishops arrested at abortion clinic protests this year, wishes more clergymen would join the blockades, which have won accolades from both New York Cardinal John O'Connor and Boston Cardinal Bernard F. Law. But he was encouraged last month when the National Conference of Bishops adopted a resolution calling abortion "the fundamental human rights issue" and declaring, "No Catholic can responsibly take a prochoice stand when the choice in question involves the taking of innocent human life."

"I saw myself in a situation akin to the German bishops in the face of Hitler's concentration camps," Vaughan said. "The only difference is that at least the German bishops could say they did not know for sure that people were dying. In our case," the Centers for Disease Control "puts out the figures on the death toll every year."

The court's decision in the Webster case to expand the power of states to regulate abortion "was a step in the right direction, but there is still so far to go before we reach the goal" that Vaughan said he expects the barricades to continue.

"The strategy has worked in the sense that abortion is no longer a non-issue," he said. "How much we can attribute to the work of the rescues is immeasurable. But lives have been saved." Operation Rescue estimates that 350 women nationwide have canceled their appointments for abortions, but this figure is impossible to confirm.

Whatever the anecdotal evidence, Vaughan said, he will be on the barricades "until some better means to stop the killing presents itself. This year was certainly a better year than last, but I can't regard anything as a victory as long as the killing continues."

In the meantime, he is due back in court in early January to face trespass charges in connection with a Good Friday demonstration last spring at an Albany abortion clinic.

The Lawyers

RACHAEL PINE: "IS PRIVACY GOING TO COME
CRASHING DOWN AS AN ESTABLISHED RIGHT?

To Rachael N. Pine, the changes taking place on the Supreme Court are less about the ascendancy of conservatism than about the decline of realism.

Somewhere along the way, the lawyer with the American Civil Liberties Union Reproductive Freedom Project said, the court lost sight of the impact of laws on human beings.

"Since Brown," she said, referring to the landmark 1954 Brown v. Board of Education school desegregation case, "the Supreme Court had looked at reality—the reality of segregation, the reality of pregnancy. Until the early '80s, it did not matter that a law looked good on its face if its impact could be demonstrated to be discriminatory or destructive of its purpose.

"But this court is less and less interested in hearing about the actual impact of laws. And since the court is not composed of poor minorities from the cities or pregnant teen-agers from the country, how can they know? The question now is: Is there a role for reality in constitutional analysis? How is the Constitution going to stay a living, breathing document if reality is constitutionally irrelevant?"

That change has added both more urgency and more frustration to Pine's work. In her office in the ACLU's New York headquarters, Pine looked back at 1989 as a "watershed year." The Roe vs. Wade decision did not fall, but it began to teeter.

"The main thing about Webster is that it did not affirm Roe," she said. "Roe has been such a strong and effective shield against state attempts to prevent reproductive choice for women that lower courts came through time and again, even when Reagan appointees would often complain about it in footnotes. Even they knew it was the law. We're in a transition phase now. Is privacy going to come crashing down as an established right? Is the door ajar for more political tampering with reproductive choice?"

One place where the door has not only been pried ajar but thrown wide opens a term at hard labor for doctors convicted of performing abortions.

Pine scoffed at the suit when it was filed. But she was no longer laughing as she gestured to the 2-foot-high pile of briefs and motions on the corner of her desk.

"I thought Connick's efforts would be perceived as more off-the-wall than I see now they were," she said. "My first reaction was, 'This is outrageous, unbelievable.' But you can't be so glib when you are looking at the assignment" of a three-judge panel instead of a single justice to hear the case and orders for more and more documentation. "It starts to look an awful lot more complicated than I would have hoped.

"The fact that it isn't easy says something about how hard it is for the federal courts to stand up for Roe after Webster, especially in Louisiana, where the entire political structure is stacked up on the other side. When you have such equivocation on the Supreme Court, it is harder for the federal courts to hold off the onslaught."

That public policy on reproductive health is reverting to the political arena gives Pine pause. "What we're seeing now is a slowed desire to restrict choice, but that is not the same as guaranteeing the right to choice."

She has no plans to abandon the fight in the courts. But she is beginning to understand how her opponents felt during the 16 years when Roe seemed an impenetrable barrier. "You have all these briefs you've filed, and you know they are excellent and you worry that it might not matter," she said. "It is hard to work that hard when you wonder if you are being heard."

JOHN S. BAKER: "ARE WE GOING TO DENY REALITY
BECAUSE WE DON'T LIKE THE CONSEQUENCES?"

John S. Baker was a law student at the University of Michigan in 1969, when he testified before legislators there, urging them to kill a move to liberalize the state's abortion laws. He did not think it was a good idea then and, 16 years after the Supreme Court nullified state prohibitions on abortion, Baker is still searching for ways to reinstate them.

He thinks he has found a way. The Louisiana State University law professor and former prosecutor is arguing the criminal statute case for New Orleans District Attorney Harry Connick, who brought the action.

Like Rachael Pine, opposing counsel in the suit to reactivate Louisiana's criminal abortion laws, Baker thinks reality has been the ultimate victim in the divisive debate.

"I'm impressed when arguing with the other side that the ACLU arguments are designed to avoid reality," he said. "Anyone who is trained as a trial lawyer respects physical evidence. The other side likes to create a fiction that we are not dealing with life here. It either is life or it isn't life. That reality is not dependent on your will. If you are happily pregnant, you are carrying a baby; unhappily so, a fetus. The reality is the same, just your view of it.

"Are we going to deny reality because we don't like the consequences? Maybe the consequences will be unhappy for the pregnant teen-ager. . . . That is sad but it's irrelevant to the reality of abortion."

Though his reasons differ, Baker, like Pine, is frustrated by the Webster decision, which stopped short of rescinding Roe. "I feel very much like Scalia," he said of Antonin Scalia, the Supreme Court justice who said in his Webster opinion that the court seemed intent on dismantling Roe "doorjamb by doorjamb."

"If we can lift the injunction on the Louisiana laws, let the ACLU fight us to the Supreme Court. We'll give O'Connor, who is obviously waiting for the perfect case, a clean target," he said referring to Justice Sandra Day O'Connor. "I want to give her a rifle shot at Roe."

The federal court in Louisiana is expected to rule on the case early in 1990.

For Baker, what is at stake is the philosophical direction of the country as well as the constitutional direction of the high court. "A good criminal law-yer always uses the competing elements of good and evil in his closing argu-ment," he said. "For better or worse, Americans look to the courts for moral sanction. When abortion became legal, for many people that meant it was moral. When Roe is reversed, it will then be illegal, and thus immoral.

"My motivations have always been prolife, but I channel them through legal argument, not political grandstanding. The whole business of plural-ism in this country is that it doesn't matter where your motivations lie. If you can make your case, you can translate those principles into social policy." . . .

The Politicians

L. DOUGLAS WILDER: "ANYONE WHO TRIES TO READ
MY TEA LEAVES FOR . . . ANOTHER ELECTION
WOULD BE MAKING A MISTAKE."

Disputed ballots were still being recounted when the pundits proclaimed L. Douglas Wilder's razor-thin victory last month in the Virginia governor's race a tribute to his abortion-rights position.

The gubernatorial elections in Virginia and New Jersey were the first tests of voter sentiment on abortion since the Webster vs. Reproductive Health Services decision, and abortion rights advocates were quick to take more credit than Wilder himself ascribes to the issue.

"It was an influence, but I don't think an overwhelming one," he said, as his reception area filled with well-wishers and aides packing boxes for the move from the lieutenant governor's office to the executive suite. "I got more crossover votes because of it, sure. But anyone who tries to read my tea leaves for advantage in another election would be making a mistake."

If it is true that all politics are local, the post-Webster political scene is demonstrating that no issue is more local than abortion. A month before abortion-rights candidates won New Jersey and Virginia, Pennsylvania Gov. Robert P. Casey signed into law the toughest restrictions in the nation. In Florida, Gov. Bob Martinez was confident that a solid antiabortion Legis-lature would pass new abortion restrictions at a special session in October. Not only did the lawmakers bury the bills, but the Florida Supreme Court declared that week that abortion is protected under the privacy provision of the state constitution.

Wilder, who will be the first black governor in the nation's history when he is sworn in Jan. 13, had to deal with the volatile issues of race and abortion as he campaigned in the heart of the old Confederacy. He did it by portraying himself as a mainstream Democrat.

"Remember, I was never a proabortion candidate," he said. "I made the argument against government interference in such a personal decision. And that is a conservative argument. The way to frame the question politically is not whether you favor abortion—I don't think anyone does. The question should be: Do you support government intervention in the most difficult, personal decision a woman can make?" Out of the same line of reasoning, Wilder supports laws that require teen-agers to obtain parental consent before having an abortion, arguing that parental rights outweigh a minor's right to privacy.

"I think the jury is still out on this issue," he said. "The Supreme Court has not decided where it is going to come down. And how much can you celebrate these last election returns? In New York City, where the registration is 5-to-1 Democratic, the prochoice candidate barely won."

If politicians can draw any lesson from the fall campaigns, Wilder said, it is that "it's a dangerous thing if the public thinks you are chameleonlike on this issue. Voters will see through it and see political expediency instead of leadership." Both J. Marshall Coleman, his Republican opponent, and New Jersey Rep. James Courter, the unsuccessful GOP gubernatorial candidate, abruptly modified their antiabortion stands in the wake of post-Webster opinion polls showing that, although the public is open to more restrictions on abortion, it does not favor overturning Roe.

Illinois Attorney General Neil Hartigan could face problems next year in his gubernatorial campaign, Wilder said, because he abandoned a Supreme Court test of a restrictive state abortion law by settling out of court. Until recently, Hartigan was seen as an antiabortion Democrat, but he is now running as an abortion rights candidate. "He has to be careful," Wilder said. "The public has to believe that your position evolved, not that you shifted overnight."

There is no natural lifespan to an issue like abortion, he said. "It will stay out there. . . . Without a national consensus on abortion, George Bush has got to run again, and he is going to face this issue, especially if the court continues to chip away at Roe."

CAROL BENTLEY: "MY OPPONENT BECAME AN INSTANT MARTYR. IT THREW THE WHOLE CAMPAIGN OUT OF CONTROL."

Were it not for the abortion issue, Carol Bentley is certain she would be the state senator from California's 39th District.

Bentley, a freshman Republican assemblywoman, was favored to win a special election three weeks ago in San Diego County, where registered Republicans outnumber Democrats 49 percent to 38 percent.

But the longshot candidacy of Lucy Killea, a 67-year-old Democrat, gained new momentum weeks before the election when San Diego Bishop Leo Y. Maher barred the Roman Catholic legislator from receiving communion until she renounced her support of abortion rights.

"My opponent became an instant martyr. It threw the whole campaign out of control," said Bentley, who is both embittered and emphatic that the backlash against religious intervention in the race cost her the Senate seat.

Calling Killea "an advocate of this most heinous crime," Bishop Maher said his sanction was "more pastoral than political." But the irony for Bentley, she said, "is that the bishop agrees with me, and he helped elect my opponent."

In addition to bringing enraged voters to the polls, the bishop apparently generated more funds for Killea's campaign coffers. In the end, Killea outspent Bentley, by a 2–1 ratio. Bentley, who opposes abortion in most cases, said she is convinced voters share her support of requirements that parents consent to a teen-ager's abortion and that public funding be limited to cases of rape, incest or hazards to maternal health.

"A lot of voters say they are prochoice but when you examine the conditions under which they support abortion, you find that they would like to see more restrictions," she said. "Very few favor abortion on demand."

Killea's victory gives abortion rights proponents a slim 21–19 majority in the California Senate.

Although she attributes her loss to fallout from the bishop's interference, Bentley said that the outcome of her campaign and the failed fortunes of other Republicans this fall underscore the need for the GOP to soften its antiabortion stand.

"My position will not change on abortion, and I think I reflect this district's abortion views more accurately than my opponent," said Bentley. "But every race is different. I think the Republican Party needs to have as broad a view as possible on this. We have to be open to all views or be prepared to lose. Candidates need to know where they stand and be prepared to defend it. When you waffle, you raise questions for the voter about your ethics. But in our next national platform, I think we should just not mention abortion."

Late next month, Bentley will formally declare her intention to run for reelection. "With any luck, the bishop of San Diego won't take any interest in this race," she said.

. . .

The year was over, but the controversy had only become worse. The beginning of the new decade brought more confusion in the law and more confrontation in the streets.

NOTES

1. Joseph R. Tybor, "Nominee Confronts Key Issues," *Chicago Tribune*, December 15, 1987, 1.

2. N. E. H. Hull and Peter Charles Hoffer, *Roe v. Wade: The Abortion Rights Controversy in American History* (Lawrence, Kans., 2001), 238.

· · ·

CHAPTER 7

Regulation and Controversy in
the Post-*Webster* Era

In the course of allowing states and municipalities to deny funding, ordain extensive consent procedures, require notification of parents, and impose one-day waiting periods for women seeking abortions at any time in the pregnancy, the Court had torn Justice Blackmun's trimester formula to tatters. Whether the Court had acted to override a woman's choice in the matter of continuing a pregnancy was another matter. Justice O'Connor did not think that substitution of the undue burden standard for the trimester formula endangered women's right to an abortion. But the new standard implied to some of her colleagues on the Court that the right to an abortion was no longer fundamental, hence state regulations no longer had to survive "strict scrutiny." She did not accept this position, but neither would she concede that states' hands were tied in the first weeks of a pregnancy, an essential part of the original *Roe* ruling.

For courts facing litigation over abortion regulations, the message of *Webster* was unclear. While the old trimester scheme afforded doctors almost unlimited discretion in the doctor-patient relationship, the undue burden test required courts to oversee the operation of every regulation. The real danger to women's rights promoters as well as pro-choice advocates in the shift of the Court's reasoning was that, framed in the language of undue burden, reproductive choice was no longer a "fundamental right" as enunciated in *Griswold* and extended in *Roe*. For legislatures, the picture was somewhat different; they could continue to pass laws that restricted access to abortion and funding for abortion, while imposing regulations regarding notification, informed consent, and medical practices in abortions. Each of these would then face challenges from abortion providers and pro-choice advocacy groups. After *Webster*, the outcome of these cases would hang on whether courts would enjoin the operation of the new law.

In 1988 and again in 1989, the Pennsylvania abortion statute voided in *Thornburgh* was amended to provide that (1) a woman seeking an abortion give her informed consent prior to the abortion procedure and at least twenty-four hours before the abortion was to be performed along with certain information concerning her decision, (2) a minor seeking an abortion obtain the informed consent of one of her parents or guardians (with a judicial "bypass" option if the minor does not wish to or cannot obtain such consent), and (3) unless certain exceptions apply, a married woman seeking an abortion sign a statement indicating that she has notified her husband of her intended abortion. Compliance with the foregoing requirements was exempted in the event of a "medical emergency" (a physician's good-faith clinical judgment that an immediate abortion would avert the woman's death or to avert a serious risk of substantial and irreversible impairment of a major bodily function). Finally, facilities providing abortion services were subject to certain reporting and record-keeping requirements, which did not include the disclosure of the identities of women who have undergone abortions but which included a requirement of reporting a married woman's failure to provide notice to her husband of her intended abortion.

Before any of these provisions took effect, five abortion clinics and one physician representing himself as well as a class of physicians who provided abortion services brought suit seeking declaratory and injunctive relief, arguing that each provision was unconstitutional on its face. The U.S. District Court for the Eastern District of Pennsylvania, after entering a preliminary injunction against enforcement of the provisions, held that all of the provisions were unconstitutional and entered a permanent injunction against the state's enforcement of the provisions. The U.S. Court of Appeals for the Third Circuit reversed the lower court ruling, upholding all of the provisions except for the spousal-notice requirement. The case, *Casey v. Planned Parenthood of Pennsylvania*, was argued before the U.S. Supreme Court in April and decided in July 1992.

It was widely expected to leave *Roe* an empty shell and to give to those state legislatures wishing to adopt them regulations of abortion practices reaching back to the moment of conception. In part the reason for this was the addition to the Court, replacing Justice Marshall, of Justice Clarence Thomas. Thomas, like Marshall an African American, was unlike Marshall in being a strong opponent of the right to an abortion. He reasoned that the Declaration of Independence, with its ringing trinity of life, liberty, and the pursuit of happiness, dictated a pro-life stance. His vote should have been sufficient to topple *Roe* and send abortion back to the state legislatures, where it had been before the Supreme Court heard the appeal of the Texas law.

New appointments to the High Court by pro-choice President Bill Clinton changed the balance of voting but not the tenor or the lines of dispute. Federal judge and former Columbia Law School professor Ruth Bader Ginsburg had argued that the right to choose to end a pregnancy should rest upon equal protection concepts rather than due process, as in *Roe*. She was nominated to the Court on June 13, 1993. While on the faculty at Columbia Law School, she became the head litigator in sex discrimination cases for the ACLU. In the 1970s, she won six women's rights cases before the High Court, using the remarkable tactic of arguing that the laws involved deprived men of equal rights. Criticized both by radical feminists and conservatives for her view that men and women should be treated strictly equally, she replied that her victories in court had helped to end the confinement of women to a separate, inferior sphere of life. When asked about *Roe* at her confirmation hearings, she reasserted what she had written years before: the Constitution must protect a woman's right to choose to terminate a pregnancy.

In July 1994, President Clinton's second nominee to the High Court, First Circuit Court of Appeals chief judge Stephen G. Breyer, also sailed through the confirmation process. Breyer, a former Harvard Law School professor and something of a conservative economic theorist, was confirmed by a vote of 87 to 9 on July 29, 1994. All of his opponents were outspoken pro-life politicians. To him fell the dubious honor of writing the majority opinion for the Court in the next round of regulatory cases.

Although the High Court had not laid out a new test for the constitutionality of abortion restrictions in *Casey*, Justice Scalia's repeated warning that "undue burden" was so indefinite and therefore susceptible to a wide variety of legislative readings bore fruit eight years after *Casey* was announced. Various states had prohibited a new procedure for late-term abortions, called "partial birth abortion" by its critics. Cases involving it arrived at the High Court by the end of the decade.

• • •

In Casey, *Justice O'Connor, Justice Kennedy, and Justice David Souter, appointed in 1990 to the Court by President George Bush in place of the retired William Brennan, announced the judgment of the Court (i.e., they had a majority of the Court with them) in the matter of the regulations themselves and the status of* Roe, *but the majority they had with them changed dramatically with respect to these two issues. In support of the Pennsylvania regulations (excepting the spousal notice), Justices Rehnquist, Thomas, and White joined the three authors of the "joint opinion." With respect to whether* Roe *should be overturned, Justices Stevens and Blackmun subscribed to the "joint opinion." Justice Kennedy wrote the first portion of the "joint opinion" in* Casey. *Did Kennedy restate the holding in* Roe *correctly? What historical examples did he offer for the protection of rights not mentioned in the Constitution? How did he factor into the opinion the unique problems of women? Why did stare decisis dictate that* Roe *remain in place? Does he seem to use a balancing test (wherein rights of the woman and rights of the fetus are balanced) rather than a test based on constitutional absolutes?*

Planned Parenthood of Southeastern Pennsylvania et al. v. Robert P. Casey, Governor of Pennsylvania, 505 U.S. 833 (1992)

Liberty finds no refuge in a jurisprudence of doubt. Yet 19 years after our holding that the Constitution protects a woman's right to terminate her pregnancy in its early stages . . . that definition of liberty is still questioned. Joining the respondents as *amicus curiae*, the United States, as it has done in five other cases in the last decade, again asks us to overrule *Roe.* . . . We acknowledge that our decisions after *Roe* cast doubt upon the meaning and reach of its holding. Further, the chief justice admits that he would overrule the central holding of *Roe* [that choice was a fundamental right and any statute infringing it had to pass a strict scrutiny test] and adopt the rational relationship test as the sole criterion of constitutionality. . . . State and federal courts as well as legislatures throughout the Union must have guidance as they seek to address this subject in conformance with the Constitution. Given these premises, we find it imperative to review once more the principles that define the rights of the woman and the legitimate authority of the State respecting the termination of pregnancies by abortion procedures.

After considering the fundamental constitutional questions resolved by *Roe*, principles of institutional integrity, and the rule of *stare decisis*, we are led to conclude this: the essential holding of *Roe v. Wade* should be retained and once again reaffirmed.

It must be stated at the outset and with clarity that *Roe*'s essential holding, the holding we reaffirm, has three parts. First is a recognition of the right of the woman to choose to have an abortion before viability and to obtain it without undue interference from the State. Before viability, the State's interests are not strong enough to support a prohibition of abortion or the imposition of a substantial obstacle to the woman's effective right to elect the procedure. Second is a confirmation of the State's power to restrict abortions after fetal viability, if the law contains exceptions for pregnancies which endanger the woman's life or health. And third is the principle that the State has legitimate interests from the outset of the pregnancy in protecting the health of the woman and the life of the fetus that may become a child. These principles do not contradict one another; and we adhere to each. . . .

It is also tempting, for the same reason, to suppose that the Due Process Clause protects only those practices, defined at the most specific level, that were protected against government interference by other rules of law when the Fourteenth Amendment was ratified. . . . But such a view would be inconsistent with our law. It is a promise of the Constitution that there is a realm of personal liberty which the government may not enter. We have vindicated this principle before. Marriage is mentioned nowhere in the Bill of Rights and interracial marriage was illegal in most States in the 19th century, but the Court was no doubt correct in finding it to be an aspect of liberty protected against state interference by the substantive component of the Due Process Clause in *Loving v. Virginia*, . . .

Neither the Bill of Rights nor the specific practices of States at the time of the adoption of the Fourteenth Amendment marks the outer limits of the substantive sphere of liberty which the Fourteenth Amendment protects. . . . It is settled now, as it was when the Court heard arguments in *Roe v. Wade*, that the Constitution places limits on a State's right to interfere with a person's most basic decisions about family and parenthood. . . .

The inescapable fact is that adjudication of substantive due process claims may call upon the Court in interpreting the Constitution to exercise that same capacity which by tradition courts always have exercised: reasoned judgment. Its boundaries are not susceptible of expression as a simple rule. That does not mean we are free to invalidate state policy choices with which we disagree; yet neither does it permit us to shrink from the duties of our office. . . . Men and women of good conscience can disagree, and we suppose some always shall disagree, about the profound moral and spiritual implications of terminating a pregnancy, even in its earliest stage. Some of us as individuals find abortion offensive to our most basic principles of morality, but that cannot control our decision. Our obligation is to define the liberty of all, not to mandate our own moral code. The underlying constitutional issue is whether the State can resolve these philosophic questions in such a definitive way that a woman lacks all choice in the matter, except perhaps in those rare circumstances in which the pregnancy is itself a danger to her own life or health, or is the result of rape or incest. . . .

These considerations begin our analysis of the woman's interest in terminating her pregnancy but cannot end it, for this reason: though the abortion decision may originate within the zone of conscience and belief, it is more than a philosophic exercise. Abortion is a unique act. It is an act fraught with consequences for others: for the woman who must live with the implications of her decision; for the persons who perform and assist in the procedure; for the spouse, family, and society which must confront the knowledge that these procedures exist, procedures some deem nothing short of an act of violence against innocent human life; and, depending on one's beliefs, for the life or potential life that is aborted. Though abortion is conduct, it does not follow that the State is entitled to proscribe it in all instances. That is because the liberty of the woman is at stake in a sense unique to the human condition and so unique to the law. The mother who carries a child to full term is subject to anxieties, to physical constraints, to pain that only she must bear.

That these sacrifices have from the beginning of the human race been endured by woman with a pride that ennobles her in the eyes of others and gives to the infant a bond of love cannot alone be grounds for the State to insist she make the sacrifice. Her suffering is too intimate and personal for the State to insist, without more, upon its own vision of the woman's role, however dominant that vision has been in the course of our history and our culture. The destiny of the woman must be shaped to a large extent on her own conception of her spiritual imperatives and her place in society.

It should be recognized, moreover, that in some critical respects the abortion decision is of the same character as the decision to use contraception, to which *Griswold v. Connecticut, Eisenstadt v. Baird*, and *Carey v. Population Services International* afford constitutional protection. We have no doubt as to the correctness of those decisions. They support the reasoning in *Roe* relating to the woman's liberty because they involve personal decisions concerning not only the meaning of procreation but also human responsibility and respect for it. As with abortion, reasonable people will have differences of opinion about these matters. One view is based on such reverence for the wonder of creation that any pregnancy ought to be welcomed and carried to full term no matter how difficult it will be to provide for the child and ensure its well-being. Another is that the inability to provide for the nurture and care of the infant is a cruelty to the child and an anguish to the parent. These are intimate views with infinite variations, and their deep, personal character underlay our decisions in *Griswold, Eisenstadt*, and *Carey*. The same concerns are present when the woman confronts the reality that, perhaps despite her attempts to avoid it, she has become pregnant.

It was this dimension of personal liberty that *Roe* sought to protect, and its holding invoked the reasoning and the tradition of the precedents we have discussed, granting protection to substantive liberties of the person. *Roe* was, of course, an extension of those cases and, as the decision itself indicated, the separate States could act in some degree to further their own legitimate interests in protecting prenatal life. The extent to which the legislatures of the States might act to outweigh the interests of the woman in choosing to terminate her pregnancy was a subject of debate both in *Roe* itself and in decisions following it.

While we appreciate the weight of the arguments made on behalf of the State in the cases before us, arguments which in their ultimate formulation conclude that *Roe* should be overruled, the reservations any of us may have in reaffirming the central holding of *Roe* are outweighed by the explication of individual liberty we have given combined with the force of *stare decisis*. We turn now to that doctrine. . . .

. . .

Justice Souter wrote the central portion of the "joint opinion." Souter, a New Hampshire lawyer and judge and a voracious reader of history, had already gained a reputation as a meticulous legal craftsman on the bench. When asked about abortion by the president's representatives, he replied that he had nothing to say about issues on which he might have to rule, and if they persisted in wanting an answer, they could count him out of the running. All during his interview with the president's aides and with Bush himself, the subject never came up. Bush later remarked, "You might just think that the whole nomination had something to do with abortion. . . . It's something much broader than that. I have too much respect for the Supreme Court for that."[1] Souter rested the constitutionality of Roe on the reliance modern women put on the right to an abortion that the Court had declared.

The obligation to follow precedent begins with necessity, and a contrary necessity marks its outer limit. . . . We recognize that no judicial system could do society's work if it eyed each issue afresh in every case that raised it. . . . Indeed, the very concept of the rule of law underlying our own Constitution requires such continuity over time that a respect for precedent is, by definition, indispensable. . . . At the other extreme, a different necessity would make itself felt if a prior judicial ruling should come to be seen so clearly as error that its enforcement was for that very reason doomed.

Even when the decision to overrule a prior case is not, as in the rare, latter instance, virtually foreordained, it is common wisdom that the rule of *stare decisis* is not an "inexorable command," and certainly it is not such in every constitutional case. . . . Rather, when this Court reexamines a prior holding, its judgment is customarily informed by a series of prudential and pragmatic considerations designed to test the consistency of overruling a prior decision with the ideal of the rule of law, and to gauge the respective costs of reaffirming and overruling a prior case. . . . whether the rule is subject to a kind of reliance that would lend a special hardship to the consequences of overruling and add inequity to the cost of repudiation . . . [and] whether related principles of law have so far developed as to have left the old rule no more than a remnant of abandoned doctrine. . . .

So in this case we may enquire whether *Roe*'s central rule has been found unworkable; whether the rule's limitation on state power could be removed without serious inequity to those who have relied upon it or significant damage to the stability of the society governed by it; whether the law's growth in the intervening years has left *Roe*'s central rule a doctrinal anachronism discounted by society; and whether *Roe*'s premises of fact have so far changed in the ensuing two decades as to render its central holding somehow irrelevant or unjustifiable in dealing with the issue it addressed.

Although *Roe* has engendered opposition, it has in no sense proven "unworkable," . . . representing as it does a simple limitation beyond which a state law is unenforceable. While *Roe* has, of course, required judicial assessment of state laws affecting the exercise of the choice guaranteed against government infringement, and although the need for such review will remain as a consequence of today's decision, the required determinations fall within judicial competence.

The inquiry into reliance counts the cost of a rule's repudiation as it would fall on those who have relied reasonably on the rule's continued application. . . . To eliminate the issue of reliance . . . one would need to limit cognizable reliance to specific instances of sexual activity. But to do this would be simply to refuse to face the fact that for two decades of economic and social developments, people have organized intimate relationships and made choices that define their views of themselves and their places in society, in reliance on the availability of abortion in the event that contraception should fail. The ability of women to participate equally in the economic and social life of the Nation has been facilitated by their ability to control their reproductive lives. . . . The Constitution serves human values, and while the effect of reliance on *Roe* cannot be exactly measured, neither can the certain cost of overruling *Roe* for people who have ordered their thinking and living around that case be dismissed.

No evolution of legal principle has left *Roe*'s doctrinal footings weaker than they were in 1973. No development of constitutional law since the case was decided has implicitly or explicitly left *Roe* behind as a mere survivor of obsolete constitutional thinking. . . .

Nor will courts building upon *Roe* be likely to hand down erroneous decisions as a consequence. Even on the assumption that the central holding of *Roe* was in error, that error would go only to the strength of the state interest in fetal protection, not to the recognition afforded by the Constitution to the woman's liberty. The latter aspect of the decision fits comfortably within the framework of the Court's prior decisions. . . . If indeed the woman's interest in deciding whether to bear and beget a child had not been recognized as in *Roe*, the State might as readily restrict a woman's right to choose to carry a pregnancy to term as to terminate it, to further asserted state interests in population control, or eugenics, for example. . . .

We have seen how time has overtaken some of *Roe*'s factual assumptions: advances in maternal health care allow for abortions safe to the mother later in pregnancy than was true in 1973 . . . and advances in neonatal care have advanced viability to a point somewhat earlier. . . . But these facts go only to the scheme of time limits on the realization of competing interests, and the divergences from the factual premises of 1973 have no bearing on the validity of *Roe*'s central holding, that viability marks the earliest point at which the State's interest in fetal life is constitutionally adequate to justify a legislative ban on nontherapeutic abortions. The soundness or unsoundness of that constitutional judgment in no sense turns on whether viability occurs at approximately 28 weeks, as was usual at the time of *Roe*, at 23 to 24 weeks, as it sometimes does today, or at some moment even slightly earlier in pregnancy, as it may if fetal respiratory capacity can somehow be enhanced in the future. Whenever it may occur, the attainment of viability may continue to serve as the critical fact, just as it has done since *Roe* was decided; which is to say that no change in *Roe*'s factual underpinning has left its central holding obsolete, and none supports an argument for overruling it. . . .

The country's loss of confidence in the Judiciary would be underscored by an equally certain and equally reasonable condemnation for another failing in overruling unnecessarily and under pressure. Some cost will be paid by anyone who approves or implements a constitutional decision where it is unpopular, or who refuses to work to undermine the decision or to force its reversal. The price may be criticism or ostracism, or it may be violence. An extra price will be paid by those who themselves disapprove of the decision's results when viewed outside of constitutional terms, but who nevertheless struggle to accept it, because they respect the rule of law. To all those who will be so tested by following [it], the Court implicitly undertakes to remain steadfast, lest in the end a price be paid for nothing. The promise of constancy, once given, binds its maker for as long as the power to stand by the decision survives and the understanding of the issue has not changed so fundamentally as to render the commitment obsolete. From the obligation of this promise this Court cannot and should not assume any exemption when duty requires it to decide a case in conformance with the Constitution. A willing breach of it would be nothing less than a breach of faith, and no Court that broke its faith with the people could sensibly expect credit for principle in the decision by which it did that. . . .

· · ·

Justice O'Connor wrote the closing portions of the "joint opinion." Although she upheld all but one of the Pennsylvania regulations, she insisted that nothing the legislature had done imposed an undue burden on the right to choose an abortion, save one requirement.

The Court of Appeals applied what it believed to be the undue burden standard and upheld each of the provisions except for the husband notification requirement. We agree generally with this conclusion, but refine the undue burden analysis in accordance with the principles articulated above. . . .

Whatever constitutional status the doctor-patient relation may have as a general matter, in the present context it is derivative of the woman's position. The doctor-patient relation does not underlie or override the two more general rights under which the abortion right is justified: the right to make family decisions and the right to physical autonomy. On its own, the doctor-patient relation here is entitled to the same solicitude it receives in other contexts. Thus, a requirement that a doctor give a woman certain information as part of obtaining her consent to an abortion is, for constitutional purposes, no different from a requirement that a doctor give certain specific information about any medical procedure. . . .

The Pennsylvania statute also requires us to reconsider the holding in *Akron I* that the State may not require that a physician, as opposed to a qualified assistant, provide information relevant to a woman's informed consent. Since there is no evidence on this record that requiring a doctor to give the information as provided by the statute would amount in practical terms to a substantial obstacle to a woman seeking an abortion, we conclude that it is not an undue burden. . . .

Our analysis of Pennsylvania's 24-hour waiting period between the provision of the information deemed necessary to informed consent and the performance of an abortion under the undue burden standard requires us to reconsider the premise behind the decision in *Akron I* invalidating a parallel requirement. . . . The idea that important decisions will be more informed and deliberate if they follow some period of reflection does not strike us as unreasonable, particularly where the statute directs that important information become part of the background of the decision. The statute, as construed by the Court of Appeals, permits avoidance of the waiting period in the event of a medical emergency and the record evidence shows that in the vast majority of cases, a 24-hour delay does not create any appreciable health risk. In theory, at least, the waiting period is a reasonable measure to implement the State's interest in protecting the life of the unborn, a measure that does not amount to an undue burden.

Whether the mandatory 24-hour waiting period is nonetheless invalid because in practice it is a substantial obstacle to a woman's choice to terminate her pregnancy is a closer question. The findings of fact by the District Court indicate that because of the distances many women must travel to reach an abortion provider, the practical effect will often be a delay of much more than a day because the waiting period requires that a woman seeking an abortion make at least two visits to the doctor. The District Court also found that in many instances this will increase the exposure of women seeking abortions to "the harassment and hostility of antiabortion protestors demonstrating outside a clinic." As a result, the District Court found that for those women who have the fewest financial resources, those who must travel long distances, and those who have difficulty explaining their whereabouts to husbands, employers, or others, the 24-hour waiting period will be "particularly burdensome."

These findings are troubling in some respects, but they do not demonstrate that the waiting period constitutes an undue burden. We do not doubt that, as the District Court held, the waiting period has the effect of "increasing the cost and risk of delay of abortions" . . . but the District Court did not conclude that the increased costs and potential delays amount to substantial obstacles. . . . As we have stated, under the undue burden standard a State is permitted to enact persuasive measures which favor childbirth over abortion, even if those measures do not further a health interest. And while the waiting period does limit a physician's discretion, that is not, standing alone, a reason to invalidate it. In light of the construction given the statute's definition of medical emergency by the Court of Appeals, and the District Court's findings, we cannot say that the waiting period imposes a real health risk. . . .

Section 3209 of Pennsylvania's abortion law provides, except in cases of medical emergency, that no physician shall perform an abortion on a married woman without receiving a signed statement from the woman that she has notified her spouse that she is about to undergo an abortion. The woman has the option of providing an alternative signed statement certifying that her husband is not the man who impregnated her; that her husband could not be located; that the pregnancy is the result of spousal sexual assault which she has reported; or that the woman believes that notifying her husband will cause him or someone else to inflict bodily injury upon her. . . .

The American Medical Association (AMA) has published a summary of the recent research in this field, which indicates that in an average 12-month period in this country, approximately two million women are the victims of severe assaults by their male partners. In a 1985 survey, women reported that nearly one of every eight husbands had assaulted their wives during the past year. The AMA views these figures as "marked underestimates," because the nature of these incidents discourages women from reporting them, and because surveys typically exclude the very poor, those who do not speak English well, and women who are homeless or in institutions or hospitals when the survey is conducted. According to the AMA, "researchers on family violence agree that the true incidence of partner violence is probably *double* the above estimates; or four million severely assaulted women per year. . . . Many of these incidents involve sexual assault. . . .

Other studies fill in the rest of this troubling picture. Physical violence is only the most visible form of abuse. Psychological abuse, particularly forced social and economic isolation of women, is also common. . . . Many victims of domestic violence remain with their abusers, perhaps because they perceive no superior alternative. . . . Many abused women who find temporary refuge in shelters return to their husbands, in large part because they have no other source of income. . . .

The vast majority of women notify their male partners of their decision to obtain an abortion. In many cases in which married women do not notify their husbands, the pregnancy is the result of an extramarital affair. Where the husband is the father, the primary reason women do not notify their husbands is that the husband and wife are experiencing marital difficulties, often accompanied by incidents of violence. . . .

This information and the District Court's findings reinforce what common sense would suggest. In well-functioning marriages, spouses discuss important intimate decisions such as whether to bear a child. But there are millions of women in this country who are the victims of regular physical and psychological abuse at the hands of their husbands. Should these women become pregnant, they may have very good reasons for not wishing to inform their husbands of their decision to obtain an abortion. Many may have justifiable fears of physical abuse, but may be no less fearful of the consequences of reporting prior abuse to the Commonwealth of Pennsylvania. Many may have a reasonable fear that notifying their husbands will provoke further instances of child abuse; these women are not exempt from §3209's notification requirement. Many may fear devastating forms of psychological abuse from their husbands, including verbal harassment, threats of future violence, the destruction of possessions, physical confinement to the home, the withdrawal of financial support, or the disclosure of the abortion to family and friends. These methods of psychological abuse may act as even more of a deterrent to notification than the possibility of physical violence, but women who are the victims of the abuse are not exempt from §3209's notification requirement. And many women who are pregnant as a result of sexual assaults by their husbands will be unable to avail themselves of the exception for spousal sexual assault, §3209(b)(3), because the exception requires that the woman has notified law enforcement authorities within 90 days of the assault, and her husband will be notified of her report once an investigation begins. . . .

The spousal notification requirement is thus likely to prevent a significant number of women from obtaining an abortion. It does not merely make abortions a little more difficult or expensive to obtain; for many women, it will impose a substantial obstacle. We must not blind ourselves to the fact that the significant number of women who fear for their safety and the safety of their children are likely to be deterred from procuring an abortion as surely as if the Commonwealth had outlawed abortion in all cases. . . .

The effect of state regulation on a woman's protected liberty is doubly deserving of scrutiny in such a case, as the State has touched not only upon the private sphere of the family but upon the very bodily integrity of the pregnant woman. . . .

· · ·

Justice Blackmun concurred with the joint opinion that Roe *was still good law, but he would have overturned all of Pennsylvania's new regulations.*

Three years ago, in *Webster v. Reproductive Health Services* (1989), four Members of this Court appeared poised to "cast into darkness the hopes and visions of every woman in this country" who had come to believe that the Constitution guaranteed her the right to reproductive choice. . . ." (Blackmun, J., dissenting). . . . All that remained between the promise of *Roe* and the darkness of the plurality was a single, flickering flame. Decisions since *Webster* gave little reason to hope that this flame would cast much light. . . . But now, just when so many expected the darkness to fall, the flame has grown bright.

I do not underestimate the significance of today's joint opinion. Yet I remain steadfast in my belief that the right to reproductive choice is entitled to the full protection afforded by this Court before *Webster*. And I fear for the darkness as four Justices anxiously await the single vote necessary to extinguish the light. . . .

Make no mistake, the joint opinion . . . is an act of personal courage and constitutional principle. In contrast to previous decisions in which Justices O'Connor and Kennedy postponed reconsideration of *Roe v. Wade*, . . . the authors of the joint opinion today join Justice Stevens and me in concluding that "the essential holding of *Roe v. Wade* should be retained and once again reaffirmed." In brief, five Members of this Court today recognize that "the Constitution protects a woman's right to terminate her pregnancy in its early stages." . . .

A fervent view of individual liberty and the force of *stare decisis* have led the Court to this conclusion. . . . Today a majority reaffirms that the Due Process Clause of the Fourteenth Amendment establishes "a realm of personal liberty which the government may not enter" . . . a realm whose outer limits cannot be determined by interpretations of the Constitution that focus only on the specific practices of States at the time the Fourteenth Amendment was adopted. . . . Finally, the Court today recognizes that in the case of abortion, "the liberty of the woman is at stake in a sense unique to the human condition and so unique to the law. The mother who carries a child to full term is subject to anxieties, to physical constraints, to pain that only she must bear." . . .

I am 83 years old. I cannot remain on this Court forever, and when I do step down, the confirmation process for my successor well may focus on the issue before us today. That, I regret, may be exactly where the choice between the two worlds will be made.

. . .

Chief Justice Rehnquist wanted to abandon Roe. *His opinion in* Casey *chastised the "joint opinion" for hiding what should have been made obvious. Was the chief justice correct that the "joint opinion" had overturned* Roe *in all but name?*

The joint opinion, following its newly minted variation on *stare decisis*, retains the outer shell of *Roe v. Wade* . . . but beats a wholesale retreat from the substance of that case. We believe that *Roe* was wrongly decided, and that it can and should be overruled consistently with our traditional approach to *stare decisis* in constitutional cases. . . . Although they reject the trimester framework that formed the underpinning of *Roe*, Justices O'Connor, Kennedy, and Souter adopt a revised undue burden standard to analyze the challenged regulations. We conclude, however, that such an outcome is an unjustified constitutional compromise, one which leaves the Court in a position to closely scrutinize all types of abortion regulations despite the fact that it lacks the power to do so under the Constitution.

In *Roe v. Wade*, the Court recognized a "guarantee of personal privacy" which "is broad enough to encompass a woman's decision whether or not to terminate her pregnancy." We are now of the view that, in terming this right fundamental, the Court in *Roe* read the earlier opinions upon which it based its decision much too broadly. Unlike marriage, procreation, and contraception, abortion "involves the purposeful termination of a potential life" [citing *Harris v. McRae*]. . . . The abortion decision must therefore "be recognized as *sui generis*, different in kind from the others that the Court has protected under the rubric of personal or family privacy and autonomy." *Thornburgh v. American College of Obstetricians and Gynecologists, supra*, at 792 (White, J., dissenting). One cannot ignore the fact that a woman is not isolated in her pregnancy, and that the decision to abort necessarily involves the destruction of a fetus. . . .

Nor do the historical traditions of the American people support the view that the right to terminate one's pregnancy is "fundamental." The common law which we inherited from England made abortion after "quickening" an offense. At the time of the adoption of the Fourteenth Amendment, statutory prohibitions or restrictions on abortion were commonplace; in 1868, at least 28 of the then-37 States and 8 Territories had statutes banning or limiting abortion. . . . By the turn of the century virtually every State had a law prohibiting or restricting abortion on its books. By the middle of the present century, a liberalization trend had set in. But 21 of the restrictive abortion laws in effect in 1868 were still in effect in 1973 when *Roe* was decided, and an overwhelming majority of the States prohibited abortion unless necessary to preserve the life or health of the mother. . . . On this record, it can scarcely be said that any deeply rooted tradition of relatively unrestricted abortion in our history supported the classification of the right to abortion as "fundamental" under the Due Process Clause of the Fourteenth Amendment.

We think, therefore, both in view of this history and of our decided cases dealing with substantive liberty under the Due Process Clause, that the Court was mistaken in *Roe* when it classified a woman's decision to terminate her pregnancy as a "fundamental right" that could be abridged only in a manner which withstood "strict scrutiny." . . .

The joint opinion . . . cannot bring itself to say that *Roe* was correct as an original matter, but the authors are of the view that "the immediate question is not the soundness of *Roe*'s resolution of the issue, but the precedential force that must be accorded to its holding." . . . Instead of claiming that *Roe* was correct as a matter of original constitutional interpretation, the opinion therefore contains an elaborate discussion of *stare decisis*. This discussion of the principle of *stare decisis* appears to be almost entirely dicta, because the joint opinion does not apply that principle in dealing with *Roe*. *Roe* decided that a woman had a fundamental right to an abortion. The joint opinion rejects that view. *Roe* decided that abortion regulations were to be subjected to "strict scrutiny" and could be justified only in the light of "compelling state interests." The joint opinion rejects that view. . . . *Roe* analyzed abortion regulation under a rigid trimester framework, a framework which has guided this Court's decisionmaking for 19 years. The joint opinion rejects that framework. . . .

• • •

Justice Scalia, writing for himself and Justices White and Thomas, along with the chief justice, penned the strongest and least conciliatory of rebukes to the three authors of the "joint opinion." In particular, the justice seemed to be opposed to what he called an "imperial judiciary."

My views on this matter are unchanged from . . . *Webster*. . . . The States may, if they wish, permit abortion on demand, but the Constitution does not *require* them to do so. The permissibility of abortion, and the limitations upon it, are to be resolved like most important questions in our democracy: by citizens trying to persuade one another and then voting. As the Court acknowledges, "where reasonable people disagree the government can adopt one position or the other." . . . The Court is correct in adding the qualification that this "assumes a state of affairs in which the choice does not intrude upon a protected liberty,"—but the crucial part of that qualification is the penultimate word. A State's choice between two positions on which reasonable people can disagree is constitutional even when (as is often the case) it intrudes upon a "liberty" in the absolute sense. Laws against bigamy, for example—with which entire societies of reasonable people disagree—intrude upon men and women's liberty to marry and live with one another. But bigamy happens not to be a liberty specially "protected" by the Constitution.

That is, quite simply, the issue in these cases: not whether the power of a woman to abort her unborn child is a "liberty" in the absolute sense; or even whether it is a liberty of great importance to many women. Of course it is both. The issue is whether it is a liberty protected by the Constitution of the United States. I am sure it is not. . . . I reach it for the same reason I reach the conclusion that bigamy is not constitutionally protected—because of two simple facts: (1) the Constitution says absolutely nothing about it, and (2) the longstanding traditions of American society have permitted it to be legally proscribed. . . .

The Imperial Judiciary lives. It is instructive to compare this Nietzschean vision of us unelected, life-tenured judges—leading a Volk who will be "tested by following," and whose very "belief in themselves" is mystically bound up in their "understanding" of a Court that "speaks before all others for their constitutional ideals"—with the somewhat more modest role envisioned for these lawyers by the Founders. . . . To make matters worse, two of the three [authors of the joint opinion], in order thus to remain steadfast, had to abandon previously stated positions. . . . It is beyond me how the Court expects these accommodations to be accepted "as grounded truly in principle, not as compromises with social and political pressures having, as such, no bearing on the principled choices that the Court is obliged to make." . . . The only principle the Court "adheres" to, it seems to me, is the principle that the Court must be seen as standing by *Roe*. That is not a principle of law (which is what I thought the Court was talking about), but a principle of *Realpolitik*—and a wrong one at that.

I cannot agree with, indeed I am appalled by, the Court's suggestion that the decision whether to stand by an erroneous constitutional decision must be strongly influenced—*against* overruling, no less—by the substantial and continuing public opposition the decision has generated. The Court's judgment that any other course would "subvert the Court's legitimacy" must be another consequence of reading the error-filled history book that described the deeply divided country brought together by *Roe*. In my history book, the Court was covered with dishonor and deprived of legitimacy by *Dred Scott v. Sandford* [in which a majority of the Court found that a person of African descent could not be a citizen, that the Congress could not bar slavery from the territories, and that Dred Scott could not gain his freedom through application of the Full Faith and Credit Clause of the Constitution], an erroneous (and widely opposed) opinion that it did not abandon. . . .

But whether it would "subvert the Court's legitimacy" or not, the notion that we would decide a case differently from the way we otherwise would have in order to show that we can stand firm against public disapproval is frightening. It is a bad enough idea, even in the head of someone like me, who believes that the text of the Constitution, and our traditions, say what they say and there is no fiddling with them. But when it is in the mind of a Court that believes the Constitution has an evolving meaning, . . . that the Ninth Amendment's reference to "other" rights is not a disclaimer, but a charter for action, . . . and that the function of this Court is to "speak before all others for [the people's] constitutional ideals" unrestrained by meaningful text or tradition—then the notion that the Court must adhere to a decision for as long as the decision faces "great opposition" and the Court is "under fire" acquires a character of almost czarist arrogance. . . . We have no Cossacks, but at least we can stubbornly refuse to abandon an erroneous opinion that we might otherwise change—to show how little they intimidate us. . . .

What makes all this relevant to the bothersome application of "political pressure" against the Court are the twin facts that the American people love democracy and the American people are not fools. As long as this Court thought (and the people thought) that we Justices were doing essentially lawyers' work up here—reading text and discerning our society's traditional understanding of that text—the public pretty much left us alone. Texts and traditions are facts to study, not convictions to demonstrate about. But if in reality our process of constitutional adjudication consists primarily of making *value judgments*, . . . The people know that their value judgments are quite as good as those taught in any law school—maybe better. If, indeed, the "liberties" protected by the Constitution are, as the Court says, undefined and unbounded, then the people *should* demonstrate, to protest that we do not implement *their* values instead of *ours*. Not only that, but confirmation hearings for new Justices *should* deteriorate into question-and-answer sessions in which Senators go through a list of their constituents' most favored and most disfavored alleged constitutional rights, and seek the nominee's commitment to support or oppose them. Value judgments, after all, should be voted on, not dictated; and if our Constitution has somehow accidently committed them to the Supreme Court, at least we can have a sort of plebiscite each time a new nominee to that body is put forward. . . .

There is a poignant aspect to today's opinion. Its length, and what might be called its epic tone, suggest that its authors believe they are bringing to an end a troublesome era in the history of our Nation and of our Court. "It is the dimension" of authority, they say, to "call the contending sides of national controversy to end their national division by accepting a common mandate rooted in the Constitution." . . . Quite to the contrary, by foreclosing all democratic outlet for the deep passions this issue arouses, by banishing the issue from the political forum that gives all participants, even the losers, the satisfaction of a fair hearing and an honest fight, by continuing the imposition of a rigid national rule instead of allowing for regional differences, the Court merely prolongs and intensifies the anguish.

We should get out of this area, where we have no right to be, and where we do neither ourselves nor the country any good by remaining.

. . .

The Court's logic did not sway law professors such as Cass Sunstein. He proposed that defenders of abortion rights in Roe *and in the later "undue burden" test had missed the best reason for guaranteeing those rights in the first place. His 1992 article restimulated an ongoing debate over abortion rights within academia.*

Cass Sunstein, "Neutrality in Constitutional Law," *Columbia Law Review* 92 (January 1992): 1–42

. . . In the context at hand, a restriction on access to abortion turns women's reproductive capacities into something to be used by fetuses. . . .

With abortion . . . two positions seem to dominate the constitutional territory. According to the first view, the fetus has the status of a human life, for religious or other reasons. Because it has that status, nearly any governmental burden on the pregnant mother, if necessary to protect the fetus, is adequately justified. This view is often closely identified with the understanding—which is not a part of the first view as a logical or necessary matter—that sexual activity should be exclusively for purposes of reproduction. At least some of the controversy over abortion lies at bottom on this issue, with many critics of abortion concerned that its free availability will promote promiscuity, remove a built-in check on sexual self-discipline, and encourage sexual activity for nonreproductive purposes. Certainly not all members of the prolife movement share these concerns; but these ideas lie close to the conceptual heart of the movement. . . .

For those who believe in the right to abortion, the right to privacy calls first and foremost for control of the body; but it bears on sexuality more generally as well. Just as the antiabortion position is linked with the view that sexuality is for purposes of reproduction, the opposing view is deeply rooted in a belief that the abortion right is part and parcel of sexual freedom, which is important for both men and women. On this view, that right is necessary in part to ensure that nonreproductive sexuality will continue to be possible. One of the harms caused by antiabortion laws is the severe practical restrictions they impose on sexuality. . . .

There are serious difficulties, however, in treating the abortion right as one of privacy, not least because the Constitution does not refer to privacy and because the abortion decision does not involve conventional privacy at all. In any case, the two views on the subject seem to have reached stalemate, with no possibility of developing criteria for mediating between them that might be acceptable to both sides.

We might therefore explore another argument on behalf of the relevant right, one that sounds in principles of equal protection. This argument sees a prohibition on abortion as invalid because it involves a cooptation of women's bodies for the protection of fetuses. It claims that abortion restrictions selectively turn women's reproductive capacities into something for the use and control of others. No parallel disability is imposed on men. Unlike the privacy view, this argument does not and need not take a position on the status of the fetus. It acknowledges the possibility that fetuses are in important respects human beings. It is entirely comfortable with the claim that the destruction of a fetus is at least a morally problematic act. But it asserts that under current conditions, the government cannot impose on women alone the obligation to protect fetuses through a legal act of bodily cooptation.

On this view, abortion should be seen not as murder of the fetus but instead as a refusal to continue to permit one's body to be used to provide assistance to it. The failure to see it in this way is simply a product of the perceived naturalness of the role of women as childbearers—whether they want to assume that role or not. And even if a general legal obligation of bodily assistance to the vulnerable might be constitutionally acceptable, such an obligation cannot be permitted if it is imposed solely on women. This is so especially because of the close real-world connection between selectivity of this sort and constitutionally illegitimate stereotypes about the appropriate role of women.

In its fullest form, the argument from equality is supported by four different points: (1) prohibiting abortion is a form of prima facie or de jure sex discrimination; (2) it is impermissibly selective; (3) it results from constitutionally unacceptable stereotypes; and (4) it fails sufficiently to protect fetal lives. Standing alone, any one of these points is probably insufficient. They derive force by their cumulative effect.

The first point is that restrictions on abortion should be seen as a form of sex discrimination. The proper analogy here is to a law that is targeted solely at women and thus contains a de jure distinction on the basis of sex. A statute that is explicitly addressed to women is of course a form of sex discrimination. A statute that involves a defining characteristic or a biological correlate of being female should be treated in precisely the same way. If a law said that "no woman" may obtain an abortion, it should readily be seen as a sex-based classification. A law saying that "no person" may obtain an abortion has the same meaning.

The fact that some men may also be punished by abortion laws—for example, male doctors—does not mean that restrictions on abortion are sex-neutral. Laws calling for racial segregation make it impermissible for whites as well as blacks to desegregate, and this does not make such laws race-neutral. . . . A law that prohibited pregnant women, or pregnant people, from appearing on the streets during daylight would readily be seen as a form of de jure sex discrimination. A restriction on abortion has the same sex-based features. . . .

The [second] point suggests that from the standpoint of equal protection, the problem with restrictions on abortion is not merely that they impose on women's bodies but also that they do so in a way that is inextricably intertwined with the prescription, by the law and thus the state, of different roles for men and women, different roles that are part of second-class citizenship for women. Far from undermining it, the fact that only men are drafted helps to confirm the claim that abortion laws represent a form of unacceptable selectivity.

The third point, buttressing the second, is that the notion that women should be compelled in this way is a product of constitutionally unacceptable stereotypes about the proper role of women in society. The connection is not a matter of logic but of past and current practice; it is fully possible to reject these stereotypes and the practice of abortion. But the history of abortion restrictions unambiguously supports the claim that in fact, such restrictions are closely tied up with, indeed in practice driven by, traditional ideas about women's proper role. To be sure, some people oppose with equal fervor both abortion and those traditional ideas. But the restrictions that do or could exist in this world would in all probability have failed to pass without the involvement and support of people holding and relying on unacceptable stereotypes. . . .

The fourth and final factor is that in the real world, the consequence of a restriction on abortion is not materially to save fetal lives, but instead to force women to seek dangerous abortions, with increased risks to women themselves. Indeed, some estimates suggest that before *Roe*, 5,000 to 10,000 women died per year as a result of incompetently performed abortions, and thousands more were admitted to hospitals for the same reason. Since *Roe*, abortion-related maternal deaths have dropped by no less than 90%, falling by 40% in the year after *Roe* alone. Moreover, the abortion rate appears not to have increased dramatically as a result of the decision in *Roe*. Even the rate of *legal* abortions increased more in the three years before *Roe* than in the three years after that decision. Indeed, some studies show that nearly as many abortions were performed before *Roe* as now. The abortion rate has increased from between 20% and 25% to about 28%; the total annual number has gone from between 1 million and 1.5 million to between 1.5 and 1.6 million.

Even if these statistics are overstated, and even if the number and rate of abortions has increased more substantially as a result of *Roe*, at least it seems clear that the principal effect of the decision was not to increase fetal deaths, but instead to produce a shift from dangerous to safe abortions. If this is so, restrictions on abortion do not materially advance the goal of protecting life at all. Instead, they increase maternal deaths while decreasing the termination of fetal lives much less than might be expected or hoped.

The evidence on the futility of antiabortion restrictions also suggests, though it certainly does not demonstrate, the presence of a discriminatory purpose. The failure of advocates of abortion laws to come to terms with that evidence suggests the possibility that at least a part of the antiabortion movement stems from punitive goals rather than an interest in protecting fetal life.

The argument for an abortion right built on principles of sex equality is thus straightforward. Restrictions on abortion burden only women, and are therefore impermissible unless persuasively justified in sex-neutral terms. . . .

. . .

Sunstein's argument that the Equal Protection Clause of the Fourteenth Amendment was a better constitutional home for the abortion right than privacy or substantive due process left him open to the counterargument that women's equality was dependent in some way on women's refusal to have children. In the next selection, Kristina M. Mentone, then a J.D. candidate at Fordham Law School and a member of the law review editorial board, disputed that identification.

Kristina M. Mentone, "When Equal Protection Fails: How the Equal Protection Justification for Abortion Undercuts the Struggle for Equality in the Workplace," *Fordham Law Review* 70 (May 2002): 2665–68, 2678–89

... In 1992, the Supreme Court again wrestled with the constitutional right to an abortion and the scope of that right in *Planned Parenthood v. Casey*. At issue in *Casey* was a Pennsylvania statute that imposed several regulations on abortion.

The joint opinion of Justices O'Connor, Kennedy, and Souter reaffirmed the central holding in *Roe*. That is, the Court affirmed the constitutional right to an abortion before viability without undue interference from state legislation, and recognized that a state has legitimate interests in the health of the mother and the potential life of the fetus from the outset of pregnancy.

Although the Court upheld the central holding of *Roe*, a woman's right to an abortion looked very different after *Casey*. *Casey* altered the holding in *Roe* in three significant ways. First, the joint opinion gave wider latitude to a state's ability to regulate abortion. ...

Additionally, *Casey* changed the standard of review required of abortion legislation. Rather than requiring strict scrutiny, *Casey* applied the undue burden standard. The undue burden standard merely prohibits "a state regulation having the purpose or effect of placing a substantial obstacle in the path of a woman seeking an abortion of a nonviable fetus." ...

The third significant change in *Casey* was that the Court intimated an alternate constitutional basis for the right to an abortion. While *Roe* based the right to an abortion on privacy rights inherent in the Fourteenth Amendment's Due Process Clause, the joint opinion in *Casey* rarely mentions privacy, and even where it does, it is merely a reference to a general right to privacy.

Instead, the opinions in *Casey* for the first time intimated that the Equal Protection Clause of the Fourteenth Amendment may provide a basis for the constitutional right to an abortion. The joint opinion states that "the ability of women to participate equally in the economic and social life of the Nation has been facilitated by their ability to control their reproductive lives." Justice Stevens also stated that there would be enormous societal costs if *Roe* were overruled because it had become "an integral part of a correct understanding of both the concept of liberty and the basic equality of men and women." Thus, if the opportunity arises to reevaluate the right to an abortion, the Court may base the right on equal protection grounds. ...

Privacy and autonomy arguments approach the right to abortion from a gender-neutral perspective, at least insofar as social roles are concerned. These arguments do not rely on the social roles of men or women, nor do they advocate for abortion primarily on the basis that women are in any way controlled by men. Rather, privacy and autonomy arguments are premised on the notion that continuing a pregnancy is a major life decision that women are capable of making. Accordingly, government should not force or coerce a woman's ultimate decision.

The idea that an individual should maintain control over her body and make decisions for herself regarding procreation is compelling. The burden and implications of pregnancy are great, and no law should require a person to serve as a human incubator. A woman's decision whether or not to bear a child should therefore be both private and autonomous.

While the privacy argument recognizes a woman's autonomy and affords sufficient protection to a woman's right to abortion, the equal protection argument does not. The latter fails to recognize the importance and seriousness of deciding to carry a pregnancy to term, regardless of the woman's situation in life. A major line of reasoning underlying the equal protection argument is that, absent abortion rights, women would be forced to become mothers and motherhood is thought to place women at a distinct disadvantage in society by hindering both their educational and professional pursuits. Mothers are considered to bear most of the weight of childrearing, which disables them from competing equally with men (even those that are fathers) in the workplace. Thus, equal protection proponents argue that abortion is necessary to allow women to postpone childbearing so that they can pursue the goals that motherhood hinders.

Additionally, the equal protection argument is based on anti-caste principles, which indicate that the law must remedy the traditional subordination of women . . . to cure the sexual and societal domination of women by men. According to this argument, a history of sexual control by men has caused women to live as second-class citizens in fear of men. . . .

Doubtless, sexual violence is a problem in society, and women are the primary targets of such violence, but the notion that all men are responsible for this problem is as stereotypical as the notion that a woman's place is in the home. Attacking men as a class in such a manner is not only unfair to men, but is also dangerous for feminism and women's equality. Such arguments can alienate men who would otherwise support women's equality. Rather than fostering additional support for the equality of women and the right to an abortion, such extreme accusations against men create a situation where men are pitted against women. Feminism need not be regarded as purely a woman's issue: equality of the sexes benefits both men and women.

Furthermore, although any woman who has walked a city street probably understands . . . that sexual violence has caused a fear in women that is not experienced by men, that fear of potential sexual violence does not in any way suggest that all or even a majority of women's sexual relations are unwanted or unequal. To suggest that women cannot or do not assert control over a significant portion of their sexual relations reinforces stereotypical views of women as being meek and submissive.

Moreover, the equal protection argument only narrowly protects abortion rights and endangers the future of those rights should women achieve social equality. . . . But, if . . . women have control over their reproductive functions by their ability to choose whether or not to have sex[,] [the equal rights argument] does not provide sufficient support for abortion rights outside the context of coercive sex.

Sunstein admits that the equal protection argument is more easily applied to cases where pregnancy resulted from rape or incest. Most pregnancies, however, are not a result of rape or incest, and most women who seek an abortion are not pregnant due to rape or incest. Sunstein even acknowledges that, "no one is likely to be in a good position to answer the question whether abortion should be available in a world of gender-based equality." . . .

Moreover, the equal protection argument endangers the right to abortion even at the present time. If the primary reason that a woman is entitled to an abortion is that she likely was coerced into having sex and did not have control over her pregnancy in the first place, or that she likely will be the primary caretaker, then perhaps states could limit abortion rights to such situations. Under such a system, a woman who voluntarily has sex, or perhaps intentionally gets pregnant, but then changes her mind, could be denied the right to an abortion. Similarly, a woman who becomes pregnant by a man who is willing to be the primary caretaker might be denied the right to have an abortion so that the father could raise the baby.

According to the equal protection theory, then, abortion is merely a means to repair women's situation in society based on discrimination. Therefore, abortion may be seen as a right limited to a time when women still experience discrimination. By contrast, the privacy argument is bound neither by a time limit nor by the individual circumstances of a particular woman. The privacy argument acknowledges that no woman, regardless of how powerless or powerful she may be, can be forced to have a baby. It protects women who intentionally get pregnant and then change their minds. It protects women who consensually have sex but accidentally get pregnant. It protects women who are pregnant due to rape or coercion. It protects women who are pregnant by men who are willing to support the baby. It protects all women, all the time. . . .

. . .

While the law professors had their eyes on the justices, political scientists were watching the other branches of government to see how they responded to the abortion/abortion rights issue in the 1990s. In a review of one of the leading surveys of political scientists' "take" on abortion rights and the American political system, political scientist Neal Devins made some points of his own about the role of the elected branches of government in the evolution of abortion law.

Neal Devins, "Through the Looking Glass: What Abortion Teaches Us about American Politics," review of *Abortion and American Politics*, by Barbara Hinkson Craig and David M. O'Brien, *Columbia Law Review* 94 (January 1994): 293–313

. . . A simple comparison of elected branch interest in abortion before and after *Roe* makes clear that the abortion dispute is not controlled by nine individuals working in isolation. Prior to *Roe*, abortion was a matter of some state and limited national attention. In the decade preceding *Roe*, after nearly a century of political dormancy, four states repealed and nineteen states—while still limiting abortion rights—liberalized their abortion laws. Congress and the White House, for the most part, were content to leave the abortion issue in the hands of state government: congressional action was limited and designed to preserve the anti-abortion status quo ante, while executive branch action was equally limited and typically reaffirmed state authority.

Elected government action since *Roe* makes clear that the Supreme Court's nationalization of abortion rights was anything but the last word on the subject. Over the past twenty years, the abortion dispute has spread throughout the American political system. *Roe v. Wade* and *Planned Parenthood v. Casey* notwithstanding, abortion is hardly the sole province of the judiciary. While abortion politics and court decision-making are closely linked—especially through the nomination and confirmation of federal judges—the sweep of abortion-related policy is far too broad for any one branch of government to dominate.

The abortion drama demonstrates that the elected branches can influence the shaping of constitutional values in many ways. The executive branch has been extremely active in its attempts to regulate abortion. Presidential appointments to courts and government agencies, the use of constitutionally specified powers to recommend as well as veto legislation, and the exercise of symbolic leadership through bully pulpit speeches all figure prominently in the abortion dispute. Furthermore, federal departments and agencies involved in health and family planning, civil rights, foreign policy, and the budget have all found themselves in the midst of the abortion controversy. Congress and its committees have also been vigorous players in the abortion dispute. Through its roles both as lawmaker and overseer of government agencies and departments, Congress is continuously involved in shaping and limiting abortion rights.

Abortion, finally, is not simply about federal decision-making. A vigorous dialogue has emerged between state legislatures and the federal courts. State legislatures regularly enact, review, and modify laws governing such areas as pre-abortion counseling, waiting periods, and juvenile and spousal rights. In conjunction with Congress, the White House, and the states, interest groups are also actively involved in this political dynamic. . . .

Congress has repeatedly shied away from taking an absolutist position on abortion. It has rejected a proposed constitutional amendment overturning *Roe* as well as human life legislation defining the beginning of life as conception and specifying that fetuses are persons for Fourteenth Amendment purposes. These proposals would have done more than overturn *Roe* and return the abortion issue to the states. The specification of fetuses as legal persons was designed to prevent states from permitting abortions unless the mother's life was in jeopardy. Congress also rejected a more modest federalism amendment in 1982 and again in 1983 that would have allowed states to regulate abortion as they saw fit. Another example of this unwillingness to endorse extremist positions, although not mentioned in *Abortion and American Politics*, is Congress' repudiation of proposals to strip federal courts, including the U.S. Supreme Court, of jurisdiction in abortion cases. These proposals would leave state courts free to follow, limit, or abandon *Roe*. Of all these measures, only the federalism amendment made it out of committee, but it was soundly defeated on the Senate floor.

Congress has also rejected pro-choice absolutism. For example, in the wake of an endorsement in *Planned Parenthood v. Casey* of a qualified right to seek an abortion, legislators began backing away from efforts to codify abortion rights. In addition to pro-life legislators, pro-choice legislators who endorse parental consent and waiting period restrictions appear unwilling to support the codification of *Roe* through the Freedom of Choice Act. Notwithstanding the Clinton administration's ostensible support for these codification efforts, the Freedom of Choice Act has stalled and is unlikely to reemerge in the near future. . . .

Another phenomenon deserving more focused attention is how Congress seeks to shape constitutional doctrine through its participation in litigation. When the Supreme Court upheld the constitutionality of the Hyde Amendment in *Harris v. McRae*, for example, a bipartisan coalition of over 200 congressional amici argued that to tamper with the inviolable and exclusive power of the purse is to tamper with the very essence of constitutional, representative government. In recent years, pro-choice and pro-life legislators have lined up on opposite sides of state regulation cases. These filings, although principally symbolic, are nonetheless instructive in measuring legislative attitudes. In *Thornburgh v. American College of Obstetricians and Gynecologists*, eighty-one pro-choice legislators publicly scolded Solicitor General Charles Fried for having taken an extraordinary and unprecedented step in calling for Roe's reversal.

In addition to the enactment of punitive legislation, congressional oversight also, and more typically, takes the form of legislative jawboning. When the Reagan administration suspended fetal tissue research, for example, House Committee on Human Resources chair Ted Weiss requested that the administration turn over all research evidence and all documents, including letters, memoranda, minutes of meetings, and internal or draft documents. Another example of congressional cajoling occurred when the Reagan administration announced its proposed regulations on family planning programs. Congressional supporters, including 106 co-signers of a letter of support to Health and Human Services Secretary Otis Bowen, encouraged the administration to stick to its guns and promulgate the regulations in final form. Opponents, in contrast, pleaded with the administration to suspend the regulations, accusing the administration of succumbing to political pressure and describing the proposal as not in the best interest of the 5,000,000 low income people that depend upon the program each year for family planning services. . . .

A factor not considered by Craig and O'Brien in their assessment of state abortion politics is the often pivotal role played by state court judges. Before *Roe*, several state courts struck down anti-abortion laws. After the Supreme Court concluded in *Harris v. McRae* that a congressional prohibition on the use of Medicaid funds for abortions did not violate the Equal Protection Clause, courts in California, Connecticut, Massachusetts, Michigan, New

Jersey, and Oregon interpreted their own constitutions to protect the right of indigent women to a state-funded abortion. The New Jersey Supreme Court pointed out that state Constitutions are separate sources of individual freedoms and restrictions on the exercise of power by the Legislature. . . . Although the state Constitution may encompass a smaller universe than the federal Constitution, our constellation of rights may be more complete.

Ten states' constitutions contain explicit privacy provisions and several others contain clauses that have been interpreted to protect the right to privacy. Some state courts have applied these provisions to protect abortion rights. For example, the California Supreme Court ruled that the federal right of privacy . . . is more limited than the corresponding right in the California Constitution and that restrictions on abortion funding for indigent women therefore violated California's explicit privacy right.

Victories in state court, moreover, do not end the political struggle. Instead, the state legislature and voters engage state courts in a dialogue over the meaning of the state constitution. Take the case of California. In 1981, the California Supreme Court declared that the legislature could not restrict state funding for abortions for indigent women, but in each of the last ten years the legislature passed laws restricting the funding. Each year the courts struck down the laws and reinstated the funding. Conservatives attempted to make use of the ballot box to remove liberal judges. California Chief Justice Rose Elizabeth Bird and two other justices were ousted in 1986 when conservatives targeted them for electoral defeat. A five-two conservative majority now dominates the court, but it continues to issue an expansive interpretation of California's privacy right.

. . .

Casey was not the last word on state regulation, as Justice Souter predicted. In the dissection and extraction (D & X) method of abortion used in the later stages of the first trimester, the fetus was pulled into the birth canal and dismembered there rather than in the womb. The procedure was supposed to be safer for the woman, but its details were appalling when recounted and led to opponents calling it a "partial birth abortion." Congress had passed bills banning the procedure, but President Clinton had vetoed them. Lower courts had granted injunctions against the state laws passed for the same purpose, and the Supreme Court heard one of these cases, from Nebraska, in 2000. The High Court had to decide if a ban on the D & X method so enhanced the danger to the pregnant woman that it posed an undue burden on her. The division on the Court was not only sharply drawn, the language was bitter, and justices took the relatively unusual step of reading their opinions in open court.

The Nebraska law at issue in Stenberg v. Carhart *prohibited any "partial birth abortion" unless the procedure was necessary to save the mother's life. It defined "partial birth abortion" as a procedure in which the doctor "partially delivers vaginally a living unborn child before killing the . . . child," defining the latter phrase to mean "intentionally delivering into the vagina a living unborn child, or a substantial portion thereof, for the purpose of performing a procedure that the [abortionist] knows will kill the . . . child and does kill the . . . child." Opponents of the law argued that the procedure, which they called the D & X, was safer for the woman, and the choice should be left to her doctor. The High Court divided five to four on Dr. Leroy Carhart's suit against the state law. The majority opinion, written by Justice Stephen Breyer, resembled in important ways Blackmun's opinion for the Court in the original* Roe.

Stenberg, Attorney General of Nebraska, et al. v. Leroy Carhart, 530 U.S. 914 (2000)

Justice Breyer delivered the opinion of the Court.

We again consider the right to an abortion. We understand the controversial nature of the problem. Millions of Americans believe that life begins at conception and consequently that an abortion is akin to causing the death of an innocent child; they recoil at the thought of a law that would permit it. Other millions fear that a law that forbids abortion would condemn many American women to lives that lack dignity, depriving them of equal liberty and leading those with least resources to undergo illegal abortions with the attendant risks of death and suffering. Taking account of these virtually irreconcilable points of view, aware that constitutional law must govern a society whose different members sincerely hold directly opposing views, and considering the matter in light of the Constitution's guarantees of fundamental individual liberty, this Court, in the course of a generation, has determined and then redetermined that the Constitution offers basic protection to the woman's right to choose. . . . We shall not revisit those legal principles. Rather, we apply them to the circumstances of this case. . . .

Because Nebraska law seeks to ban one method of aborting a pregnancy, we must describe and then discuss several different abortion procedures. Considering the fact that those procedures seek to terminate a potential human life, our discussion may seem clinically cold or callous to some, perhaps horrifying to others. There is no alternative way, however, to acquaint the reader with the technical distinctions among different abortion methods and related factual matters, upon which the outcome of this case depends. . . .

1. About 90% of all abortions performed in the United States take place during the first trimester of pregnancy, before 12 weeks of gestational age. . . . During the first trimester, the predominant abortion method is "vacuum aspiration," which involves insertion of a vacuum tube (cannula) into the uterus to evacuate the contents. Such an abortion is typically performed on an outpatient basis under local anesthesia. . . . Vacuum aspiration is considered particularly safe. . . . As the fetus grows in size, however, the vacuum aspiration method becomes increasingly difficult to use. . . .

2. Approximately 10% of all abortions are performed during the second trimester of pregnancy (12 to 24 weeks). . . . In the early 1970's, inducing labor through the injection of saline into the uterus was the predominant method of second trimester abortion. . . . Today, however, the medical profession has switched from medical induction of labor to surgical procedures for most second trimester abortions. The most commonly used procedure is called "dilation and evacuation" (D & E). That procedure (together with a modified form of vacuum aspiration used in the early second trimester) accounts for about 95% of all abortions performed from 12 to 20 weeks of gestational age. . . .

3. . . . "D & E is similar to vacuum aspiration except that the cervix must be dilated more widely because surgical instruments are used to remove larger pieces of tissue. . . . Because fetal tissue is friable and easily broken, the fetus may not be removed intact. The walls of the uterus are scraped with a curette to ensure that no tissue remains." After 15 weeks: "Because the fetus is larger at this stage of gestation (particularly the head), and because bones are more rigid, dismemberment or other destructive procedures are more likely to be required than at earlier gestational ages to remove fetal and placental tissue." After 20 weeks: "Some physicians use intrafetal potassium chloride or digoxin to induce fetal demise prior to a late D & E (after 20 weeks), to facilitate evacuation." . . .

4. When instrumental disarticulation incident to D & E is necessary, it typically occurs as the doctor pulls a portion of the fetus through the cervix into the birth canal. . . .

5. The D & E procedure carries certain risks. The use of instruments within the uterus creates a danger of accidental perforation and damage to neighboring organs. Sharp fetal bone fragments create similar dangers. And fetal tissue accidentally left behind can cause infection and various other complications. . . . Nonetheless studies show that the risks of mortality and complication that accompany the D & E procedure between the 12th and 20th weeks of gestation are significantly lower than those accompanying induced labor procedures (the next safest midsecond trimester procedures). . . .

8. The American College of Obstetricians and Gynecologists describes the D & X procedure in a manner corresponding to a breech-conversion intact D & E [described in number 3 above], including the following steps:

1. deliberate dilatation of the cervix, usually over a sequence of days;
2. instrumental conversion of the fetus to a footling breech;
3. breech extraction of the body excepting the head; and
4. partial evacuation of the intracranial contents of a living fetus to effect vaginal delivery of a dead but otherwise intact fetus." ...

10. The materials presented at trial referred to the potential benefits of the D & X procedure in circumstances involving nonviable fetuses, such as fetuses with abnormal fluid accumulation in the brain (hydrocephaly). ... Others have emphasized its potential for women with prior uterine scars, or for women for whom induction of labor would be particularly dangerous. ...

The question before us is whether Nebraska's statute, making criminal the performance of a "partial birth abortion," violates the Federal Constitution, as interpreted in *Planned Parenthood of Southeastern Pa. v. Casey*. ... We conclude that it does for at least two independent reasons. First, the law lacks any exception "'for the preservation of the . . . health of the mother.'" ... Second, it "imposes an undue burden on a woman's ability" to choose a D & E abortion [which fits the statute's definition of a "partial birth abortion" as well], thereby unduly burdening the right to choose abortion itself. ...

The Nebraska law, of course, does not directly further an interest "in the potentiality of human life" by saving the fetus in question from destruction, as it regulates only a *method* of performing abortion. Nebraska describes its interests differently. It says the law "'shows concern for the life of the unborn,'" "prevents cruelty to partially born children," and "preserves the integrity of the medical profession." ... But we cannot see how the interest-related differences could make any difference to the question at hand, namely, the application of the "health" requirement. Consequently, the governing standard [set by the Court] requires an exception [in state regulatory statutes that reads] "where it is necessary, in appropriate medical judgment for the preservation of the life or health of the mother," ... for this Court has made clear that a State may promote but not endanger a woman's health when it regulates the methods of abortion. ...

Justice Thomas says that the cases just cited limit this principle to situations where the pregnancy *itself* creates a threat to health. ... He is wrong. The cited cases [*Danforth* and *Thornburgh*], reaffirmed in *Casey*, recognize that a State cannot subject women's health to significant risks both in that context, AND ALSO where state regulations force women to use riskier methods of abortion. Our cases have repeatedly invalidated statutes that in the process of regulating the *methods* of abortion, imposed significant health risks [on women]. They make clear that a risk to a women's health is the same whether it happens to arise from regulating a particular method of abortion, or from barring abortion entirely. Our holding does not go beyond those cases, as ratified in *Casey*. . . .

Nebraska, along with supporting *amici*, replies that these findings are irrelevant, wrong, or applicable only in a tiny number of instances. It says (1) that the D & X procedure is "little-used," (2) by only "a handful of doctors." . . . It argues (3) that D & E and labor induction are at all times "safe alternative procedures." It refers to the testimony of petitioners' medical expert, who testified (4) that the ban would not increase a woman's risk of several rare abortion complications. . . .

We find these . . . arguments insufficient to demonstrate that Nebraska's law needs no [women's] health exception. For one thing, certain of the arguments are beside the point. The D & X procedure's relative rarity (argument [1]) is not highly relevant. The D & X is an infrequently used abortion procedure; but the health exception question is whether protecting women's health requires an exception for those infrequent occasions. A rarely used treatment might be necessary to treat a rarely occurring disease that could strike anyone—the State cannot prohibit a person from obtaining treatment simply by pointing out that most people do not need it. Nor can we know whether the fact that only a "handful" of doctors use the procedure (argument [2]) reflects the comparative rarity of late second term abortions, the procedure's recent development[,] . . . the controversy surrounding it, or, as Nebraska suggests, the procedure's lack of utility.

. . . In respect to argument (3), for example, the District Court agreed that alternatives, such as D&E and induced labor, are "safe" but found that the D & X method was significantly *safer* in certain circumstances. . . . In respect to argument (4), the District Court simply relied on different expert testimony—testimony stating that "'another advantage of the Intact D & E is that it eliminates the risk of embolism of cerebral tissue into the woman's blood stream.'" . . .

The Eighth Circuit found the Nebraska statute unconstitutional because, in *Casey*'s words, it has the "effect of placing a substantial obstacle in the path of a woman seeking an abortion of a nonviable fetus." It thereby places an "undue burden" upon a woman's right to terminate her pregnancy before viability. Nebraska does not deny that the statute imposes an "undue burden" *if* it applies to the more commonly used D & E procedure as well as to D & X. . . .

Our earlier discussion of the D & E procedure, shows that it falls within the statutory prohibition. The statute forbids "deliberately and intentionally delivering into the vagina a living unborn child, or a substantial portion thereof, for the purpose of performing a procedure that the person performing such procedure knows will kill the unborn child." We do not understand how one could distinguish, using this language, between D & E (where a foot or arm is drawn through the cervix) and D & X (where the body up to the head is drawn through the cervix). Evidence before the trial court makes clear that D & E will often involve a physician pulling a "substantial portion" of a still living fetus, say, an arm or leg, into the vagina prior to the death of the fetus. . . . Even if the statute's basic aim is to ban D & X, its language makes clear that it also covers a much broader category of procedures . . . though it would have been a simple matter, for example, to provide an exception for the performance of D&E and other abortion procedures. . . . The relevant question is *not* whether the legislature wanted to ban D & X; it is whether the law was intended to apply *only* to D & X. . . . Both procedures can involve the introduction of a "substantial portion" of a still living fetus, through the cervix, into the vagina—the very feature of an abortion that leads Justice Thomas to characterize such a procedure as involving "partial birth."

The Nebraska State Attorney General argues that the statute does differentiate between the two procedures. He says that the statutory words "substantial portion" mean "the child up to the head." He consequently denies the statute's application where the physician introduces into the birth canal a fetal arm or leg or anything less than the entire fetal body. He argues further that we must defer to his views about the meaning of the state statute.

We cannot accept the Attorney General's narrowing interpretation of the Nebraska statute. This Court's case law makes clear that we are not to give the Attorney General's interpretative views controlling weight. . . .

The Attorney General also points to the Nebraska Legislature's debates, where the term "partial birth abortion" appeared frequently. But those debates hurt his argument more than they help it. Nebraska's legislators focused directly upon the meaning of the word "substantial." One senator asked the bill's sponsor, "You said that as small a portion of the fetus as a foot would constitute a substantial portion in your opinion. Is that correct?" The sponsoring senator replied, "Yes, I believe that's correct." . . .

In sum, using this law some present prosecutors and future Attorneys

General may choose to pursue physicians who use D & E procedures, the most commonly used method for performing previability second trimester abortions. All those who perform abortion procedures using that method must fear prosecution, conviction, and imprisonment. The result is an undue burden upon a woman's right to make an abortion decision. We must consequently find the statute unconstitutional.

. . .

Justice O'Connor wrote a concurring opinion to explain her views. (Of all of the justices, only David Souter did not write an opinion.) The number of concurrences and dissents suggests that even though the Court had come to a decision, no one was entirely satisfied with it. Ironically, Justice O'Connor had found herself, in a way, in the same situation as Justice Blackmun when he faced her challenge to his trimester formula.

Justice O'Connor, concurring:

The issue of abortion is one of the most contentious and controversial in contemporary American society. It presents extraordinarily difficult questions that, as the Court recognizes, involve "virtually irreconcilable points of view." The specific question we face today is whether Nebraska's attempt to proscribe a particular method of abortion, commonly known as "partial-birth abortion," is constitutional. For the reasons stated in the Court's opinion, I agree that Nebraska's statute cannot be reconciled with our decision in *Planned Parenthood of Southeastern Pa.* v. *Casey* (1992), and is therefore unconstitutional. I write separately to emphasize the following points.

First, the Nebraska statute is inconsistent with *Casey* because it lacks an exception for those instances when the banned procedure is necessary to preserve the health of the mother. . . . Contrary to the assertions of Justice Kennedy and Justice Thomas the need for a health exception does not arise from "the individual views of Dr. Carhart and his supporters." . . . Rather, as the majority explains, where, as here, "a significant body of medical opinion believes a procedure may bring with it greater safety for some patients and explains the medical reasons supporting that view," then Nebraska cannot say that the procedure will not, in some circumstances, be "necessary to preserve the life or health of the mother." Accordingly, our precedent requires that the statute include a health exception.

Second, Nebraska's statute is unconstitutional on the alternative and independent ground that it imposes an undue burden on a woman's right to choose to terminate her pregnancy before viability. Nebraska's ban covers not just the dilation and extraction (D & X) procedure, but also the dilation and evacuation (D & E) procedure, "the most commonly used method for performing previability second trimester abortions." . . .

It is important to note that, unlike Nebraska, some other States have enacted statutes more narrowly tailored to proscribing the D & X procedure alone. Some of those statutes have done so by specifically excluding from their coverage the most common methods of abortion, such as the D & E and vacuum aspiration procedures. For example, the Kansas statute states that its ban does not apply to the "(A) suction curettage abortion procedure; (B) suction aspiration abortion procedure; or (C) dilation and evacuation abortion procedure involving dismemberment of the fetus prior to removal from the body of the pregnant woman." . . . The Utah statute similarly provides that its prohibition "does not include the dilation and evacuation procedure involving dismemberment prior to removal, the suction curettage procedure, or the suction aspiration procedure for abortion." . . . Likewise, the Montana statute defines the banned procedure as one in which "(A) the living fetus is removed intact from the uterus until only the head remains in the uterus; (B) all or a part of the intracranial contents of the fetus are evacuated; (C) the head of the fetus is compressed; and (D) following fetal demise, the fetus is removed from the birth canal." . . . By restricting their prohibitions to the D & X procedure exclusively, the Kansas, Utah, and Montana statutes avoid a principal defect of the Nebraska law.

If Nebraska's statute limited its application to the D & X procedure and included an exception for the life and health of the mother, the question presented would be quite different than the one we face today. As we held in *Casey*, an abortion regulation constitutes an undue burden if it "has the purpose or effect of placing a substantial obstacle in the path of a woman seeking an abortion of a nonviable fetus." . . .

· · ·

Justice Ginsburg, joined by Justice Stevens, wrote to reiterate a point that might have seemed buried in Breyer's opinion.

Justice Ginsburg, concurring:

I write separately only to stress that amidst all the emotional uproar caused by an abortion case, we should not lose sight of the character of Nebraska's "partial birth abortion" law. As the Court observes, this law does not save any fetus from destruction, for it targets only "a *method* of performing abortion." . . . Seventh Circuit Chief Judge Posner correspondingly observed, regarding similar bans in Wisconsin and Illinois, that the law prohibits the D & X procedure "not because the procedure kills the fetus, not because it risks worse complications for the woman than alternative procedures would do, not because it is a crueler or more painful or more disgusting method of terminating a pregnancy." . . . Rather, Chief Judge Posner commented, the law prohibits the procedure because the State legislators seek to chip away at the private choice shielded by *Roe* v. *Wade*, even as modified by *Casey*. . . .

. . .

Justice Scalia dissented, again reminding his colleagues of his strong comments in Casey. *Can it be argued that he had given a kind of support to state legislatures to press for further narrowing of O'Connor's "undue burden" standard, and Nebraska's law was one outcome?*

Justice Scalia, dissenting.

I am optimistic enough to believe that, one day, *Stenberg* v. *Carhart* will be assigned its rightful place in the history of this Court's jurisprudence beside *Korematsu* and *Dred Scott*. The method of killing a human child—one cannot even accurately say an entirely unborn human child—proscribed by this statute is so horrible that the most clinical description of it evokes a shudder of revulsion. And the Court must know (as most state legislatures banning this procedure have concluded) that demanding a "health exception"—which requires the abortionist to assure himself that, in his expert medical judgment, this method is, in the case at hand, marginally safer than others (how can one prove the contrary beyond a reasonable doubt?)—is to give live-birth abortion free rein. The notion that the Constitution of the United States, designed, among other things, "to establish Justice, insure domestic Tranquility, . . . and secure the Blessings of Liberty to ourselves and our Posterity," prohibits the States from simply banning this visibly brutal means of eliminating our half-born posterity is quite simply absurd.

Even so, I had not intended to write separately here until the focus of the other separate writings (including the one I have joined) gave me cause to fear that this case might be taken to stand for an error different from the one that it actually exemplifies. Because of the Court's practice of publishing dissents in the order of the seniority of their authors, this writing will appear in the reports before those others, but the reader will not comprehend what follows unless he reads them first.

The two lengthy dissents in this case have, appropriately enough, set out to establish that today's result does not follow from this Court's most recent pronouncement on the matter of abortion, *Planned Parenthood of Southeastern Pa.* v. *Casey* (1992). It would be unfortunate, however, if those who disagree with the result were induced to regard it as merely a regrettable misapplication of *Casey*. It is not that, but is *Casey*'s logical and entirely predictable consequence.

To be sure, the Court's construction of this statute so as to make it include procedures other than live-birth abortion involves not only a disregard of fair meaning, but an abandonment of the principle that even ambiguous statutes should be interpreted in such fashion as to render them valid rather than void. *Casey* does not permit *that* jurisprudential novelty— which must be chalked up to the Court's inclination to bend the rules when any effort to limit abortion, or even to speak in opposition to abortion, is at issue. . . .

But the Court gives a second and independent reason for invalidating this humane (not to say anti-barbarian) law: That it fails to allow an exception for the situation in which the abortionist believes that this live-birth method of destroying the child might be safer for the woman. (As pointed out by Justice Thomas, and elaborated upon by Justice Kennedy, there is no good reason to believe this is ever the case, but—who knows?—it sometime *might* be.)

I have joined Justice Thomas's dissent because I agree that today's decision is an "unprecedented expansion" of our prior cases, "is not mandated" by *Casey*'s "undue burden" test, and can even be called (though this pushes me to the limit of my belief) "obviously irreconcilable with *Casey*'s explication of what its undue-burden standard requires." But I never put much stock in *Casey*'s explication of the inexplicable. In the last analysis, my judgment that *Casey* does not support today's tragic result can be traced to the fact that what I consider to be an "undue burden" is different from what the majority considers to be an "undue burden"—a conclusion that cannot be demonstrated true or false by factual inquiry or legal reasoning. It is a value judgment, dependent upon how much one respects (or believes society ought to respect) the life of a partially delivered fetus, and how much one respects (or believes society ought to respect) the freedom of the woman who gave it life to kill it. Evidently, the five Justices in today's majority value the former less, or the latter more, (or both), than the four of us in dissent. Case closed. There is no cause for anyone who believes in *Casey* to feel betrayed by this outcome. It has been arrived at by precisely the process *Casey* promised—a democratic vote by nine lawyers, not on the question whether the text of the Constitution has anything to say about this subject (it obviously does not); nor even on the question (also appropriate for lawyers) whether the legal traditions of the American people would have sustained such a limitation upon abortion (they obviously would); but upon the pure policy question whether this limitation upon abortion is "undue"—*i.e.*, goes too far.

In my dissent in *Casey*, I wrote that the "undue burden" test made law by the joint opinion created a standard that was "as doubtful in application as it is unprincipled in origin," *Casey*, 505 U.S. at 985; "hopelessly unworkable in practice," 505 U.S. at 986; "ultimately standardless," 505 U.S. at 987. Today's decision is the proof. As long as we are debating this issue of necessity for a health-of-the-mother exception on the basis of *Casey*, it is really quite impossible for us dissenters to contend that the majority is *wrong* on the law—any more than it could be said that one is *wrong in law* to support or oppose the death penalty, or to support or oppose mandatory minimum sentences. The most that we can honestly say is that we disagree with the majority on their policy-judgment-couched-as-law. And those who believe that a 5-to-4 vote on a policy matter by unelected lawyers should not overcome the judgment of 30 state legislatures have a problem, not with the *application* of *Casey*, but with its *existence*. *Casey* must be overruled.

While I am in an I-told-you-so mood, I must recall my bemusement, in *Casey*, at the joint opinion's expressed belief that *Roe* v. *Wade* had "called the contending sides of a national controversy to end their national division by accepting a common mandate rooted in the Constitution," and that the decision in *Casey* would ratify that happy truce. It seemed to me, quite to the contrary, that "*Roe* fanned into life an issue that has inflamed our national politics in general, and has obscured with its smoke the selection of Justices to this Court in particular, ever since"; and that, "by keeping us in the abortion-umpiring business, it is the perpetuation of that disruption, rather than of any *Pax Roeana*, that the Court's new majority decrees." Today's decision, that the Constitution of the United States prevents the prohibition of a horrible mode of abortion, will be greeted by a firestorm of criticism—as well it should. I cannot understand why those who *acknowledge* that, in the opening words of Justice O'Connor's concurrence, "the issue of abortion is one of the most contentious and controversial in contemporary American society," persist in the belief that this Court, armed with neither constitutional text nor accepted tradition, can resolve that contention and controversy rather than be consumed by it. If only for the sake of its own preservation, the Court should return this matter to the people—where the Constitution, by its silence on the subject, left it—and let *them* decide, State by State, whether this practice should be allowed. *Casey* must be overruled.

. . .

Justice Kennedy had coauthored the joint opinion in Casey, *but here he parted company with his coauthors, Justices O'Connor and Souter.*

Justice Kennedy, with whom the Chief Justice joins, dissenting.

For close to two decades after *Roe* v. *Wade*, the Court gave but slight weight to the interests of the separate States when their legislatures sought to address persisting concerns raised by the existence of a woman's right to elect an abortion in defined circumstances. When the Court reaffirmed the essential holding of *Roe*, a central premise was that the States retain a critical and legitimate role in legislating on the subject of abortion, as limited by the woman's right the Court restated and again guaranteed. . . . The political processes of the State are not to be foreclosed from enacting laws to promote the life of the unborn and to ensure respect for all human life and its potential. The State's constitutional authority is a vital means for citizens to address these grave and serious issues, as they must if we are to progress in knowledge and understanding and in the attainment of some degree of consensus.

The Court's decision today, in my submission, repudiates this understanding by invalidating a statute advancing critical state interests, even though the law denies no woman the right to choose an abortion and places no undue burden upon the right. The legislation is well within the State's competence to enact. Having concluded Nebraska's law survives the scrutiny dictated by a proper understanding of *Casey*, I dissent from the judgment invalidating it.

The Court's failure to accord any weight to Nebraska's interest in prohibiting partial-birth abortion is erroneous and undermines its discussion and holding. The Court's approach in this regard is revealed by its description of the abortion methods at issue, which the Court is correct to describe as "clinically cold or callous." The majority views the procedures from the perspective of the abortionist, rather than from the perspective of a society shocked when confronted with a new method of ending human life. Words invoked by the majority, such as "transcervical procedures," "osmotic dilators," "instrumental disarticulation," and "paracervical block," may be accurate and are to some extent necessary, but for citizens who seek to know why laws on this subject have been enacted across the Nation, the words are insufficient. Repeated references to sources understandable only to a trained physician may obscure matters for persons not trained in medical terminology. Thus it seems necessary at the outset to set forth what may happen during an abortion.

The person challenging Nebraska's law is Dr. Leroy Carhart, a physician who received his medical degree from Hahnemann Hospital and University in 1973. Dr. Carhart performs the procedures in a clinic in Nebraska, and will also travel to Ohio to perform abortions there, *id.* at 86. Dr. Carhart has no specialty certifications in a field related to childbirth or abortion and lacks admitting privileges at any hospital. He performs abortions throughout pregnancy, including when he is unsure whether the fetus is viable. In contrast to the physicians who provided expert testimony in this case (who are board certified instructors at leading medical education institutions and members of the American Board of Obstetricians and Gynecologists), Dr. Carhart performs the partial-birth abortion procedure (D & X) that Nebraska seeks to ban. He also performs the other method of abortion at issue in the case, the D & E.

As described by Dr. Carhart, the D & E procedure requires the abortionist to use instruments to grasp a portion (such as a foot or hand) of a developed and living fetus and drag the grasped portion out of the uterus into the vagina. Dr. Carhart uses the traction created by the opening between the uterus and vagina to dismember the fetus, tearing the grasped portion away from the remainder of the body. The traction between the uterus and vagina is essential to the procedure because attempting to abort a fetus without using that traction is described by Dr. Carhart as "pulling the cat's tail" or "dragging a string across the floor. . . . It's not until something grabs the other end that you are going to develop traction." The fetus, in many cases, dies just as a human adult or child would: It bleeds to death as it is torn limb from limb. The fetus can be alive at the beginning of the dismemberment process and can survive for a time while its limbs are being torn off. Dr. Carhart agreed that "when you pull out a piece of the fetus, let's say, an arm or a leg and remove that, at the time just prior to removal of the portion of the fetus, . . . the fetus [is] alive." Dr. Carhart has observed fetal heartbeat via ultrasound with "extensive parts of the fetus removed," and testified that mere dismemberment of a limb does not always cause death because he knows of a physician who removed the arm of a fetus only to have the fetus go on to be born "as a living child with one arm." At the conclusion of a D & E abortion no intact fetus remains. In Dr. Carhart's words, the abortionist is left with "a tray full of pieces."

The other procedure implicated today is called "partial-birth abortion" or the D & X. The D & X can be used, as a general matter, after 19 weeks gestation because the fetus has become so developed that it may survive intact partial delivery from the uterus into the vagina. In the D & X, the abortionist initiates the woman's natural delivery process by causing the cervix of the woman to be dilated, sometimes over a sequence of days. The fetus' arms and legs are delivered outside the uterus while the fetus is alive; witnesses to the procedure report seeing the body of the fetus moving outside the woman's body. At this point, the abortion procedure has the appearance of a live birth. As stated by one group of physicians, "as the physician manually performs breech extraction of the body of a live fetus, excepting the head, she continues in the apparent role of an obstetrician delivering a child." With only the head of the fetus remaining in utero, the abortionist tears open the skull. According to Dr. Martin Haskell, a leading proponent of the procedure, the appropriate instrument to be used at this stage of the abortion is a pair of scissors. . . . Witnesses report observing the portion of the fetus outside the woman react to the skull penetration. The abortionist then inserts a suction tube and vacuums out the developing brain and other matter found within the skull. The process of making the size of the fetus' head smaller is given the clinically neutral term "reduction procedure." Brain death does not occur until after the skull invasion, and, according to Dr. Carhart, the heart of the fetus may continue to beat for minutes after the contents of the skull are vacuumed out. The abortionist next completes the delivery of a dead fetus, intact except for the damage to the head and the missing contents of the skull.

Of the two described procedures, Nebraska seeks only to ban the D & X. In light of the description of the D & X procedure, it should go without saying that Nebraska's ban on partial-birth abortion furthers purposes States are entitled to pursue. Dr. Carhart nevertheless maintains the State has no legitimate interest in forbidding the D & X. As he interprets the controlling cases in this Court, the only two interests the State may advance through regulation of abortion are in the health of the woman who is considering the procedure and in the life of the fetus she carries. The Court, as I read its opinion, accedes to his views, misunderstanding *Casey* and the authorities it confirmed. . . . *Casey* demonstrates that the interests asserted by the State are legitimate and recognized by law. It is argued, however, that a ban on the D & X does not further these interests. This is because, the reasoning continues, the D & E method, which Nebraska claims to be beyond its intent to regulate, can still be used to abort a fetus and is no less dehumanizing than the D & X method. While not adopting the argument in express terms, the Court indicates tacit approval of it by refusing to reject it in a forthright manner. Rendering express what is only implicit in the majority opinion, Justice Stevens and Justice Ginsburg are forthright in declaring that the two procedures are indistinguishable and that Nebraska has acted both irrationally and without a proper purpose in enacting the law. The issue is not whether members of the judiciary can see a difference between the two procedures. It is whether Nebraska can. The Court's refusal to recognize Nebraska's right to declare a moral difference between the procedure is a dispiriting disclosure of the illogic and illegitimacy of the Court's approach to the entire case.

Nebraska was entitled to find the existence of a consequential moral difference between the procedures. . . . Witnesses to the procedure relate that the fingers and feet of the fetus are moving prior to the piercing of the skull; when the scissors are inserted in the back of the head, the fetus' body, wholly outside the woman's body and alive, reacts as though startled and goes limp. D & X's stronger resemblance to infanticide means Nebraska could conclude the procedure presents a greater risk of disrespect for life and a consequent greater risk to the profession and society, which depend for their sustenance upon reciprocal recognition of dignity and respect. The Court is without authority to second-guess this conclusion. . . .

· · ·

The dissents seemed to return to the old theme of deference to the legislatures. In the spring of 2003, Congress once again passed a bill that would bar anyone from performing the D & X, an instruction to the nation's doctors that opponents viewed as equal in scope and intrusiveness to the Comstock Act's ban on birth control itself. As NARAL president Kate Michelman wrote in the "On-line Newsroom" release of February 13, 2003, "anti-choice members [of Congress] are playing politics with women's lives, health and rights by pushing an unconstitutional bill banning abortion procedures."[2] The National Right to Life Committee took a different view. They called the NARAL and other warnings "the pro-abortion disinformation campaign."[3]

Would the horrors of the D & X as depicted so graphically in the dissents and the speeches in Congress have passed constitutional muster if the Nebraska legislature had passed a law explicitly allowing the procedure? Was not the "disrespect for life and a consequent greater risk to the profession [of medicine] and society, which depend for their sustenance upon reciprocal recognition of dignity and respect" in the D & X a bar to its employment whatever a state legislature might say? Thus the argument against the "partial birth abortion" could not lie solely in deference to popularly elected bodies. It must lie in the constitutional protection of the right to life of the unborn. Yet this would seem to require a total ban on abortion, even that which saved the life of the mother when such abortions cost the "innocent" life of the infant.

The confusion within the Court on the exact application of the Nebraska law on partial birth abortion reflected a larger confusion throughout the country over a wide range of abortion procedure regulations. Various states had a wide variety of rules, some of which were exactly the opposite of other states' rules. While New Jersey, for example, keeps the identity of women seeking abortions confidential, South Carolina law allows the state to go into a birth control or abortion clinic and copy the names and addresses of every woman who has used the facility and make the record public. On April 29, 2003, the Supreme Court declined to review the constitutionality of the South Carolina law, leaving open questions of whether the law also applied to other doctor-patient confidences or to other surgical procedures. The same confusing and contradictory array of regulations concerning laws exempting medical personnel from performing abortions, exempting pharmacists from filling prescriptions for medications that might be used as abortifacients, and requiring parental notification or consent for minors to have abortions create a crazy quilt of abortion law across the land.

NOTES

1. Quoted in N. E. H. Hull and Peter Charles Hoffer, *Roe v. Wade: The Abortion Rights Controversy in American History* (Lawrence, Kans., 2001), 243.

2. <www.Naral.org/mediaresources/press/2003/pr021303—socalled.html> (accessed March 19, 2003).

3. <www.nrlc.org/abortion/pba/PartialBirthAbortionRecentDevelopments .html> (accessed March 19, 2003).

CHAPTER 8

· · ·

Freedom of Speech versus Free Access to Clinics

The final piece of the abortion/abortion rights debate returns us to the First Amendment. We have seen how the controversy touched the Establishment of Religion and Free Exercise Clauses of the amendment. It also reached out to the Freedom of Speech provisions. Even as the abortion regulation controversy continued in the legislatures and courts of the nation, a new issue arose to trouble advocates on both sides. Could local, state, and federal governments regulate anti-abortion protests? Was the right to free speech unconstitutionally restricted when protesters at abortion clinics were either curbed by regulations or jailed for their activities? On the other side of the question, could the federal government muzzle doctors and health care professionals who wanted to counsel women about abortion?

The latter question seemed to be answered in the affirmative by the High Court in 1990. Twenty years before, the federal government had established a program for family planning under Title X of the Public Health Services Act. It was intended as an alternative to abortion counseling, and one of its provisions required that no funds could go to abortion clinics. In 1988, the last year of President Reagan's administration, personnel, including doctors, at clinics receiving federal money were told not to mention abortion. If asked about it by a client, the health care or social work professional had to say that the clinic did not consider abortion an "appropriate method" of birth control. Dr. Irving Rust, a New York City practitioner and a recipient of Title X funds, sued U.S. Secretary of Health and Human Services Louis Sullivan, alleging that the regulations the secretary promulgated under authority of the act violated the terms of the act itself as well as Dr. Rust's and his patients' free speech and due process rights under the Constitution. When the case came to the High Court, Chief Justice Rehnquist wrote for the majority, including Justices Souter, White, Kennedy, and Scalia. He found that the Court had to defer to the interpretation of the statute given it by the federal agency (Health and Human Services) charged with administering the act and that the secretary's interpretation was in line with the general purposes of the act and did not violate the free speech rights of the doctors. It simply required that referral to abortion services be made outside of the confines of the Title X–funded clinic. Nor was the patient's right to an abortion constrained, for she could always go to a family planning center that was not underwritten by federal funds—the same option she would have if Title X did not fund any clinics.

Justices O'Connor, Blackmun, and Marshall dissented. They insisted that the government could not attach an unconstitutional requirement to a funding bill and then say, in effect, if you don't want to give up your constitutional rights, don't apply for the funding. The latter two justices also contended, with Justice Stevens in agreement, that the government was using funding as a way to promote one viewpoint on abortion. The so-called gag rule prevented women from getting an answer to their questions about abortion, even when these questions touched immediate and permanent medical concerns. Women relying on doctors in these clinics would be placed in peril if the doctors could not warn them that their medical condition might require an abortion. Women misled in this fashion were not in the same position they would have been in if Title X clinics had never existed.

For protesters at the clinics, the state and federal limitations on picketing seemed another unacceptable form of gag rule. Foremost among the many street groups that opposed abortion was Operation Rescue, founded in the late 1980s by Randall Terry and other anti-abortion advocates. It targeted the clinics that provided abortions, the doctors who performed them, and the women who sought them. Some of these demonstrations were peaceful, others involved verbal abuse, and some advocated violence. In all of them, the demonstrators tried to dissuade women from entering the clinics. Some of the protest groups also targeted the people who worked at the clinics, picketing their homes, calling their phone numbers, and passing out posters with their pictures, addresses, and phone numbers.

The violence feared by clinic doctors and their staffs was not far away. In the late 1980s, extremists within anti-abortion groups engaged in a campaign of bombings. These largely ended when the leading perpetrator was caught, tried, and sentenced. But the weapons of assault on the clinics and the doctors did not end. On March 10, 1993, Dr. David Gunn, already the target of death threats, was murdered during a Pensacola, Florida, anti-abortion rally, shot in the back three times by Michael F. Griffin, an anti-abortion activist. Operation Rescue had printed Gunn's photograph, home phone number, and address on a "wanted poster" the year before. On August 19, 1993, Dr. George Tiller was shot in both arms by Rachelle Shannon, a woman protester at a Wichita, Kansas, anti-abortion rally. She had been sending letters of support to the jailed Griffin and hailed the murderer of Dr. Gunn as a "hero of our time." The next day, Dr. George Patterson, owner of four southeastern abortion clinics, was bushwhacked; his killer has never been caught. On July 29, 1994, former evangelical minister Paul Hill, director of the anti-abortion group Defensive Action, murdered Dr. John Britton and his elderly escort, James H. Barrett, outside a Pensacola abortion clinic. A woman who was also chaperoning the doctor was badly wounded. Hill announced that the "infants" he was saving from the abortionist justified the murderous assault on the doctor and his escorts and was unrepentant at his trial and sentencing. In 1998, abortion provider Barnett Slepian was assassinated by James Kopp, who fled, was captured, and admitted the act. His conduct was condemned widely by the pro-life movement. He was convicted of the offense on March 18, 2003.

Various state and local government police forces intervened in the clinic protests to keep order. Clinics and doctors who provided their services to the clinics claimed that Operation Rescue tactics prevented these police forces from effectively guaranteeing access to the clinics. The National Organization for Women (NOW) and other pro-choice groups attempted to curb the demonstrations by bringing suits against the organizations and individuals who led them. The problem for NOW was finding a legal ground on which courts could restrict the activities of the protesters. Lawyers for NOW turned first to an 1871 anti–Ku Klux Klan act and then, when the High Court rejected that approach, to the Racketeer Influenced Corrupt Organizations Act (RICO) deployed by the federal government against organized crime. Although the Court was at first willing to allow NOW to proceed against clinic protests using the latter, on February 2003 the Court decided (in *Scheidler v. NOW* and *Operation Rescue v. NOW*) that prosecutions under RICO had to prove that the protesters had taken the victims' property by the threat of force and had not so proven.

While NOW battled pro-life groups in the courts and protesters argued with police in the streets, lobbying groups on both sides continued to look to politicians for support. From 1993 to 2000, pro-choice forces found an ally in President Bill Clinton. With his support, they asked Congress to pass a law insuring free access to the clinics, which resulted in the Free Access to Clinic Entrances Act (FACE). This act provided that "whoever by force or threat of force or by physical obstruction, intentionally injures, intimidates, or interferes with or attempts to injure, intimidate or interfere with any person . . . [to hinder that person or class of persons] from obtaining or providing reproductive health services shall be subject to criminal penalties and civil remedies." The latter included injunctive relief and monetary damages. Clinton signed the bill into law in 1994, saying that "this bill is designed to eliminate violence and coercion. It is not a strike against the First Amendment. . . . We simply cannot, we must not continue to allow the attacks, the incidents of arson, the campaigns of intimidation upon law-abiding citizens that has given rise to this law."[1]

Pro-life groups immediately challenged FACE's constitutionality as well as its application to their activities. In a series of cases, notably *Terry v. Reno* and *American Life League v. Reno*, federal courts held that the statute did not violate the First Amendment, and in *U.S. v. Dinwiddie* the courts held that the statute did not exceed Congress's authority under the Commerce Clause of the Constitution. By 1999, in fifteen out of seventeen criminal prosecutions brought by the Department of Justice under the law, defendants had been convicted. In fourteen out of seventeen cases seeking civil damages, courts found defendants liable. The U.S. Supreme Court has declined to review these cases, but in 2001, the High Court found, in a decision without an opinion (*Gregg v. U.S.*), that the law did not violate the constitutional guarantees of free speech and assembly.

The political battle over abortion rights in Congress shifted course when pro-life Republicans won a majority of the House of Representatives in 1994. In 1995, the lower house voted to reverse the 1993 extension of funding to rape and incest victims, but the Senate refused to concur. The House tried again in 1996, and once more the Senate blocked the return to the more restrictive funding formula. Thereafter, the pro-life representatives shifted to legislation that would prevent all federally funded health care professionals from providing information about or referrals to abortion clinics. The anti–abortion rights leaders also drafted a Child Custody Protection Act that would make it a federal crime for any person other than a parent to knowingly transport a minor across state lines for the purpose of obtaining an abortion, if the minor had not complied with the state of origin's laws regarding parental notification and consent.

Pro-choice advocates now found themselves swimming against the tide in Congress. From 1996 to 2000, President Clinton's proposed Family Planning and Choice Protection Act, which would have increased funding for family planning clinics under Title X, permanently remove the gag rule on counseling contraceptive and abortion services when appropriate, require health insurance plans to cover contraception, and protect women's access to abortion clinics, failed to gain approval in Congress.

By the end of the decade, disputes over the conflicting rights of the picketers and the clinic users seemed just as unresolvable as the underlying dispute over the right to an abortion. The variety and specificity of the local and state rules on picketing were as bewildering as the states' regulations of abortions, and the Court's rulings exhibited the same divisive, bitterly contested, and complex character as they did in the abortion regulation cases. In *Schenck v. Pro-Choice Network* (1997), the Court, voting 8 to 1, invalidated a New York court's "floating buffer zone" of fifteen feet between persons seeking to enter or leave a clinic and all demonstrators on the grounds that the imposition burdened speech too much. A Colorado statute, requiring only eight feet of separation, came before the High Court in January 2000 (*Hill v. Colorado*) on an appeal from the Colorado Supreme Court's decision upholding the law. The Court, in a 6 to 3 opinion, upheld the state's statute on June 28, 2000.

. . .

When clinic operators first sued Operation Rescue, they based their suit on the Civil Rights Act of 1871, a law that went back to Reconstruction. The act was passed to make illegal the Ku Klux Klan and other similar organizations' attacks on freedmen and freedwomen in the South. The NOW lawyers argued that the anti-abortion demonstrators were a conspiracy like the Klan, attempting on this occasion to deprive women of their right to an abortion. Their case hinged on an analogy. In Bray v. Alexandria Women's Health Clinic, *Justice Antonin Scalia delivered the opinion of the Court, in which Chief Justice Rehnquist and Justices White, Kennedy, and Thomas joined. Justice Stevens dissented, joined by Justice Blackmun. Justice O'Connor filed her own dissent, in which Justice Blackmun joined.*

Jayne Bray et al., Petitioners, v. Alexandria Women's Health Clinic et al., 506 U.S. 263 (1993)

Justice Scalia delivered the opinion of the Court.

This case presents the question whether the first clause of Rev. Stat. §1980, 42 U.S.C. §1985(3)—the surviving version of §2 of the Civil Rights Act of 1871—provides a federal cause of action against persons obstructing access to abortion clinics. Respondents are clinics that perform abortions and organizations that support legalized abortion and that have members who may wish to use abortion clinics. Petitioners are Operation Rescue, an unincorporated association whose members oppose abortion, and six individuals. Among its activities, Operation Rescue organizes antiabortion demonstrations in which participants trespass on, and obstruct general access to, the premises of abortion clinics. The individual petitioners organize and coordinate these demonstrations. . . .

Our precedents establish that in order to prove a private conspiracy in violation of the first clause of §1985(3), a plaintiff must show, *inter alia* [among other things], (1) that "some racial, or perhaps otherwise class-based, invidiously discriminatory animus [lay] behind the conspirators' action" . . . and (2) that the conspiracy "aimed at interfering with rights" that are "protected against private, as well as official, encroachment." . . . We think neither showing has been made in the present case. . . .

To begin with, we reject the apparent conclusion of the District Court (which respondents make no effort to defend) that opposition to abortion constitutes discrimination against the "class" of "women seeking abortion." Whatever may be the precise meaning of a "class" . . . the term unquestionably connotes something more than a group of individuals who share a desire to engage in conduct that the §1985(3) defendant disfavors. . . .

Respondents' contention, however, is that the alleged class-based discrimination is directed not at "women seeking abortion" but at women in general. We find it unnecessary to decide whether *that* is a qualifying class under §1985(3), since the claim that petitioners' opposition to abortion reflects an animus against women in general must be rejected. . . . The record in this case does not indicate that petitioners' demonstrations are motivated by a purpose (malevolent *or* benign) directed specifically at women as a class. . . .

Respondents' case comes down, then, to the proposition that intent is legally irrelevant; that since voluntary abortion is an activity engaged in only by women, to disfavor it is *ipso facto* [automatically] to discriminate invidiously against women as a class. Our cases do not support that proposition. . . .

In any event, the characteristic that formed the basis of the targeting here was not womanhood, but the seeking of abortion—so that the class the dissenters identify is the one we have rejected earlier: women seeking abortion. The approach of equating opposition to an activity (abortion) that can be engaged in only by a certain class (women) with opposition to that class leads to absurd conclusions. . . .

The other right alleged by respondents to have been intentionally infringed is the right to abortion. . . . It would be most peculiar to accord [the right to an abortion] that preferred position, since it is much less explicitly protected by the Constitution than, for example, the right of free speech. . . . Moreover, the right to abortion has been described in our opinions as one element of a more general right of privacy . . . or of Fourteenth Amendment liberty . . . and the other elements of those more general rights are obviously *not* protected against private infringement. . . .

. . .

Justice Souter saw the issue somewhat differently.

Justice Souter, concurring in the judgment in part and dissenting in part.

This case turns on the meaning of two clauses of 42 U.S.C. §1985(3) which render certain conspiracies civilly actionable. . . .

Respondents' complaint . . . alleges simply that petitioners "have conspired with each other and other parties presently unknown for the purpose of denying women seeking abortions at targeted facilities their right to privacy, in violation of 42 U.S.C. §1985(3)." Evidence presented at a hearing before the District Court addressed the issue of prevention or hindrance, leading that court to note that the demonstrators so far outnumbered local police that "even though 240 rescuers were arrested, the police were unable to prevent the closing of the clinic for more than six (6) hours." . . .

We may recall that in holding racial or other class-based animus a necessary element of the requisite purpose to deprive of equal protection, the . . . Court was mindful of the congressional apprehension that the statute might otherwise turn out to be "a general federal tort [civil wrong] law." . . . [This is] understandable when one sees that the scope of conspiracies actionable under the deprivation clause has virtually no textual limit. . . .

The prevention clause carries no such premonition of liability, however. Its most distinctive requirement, to prove a conspiratorial purpose to "prevent or hinder the constituted authorities of any State or Territory from giving or securing . . . the equal protection of the laws," is both an additional element unknown to the deprivation clause and a significantly limiting condition. Private conspiracies to injure according to class or classification are not enough here; they must be conspiracies to act with enough force, of whatever sort, to overwhelm the capacity of legal authority to act evenhandedly in administering the law. . . .

The requirement of an object to thwart the capacity of law enforcement authority to provide equal protection of the laws thus narrows the scope of conspiracies actionable under the prevention clause. It does so to such a degree that no reason appears for narrowing it even more by a view of equal protection more restrictive than that of the Fourteenth Amendment. . . . Accordingly, I conclude that the prevention clause [of the Civil Rights

Act of 1871] may be applied to a conspiracy intended to hobble or overwhelm the capacity of duly constituted state police authorities to secure equal protection of the laws, even when the conspirators' animus is not based on race or a like class characteristic, and even when the ultimate object of the conspiracy is to violate a constitutional guarantee that applies solely against state action. . . . When private individuals conspire for the purpose of arrogating and, in effect, exercising the State's power in a way that would thus violate equal protection if so exercised by state officials, the conspiracy becomes actionable when implemented by an act "whereby [a person] is injured in his person or property, or deprived of . . . any right or privilege of a citizen of the United States." §1985(3). . . .

· · ·

Justices Blackmun and Stevens also dissented; Justice Stevens's opinion directly confuted key points in that of Justice Scalia.

Justice Stevens, with whom Justice Blackmun joins, dissenting.

After the Civil War, Congress enacted legislation imposing on the Federal Judiciary the responsibility to remedy both abuses of power by persons acting under color of state law and lawless conduct that state courts are neither fully competent, nor always certain, to prevent. . . . a response to the massive, organized lawlessness that infected our Southern States during the post–Civil War era. When a question concerning this statute's coverage arises, it is appropriate to consider whether the controversy has a purely local character or the kind of federal dimension that gave rise to the legislation.

Based on detailed, undisputed findings of fact, the District Court concluded that the portion of §2 of the Ku Klux [Klan] Act now codified at 42 U.S.C. §1985(3) provides a federal remedy for petitioners' violent concerted activities on the public streets and private property of law-abiding citizens. . . . The holdings of the courts below are supported by the text and the legislative history of the statute and are fully consistent with this Court's precedents. Admittedly, important questions concerning the meaning of §1985(3) have been left open in our prior cases, including whether the statute covers gender-based discrimination and whether it provides a remedy for the kind of interference with a woman's right to travel to another State to obtain an abortion revealed by this record. Like the overwhelming majority of federal judges who have spoken to the issue, I am persuaded that traditional principles of statutory construction readily provide affirmative answers to these questions. . . .

It is unfortunate that the Court has analyzed this case as though it presented an abstract question of logical deduction rather than a question concerning the exercise and allocation of power in our federal system of government. The Court ignores the obvious (and entirely constitutional) congressional intent behind §1985(3) to protect this Nation's citizens from what amounts to the theft of their constitutional rights by organized and violent mobs across the country. . . .

Petitioners are dedicated to a cause that they profoundly believe is far more important than mere obedience to the laws of the Commonwealth of Virginia or the police power of its cities. To achieve their goals, the individual petitioners "have agreed and combined with one another and with defendant Operation Rescue to organize, coordinate and participate in 'rescue' demonstrations at abortion clinics in various parts of the country, including the Washington metropolitan area. The purpose of these 'rescue' demonstrations is to disrupt operations at the target clinic and indeed ultimately to cause the clinic to cease operations entirely."

The scope of petitioners' conspiracy is nationwide; it far exceeds the bounds or jurisdiction of any one State. They have blockaded clinics across the country, and their activities have been enjoined in New York, Pennsylvania, Washington, Connecticut, California, Kansas, and Nevada, as well as the District of Columbia metropolitan area. They have carried out their "rescue" operations in the District of Columbia and Maryland in defiance of federal injunctions. Pursuant to their overall conspiracy, petitioners have repeatedly engaged in "rescue" operations that violate local law and harm innocent women. Petitioners trespass on clinic property and physically block access to the clinic, preventing patients, as well as physicians and medical staff, from entering the clinic to render or receive medical or counseling services. Uncontradicted trial testimony demonstrates that petitioners' conduct created a "substantial risk that existing or prospective patients may suffer physical or mental harm." Petitioners make no claim that their conduct is a legitimate form of "protected expression."

Petitioners' intent to engage in repeated violations of law is not contested. They trespass on private property, interfere with the ability of patients to obtain medical and counseling services, and incite others to engage in similar unlawful activity. They also engage in malicious conduct, such as defacing clinic signs, damaging clinic property, and strewing nails in clinic parking lots and on nearby public streets. This unlawful conduct is "vital to [petitioners'] avowed purposes and goals." They show no signs of abandoning their chosen method for advancing their goals.

Rescue operations effectively hinder and prevent the constituted authorities of the targeted community from providing local citizens with adequate protection. The lack of advance warning of petitioners' activities, combined with limited police department resources, makes it difficult for the police to prevent petitioners' ambush by "rescue" from closing a clinic for many hours at a time. The trial record is replete with examples of petitioners overwhelming local law enforcement officials by sheer force of numbers. . . .

Petitioners' conspiracy had both the purpose and effect of interfering with interstate travel. The number of patients who cross state lines to obtain an abortion obviously depends, to some extent, on the location of the clinic and the quality of its services. In the Washington metropolitan area, where interstate travel is routine, 20 to 30 percent of the patients at some clinics were from out of State, while at least one clinic obtained over half its patients from other States. . . .

The text of the statute makes plain the reasons Congress considered a federal remedy for such conspiracies both necessary and appropriate. . . . The plain language of the statute is surely broad enough to cover petitioners' conspiracy. Their concerted activities took place on both the public "highway" and the private "premises of another." The women targeted by their blockade fit comfortably within the statutory category described as "any person or class of persons." Petitioners' interference with police protection of women seeking access to abortion clinics "directly or indirectly" deprived them of equal protection of the laws and of their privilege of engaging in lawful travel. Moreover, a literal reading of the second clause of the statute describes petitioners' proven "purpose of preventing or hindering the constituted authorities of any State or Territory" from securing "to all persons within such State or Territory the equal protection of the laws."

No one has suggested that there would be any constitutional objection to the application of this statute to petitioners' nationwide conspiracy; it is obvious that any such constitutional claim would be frivolous. Accordingly, if, as it sometimes does, the Court limited its analysis to the statutory text, it would certainly affirm the judgment of the Court of Appeals. For both the first clause and the second clause of §1985(3) plainly describe petitioners' conspiracy. . . .

Once concerns about the constitutionality of §1985(3) are properly put aside, we can focus more appropriately on giving the statute its intended effect. On the facts disclosed by this record, I am convinced that both the text of the statute and its underlying purpose support the conclusion that petitioners' conspiracy was motivated by a discriminatory animus and violated respondents' protected right to engage in interstate travel. . . .

It should be noted that a finding of class-based animus in this case does not require finding that to disfavor abortion is "*ipso facto*" to discriminate invidiously against women. . . . Respondents do not take that position, and they do not rely on abstract propositions about "opposition to abortion" *per se*. . . . Instead, they call our attention to a factual record showing a particular lawless conspiracy employing force to prevent women from exercising their constitutional rights. Such a conspiracy, in the terms of the Court's first proposition, may "reasonably be presumed to reflect a sex-based intent." . . .

. . .

Pro-choice groups did not give up the idea of prosecuting violent anti-abortion demonstrators in the courts when Bray *was decided. Instead, the clinics turned to another innovative idea, using the Racketeer Influenced Corrupt Organizations Act chapter of the Organized Crime Control Act of 1970, 18 U.S.C. §§1961–68. Although it was in origin a way to dismantle the Cosa Nostra and other well-entrenched, well-financed criminal organizations, in* NOW v. Scheidler *it was argued that the Pro-Life Action Network (PLAN) and others were members of a nationwide conspiracy to shut down abortion clinics through a pattern of racketeering activity, including extortion, threatened or actual force, violence, or fear to induce clinic employees, doctors, and patients to give up their jobs, their right to practice medicine, and their right to obtain clinic services. Chief Justice Rehnquist read the opinion of the Court. Justice Souter filed a concurring opinion, in which Justice Kennedy joined.*

National Organization for Women, Inc., et al. v. Joseph Scheidler et al., 510 U.S. 249 (1994)

Chief Justice Rehnquist delivered the opinion of the Court.

We are required once again to interpret the provisions of the Racketeer Influenced Corrupt Organizations Act. . . . We granted certiorari to determine whether RICO requires proof that either the racketeering enterprise or the predicate acts of racketeering were motivated by an economic purpose. We hold that RICO requires no such economic motive. . . .

. . . According to respondent Scheidler's congressional testimony, these protesters aim to shut down the clinics and persuade women not to have abortions. . . . The . . . complaint alleged that respondents were members of a nationwide conspiracy to shut down abortion clinics through a pattern of racketeering activity. . . .

We turn to the question whether the racketeering enterprise or the racketeering predicate acts must be accompanied by an underlying economic motive. . . .

The phrase "any enterprise engaged in, or the activities of which affect, interstate or foreign commerce" comes the closest of any language in subsection (C) to suggesting a need for an economic motive. Arguably an enterprise engaged in interstate or foreign commerce would have a profit-seeking motive, but the language in §1962(C) does not stop there; it includes enterprises whose activities "affect" interstate or foreign commerce. *Webster's Third New International Dictionary* defines "affect" as "to have a detrimental influence on—used especially in the phrase *affecting commerce*." An enterprise surely can have a detrimental influence on interstate or foreign commerce without having its own profit-seeking motives. . . . Respondents and the two Courts of Appeals, we think, overlook the fact that predicate acts, such as the alleged extortion, may not benefit the protesters financially but still may drain money from the economy by harming businesses such as the clinics which are petitioners in this case.

We also think that the quoted statement of congressional findings is a rather thin reed upon which to base a requirement of economic motive neither expressed nor, we think, fairly implied in the operative sections of the Act. . . . Congress has not, either in the definitional section or in the operative language, required that an "enterprise" in §1962(c) have an economic motive. . . .

We therefore hold that petitioners may maintain this action if respondents conducted the enterprise through a pattern of racketeering activity. The questions whether respondents committed the requisite predicate acts, and whether the commission of these acts fell into a pattern, are not before us. We hold only that RICO contains no economic motive requirement. . . .

. . .

But the verdict on the application of RICO to protests was still out. In Scheidler v. NOW *(2003), Chief Justice Rehnquist, writing for an 8 to 1 majority, opined that "there is no dispute in these cases that petitioners [the demonstrators, convicted in a jury trial of violation of RICO] interfered with, disrupted, and in some instances completely deprived respondents of their ability to exercise their property rights. Likewise, petitioners' counsel readily acknowledged at oral argument [before the Supreme Court] that aspects of his client's conduct were criminal. But . . . such acts did not constitute extortion [under the meaning given that word in federal law] because petitioners did not 'obtain' respondent's property."[2]*

While the courts were hearing suits about court-imposed injunctions, the methods of Operation Rescue in blocking access to clinics and harassing clinic users and staff were also the subject of hearings in Congress. The members of the committee first read their own statements into the record. Of course, these were political in the sense that they were meant for distribution to the representatives' constituents. At the same time, they seem to be sincere.

Opening statements, *Hearings before the Subcommittee on Crime and Criminal Justice of the Committee on the Judiciary, House of Representatives, April 1, 1993*, serial no. 39 (Washington, D.C.: U.S. Government Printing Office, 1994)

Present: Representatives Charles E. Schumer, Don Edwards, John Conyers, Jr., Dan Glickman, David Mann, F. James Sensenbrenner, Jr., Steven Schiff, and Jim Ramstad.

Also present: Andrew Fois, counsel; Gabrielle Gallegos, assistant counsel; Rachel Jacobson, secretary; Lyle Nirenberg, minority counsel; and Mark Curtis, congressional fellow.

Opening Statement of Chairman Schumer

Mr. Schumer. The hearing will coming to order.

First, the Chair has received a request to cover this hearing in whole or in part by television broadcast, radio broadcast, still photography or other similar methods. In accordance with rule V, permission will be granted unless there is objection.

Without objection.

Good morning. Today we are having a hearing on "Beyond Blockades" and what we should do about those. Why are we having this hearing? Well, it seems some have gone beyond peaceful means to try to exercise their rights to protest abortion and have had a dramatic change in tactics. Blockades are no longer the only thing done. Individuals have been targeted. Newly announced targets of the antichoice movement are individuals who provide or seek abortions rather than the system that makes abortion legal. The advocates of this strategy have intentionally targeted what they see as the weak link—their words—in the chain of legal abortions with tactics the originators have proudly given such language to as the "No Place to Hide Campaign."

What do they do? They trace doctors, staffers, and patients through their license plate numbers. They videotape and eavesdrop on them in their homes. They follow and harass them in stores, restaurants, and theaters. They bother their neighbors, picket their homes at all hours. They make phone calls to them both threatening and designed to jam lines.

We will hear testimony that certain doctors are—there are 50 people dialing their number over and over and over again immobilizing their phone lines because they might choose to perform abortion. They are putting them on wanted posters, sending hate mail, following and harassing their children in school. In other words, a doctor performs an abortion, the people follow the children to school and tell the children's friends your daddy is a baby killer.

There has also been increased violence. We have seen a general and possibly related increase in abortion-related violence, death threats, vandalism, acid arson and now in one case, murder.

In the last few years, there were 28 bombings, 61 arsons, 266 bomb threats, 57 acid attacks in 1992 alone, 395 incidents of vandalism, 68 assaults and hundreds of death threats by phone and by mail.

In 1993 alone, 1 murder, 3 assaults, 3 arsons, with 2, 1 in Montana and 1 in Texas, burning the clinic to the ground, and 11 acid attacks.

So clearly the tactics have changed beyond blockades. Today we are here to examine that and see what should be done about it.

The damages to clinics in 1993 already total nearly $2 million. These tactics are having a serious and sad effect. The stated goal of the tactics is to drive doctors and clinics out of the business of providing abortions and the tactics appear to be working. There are only 2,100 doctors left that perform abortions; 83 percent of U.S. counties are without a provider. Only 12.4 percent of medical schools routinely teach abortion. One-third of medical schools do not teach abortion at all. Two doctors stopped working at a Florida clinic where Dr. Gunn was murdered, for instance, the day after the shooting.

There also seem to be, and we will have to explore this at some length, insufficient State resources either in terms of law or in terms of will and ability to prevent these things from happening. Law enforcement is overwhelmed. Blockades, we know, are enormously expensive. Five million dollars in costs to Atlanta in 1991; $1 million to Wichita in 1991; and $1.5 million in 1992 in Milwaukee. Police cannot provide around-the-clock protection against the targeted 7-day a week stalking that presently occurs. As Dr. Tompkins will testify, he has had to pay for his own personal bodyguards.

Of the 28 cases of arson at abortion clinics during 1990 through 1992, only 3 resulted in an arrest.

Second, localities may not have adequate laws on the books. The State laws are inadequate to deal with the problem. Thirty States have enacted stalking laws; but many of these cover only domestic stalking and would not cover abortion providers.

Finally, even if State laws exist, the States must be willing to enforce them. As we will hear today from our first panel of witnesses, police sometimes are reluctant to arrest, and State judges who must face reelection are reluctant to sentence.

So the whole panoply of actions against the federally protected right to choose is at stake. . . .

Mr. Sensenbrenner. Thank you very much, Mr. Chairman. Today we are having a hearing on a very touchy and emotional subject. We are going to be hearing testimony from people who have strongly held views on both sides of the issue. Even though I consider myself prolife, I respect those people who take the other side of the issue; and even though I oppose the legislation that was reported from this committee last week, I respect the arguments of the people who promote that legislation even though I disagree with them.

Let me say at the outset that in my opinion, violence has no place in any protest movement. However, I believe very strongly there are adequate State and Federal laws on the books to protect people against violence; laws against murder, laws against arson, laws against assault, laws against disorderly conduct. It seems to me also that rather than trying to solve the problems by passing a new law of questionable constitutionality, we should be enforcing the existing laws that are on the books and prosecuting those people who have been accused of violating those laws.

I would like to express my personal sympathy to Dr. Gunn's son. What the assailant of his father did set back the prolife movement a good 10 years. That type of activity has no place in the prolife movement, and practically everybody within that movement has condemned the assassination and the murder of Dr. Gunn in Pensacola, FL.

However, there has been violence and threats of violence on both sides of this issue. The chairman, in his opening statement, talked about wanted posters of physicians who perform abortions. I have one here put out by the other side of a wanted poster with the picture of the archbishop of Los Angeles, Roger Cardinal Maloney: Wanted, Cardinal Maloney, for crimes against humanity, hate crimes against women, attempting to deny women legal access to health care, teaching hatred of women, gay bashing, teaching ignorance instead of safe sex, undermining the Constitution by denying separation of church and State, union busting, and censorship.

So this is going on on both sides. There have been quotations in the newspaper within the last 2 weeks of people who take the prochoice saying "I would like a submachine gun on my roof, but short of that extreme measure, I am not sure what we do."

Now, those types of statements on the prochoice side are just as reprehensible as threats on the prolife side. It seems to me that everybody who is involved in this controversy ought to step back and cool it a bit so that we can debate the issue of whether abortion should be legal in the United States; and if so, under what circumstances and what restrictions, if any. Because that is the public policy question; and yes, indeed, the moral question. The people who are engaged in this debate, as well as we as elected representatives, are going to have to face and reach our own personal decisions; in the case of the Congress, what we think our constituency wants.

However, despite how strongly each of us holds our individual views on this particular issue, the Constitution of the United States, particularly the first amendment, still applies.

The first amendment was never intended to protect politically correct speech. We do not need a first amendment if the only thing it is to do is to protect speech that is politically correct. The right to protest and to picket and to stage sit-ins in order to bring to the public's attention what one's viewpoint is [is] something that is ingrained in American society, for the past 100 years.

It seems to me that whatever we do in terms of responding to the problems that have arisen over the past few years, we should keep that in mind because we do not want to have a chilling effect on free speech. We do not want to prevent people from expressing that free speech to others.

Mr. Edwards. Thank you, Mr. Chairman.

I want to get along with the hearings so I will not make any kind of statement other than to say, Mr. Chairman, that I thought the Chair's opening statement was very moving and I subscribe to every word in it.

I would also like to add Mr. Schumer, my chairman, is known for his fairness. He has never been accused of being unfair and is not in this case at all.

Lastly, I am one of the few members left who was here in Congress in the early sixties when we had a similar situation in certain States of the Old Confederacy, I am sorry to say, where the people's constitutional rights were not being defended by the local officers, by the local police, of the State police; and pursuant to our constitutional responsibilities, we moved in and passed the omnibus civil rights bill of 1964 and the Voting Rights Act to enforce the Constitution.

I have a real sense of deja vu. Almost exactly the same things are going on with the prolife people, harassment, abuse, criminal conduct, that [were] going on in the Old South; and we are doing exactly the right thing in inserting the Federal Government, as we are required to do under the Constitution, into this very serious situation.

Mr. Conyers. Thank you very much, Mr. Chairman.

Ladies and gentlemen, members of this committee, this is a very sensitive and timely subject. I am very pleased that the Judiciary Committee has chosen to have a public forum where the American people can listen to the legal, the moral, the Federal, and the local implications of a very important issue that confronts us at this point in time.

I think that we need to recognize what has happened now with the shooting of Dr. David Gunn has incrementally transformed the nature and subject of this discussion; because his shooting in front of a Pensacola clinic by an antichoice activist named Michael Griffin demonstrates that Operation Rescue and others are determined to prevent the delivery of reproductive services by any means necessary. Donald Tresham, executive director of Rescue America, stated that while he did not condone Griffin's action, "the casualties have always been on one side up until now."

So a strong Federal directive to protect not only a woman's right to choose, but her right to actualize that choice is not only necessary but could be the difference between life and death. As the antichoice groups correctly advocate, without the ability to realize the services, the right is useless. Women must also have access to information. Women must have access to counseling provided by the clinics. Without these resources, their ability to choose is once again seriously impaired.

The tactics of organized abortion opponents have disturbed not only women seeking to exercise their rights, but the communities in which these protests occur. The summer-long campaign of clinic blockades in Kansas in 1991 is a perfect example of the disruptive nature of these protests and their long-term ramifications. State and local police were forced to expend precious resources to deal with the protesters, making it very difficult for them to meet the policing needs of their communities.

Wichita spent in excess of a half-a-million dollars to respond to a 46-day blockade. Our colleague and distinguished member of this committee is probably—has a far more detail on that point.

The ongoing blockade in Milwaukee, WI, has cost that city in excess of $1.5 million with over 2,000 arrests.

When the U.S. Supreme Court decided in the case of *Bray* and the *Alexandria Women's Health Clinic* that women seeking abortions were not covered by laws against blockaders, it created a huge problem for us as lawmakers. Picketing and protests are a viable means to communicate that should be protected under the first amendment. I doubt if there is a person in this room that would disagree with that assertion.

So from one point of view, this is not an awfully difficult subject. We are the Judiciary Committee. We deal with criminal law. If there are crimes being committed or offenses that need to be criminalized, that is what the Judiciary Committee was created for. If in the determination of this committee we decide there needs to be adequate criminal laws added to the books because of the unusual tactics that are now apparently going to be standardized across the country, then it is our job to do so.

If, on the other hand, a majority feel that that is not the case, then, of course, we obviously will not do so.

So I am very pleased to be here to listen very carefully to all of the witnesses' testimony.

Thank you, Mr. Chairman.

Mr. Schumer. Thank you. . . .

Mr. Glickman, the final opening statement.

Mr. Glickman. First of all, let me say there are many things one can say about the chairman of this subcommittee, but one thing you must say is he is a very fair individual. I think these hearings have been constructed extremely fairly, both in terms of numbers, and in terms of qualitative and quantitative aspects of who is here testifying. I think, Chuck, you have done it correctly. I want to support you on that.

I don't think, however, that you can talk about this issue of violence without talking a little bit about the underlying issue of abortion. While this is not a prochoice/prolife hearing, as Mr. Schumer said, I don't think you can consider this issue in the abstract. I come from Wichita. We had the first major Operation Rescue demonstration there.

I want to talk about it as I see it and as I feel it for my constituents. Let me start by saying I am absolutely torn by this issue. I think my constituents are torn by this issue. I think America is torn by this issue.

I don't think in America we have seen anything like this for several generations. It is balkanizing this country, taking a cue a little bit from what is happening in another part of the world. There is increasing violence in America, anyway, with the proliferation of guns and weapons.

What disturbs me is that you take this issue which so divides the country and add it to the increasing violence taking place in America and the recipe for disaster is here.

We are here discussing an issue that is dividing this country reminiscent of the way the country was divided during the Civil War. It is proving to be just as divisive, even though the issues are different. Like a war, it certainly has become violent.

It is obvious by the need for this type of hearing that it is imperative we come together on some common ground to start a dialog of understanding and a commitment to working together to reach workable and acceptable solutions wherever possible, looking to stopping the violence and to laws defining a Federal remedy.

I am a firm believer that we in the Government are in the business of protecting citizens' constitutional rights. Abortion is a right guaranteed by the Constitution. But I also subscribe to the philosophy espoused by then-candidate Clinton who said abortion should be safe, legal, and rare.

I recognize this is a deeply moral and philosophical issue that must be individually determined. However, I think we should be expending at least as much energy dealing with this issue in other ways. We need to educate and provide resources to prevent unwanted pregnancies in the first place. Education is a valuable tool. We should not be afraid to start education at a young age, because given the statistics of the ages of the young girls—and I use that word deliberately—who are having abortions, they are learning how to get pregnant at an early age.

We should also promote adoption and other alternatives, looking at our tax laws and our health care system, for example, to encourage that abortion will not occur in the first place. We should look to alternatives which will help us come to some resolution in this disturbing battle; and the prolife and prochoice communities can work together on these things. What I am saying is government should be doing more to provide responsible alternatives to abortion. Government should not be in the position of actively encouraging abortions.

Furthermore, it is not a protected first amendment right to harass and threaten people into submission. I think it is incomprehensible how it can be morally justified that in the name of life, people are destroying the lives and peace of innocent family members by going to children's schools and showing up at a spouse's workplaces. Some say the end justifies the means because of the deep moral issues involved. But in a democracy, means never justify ends. That is the hallmark of a totalitarian society and under that theory, two wrongs make a right. That is not my belief about America.

This subject and this unnecessary violence is all too familiar to me and my fellow citizens from Wichita. As most of you remember, as Mr. Conyers talked about, we were targeted as an Operation Rescue city in the summer of 1991. Although many good, hardworking nonviolent Kansans came out to protest, there were thousands of out-of-towners bused into Wichita, and the result was destruction of property and harassment of some innocent citizens.

The transformation of our peaceful city into a virtual war zone was incredible. I cannot protect this kind of protest. Sadly, the extremism like what we witnessed in Wichita has only accelerated. How are we going to stop this constant battle in cities around the country? I really do not know.

There are deep moral divisions. Prochoice and prolife people or they are called—every side uses terms in order to buttress their own position—must develop a dialog.

I know, however, violence and destruction and murder certainly are not helping anyone. It certainly is not persuading people in the nonviolent dialog-based manner that was envisioned by the first amendment. I think by putting our heads together instead of our weapons, we could stop the violence and protect everybody's constitutional rights.

· · ·

After the members of the subcommittee had made their statements for the record, they welcomed a number of witnesses. Such hearings are designed to help Congress gather information. They are also a showcase for various interest groups to present their positions on issues. C-Span and other news networks often cover at least a part of the hearings. In this case, however, the witnesses had a personal stake in the outcome of the legislation.

Statement of David Gunn, Jr.

Mr. Gunn. I just want to say thanks for having me here. I don't have anything prepared. I would like to say my father—

Mr. Schumer. Bring the microphone a little closer to you so everyone can hear you.

Mr. Gunn [continuing]. My father had been targeted by these organizations for some time in early 1992. He was the victim of wanted posters and on these posters were listed his schedule, the clinics he went to, his time of arrival and departure. It takes diligent research to find out such things about these doctors that I don't think is covered under the first amendment. That is invasion of privacy and harassment.

I would also like to say I have Operation Rescue's abortion-busters manual which is their manifesto of terrorist acts. It is this right here. It outlines how to achieve getting information on physicians, how to use tax records, malpractice suits, license plates, and other various means to track and trail these citizens.

My father told me numerous times about the harassment that he was receiving. He was being followed from clinic to clinic. I know he would sometimes divert his routine to compensate for that following. He had begun to arm himself because he was feeling so threatened by these people that he was afraid they would pull him over somehow on the side of the road and he would have no way to defend himself.

I know in Pensacola, the Friday before the shooting, a clinic worker advised the Pensacola authorities that the harassment was getting worse; that he was being followed to restaurants, he was being harassed in restaurants. He didn't have a home. He couldn't have a home. He lived out of hotel rooms because of this harassment. They did nothing. They did not offer any help. They said that is not our problem, we do not see it as a threat; we will—see what ignorance has brought about now.

These antichoice organizations, I can't refer to them as prolife any more, they are antichoice—are employing terrorist tactics. They are employing harassment, intimidation; the same tactics we saw the Ku Klux Klan use in the early 1960's. That was put a stop to. I think this also should be put a stop to.

Statement of Jeri Rasmussen, Executive Director, Midwest Health Center for Women, Minneapolis, MN

Ms. Rasmussen. Mr. Chairman, members of the committee, I have been actively involved in the struggle for reproductive choices since 1968 as an organizer, speaker, chief lobbyist both State and Federal; and since 1988 as the director of Midwest Health Center for Women in Minneapolis, MN. Midwest is a nonprofit clinic. I do not intend—

Mr. Conyers. Could you pull your mike forward, Ms. Rasmussen?

Ms. Rasmussen. I am not going to spend any time today on what has happened at the clinic scene in Minnesota but it is not unlike other States. I am proud of the work I do. I feel privileged to have as my life's work the role of dignifying the choices women make. What we are experiencing today is 20 years of naming women and health care providers murderers, thus creating a climate for the insanity that prevails today.

I hope to make real for you what it is like to go to work in the morning and not know if you will make it home at night; and when you are home, to know that the latter-day Ku Klux Klan has plans for you; how one checks one's yard daily and car to see if someone stuffed a bomb into the tailpipe; looking at your mail closely to see if it has a postmark and a return address —normalizing life in this manner.

I ask you to consider my life for the past 3 years as I have struggled with hate-filled action directed at me and at my home. Why this terrorism? Why this hatred? Because I am employed as the director of a woman's health clinic.

In March 1990, I received a telephone call from a neighbor telling me about a flyer that had been left at his home. The flyer contained no disclaimer. It purported to inform in graphic misinformation how I regularly "kill or murder babies" at Midwest Health Center for Women. The flyer invited anyone to visit, call, write or pray for me at my home or at the clinic. I was shocked. My home has always been a refuge, private, and a place of comfort and enjoyment.

My name was never listed in the telephone directory. I enjoyed privacy. But that all changed when a former high school classmate filled with some kind of religious zeal wrote me a letter and subsequently revealed my home address to her associates. She has robbed me of something very precious: my privacy.

I am and I remain a private person, yet I am changed.

I endured six incursions into my neighborhood and finally sought an ordinance that would protect targeted picketing of a private residence. It was enacted. It did not stop anyone.

In 1990, a new law was passed in Minnesota providing for an individual to seek an order for protection based upon harassment. What you had to do was to be able to identify the people in order to cease the harassment. The police would not identify people for me. I had to photograph and compare photos with other clinics to help establish who they were before I could even go to court.

I was stalked on the freeway for a considerable frightening distance by a St. Paul City firefighter. He and his wife have been at my home for over 3 years.

I have been assailed by him in a restaurant, on my walking path and elsewhere. I have ugly signs left on my property. Thirty men at my home, one with an attack dog, were not considered threatening by the police.

I want to conclude my statement with the plea to the Congress of the United States to say no to these domestic terrorists. We need the Congress of the United States to understand what this is about, to understand as

Congress now does that rape is not something women enjoy and men brag about and that battered women is a societal horror that is now understood. Congress is learning the meaning of sexual harassment.

I ask after 15 years of blatant attacks Congress has the responsibility and the obligation to make certain that harassment, terrorism, and murder are not equated with free speech or first amendment guarantees and that the penalties for interfering with the free exercise of one's right to privacy and safety is an offense with severe penalties.

Do I fear? Does my family fear for my personal safety, my life?

The answer is yes.

Thank you.

Statement of Susan Hill, President, National Women's Health Organization, Raleigh, NC

Ms. Hill. My thanks first to the members of the committee for allowing us to testify on the issues of violence and harassment against abortion providers in this country.

Mr. Schumer. If you could pull the microphone closer? The microphones on the table seem to be a little muted today.

Ms. Hill. We believe this is a campaign of terrorism that has been allowed to fester in every city where there is a clinic.

Dr. David Gunn had worked with our Columbus, GA, clinic since 1985. I received a phone call on March 10, 1993, with a simple frightening message "They shot Dr. Gunn. He is dead." In reflecting on this moment, I realize that the shocking thing about the message was not the incident; it was that for a moment I thought it was about two other physicians who had been living under death threats for months. We had believed that Dr. Gunn was in less danger than five of our other physicians.

How is it possible that in a country founded on religious freedom and individual rights, we providers of abortion care have come to live in fear of religious groups, who pronounce themselves the judge and jury of our fate?

Abortion providers have been told to use the legal system and we have to no avail. My organization has obtained Federal court injunctions against protesters' illegal activity. We have obtained State court injunctions against unlawful activity by protesters. We have obtained over 1,000 arrests. We have spent over $500,000 in legal fees. We have been awarded damages and attorney's fees of over $100,000. We have collected zero. In Delaware, out of 225 protesters arrested, the average fine was $25 with no jail time. In Ft. Wayne, IN, 455 protesters were arrested. All charges were dropped. In

Milwaukee, WI, in the last year, there were 2,100 arrests with only 20 prosecutions. All charges were dropped.

We are attacked by a group of people who have been taught how to be judgment-proof, and how to beat the system. They have workshops on beating the system. They do it with pride and defiance.

We have lost scores of physicians and staff due to the direct threats to themselves and their families. Antiabortion activists have camped in front of physician's and administration's homes all night long. They have rolled cement-filled barrels across driveways, blocking the ingress and egress of a private home. Doctors have had to walk through woods behind their houses in order to get out of their houses safely. Antiabortion activists have posed as interested home buyers, in order to obtain names and identities of children of physicians. They have stalked children on their way to school, at school and after school. Several children have been driven to and from school by local police due to the stalking. They have stalked a physician's 80-year-old mother, picketed her home, and called her late at night to report that her son had been killed, a false story. Wanted posters, identical to Dr. Gunn's have been circulated on most of our physicians, and sent to their homes with warnings to their families. They called and harassed my twin sister dying of cancer, telling her that she was dying because of what I did. They have even picketed the graveside services of a friend who ran women's clinics in Texas. As we drove up to the grave, I realized that the antiabortion picketer was a protester we had arrested in Delaware the year before. These are not isolated incidents. These are not individuals acting alone. I have seen missionaries for the Preborn and Lambs of Christ in Fargo, ND, then seen the same people a few weeks later in Milwaukee, WI, and later in Ft. Wayne, IN. They claim no income, but they travel easily and quickly.

We have had arsons at eight of our facilities and only one arrest by the Federal authorities. That arrest was of an antiabortion activist, Marjorie Reed, who was fleeing arson charges, concerning a clinic fire in Ohio. The real story is that Ms. Reed was being given refuge by another antiabortion activist in New Jersey in what they referred to as a safehouse. None of the people hiding her were charged with anything.

You must not believe these are all well meaning local church-goers who are merely exercising their first amendment rights. This is a holy war. There is no difference between this group of traveling terrorists and groups of terrorists in the Middle East. These are terrorists who believe the law of God is above all other laws. Check the transcripts of court hearings across the country in antiabortion cases. God's law is used throughout all of their defense.

Statement of Randall A. Terry, Founder, Operation Rescue

Mr. Terry. Mr. Chairman, members of the House of Representatives, thank you for the opportunity to be with you. I think what we are seeing here is a low-tech lynching.

I am distressed by the mischaracterizations, the outright lies, the character assassination that has gone on of decent men and women all over this country who have conscientiously and nonviolently sought to save children from abortion. It is our hope that during the time of questioning we can set the record straight and not only diffuse any further amendments to the freedom of access to clinic entrances but also to kill the bill, frankly.

I founded Operation Rescue in 1978 with the express purpose of calling the church of Jesus Christ and the Nation to repentance over the national sin of child killing. Part of that repentance is for people to nonviolently place their body between the killer and his intended victim.

I would insert at this point—we have a pledge our participants are required to sign that they commit to nonviolence in word and in deed. Since the beginning of Operation Rescue, over 60,000 arrests have been made nationwide perhaps making Operation Rescue the largest civil disobedience movement in the history of America. To say we are somehow not mainstream is to defy American history and the numbers.

What is the profile of the average person who is at one of these events? There are grandmothers praying the rosary; moms with small children of their own; there are businessmen, owners of businesses in the community; doctors, lawyers, firemen; yes, there are even policemen who have been arrested with us in our efforts to save children.

To in any way call this diverse cross-section of Americans terrorists is to insult intelligence, is to insult the true victims of terrorism all over the world, and is to betray the meaning of the word.

It is important to note the average charge of the rescuers: Trespass, disorderly conduct, failure to disburse, and we are arrested, arrested regularly as the record will clearly reflect.

I think what I would like to point out here is that rather than us being terrorists, the truth be known, we have been singled out as an organization, really as a movement, to be hammered by law enforcement officials and judges.

Compare the sentences that profile citizens have received at the hands of judges or the treatment we have received at the hands of police with other protest civil disobedience groups. I want to say something here. Please hear this. We understand the difference between protected first amendment speech and civil disobedience.

The activities of blockading abortion clinics are not first amendment speech. We understand that. However America has a rich heritage from Susan B. Anthony to Rosa Parks, from Dr. King to the heavy coffin of the underground railroad. We have a rich heritage of civil disobedience and tolerance of civil disobedience.

It is a form of political protest.

We patterned much of our activity, much of our training, and much of our literature after the writings of Dr. King and the civil rights leaders.

Now, if you compare the sentences we have been given to those given by [sic] other groups, for example, homosexuals going into St. Patrick's Cathedral desecrating the Eucharist, cursing, blasphemy. They were given a hundred dollar fine and released.

We have been fined hundreds of thousands of dollars in New York City. I personally spent 7 months behind bars while people who committed violations, people convicted of drug abuse were freed. In L.A., when Martin Sheen, the actor, was arrested for his 18th civil disobedience protest, he was given a small fine and community service.

Contrast that with the prolifers who on their first arrest were given weeks and months in jail for their first offense. Operation Rescue is civil disobedience. We acknowledge it is an effort to save children.

However for our opponents to say it is not civil disobedience in the traditional sense of the word is a very hollow argument, to say Operation Rescue is not politically correct civil disobedience.

We believe this legislation strikes at the heart of what it means to live in political freedom. That is the right to dissent. Sometimes vigorously. Sometimes with nonviolent civil disobedience without the fear of oppressive crushing retaliation from a government.

Compare the treatment we have received with every other protest group, whether animal rights activists, homosexual activists, people protesting on behalf of trees, people protesting on behalf of the homeless. We have been singled out and hammered.

I want to ask a question of the members of this board: Will the homosexuals who continue to sit in at our churches be targeted with a Federal offense? Will the AIDS activists who blockade Federal buildings sitting in, will they be charged with a Federal offense? Will the activists for the homeless or animal rights, the people who blockade research laboratories because they don't want animals used in research, will they be charged with a Federal offense? Or is this selective prosecution and persecution because we have dared to confront the crown jewel of the politically correct? Child killing.

Thank you for the opportunity of being with you. It is my hope that death industries' frenzied attempts to keep child killing legal at all costs will not blind this body and the larger committee to what is really happening here. That is that abortion kills children. We are being singled out because we are trying to save them.

Finally, we are not the new kids on the block, Mr. Chairman. Abortion was illegal for a hundred years before *Roe* and would never have been tolerated by the Founding Fathers of this country in its current stature. Beyond that, God has plainly said through the law of Moses thou shalt not murder.

We will give an account as a nation for the blood that is now crying from the ground for vengeance.

Thank you. . . .

Statement of Rev. Joseph Foreman, President, Missionaries to the Preborn

Reverend Foreman. I wanted to thank you very much for this opportunity to testify.

The history of the abortion lobby has been to use every possible tactic to crush all dissent, thereby making abortion the only choice by default. One of the major tactics has been to label all street activity as violent and extremist. I mean all street activity.

Because the prolife movement has been distinctly lacking in violence and extremism among its demonstrators, the abortion movement feels compelled to create the violence themselves. They focus the media on one or two picketers who might shout in order to tar all prolife people. Under the guise of stopping people who block doors, they seek injunctions that, in fact, freeze the first amendment rights of picketers by establishing bubble zones where the first amendment is suspended.

These injunctions have nothing to do with blocking doors but everything to do with violating first amendment rights of picketers.

Now we see them using the fact that a man was shot, a tragedy, in order to target people who neither shoot nor advocate the shooting of an abortionist. What is wrong? Are the murder laws not strict enough, or arson laws too lax, or assault and battery laws incapable of enforcement? If there were actually "an acceleration of violence at abortion clinics" which is most a universal claim of the media, why are jails filling up with people guilty of sit-ins instead of assault and batteries? I will tell you why. It is because in terms of the actual street activity, there is almost no increase in assault and battery.

Let me give you an example. In Milwaukee, we have 49 documented incidents—in other words videotaped footage of police bringing assault and battery charges only to be forced to drop them when the videotaped footage clearly demonstrated either there was no assault at all or that it was the proabortion person who did the assaulting.

By the way, they never bring reverse charges even when the videotape demonstrates it. The police have been documented as lying 49 times. They are not called to account by the courts. This is typical of all the escalating violence type of lies. I am talking now about street activity.

Like everything else they do, the legislation is designed to eliminate the moderate element of the prolife movement. If successful, you are gong to have a disaster on your hands.

Let me paint you the picture of why I say that. There is an ethical crisis that exists at the doors of every abortion clinic in the country. There is a man committed to killing a number of children each day. How can we both stop him and yet still respect his right to life?

The only solution that a secular world can offer is a false solution which comes straight out of the row-boat games of their own values. In those games the ship is sunk, there is not enough food, the class must decide who must die. Do you kill the children? Do you kill the doctor?

Instead we have rejected his as a false dilemma and say no, there is another solution. You separate the doctor from his victim in a passive way. Rescue blocking the doors of the abortion clinic supplies the only solution in which everyone walks away from the death camp alive.

The abortionist lobby, they don't want everyone alive. Their agenda was crumbling in the face of their harmless protection of everyone. They desperately needed a dead abortionist to give their distortionists credibility. When they finally got their kill, their plan worked. They have successfully intimidated the Congress of the United States into attacking people who have no earthly connection with this killing. You must not allow the distorted agenda of the abortion lobby to make you act as if nonviolently separating a killer from the victim is the same as using force to either destroy his building or him.

Mr. Terry made the distinction between first amendment activity and a blockade. I agree with that distinction. I am going to go on to make the distinction between a blockade and the use of violence or other sorts of activities. We have consistently been against anything that is violent. We have consistently spoken against it.

One of the reasons why in Milwaukee we no longer have people sign a statement or pledge of nonviolence is for the simple fact that that is used as conspiracy when we go to court. And so conspiracy charges can be brought against us because we are charging nonviolence.

Don't be confused about what is at stake here. Hundreds of thousands of middle Americans have come into the street to directly confront evil and offer their own homes to any mother in need. It is possible to crush them by singling them out because of their political incorrectness with unconstitutional remedies like this proposed legislation.

What is the result going to be? You are going to remove the middle of the road element committed to nonviolence. Please think. See through the media's feeding frenzy. If you refuse to distinguish violent from nonviolent, if you go on to crush the nonviolent claiming to go after the violent, I am against the rock throwers. They shouldn't be doing that.

Then you inevitably leave the arena to the true extremists. Believe me, I know the extremist mind set. I have not spent the last 5 years polishing a media image. I don't care what you think of me or the so-called prolife movement. I have spent almost a year and a half of that time in jail. I am telling you what I have seen and heard out there. The extremist is not a demonstrator.

We hear Michael Griffin described as a protester. He has never protested or demonstrated against anything in his whole life.

I am simply telling you that to them, rescuing and going to jail is foolish. Their reason is the doctor comes back the next day. With all due respect to my fellow people on the panel, they view us as halfhearted. Their type was careful how we handle things like the killing of Dr. Gunn. They watch to see whether or not people like Jeff White, Randall Terry or me have folded in our defense of the children.

While the media savage us for aggressively speaking up for the children who would have been killed, the Michael Griffins out there see our stand for the children and they are clearly deterred.

Why? Because they see us as taking a stand and therefore they don't take matters into their own hands. They see the moderate element may be bloodied but we are unbowed.

Now our actions tell that we are not crushed. All our means have not been exhausted. You pray for the extremist. An antiabortionist does not come to the conclusion that Operation Rescue or the Missionaries of the Preborn have failed. I know you don't like these words. You know they are true. Like the media. you find it convenient to twist them as if I were threatening something. You know I am not. You know the mind set of the extremists and what triggers it. You know in this legislation you are holding the trigger to their violence. Don't pull it.

In May 1994, Congress passed the Freedom of Access to Clinic Entrances Act. What actions did FACE prohibit? What did it allow? What kinds of criminal penalties applied? How could an individual bring a suit against a violator of the act? How could a state or local government bring a suit under the act? How was the act a compromise measure? In your opinion, does it give too much power to the law enforcement officials?

Freedom of Access to Clinic Entrances Act, 103 Public Laws 259, May 26, 1994

An Act . . . to assure freedom of access to reproductive services. This Act may be cited as the "Freedom of Access to Clinic Entrances Act of 1994."

Pursuant to the affirmative power of Congress to enact this legislation under section 8 of article I of the Constitution, as well as under section 5 of the fourteenth amendment to the Constitution, it is the purpose of this Act to protect and promote the public safety and health and activities affecting interstate commerce by establishing Federal criminal penalties and civil remedies for certain violent, threatening, obstructive and destructive conduct that is intended to injure, intimidate or interfere with persons seeking to obtain or provide reproductive health services. . . .

(a) Prohibited Activities.—Whoever—

(1) by force or threat of force or by physical obstruction, intentionally injures, intimidates or interferes with or attempts to injure, intimidate or interfere with any person because that person is or has been, or in order to intimidate such person or any other person or any class of persons from, obtaining or providing reproductive health services;

(2) by force or threat of force or by physical obstruction, intentionally injures, intimidates or interferes with or attempts to injure, intimidate or interfere with any person lawfully exercising or seeking to exercise the First Amendment right of religious freedom at a place of religious worship; or

(3) intentionally damages or destroys the property of a facility, or attempts to do so, because such facility provides reproductive health services, or intentionally damages or destroys the property of a place of religious worship,

shall be subject to the penalties provided in subsection (b) and the civil remedies provided in subsection (c), except that a parent or legal guardian of a minor shall not be subject to any penalties or civil remedies under this section for such activities insofar as they are directed exclusively at that minor.

(b) Penalties.—Whoever violates this section shall—

(1) in the case of a first offense, be fined in accordance with this title, or imprisoned not more than one year, or both; and

(2) in the case of a second or subsequent offense after a prior conviction under this section, be fined in accordance with this title, or imprisoned not more than 3 years, or both; except that for an offense involving exclusively a nonviolent physical obstruction, the fine shall be not more than $10,000 and the length of imprisonment shall be not more than six months, or both, for the first offense; and the fine shall be not more than $25,000 and the length of imprisonment shall be not more than 18 months, or both, for a subsequent offense; and except that if bodily injury results, the length of imprisonment shall be not more than 10 years, and if death results, it shall be for any term of years or for life.

(c) Civil Remedies.—

(1) Right of action.—

(A) In general.—Any person aggrieved by reason of the conduct prohibited by subsection (a) may commence a civil action for the relief set forth in subparagraph (B), except that such an action may be brought under subsection (a)(1) only by a person involved in providing or seeking to provide, or obtaining or seeking to obtain, services in a facility that provides reproductive health services, and such an action may be brought under subsection (a)(2) only by a person lawfully exercising or seeking to exercise the First Amendment right of religious freedom at a place of religious worship or by the entity that owns or operates such place of religious worship.

(B) Relief.—In any action under subparagraph (A), the court may award appropriate relief, including temporary, preliminary or permanent injunctive relief and compensatory and punitive damages, as well as the costs of suit and reasonable fees for attorneys and expert witnesses. With respect to compensatory damages, the plaintiff may elect, at any time prior to the rendering of final judgment, to recover, in lieu of actual damages, an award of statutory damages in the amount of $5,000 per violation.

(2) Action by Attorney General of the United States.—

(A) In general.—If the Attorney General of the United States has reasonable cause to believe that any person or group of persons is being, has been, or may be injured by conduct constituting a violation of this section, the Attorney General may commence a civil action in any appropriate United States District Court.

(B) Relief.—In any action under subparagraph (A), the court may award appropriate relief, including temporary, preliminary or permanent injunctive relief, and compensatory damages to persons aggrieved as described in paragraph (1)(B). The court, to vindicate the public interest, may also assess a civil penalty against each respondent—

(i) in an amount not exceeding $10,000 for a nonviolent physical obstruction and $15,000 for other first violations; and

(ii) in an amount not exceeding $15,000 for a nonviolent physical obstruction and $25,000 for any other subsequent violation.

(3) Actions by state attorneys general.—

(A) In general.—If the Attorney General of a State has reasonable cause to believe that any person or group of persons is being, has been, or may be injured by conduct constituting a violation of this section, such Attorney General may commence a civil action in the name of such State, as parens patriae on behalf of natural persons residing in such State, in any appropriate United States District Court.

(B) Relief.—In any action under subparagraph (A), the court may award appropriate relief, including temporary, preliminary or permanent injunctive relief, compensatory damages, and civil penalties as described in paragraph (2)(B).

(d) Rules of Construction.—Nothing in this section shall be construed—

(1) to prohibit any expressive conduct (including peaceful picketing or other peaceful demonstration) protected from legal prohibition by the First Amendment to the Constitution;

(2) to create new remedies for interference with activities protected by the free speech or free exercise clauses of the First Amendment to the Constitution, occurring outside a facility, regardless of the point of view expressed, or to limit any existing legal remedies for such interference;

(3) to provide exclusive criminal penalties or civil remedies with respect to the conduct prohibited by this section, or to preempt State or local laws that may provide such penalties or remedies; or

(4) to interfere with the enforcement of State or local laws regulating the performance of abortions or other reproductive health services.

(e) Definitions.—As used in this section:

(1) Facility.—The term "facility" includes a hospital, clinic, physician's office, or other facility that provides reproductive health services, and includes the building or structure in which the facility is located.

(2) Interfere with.—The term "interfere with" means to restrict a person's freedom of movement.

(3) Intimidate.—The term "intimidate" means to place a person in reasonable apprehension of bodily harm to him- or herself or to another.

(4) Physical obstruction.—The term "physical obstruction" means ren-

dering impassable ingress to or egress from a facility that provides reproductive health services or to or from a place of religious worship, or rendering passage to or from such a facility or place of religious worship unreasonably difficult or hazardous.

(5) Reproductive health services.—The term "reproductive health services" means reproductive health services provided in a hospital, clinic, physician's office, or other facility, and includes medical, surgical, counselling or referral services relating to the human reproductive system, including services relating to pregnancy or the termination of a pregnancy.

(6) State.—The term "State" includes a State of the United States, the District of Columbia, and any commonwealth, territory, or possession of the United States." . . .

. . .

While FACE was being debated in Congress and the federal courts were hearing suits against Operation Rescue, PLAN, and other direct-action groups, the High Court heard another of the many cases involving the clash of rights between defenders of the protests and defenders of the clinics. The case came from Florida in 1993. In response to a suit against protesters who closely crowded the streets and sidewalks of a Melbourne, Florida, abortion clinic, the state court issued an injunction against certain kinds of intrusive rescue. Operation Rescue appealed to the federal circuit court of appeals, arguing that the injunction was overly burdensome on their right to free speech. The appeals court agreed and vacated the injunction. The clinic turned to the Supreme Court. Chief Justice Rehnquist delivered the opinion of the Court, in which Justices Blackmun, O'Connor, Souter, and Ginsburg joined, and in which Justice Stevens joined in part. Justice Souter filed a concurring opinion, as did Stevens. Justice Scalia filed an opinion concurring in the judgment in part and dissenting in part, in which Justices Kennedy and Thomas joined.

Judy Madsen et al., Petitioners v. Women's Health Center, Inc., 512 U.S. 753 (1994)

Chief Justice Rehnquist delivered the opinion of the Court.

Petitioners challenge the constitutionality of an injunction entered by a Florida state court which prohibits antiabortion protesters from demonstrating in certain places and in various ways outside of a health clinic that performs abortions. . . .

Respondents operate abortion clinics throughout central Florida. Petitioners and other groups and individuals are engaged in activities near the site of one such clinic in Melbourne, Florida. They picketed and demonstrated where the public street gives access to the clinic. In September 1992, a Florida state court permanently enjoined petitioners from blocking or interfering with public access to the clinic, and from physically abusing persons entering or leaving the clinic. Six months later, respondents sought to broaden the injunction, complaining that access to the clinic was still impeded by petitioners' activities and that such activities had also discouraged some potential patients from entering the clinic, and had deleterious physical effects on others. The trial court thereupon issued a broader injunction, which is challenged here.

The court found that, despite the initial injunction, protesters continued to impede access to the clinic by congregating on the paved portion of the street—Dixie Way—leading up to the clinic, and by marching in front of the clinic's driveways. It found that as vehicles heading toward the clinic slowed to allow the protesters to move out of the way, "sidewalk counselors" would approach and attempt to give the vehicle's occupants anti-abortion literature. The number of people congregating varied from a handful to 400, and the noise varied from singing and chanting to the use of loudspeakers and bullhorns.

The protests, the court found, took their toll on the clinic's patients. A clinic doctor testified that, as a result of having to run such a gauntlet to enter the clinic, the patients "manifested a higher level of anxiety and hypertension causing those patients to need a higher level of sedation to undergo the surgical procedures, thereby increasing the risk associated with such procedures." . . . The noise produced by the protesters could be heard within the clinic, causing stress in the patients both during surgical procedures and while recuperating in the recovery rooms. And those patients who turned away because of the crowd to return at a later date, the doctor testified, increased their health risks by reason of the delay.

Doctors and clinic workers, in turn, were not immune even in their homes. Petitioners picketed in front of clinic employees' residences; shouted at passersby; rang the doorbells of neighbors and provided literature identifying the particular clinic employee as a "baby killer." Occasionally, the protesters would confront minor children of clinic employees who were home alone.

This and similar testimony led the state court to conclude that its original injunction had proved insufficient "to protect the health, safety and rights of women in Brevard and Seminole County, Florida and surrounding counties seeking access to [medical and counseling] services." . . . The state court therefore amended its prior order, enjoining a broader array of activities. . . . The Florida Supreme Court upheld the constitutionality of the trial court's amended injunction. . . . The court analyzed the injunction to determine whether the restrictions are "narrowly tailored to serve a significant government interest, and leave open ample alternative channels of communication." It concluded that they were.

Shortly before the Florida Supreme Court's opinion was announced, the United States Court of Appeals for the Eleventh Circuit heard a separate challenge to the same injunction. The Court of Appeals struck down the injunction, characterizing the dispute as a clash "between an actual prohibition of speech and a potential hindrance to the free exercise of abortion rights." . . . It stated that the asserted interests in public safety and order were already protected by other applicable laws and that these interests could be protected adequately without infringing upon the First Amendment rights of others. The Court of Appeals found the injunction to be content based and neither necessary to serve a compelling state interest nor narrowly drawn to achieve that end. . . .

We begin by addressing petitioners' contention that the state court's order, because it is an injunction that restricts only the speech of antiabortion protesters, is necessarily content or viewpoint based. Accordingly, they argue, we should examine the entire injunction under the strictest standard of scrutiny. . . . We disagree. To accept petitioners' claim would be to classify virtually every injunction as content or viewpoint based. An injunction, by its very nature, applies only to a particular group (or individuals) and regulates the activities, and perhaps the speech, of that group. It does so, however, because of the group's past actions in the context of a specific dispute between real parties. The parties seeking the injunction assert a violation of their rights; the court hearing the action is charged with fashioning a remedy for a specific deprivation, not with the drafting of a statute addressed to the general public. . . .

The Florida Supreme Court concluded that numerous significant government interests are protected by the injunction. It noted that the State has a strong interest in protecting a woman's freedom to seek lawful medical or counseling services in connection with her pregnancy. . . . The State also has a strong interest in ensuring the public safety and order, in promoting the free flow of traffic on public streets and sidewalks, and in protecting the property rights of all its citizens. . . . In addition, the court believed that the State's strong interest in residential privacy . . . applied by analogy to medical privacy. . . . The court observed that while targeted picketing of the home threatens the psychological well-being of the "captive" resident, targeted picketing of a hospital or clinic threatens not only the psychological, but also the physical, well-being of the patient held "captive" by medical circumstance. . . . We agree with the Supreme Court of Florida that the combination of these governmental interests is quite sufficient to justify an appropriately tailored injunction to protect them. We now examine each contested provision of the injunction to see if it burdens more speech than necessary to accomplish its goal. . . .

We begin with the 36-foot buffer zone. The state court prohibited petitioners from "congregating, picketing, patrolling, demonstrating or entering" any portion of the public right-of-way or private property within 36 feet of the property line of the clinic as a way of ensuring access to the clinic. This speech-free buffer zone requires that petitioners move to the other side of Dixie Way and away from the driveway of the clinic, where the state court found that they repeatedly had interfered with the free access of patients and staff. . . . The buffer zone also applies to private property to the north and west of the clinic property. . . .

The 36-foot buffer zone protecting the entrances to the clinic and the parking lot is a means of protecting unfettered ingress to and egress from the clinic, and ensuring that petitioners do not block traffic on Dixie Way. The state court seems to have had few other options to protect access given the narrow confines around the clinic. As the Florida Supreme Court noted, Dixie Way is only 21 feet wide in the area of the clinic. . . . The state court was convinced that allowing petitioners to remain on the clinic's sidewalk and driveway was not a viable option in view of the failure of the first injunction to protect access. And allowing the petitioners to stand in the middle of Dixie Way would obviously block vehicular traffic.

The need for a complete buffer zone near the clinic entrances and driveway may be debatable, but some deference must be given to the state court's familiarity with the facts and the background of the dispute between the parties even under our heightened review. . . . Moreover, one of petitioners' witnesses during the evidentiary hearing before the state court conceded that the buffer zone was narrow enough to place petitioners at a distance of no greater than 10 to 12 feet from cars approaching and leaving the clinic. . . . Protesters standing across the narrow street from the clinic can still be seen and heard from the clinic parking lots. . . .

The inclusion of private property on the back and side of the clinic in the 36-foot buffer zone raises different concerns. The accepted purpose of the buffer zone is to protect access to the clinic and to facilitate the orderly flow of traffic on Dixie Way. Patients and staff wishing to reach the clinic do not have to cross the private property abutting the clinic property on the north and west, and nothing in the record indicates that petitioners' activities on the private property have obstructed access to the clinic. Nor was evidence presented that protestors located on the private property blocked vehicular traffic on Dixie Way. Absent evidence that petitioners standing on the private property have obstructed access to the clinic, blocked vehicular traffic, or otherwise unlawfully interfered with the clinic's operation, this portion of the buffer zone fails to serve the significant government interests relied on by the Florida Supreme Court. We hold that on the record before us the 36-foot buffer zone as applied to the private property to the north and west of the clinic burdens more speech than necessary to protect access to the clinic.

In response to high noise levels outside the clinic, the state court restrained the petitioners from "singing, chanting, whistling, shouting, yelling, use of bullhorns, auto horns, sound amplification equipment or other sounds or images observable to or within earshot of the patients inside the clinic" during the hours of 7:30 a.m. through noon on Mondays through Saturdays. We must, of course, take account of the place to which the regulations apply in determining whether these restrictions burden more speech than necessary. We have upheld similar noise restrictions in the past, and as we noted in upholding a local noise ordinance around public schools, "the nature of a place, 'the pattern of its normal activities, dictate the kinds of regulations . . . that are reasonable.'" . . . Noise control is particularly important around hospitals and medical facilities during surgery and recovery periods. . . .

We hold that the limited noise restrictions imposed by the state court order burden no more speech than necessary to ensure the health and well-being of the patients at the clinic. The First Amendment does not demand that patients at a medical facility undertake Herculean efforts to escape the cacophony of political protests." . . .

The same, however, cannot be said for the "images observable" provision of the state court's order. Clearly, threats to patients or their families, however communicated, are proscribable under the First Amendment. But rather than prohibiting the display of signs that could be interpreted as threats or veiled threats, the state court issued a blanket ban on all "images observable." This broad prohibition on all "images observable" burdens more speech than necessary to achieve the purpose of limiting threats to clinic patients or their families. . . .

The state court ordered that petitioners refrain from physically approaching any person seeking services of the clinic "unless such person indicates a desire to communicate" in an area within 300 feet of the clinic. The state court was attempting to prevent clinic patients and staff from being "stalked" or "shadowed" by the petitioners as they approached the clinic. . . . "The skillful, and unprincipled, solicitor can target the most vulnerable, including those accompanying children or those suffering physical impairment and who cannot easily avoid the solicitation."

But it is difficult, indeed, to justify a prohibition on *all* uninvited approaches of persons seeking the services of the clinic, regardless of how peaceful the contact may be, without burdening more speech than necessary to prevent intimidation and to ensure access to the clinic. Absent evidence that the protesters' speech is independently proscribable (*i.e.*, "fighting words" or threats), or is so infused with violence as to be indistinguishable from a threat of physical harm . . . this provision cannot stand. . . .

. . .

Justice Scalia, with whom Justice Kennedy and Justice Thomas joined, concurred in the judgment in part and dissented in part.

Justice Scalia, concurring in part and dissenting in part. . . .

The judgment in today's case has an appearance of moderation and Solomonic wisdom, upholding as it does some portions of the injunction while disallowing others. That appearance is deceptive. The entire injunction in this case departs so far from the established course of our jurisprudence that in any other context it would have been regarded as a candidate for summary reversal.

But the context here is abortion. A long time ago, in dissent from another abortion-related case, Justice O'Connor, joined by then-justice Rehnquist, wrote: "This Court's abortion decisions have already worked a major distortion in the Court's constitutional jurisprudence. Today's decision goes further, and makes it painfully clear that no legal rule or doctrine is safe from ad hoc nullification by this Court when an occasion for its application arises in a case involving state regulation of abortion. The permissible scope of abortion regulation is not the only constitutional issue on which this Court is divided, but—except when it comes to abortion—the Court has generally refused to let such disagreements, however longstanding or deeply felt, prevent it from evenhandedly applying uncontroversial legal doctrines to cases that come before it." *Thornburgh* v. *American College of Obstetricians and Gynecologists*, 476 U.S. 747, 814. . . . Today the ad hoc nullification machine claims its latest, greatest, and most surprising victim: the First Amendment.

Because I believe that the judicial creation of a 36-foot zone in which only a particular group, which had broken no law, cannot exercise its rights of speech, assembly, and association, and the judicial enactment of a noise prohibition, applicable to that group and that group alone, are profoundly at odds with our First Amendment precedents and traditions, I dissent. . . . Anyone . . . who is familiar with run-of-the-mine labor picketing, not to mention some other social protests, will be aghast at what it shows we have today permitted an individual judge to do. . . .

The videotape [of a day's picketing presented to the trial court] and the rest of the record, including the trial court's findings, show that a great many forms of expression and conduct occurred in the vicinity of the clinic. These include singing, chanting, praying, shouting, the playing of music both from the clinic and from handheld boom boxes, speeches, peaceful picketing, communication of familiar political messages, handbilling, persuasive speech directed at opposing groups on the issue of abortion, efforts to persuade individuals not to have abortions, personal testimony, interviews with the press, and media efforts to report on the protest. What the videotape, the rest of the record, and the trial court's findings do not contain is any suggestion of violence near the clinic, nor do they establish any attempt to prevent entry or exit. . . .

[The constitutionality of the injunction should be weighed under the strict scrutiny standard.] The danger of content-based statutory restrictions upon speech is that they may be designed and used precisely to suppress the ideas in question rather than to achieve any other proper governmental aim. But that same danger exists with injunctions. Although a speech-restricting injunction may not attack content *as content* (in the present case, as I shall discuss, even that is not true), it lends itself just as readily to the targeted suppression of particular ideas.

When a judge, on the motion of an employer, enjoins picketing at the site of a labor dispute, he enjoins (and he *knows* he is enjoining) the expression of pro-union views. Such targeting of one or the other side of an ideological dispute cannot readily be achieved in speech-restricting general legislation except by making content the basis of the restriction; it is achieved in speech-restricting injunctions almost invariably. The proceedings before us here illustrate well enough what I mean. The injunction was sought against a single-issue advocacy group by persons and organizations with a business or social interest in suppressing that group's point of view.

The second reason speech-restricting injunctions are at least as deserving of strict scrutiny is obvious enough: They are the product of individual judges rather than of legislatures—and often of judges who have been chagrined by prior disobedience of their orders. The right to free speech should not lightly be placed within the control of a single man or woman. And the third reason is that the injunction is a much more powerful weapon than a statute, and so should be subjected to greater safeguards. . . .

Finally, though I believe speech-restricting injunctions are dangerous enough to warrant strict scrutiny even when they are not technically content based, I think the injunction in the present case was content based (indeed, viewpoint based) to boot. The Court claims that it was directed, not at those who *spoke* certain things (antiabortion sentiments), but at those who *did* certain things (violated the earlier injunction). If that were true, then the injunction's residual coverage of "all persons acting in concert or participation with [the named individuals and organizations], or on their behalf," would not include those who merely entertained the same beliefs and wished to express the same views as the named defendants. But the construction given to the injunction by the issuing judge, which is entitled to great weight . . . is to the contrary: All those who wish to express the same views as the named defendants are deemed to be "acting in concert or participation." . . .

. . . An injunction against speech is the very prototype of the greatest threat to First Amendment values, the prior restraint. . . .

The Court has left a powerful loaded weapon lying about today. What we have decided seems to be, and will be reported by the media as, an abortion case. But it will go down in the lawbooks, it will be cited, as a free-speech injunction case—and the damage its novel principles produce will be considerable. The proposition that injunctions against speech are subject to a standard indistinguishable from (unless perhaps more lenient in its application than) the "intermediate scrutiny" standard we have used for "time, place, and manner" legislative restrictions; the notion that injunctions against speech need not be closely tied to any violation of law, but may simply implement sound social policy; and the practice of accepting trial-court conclusions permitting injunctions without considering whether those conclusions are supported by any findings of fact—these latest by-products of our abortion jurisprudence ought to give all friends of liberty great concern.

• • •

By the beginning of the new millennium, the cast of characters in the free speech–free access debate had changed. Operation Rescue had become Operation Save America. Its leaders celebrated that "all across this nation, Christians are coming to the streets of their cities, they come to the streets remembering the horrible holocaust that has taken the lives of over 45

FREEDOM OF SPEECH

million pre-born children in 30 years of legalized slaughter."[3] An op-ed piece in the *New York Times* noted that the new terminology of "pre-born" and "un-born" was a centerpiece of President George W. Bush and Attorney General John Ashcroft's attack on all forms of birth control, not just abortion: "A big thrust of Mr. Bush's aggressive anti-choice crusade has been to undermine the legal foundation of the Roe decision by elevating the status of a fetus, or even a fertilized egg, to that of a person. . . . If abortion were the only target, the administration would not be attempting to block women's access to contraceptives, which drive down the number of abortions. His administration would not be declaring war on any sex education that discusses ways, beyond abstinence, to prevent pregnancy and sexually transmitted diseases."[4]

The appetite of the abortion–abortion rights controversy was voracious. The debate spilled over from the courts into the streets, from editorial pages, the evening news, and numerous websites into the chambers of state legislatures and the halls of Congress. It swallowed up First Amendment questions along with women's rights, privacy, and equal protection doctrine. And it seemed to have no end. But the portion of the controversy that focused all of the branches of government's attention on free speech had forced both sides to compromise. There would be free access to clinics, but the protesters would not be entirely silenced. They could not harass clinic workers, but they could make their points in a reasonable fashion. And they would be heard.

NOTES

1. Ruth Marcus, "Clinton Approves Bill Limiting Protests at Abortion Clinics," *Washington Post*, May 24, 1994, 2.

2. *Scheidler v. NOW*, 537 U.S. 393 (2003), 21 (Rehnquist, c.j.).

3. Posting January 16, 2003, Operation Save America website, <www.operationsaveamerica.org/index.html> (accessed March 19, 2003).

4. *New York Times*, January 12, 2003, editorial page.

CONCLUSION

. . .

In the preceding pages, we have presented a documentary account of the abortion and abortion rights controversy in chronological fashion, with the intention of showing the impact that changing social, political, and cultural contexts had on legal developments. We realize that the legal story is not the only one, and in Recommended Reading we include anthologies and collections focusing on the personal accounts of men and women who performed or underwent abortions. At the same time, the documents we have assembled here make clear that without the intervention of lawmaking bodies—for example, legislatures passing statutes that criminalized abortion, individuals bringing lawsuits, and appeals courts handing down decisions interpreting anti-abortion statutes—the issue of abortion rights would not have its present form.

To be sure, it was not inevitable that abortion would become an object of any legal action, much less a centerpiece of constitutional debate. We can conceive of an alternate historical reality in which abortion remained a matter for women and men to determine for themselves—the same way that whether to have or not to have a child is a matter today for women and men to decide. In historical scholarship this is called a "contrary to fact" hypothesis. In legal education it is termed a "hypothetical." By pursuing it for a moment, we can see how abortion and abortion rights in law intersected.

We can only speculate about the frequency of abortion in our country if abortion had never been a subject of the law. We do know that it was common before it was made a crime and remained common after it became illegal. Did making abortion a crime reduce the number of attempted abortions? Surely it had some dampening effect, but as Sanger and other observers reported, that effect was minimal. Poor people simply resorted to self-remedies or sought cheap but unsafe abortions and suffered the consequences. The difference between then and now is the number of women then, thousands upon thousands, who died from unsafe abortions. By the same token, before modern times, successful abortions certainly reduced the number of live births, but compared with the incidence of spontaneous abortion (miscarriage), infant death from diseases that are now prevented by inoculations, poor sanitation and nutrition, and neglect, abortion had relatively little impact on the overall number of children surviving into adulthood. The same is true today, when abortion for most women is legal and safe. Criminalizing and then legalizing abortion did not change the overall number of cases. The only certain answer to the hypothetical is that legal abortion saves the lives of pregnant women. Overall, making abortion criminal does not save the lives of large numbers of the unborn.

If our hypothetical tells us that the twists and turns over time of abortion law might not, in the end, have altered the number of abortion cases, it is clear that the laws did create the occasion for an ongoing national debate over abortion and abortion rights and, within that, a public conversation about how law affects the family and society. American history features a number of such public discussions involving some vital facet of law, such as the struggle against slavery and the battle for civil rights. The lawmaking process acts as a lens, focusing the dialogue over our values.

We now need to summarize what the documents as a whole have to tell us about this ongoing discourse. One way to gain a kind of perspective on the debate as a whole, rather than its development over time, is to think about the documents topically. If law did not categorize issues by theme or topic, it would be a mass of prescriptions without order or method. But into which category or categories of law do abortion and abortion rights best fit? There is no single category, and of those that do seem appropriate, there are many complications.

Certainly abortion should be analyzed as a part of criminal law. *Roe v. Wade* concerned a Texas statute that penalized doctors who performed or attempted to perform abortions. The statute went back to the 1850s, but unlike the New York State laws on which it was modeled, in Texas no therapeutic exceptions to the law were allowed except to save the pregnant woman's life. Within the category of criminal law, abortion occupies a contested space. For example, lawmakers disagree over the identity of the crime victim. The first state laws saw the pregnant woman as the victim. Later legislation regarded the fetus as the victim. Today, some opponents of abortion argue that abortion is the intentional taking of an innocent "life in being" and should be equated with murder. If so, then the woman who sought an abortion would be an accessory to a heinous felony. But no state law ever had this provision.

Other scholars and jurists see abortion as part of family law. States have passed and courts have reviewed a myriad of laws about the family, including most recently the duties that parents owe to children and children to parents, including care of pregnant women. States have moved away from prohibitions on birth control, however, and the Supreme Court has found that women and men have a fundamental privacy right that includes the use of birth control. At the same time, many states passed laws regulating abortion since *Roe* with the avowed purpose of insuring that parents and husbands can prevent a woman from gaining an abortion. These laws expressly define reproduction as a family event, indeed as the beginning of a family.

The abortion and abortion rights controversy has reached out to economic studies of the function of law. This category is sometimes termed "law and economics." For example, one can find in legal opinions and "friends of the court" briefs economic calculations of the costs of providing public assistance for infants of poor mothers should abortion not be available to the women. One article in a journal of economics even argues that violent crimes in this country have sharply declined in number because of the access that poor people have to abortion. John J. Donohue and Steven D. Levitt suggested that legalized abortion allows the poor to limit family size or delay starting a family until they can provide for their children. Without the abortion option, families have children they cannot oversee, and the offspring of these families drift into criminal careers. Critics of the research reply that no correlation exists between access to abortion and reduced crime rates.[1]

The language of judges' opinions in abortion rights cases rests most firmly on constitutional law, rather than on criminal or domestic law concepts or on law and economics. As written in 1973, *Roe* was an extension of certain constitutional protections to women seeking abortions. The Court's majority found a fundamental right to privacy in the Constitution that included reproductive choice. Opponents of the decision argued that the state also had a constitutional duty to protect potential human life, particularly after "viability" (the ability of the fetus to live outside the uterus). But even friends of the pro-choice position argued that the decision in *Roe* was incorrectly framed and should have rested not on inchoate concepts like privacy but on the Equal Protection Clause of the Fourteenth Amendment. Thus the language of the decision itself has been controversial.

If abortion is a fundamental right arising from the constitutional protection of privacy, debates over abortion would have confined themselves to constitutional language and logic. Instead, much of the controversy over abortion revolves around disputes over when life begins. For some, that beginning is defined by religious concepts. As Philadelphia Roman Catholic archbishop Anthony Bevilacqua said on the thirtieth anniversary of *Roe*, it was long past time to reverse "this immoral, unjust, illogical decision." Following the archbishop's logic, the abortion issue belongs to the category of law and religion. As the official National Right to Life Committee website spells out the mission of "pro-life," it is "to restore legal protection to innocent human life."[2] The phrase "innocent life" in the National Right to Life Committee mission statement also has a religious origin: the unborn are without sin; why should they be victimized by legal abortion? In 2002 Congress passed and President George W. Bush signed into law the Born-Alive Infant Protection Act, which proponents of a religious definition of life applauded.[3]

But does enactment into law of any particular religious definition of the inception of life—in this case a concept that a legal life begins with "ensoulment" and God gives a soul to the infant at conception—violate the constitutional protection against the establishment of a state theology? The Constitution's First and Fourteenth Amendments forbid the federal government and the states from establishing one religion over all others. Pro-choice lawyers question whether our courts should allow any one religious doctrine to become the very foundation of our laws.

For other observers, the question of when life begins calls for a scientific answer. *Roe* relied on literature about fetal development that medical science provided. Both sides in the case presented their own versions of this evidence in their briefs, and both relied on the authority of doctors. Clearly, doctors and researchers did not agree about the moment when a fetus became a person. One of the reasons why Justice Sandra Day O'Connor leveled such withering criticism at Justice Harry Blackmun's use of medical evidence was that medical treatment of early fetal development was likely to improve over time.

The intractability of the continuing debate suggests that law courts and judge-made law may not be able to provide a definitive resolution to the abortion rights controversy. Justice Antonin Scalia has argued consistently that the answer lies in the realm of democratic politics. After all, legislatures and executives make law too, and perhaps determinations of abortion rights should be a matter of policy rather than constitutional adjudication and belong to the elected branches of government rather than the appointed judiciary. The danger here is that access to abortion might become merely a matter of politics and thus an artifact of the struggle of different groups to control state and federal legislatures and administrations. We say "danger" because past experience has shown that controversy over abortion rights in elected bodies can lead to their paralysis.

Although a review of all of the inaugural addresses and State of the Union messages of the presidents of the United States from Jimmy Carter in 1977 to George W. Bush in 2002 did not reveal a single explicit mention of

Roe, every one of those presidents took a position on the issue. Carter opposed abortion, and President Ronald Reagan wanted a constitutional amendment outlawing it in all forms. President Bill Clinton was pro-choice and vetoed anti-abortion bills passed in Congress. President George W. Bush has made the pro-life position a staple theme of his administration, and in a January 22, 2003, address in St. Louis, the site of many abortion rights battles, he proclaimed that he would "protect the lives of innocent children waiting to be born."[4] The two major national parties have also registered their views. The National Republican Party platform since 1980 has asked for the restriction of abortion, whereas the National Democratic Party platform has left the question of terminating a pregnancy to the conscience of the pregnant woman. At a January 21, 2003, dinner on the thirtieth anniversary of *Roe*, all of the announced Democratic candidates for the presidency endorsed the right to choose an abortion. Representative Richard Gephardt, who had earlier opposed abortion, admitted that "wisdom gained over time" had changed his mind.[5] The same division in the parties can be seen in state party platforms.[6]

Without doubt, abortion and abortion rights are now political footballs. As political scientist Karen O'Connor has written, "The abortion issue has indeed been defined and redefined as it has made its way onto the public agenda. . . . Throughout all of the stages, the scope of the conflict has widened and narrowed, the arenas of lobbying have shifted, and the policy implementation and evaluation processes have been realigned. In the final analysis, then, the abortion issue may not be all that different from other policy issues, including civil rights and the environment."[7] The unfortunate side effect of this fact is the uncertainty of the law as various states' elected representatives have given different answers to the practical questions that abortion raises. For example, in California and New York, abortion before viability is only subject to normal health regulations. In Utah, it is all but illegal. In Pennsylvania and Missouri, it is heavily regulated. Such variability among states is not uncommon—for example, in divorce law—but in abortion law it leads to confusion and inequality.

Laurence Tribe, a law professor who argued one of the abortion rights cases before the U.S. Supreme Court, has written that we should be looking not to law or government to settle the "clash of absolutes" but to deeper cultural values. If he is right, the debate over abortion and abortion rights is really a debate over the role of women in society. If women's central role is childbearing and care, then abortion strikes at the heart of social order—the very point that Theodore Roosevelt made in 1905. If women's roles and men's roles are fungible, then women should not be viewed as carriers of the next generation unless they so choose.[8]

The editors of this reader hope that it may contribute to the time when abortion and abortion rights are no longer divisive issues, but fear that this time will not come soon. We are an intensely moralistic nation. We frame our foreign affairs and our wars, our politics and our economics in terms of moral precepts. This has been true of the controversy over abortion and abortion rights. For pro–abortion rights forces, choice was a moral principle that went far beyond abortion rights to protecting the dignity, health, and autonomy of all women; for anti–abortion rights groups, fetal life was a moral principle that reached out to the sacred memory of traditional families and motherhood as well as basic religious values. Such strongly held moral opposites are not easily compromised. True, our history teaches us that some impassioned legal and political debates do not retain their acute divisiveness forever. The controversy over civil rights for minorities once led to violent confrontations, assassinations, and bombings. Now almost all Americans accept the basic ideas of civil rights, though there is still dispute over affirmative action programs. As yet, the abortion/abortion rights debate does not show any signs of abating.

Perhaps, over time, abortion providers' clinics and referral services may become so familiar that they blend into the medical landscape. As Justice David Souter opined in *Casey*, so many women have come to rely on the availability of some kind of legal and safe abortion provider, states may find it impossible to make abortion criminal again, however much they may regulate its practice. Even if a shift in composition of the High Court leads it to narrow *Roe* still further, it is very unlikely that any Supreme Court would overturn it. But recent activity among anti-abortion protesters at clinics and recent High Court decisions protecting these protests may give new life to the anticlinic movement.

Perhaps medical technology will play the decisive part in a mitigation, if not a resolution, of the dispute. More effective and longer-lasting contraceptive methods and various kinds of morning-after pills such as RU 486 will certainly reduce the number of unwanted pregnancies in coming years, which may result in a dramatic decline in the number of abortions sought. But the same technological advances that may reduce the conflict could just as easily prolong or even worsen it. Embryonic and fetal tissue are composed of stem cells that can be vital components in highly promising medical research on Parkinson's disease and other disorders of the brain and spinal cord, as well as liver and kidney dysfunction. Stem cells reproduce rapidly and can take on the function of a myriad of the body's building blocks, offering relief and perhaps even a cure for diseases as varied as Alzheimer's and sickle cell anemia. Pregnant women can give permission for the tissue of their aborted fetus to be used in such fashion, but the consent must be in writing. Opponents of abortion also oppose research with stem cells when it is used as a defense of abortion. President George W. Bush and Congress both wrestled with the implications of stem cell research and have refused to bar it, but as long as stem cell research continues and the uses of stem cells diversify, the connection between new technologies and abortion will fuel the controversy.

NOTES

1. Vivian Berger, "Abortion and Crime," *National Law Journal*, June 24, 2002.

2. National Right to Life Committee mission statement, at <www.nrlc.org>.

3. 1 USCS §8 (2002):

§8. "Person," "human being," "child," and "individual" as including born-alive infant

(a) In determining the meaning of any Act of Congress, or of any ruling, regulation, or interpretation of the various administrative bureaus and agencies of the United States, the words "person," "human being," "child," and "individual," shall include every infant member of the species homo sapiens who is born alive at any stage of development.

(b) As used in this section, the term "born alive," with respect to a member of the species homo sapiens, means the complete expulsion or extraction from his or her mother of that member, at any stage of development, who after such expulsion or extraction breathes or has a beating heart, pulsation of the umbilical cord, or definite movement of voluntary muscles, regardless of whether the umbilical cord has been cut, and regardless of whether the expulsion or extraction occurs as a result of natural or induced labor, cesarean section, or induced abortion.

(c) Nothing in this section shall be construed to affirm, deny, expand, or contract any legal status or legal right applicable to any member of the species homo sapiens at any point prior to being "born alive" as defined in this section. (Added Aug. 5, 2002, P.L. 107–207, §2(a), 116 Stat. 926.)

4. George W. Bush to Right for Life Rally, January 22, 2003, <www.euthenasia .com/bushmarch2003.html> (accessed October 16, 2003).

5. Quoted in *New York Times*, January 22, 2003, A18.

6. "The Powers of the President: Reproductive Freedom and Choice," NARAL online newsroom, January 19, 2003, <www.naral.org/mediaresources/publica-tions/president>; National Right to Life Committee, "Citizens for Life Endorse

Bush," February 9, 2000, <www.nrlc.org/press—releases—new/Release020900 .html> (both accessed March 19, 2003).

7. Karen O'Connor, *No Neutral Ground?: Abortion Politics in an Age of Absolutes* (New York, 1996), 181.

8. Laurence H. Tribe, *Abortion: The Clash of Absolutes* (New York, 1990), 237.

RECOMMENDED READING

. . .

The reading suggestions below are not encyclopedic. There are many firsthand accounts, polemical treatments, and political manifestos that we have omitted for reasons of space. The list below is intended to supplement the documents in this book and to permit interested students to pursue further reading in scholarly sources.

Modern abortion law focuses on state and federal statutes and federal court decisions. The district court cases we discuss can be found in the West Law Reporter called the *Federal Supplement* (abbreviated F. Supp.). For example, *Roe v. Wade* is 314 F. Supp. 1217 (1970), which means that the court's opinion starts on page 1217 of volume 314 of the *Federal Supplement* reporter. *Doe v. Bolton*, the companion case from Georgia, is 319 F. Supp. 1048 (1970). The three major abortion rights cases in the U.S. Supreme Court can be found in the *United States Supreme Court Reports* (the official Supreme Court reporter) as *Roe v. Wade*, 410 U.S. 113 (1973); *Webster v. Reproductive Health Services*, 492 U.S. 490 (1989); and *Planned Parenthood of Southeastern Pennsylvania v. Casey*, 505 U.S. 833 (1992). The briefs of friends of the court and the oral arguments are in the public domain, like the opinions of the justices and judges, but a convenient text of leading cases' material appears in volumes of *Landmark Briefs and Arguments of the Supreme Court of the United States: Constitutional Law*, ed. Philip B. Kurland and Gerhardt Casper (Arlington, Va., 1975–), as well as on the Lexis website. In addition, an audiotape of selections of the oral arguments in *Roe*, *Webster*, *Casey*, and other abortion-related cases appears as a supplement to Stephanie Guitton and Peter Irons's collection, *May It Please the Court* (New York, 1993). The cassettes, available from New Press, are narrated by Irons, Sylvia Law, Eleanor Holmes Norton, and Nadine Stroesser.

So important, and so complicated, have the abortion laws and opinions become that there are now two encyclopedias that cover the field: Judith A. Baer, ed., *Historical and Multicultural Encyclopedia of Women's Reproductive Rights in the United States* (Westport, Conn., 2002), and Louis J. Palmer, ed., *Encyclopedia of Abortion in the United States* (Jefferson, N.C., 2002). But even these cannot keep up with the changes in state law.

Roe v. Wade itself is the subject of many books. The better known include Marian Faux, *Roe v. Wade: The Untold Story of the Landmark Supreme Court Decision That Made Abortion Legal* (New York, 2001); David Garrow, *Liberty and Sexuality: The Right to Privacy and the Making of Roe v. Wade* (New York, 1994); N. E. H. Hull and Peter Charles Hoffer, *Roe v. Wade: The Abortion Rights Controversy in American History* (Lawrence, Kans., 2001); Norma McCorvey and Andy Meisler, *I Am Roe: My Life, Roe v. Wade, and Freedom of Choice* (New York, 1994); and Sarah Weddington, *A Question of Choice* (New York, 1992).

Other accounts of the "abortion wars" include Cynthia Gorney's *Articles of Faith:*

A Frontline History of the Abortion Wars (New York, 1998); Laura Kaplan, *The Story of Jane: The Legendary Underground Feminist Abortion Service* (New York, 1997); Carole Joffe, *Doctors of Conscience: The Stuggle to Provide Abortion before and after Roe v. Wade* (Boston, 1995); Rosemary Nossiff, *Before Roe: Abortion Policy in the States* (Philadelphia, 2001); Rickie Solinger, *Beggars and Choosers: How the Politics of Choice Shapes Adoption, Abortion, and Welfare in the United States* (New York, 2001); and Rickie Solinger, ed., *Abortion Wars: A Half Century of Struggle, 1950–2000* (Berkeley, 1998).

As a subject in law, abortion has filled pages of law reviews and books. These include Sylvia Law, "Rethinking Sex and the Constitution," 132 *Pennsylvania Law Review* 955 (1984); Nancy Ehrenreich, "The Colonization of the Womb," 43 *Duke Law Journal* 492 (1993); and Eileen L. McDonagh, "My Body, My Consent: Securing the Constitutional Right to Abortion Funding," 62 *Albany Law Review* 1057 (1999), on feminist constitutional thinking and abortion rights. Broader reviews of these issues include Laurence H. Tribe, *Abortion: The Clash of Absolutes* (New York, 1990), and Mark Tushnet, *Abortion: Constitutional Issues* (New York, 1996).

Philosophical approaches to the subject include Hadley Arkes, *Natural Rights and the Right to Choose* (Cambridge, Eng., 2002); Robert M. Baird and Stuart E. Rosenbaum, eds., *The Ethics of Abortion: Pro-Life vs. Pro-Choice* (Amherst, N.Y., 2001); Daniel A. Dombrowski and Robert Deltete, *A Brief, Liberal, Catholic Defense of Abortion* (Urbana, Ill., 2000); Peter Kreeft, *The Unaborted Socrates* (Downers Grove, Ill., 1983); and Mary Ann Glendon, *Abortion and Divorce in Western Law* (Cambridge, Mass., 1987).

The line between politics and law in these cases is hardly clear, but students of American political life have tried to trace it. See Donald T. Critchlow, *The Politics of Abortion and Birth Control in Historical Perspective* (New York, 1996); Faye Ginsburg, *Contested Lives: The Abortion Debate in an American Community* (Berkeley, Calif., 1998); Malcolm Goggin, ed., *Understanding the New Politics of Abortion* (Newberry Park, Calif., 1993); and Ted G. Jelen, ed., *Perspectives on the Politics of Abortion* (Westport, Conn., 1995).

Studies of pro-life groups include Sara Diamond, *Not by Politics Alone: The Enduring Influence of the Christian Right* (New York, 1998); Michele McKegan, *Abortion Politics: Mutiny in the Ranks of the Right* (New York, 1992); Carol J. C. Maxwell, *Pro-Life Activists in America: Meaning, Motivation, and Direct Action* (Cambridge, Eng., 2002); and James Risen and Judy L. Thomas, *Wrath of Angels: The American Abortion War* (New York, 1998).

The history of abortion is as fascinating as the law surrounding it. Of course, abortion and birth control are related subjects if not complementary ones. Among the excellent books on abortion and birth control are Janet Farrell Brodie, *Contraception and Abortion in Nineteenth-Century America* (Ithaca, N.Y., 1994); Frederick N. Dyer, *Champion of Women and the Unborn: Horatio Robinson Storer, M.D.* (Canton, Mass., 1999); Linda Gordon, *Woman's Body, Woman's Right: A Social History of Birth Control in America* (New York, 1976); David Kennedy, *Birth Control in America: The Career of Margaret Sanger* (New Haven, Conn., 1977); James C. Mohr, *Abortion in America: The Origins and Evolution of National Policy* (New York,

1978); Marvin Olasky, *Abortion Rights: A Social History of Abortion in America* (Washington, D.C., 1992); Leslie J. Reagan, *When Abortion Was a Crime: Women, Medicine, and the Law in the United States, 1867–1973* (Berkeley, Calif., 1997); and James Reed, *The Birth Control Movement and American Society: From Private Vice to Public Virtue* (Princeton, N.J., 1983). On the impact of Comstock and his program, see Helen Lefkowitz Horowitz, "Victoria Woodhull, Anthony Comstock, and Conflict over Sex in the United States in the 1870s," and Andrea Tone, "Black Market Birth Control: Contraceptive Entrepreneurship and Criminality in the Gilded Age," *Journal of American History* 87 (2000): 403–34, 435–59.

The relation between the medical profession and abortion is essential background for understanding the controversy. On the nineteenth century, see G. J. Barker-Benfield, *Horrors of the Half-Known Life: Male Attitudes toward Women in Nineteenth-Century America* (New York, 2000); John S. Haller Jr. and Robin M. Haller, *The Physician and Sexuality in Victorian America* (Urbana, Ill., 1974); and Regina Morantz-Sanchez, *Conduct Unbecoming a Woman: Medicine on Trial in Turn-of-the-Century Brooklyn* (New York, 1999). The twists and turns of AMA policy on women and child care are the subject of the final chapter of Richard A. Meckel, *Save the Babies: American Public Health Reform and the Prevention of Infant Mortality, 1850–1929* (Baltimore, Md., 1990). Donald T. Critchlow, *Intended Consequences: Birth Control, Abortion, and the Federal Government in Modern America* (New York, 1999), follows the path of federal family planning policy in the 1960s, 1970s, and 1980s.

The abortion/abortion rights controversy should be studied in the context of more general issues in women's history. For example, see the more recent treatment in Ruth Rosen, *The World Split Open: How the Modern Women's Movement Changed America* (New York, 2000).

It is almost a full-time job to keep up with current events regarding abortion and abortion rights. Three websites help. A superb source of legal materials, including courts' opinions and briefs of cases submitted to the Supreme Court, is <www.lexis.com>. Lexis also has a news service that covers most of the major dailies, magazines of opinion, and testimony before congressional committees. More narrowly focused on abortion matters, the National Abortion Rights Action League (NARAL, now NARAL Pro-Choice America) website is <www.naral.org>. On the other side of the issue, the National Right to Life Committee's website is <www.nrlc.org>. Operation Rescue (now calling itself Operation Save America), Planned Parenthood Federation of America, NOW, and various health advisory and church groups also have websites that focus on abortion. Some of these sites also serve fund-raising and political action functions.